The
Employee

Human Resources Management Series

The

Employee

Contemporary Viewpoints

Marie S. Ensign and
Laurie Nogg Adler, Editors

Foreword by
RONALD C. PILENZO,
President and Chief Operating Officer
American Society for Personnel
Administration

ABC-Clio Information Services
Santa Barbara, California
Denver, Colorado
Oxford, England

This book is Smyth sewn and printed on acid-free paper to meet library standards.

Cover and book design by Terri Wright

Library of Congress Cataloging in Publication Data

Main entry under title:

The Employee, contemporary viewpoints.

   (Human resources management series)
   Includes indexes.
   1. Quality of work life—Abstracts. 2. Personnel management—Abstracts.   3. Job satisfaction—Abstracts.
I. Ensign, Marie S.   II. Adler, Laurie Nogg.   III. Series.
HD6955.E53 1985   306'.3   85-6243
ISBN 0-87436-449-3 (alk. paper)

10 9 8 7 6 5 4 3 2 1

ABC-Clio Information Services
2040 Alameda Padre Serra, Box 4397
Santa Barbara, California 93103

Clio Press Ltd.
55 St. Thomas Street
Oxford OX1, 1JG, England

Manufactured in the United States of America

Digests of contemporary articles
by business experts worldwide
compiled from ABI/INFORM®
the leading business database.

Contents

Foreword _____

THE PAST FEW YEARS have brought rapid and turbulent changes in the relationships between employer and employee. New attitudes by Americans toward their goals and lifestyles have been reflected quickly and with great force in the workplace—creating what might best be termed the "alternative workstyle."

Single parents, "empty nest" mothers rejoining the work force, older workers, dual-career families—10 years ago none of these groups was a significant force in the workplace. Today, their special contributions to the world of work are critical, and their special needs are reshaping that world. In some areas of benefits administration and employment practices, corporate human resource policy is barely keeping pace with the explosion of new ideas. Telecommuting, spouse relocation assistance, paternity leave, employer-funded child care, flexitime, job-sharing, quality circles, ergonomics, employee leasing, equity-sharing, profit-sharing, benefit cost-sharing are just a few of the better known concepts. A personnel "alphabet soup" is on the menu of every human resource manager today: IIMOs, PPOs and PCNs; ESOPs, TRASOPs and ZEBRAS; DEFRA, ERISA, REACT and ADEA; CAT, CBT and CAI -and many more. What they constitute is a profound challenge to today's top management; what they reflect is a fundamental change in the employer/employee relationship. As one top-level human resource executive said recently, "I don't think we have yet focused on how we might help people to better deal with their lives and, in turn, with their jobs. In the past, we just focused on the job, and that was it."

Today two demographic forces are growing in significance. First, the American population is aging. The greying of the work force is here, and will be a basic condition of business life for a long time to come. In organizations which are dealing most successfully with their older workers, programs and policies are colored by recognition of the value of the older worker, not just by the stipulation of federal compliance. Options for better utilization of older workers include job sharing; phased retirement; benefits tailored to their unique situations; and their use in community relations, new hire orientation and in-house training. All these ideas have proved to be successful in recent years. Together with rising health care costs, the greying of the work force is also viewed as being largely responsible for today's emphasis on employer-funded proactive health care—wellness, diet, and physical fitness programs.

Second, the population bulge caused by the maturation of the "baby boom" generation will combine with the impact of more older workers (most of whom are now at the peak of their careers) to create an explosive mix in the years to come. Career development paths to middle and upper management positions traditionally used by younger workers will become truncated, or at least constricted, as more managers vie for essentially the same number of jobs. For the employer, the problems caused by this dilemma will be dealing with more stress-related ailments, persuading employees to adapt to lateral instead of upward career moves, and difficulties in fulfilling employees' needs for personal growth. One human resource executive summed this up not long ago: "All this boils down to an emerging need for restructuring jobs and how people move in and out of them," she said, "so that we can accommodate a wider range of personal needs and lifestyles, as well as corporate needs that may change as we deal with a surplus of people vying for upper management jobs."

People who have served in management positions more than 10 years or so must now accustom themselves to a new barometer of current management theory—the bestseller list. A quick look at today's popular reading reveals not just suspense novels and spy stories, but also books on one minute managers, corporate cultures, the nation's top-rated employers and searches for corporate excellence. Productivity, long the purview of top executives and management professors, has become a pop trend.

One may actually trace this trend back to the influx of Japanese management techniques that began in the early '70s when that country's "secret" was revealed: employee participation. Products are produced in greater volumes and at higher quality standards, Americans "discovered," by workers who are given a stake in the success of the enterprise, a voice in decision-making, and an opportunity to assume greater responsibility and independence.

This trend has entered the mainstream of U.S. business in the intervening years and has grown in sophistication as well—predictably, it has become "Americanized." Nineteen eighty five's refinement of the participative management theme is the newly-coined term "intrapreneur," following closely on the heels of one of last year's themes: the re-emergence of the entrepreneur. "Intrapreneurs" are creative, innovative managers who share many traits of the entrepreneur but who, unlike entrepreneurs, thrive within the constraints that hierarchical organizations place on creativity and innovation.

Another reflection of today's renewed emphasis on productivity may be found in a sharper focus on the role of line management. Increasingly these employees are being included in program development activities, and are gaining greater autonomy as flatter and "matrix" organizational structures replace the traditional line-of-authority structure. Significant investment is being made by employers in these managers; even firms with large, comprehensive skills-training programs are witnessing tremendous growth in their management development efforts.

Finally, the most prominent business-related technological development of today, the introduction of "high tech" into the workplace has, at the very same time, created both a tremendous need to train (and retrain) workers to utilize new equipment and techniques and a new, highly efficient way to administer that training. In just the last three years the microcomputer has turned the world of skills training upside down. New equipment and software now allow interactive training on an individual basis and at the student's pace ("synergogy" in the trainer's argot), which was nearly impossible in traditional "stand up" training programs.

Further, many observers have noted that the introduction of "high tech" into the workplace has resulted in symptoms of dislocation, alienation, and discomfort in some workers who operate the new equipment. Thus, "high tech" has already spawned at least one new issue. Called "high touch," it focuses on the need for balancing the impersonal, computer-dominated nature of the computer/operator relationship with familiar, tactile environmental factors that emphasize the operator's comfort and safety. The first manifestation of "high tech/high touch" as an issue in the workplace, of course, is the current debate concerning possible harmful effects of video display terminals (VDTs), particularly on pregnant women. Similar debates can be expected in the future.

Some of the changes which we are seeing in today's workplace result from changes in society; some from changes in individuals. Some are natural; others are mandated or even contrived. Most reflect changes for employer and employee alike in the years to come.

— RONALD C. PILENZO, APD
President and Chief Operating Officer
American Society for Personnel Administration

Introduction

INCREASED RECOGNITION of the importance of the employees in enabling an organization to attain its goals is evident in the frequent reference to "human resources management" as an area of concern. At the same time, as noted in Ronald Pilenzo's Foreword to this book, rapid and turbulent changes are occurring in employees' attitudes toward their own goals and in their relationships with employers.

In order to provide current information in this dynamic area, ABC-Clio is introducing its new Human Resources Management series. This first title, **The Employee,** addresses areas of primary concern to employees—job satisfaction, career advancement, balancing personal and career goals, stress, and burnout, as well as the particular problems of dual career couples and working mothers. Other titles in the series will focus on the viewpoint of the business organization in such areas as motivation, productivity, recruitment, training, employee counseling, and turnover.

As the source for these titles, we have chosen the leading business database, Data Courier's ABI/INFORM®. ABI/INFORM was designed for business professionals who need timely information but are unable to scan the hundreds of news magazines, journals, and trade publications that are important to them. To build this database, abstractors, who are experts in law, employee benefits, business-government relations, data processing, finance, and other business fields, condense the international business literature into 200-word article summaries.

For this book, the more than 300,000 records in the database were searched for appropriate articles. From the resulting list, the editors selected over 500 articles, published from 1980 to the present, especially relevant to the topic, and arranged them in chapters for easy browsing. A detailed subject index gives quick access to specific concepts, and an author index leads the reader to the variety of writers represented.

At the request of librarians and other information professionals, the editors have included a list of the database index terms (descriptors) following each article summary. These terms may be used as a guide for online searches for related articles or those appearing after the publication of this book.

How to Order Articles

The full text of most articles cited here (all articles identified as "Avail. ABI") are available through Data Courier's fast, convenient photocopy service. Call their Article Delivery Service Department toll-free at 800/626-2823 (continental United States) or 800/626-0307 (Canada), Monday through Friday from 9 a.m. to

5 p.m. or write to: Article Delivery Service, Data Courier Inc, 620 S. Fifth Street, Louisville, KY 40202. Enclose a photocopy of the citation from this book or full order information including accession number, title, author, and journal title, date, and page numbers. Full-text articles are available from Data Courier at the following rates (subject to change) and can be charged to American Express, Master-Card, or VISA:

> Deposit account customers — $6.75
> All other customers — $8.25
> Add $2.00 per article for shipment outside the United
> States.

A few of the articles (identified by the abbreviations following the word Avail.) must be ordered direct from the publisher. A key to the abbreviations and publisher addresses is given below. Prices vary with publisher.

ABA	American Bar Association 115 E. 60th Street Chicago, IL 60637
ABI	Data Courier Inc Article Delivery Service 620 S. Fifth Street Louisville, KY 40202
AGA	Association of Government Accountants 727 S. 23rd Street Arlington, VA 22202
ASPA	American Society for Personnel Administration 1225 Connecticut Avenue NW Washington, DC 20036
Drug	Drug Topics Oradell, NJ 07649
JAI	JAI Press P.O. Box 1678 Greenwich, CT 06830
MCB	MCB Publications, Ltd. 200 Keighley Rd. Bradford, W. Yorkshire BD9 4JG England
Money	Money Time & Life Building Rockefeller Center New York, NY 10020
Sharpe	M. E. Sharpe, Inc. 901 N. Broadway White Plains, NY 10603

Tieto	Tieto Ltd.
	Bank House
	8a Hill Road
	Clevedon, Avon BS21 7HH
	England

ABI/INFORM, the Business Database

Data Courier Inc, a Courier-Journal and Louisville Times Co. subsidiary, is the leader in providing online business information worldwide. To produce the ABI/INFORM database, their editors index business articles appearing in more than 700 magazines and journals, and professionals in a number of business fields summarize the articles. For any topic of interest in the field virtually every significant periodical article is included in the database.

ABI/INFORM is available online through the following timesharing systems:

Bibliographic Retrieval Services (BRS)
BRS After Dark
Data-Star
ITT Dialcom, Inc.
DIALOG Information Services, Inc.
DIALOG's Knowledge Index
European Space Agency Information Retrieval Service (ESA-QUEST)
Innerline
Systems Development Corporation Search Service (ORBIT)
VU/TEXT

Data Courier provides a wide range of customer support services. Information specialists trained in online searching are available each working day toll-free at 800/626-2823 from 9 a.m. to 5 p.m. (Eastern time) to answer questions about ABI/INFORM and the firm's other products. Training specialists travel worldwide to teach groups of new and experienced searchers time-efficient and cost-saving search techniques. For more information contact:

DATA COURIER INC
620 South Fifth Street
Louisville, KY 40202-2297

Sample Entry

Title

Entry Number
(This is the
number referred
to in the index)

Probing the Telecommuting Debate (72)

Telecommuting, where employees work in their homes using computer terminals, has not been adopted by any major company on a wide scale. Instead, it is evolving on an experimental, by-exception basis. With telecommuting, managers often worry about how to get and how to measure employee productivity. Similarly, employees are concerned over the possibility of stunted careers. Unions want to ban the "electronic cottage" altogether. Control Data Corp. (CDC) is a pioneer in telecommuting. The company set up a framework for its computer designers and programmers to work in their homes. CDC has experienced several payoffs, including: 1. the retention of experienced and valuable employees, 2. increased productivity, 3. the ability to tap talented personnel in a laborforce short on skilled workers, and 4. savings in facilities overhead. CDC also claims performance has improved and deadlines are met more frequently. The experiences of many other companies have been more problematical.

200-word
Article Summary

Author

Lallande, Ann; *Business Computer Systems*, Apr 1984, 3(4): pp. 102-113. Avail. ABI 84-16724

Accession No.

Journal Title   Date of   Volume &   Page Numbers   Where to Order Copy
                   Publication   Issue Number   of Article   of Entire Article
                                                                      (see Introduction)

Telecommunications, Cottage industries, Productivity, Programmers, Cost reduction, Advantages, Disadvantages

Descriptors for
Online Access

1

Humanization of the Workplace

IMPROVING THE QUALITY OF WORKLIFE

Arbeitsmotivation und Krankheitsrisiko (Motivation to (1)
Work and the Risk of Illness)
The only universal solution to minimizing welfare costs is to foster
motivation and avoid physical and mental stress for the workers - to
humanize the workplace. Performance at work and work satisfaction are
determined by physical and social factors, such as mental attitude, security,
the need for activity, the relationship between reward and performance, and
the environment. It is widely recognized that the causes of illness are not
necessarily purely physical, but the definition of illness is complicated by
such factors as social behavior patterns, role expectations, the doctor's
expectations, and the government health insurance plan (the greater the
benefits, the less the desire to work). Other problems are introduced by the
consequences of unhealthy lifestyles. Tighter external and internal controls
have negative social and mental effects and are costly to operate. An
alternative might be an incentive scheme which provides financial
advantages to the insured worker, but such a plan must be very carefully
devised if it is to be effective and not discriminatory against truly sick people.
A personal contribution which both employers and employees would accept
would be an agreement on a certain number of days absent which would not
be covered. References. —Forster, Edgar; *Fortschrittliche Betriebsfuehrung und Industrial
Engineering (Germany),* Dec 1981, 30(6): pp. 426-429. Avail. ABI 82-14645

   Germany, Work environment, Working conditions, Humanization of work, Motivation,
   Psychological aspects, Illnesses, Controls

The Continuing Personnel Challenge (2)
A panel of personnel experts discuss ways to improve the quality of working
life. On the question of why people work, Eli Ginzberg responds that it is the
major source for social interaction. Roy Walters states that people have a
need to grow psychologically, and work should reflect this. Rosabeth Moss
Kanter sees security and pay as employee issues of the future. Virginia

McDermott sees employee expectations tied to the economy and expects that management will become more aware of the value of losing a trained employee because of the rising importance of benefits. Ginzberg thinks that educational benefits for employees' children will also become important. Milton Rock believes that pay is based more on productivity than entitlement now, and that the trend will continue. Employees are demanding more say in the running of the workplace, but this leads to certain risks for which they will have to be responsible. This form of management is growing at a modest rate, according to Jerome Rosow. Flexible work schedules are being used more by single men for recreation than by working mothers or others they were intended to benefit, says Kanter. Work at home is expected to supplement office work rather than replace it. Rock believes the major disadvantage to flextime is the recordkeeping involved. Many workers are delaying retirement or returning after retirement. Rock says business needs those workers. Walters maintains that the best way for management to handle retirement is to prepare workers for it, then ease them into it gradually. —Debats, Karen E.; *Personnel Jrnl,* May 1982, 61(5): pp. 332-344. Avail. ABI 82-12841

Work, Employees, Expectations, Employee benefits, Productivity, Participatory management, Flexible hours, Retirement, Opinions, Manypeople

Corporate Approaches to the Quality of Work Life (3)
At the Third National Conference on Business Ethics, sponsored by Bentley College, a panel discussed various corporate approaches to the quality of working life.At General Motors, quality of work life means: 1. more employee involvement, 2. improving relationships between supervisors and subordinates, 3. better cooperation between union and management, 4. innovative and more effective designs of jobs and organizations, and 5. improved integration of people and technology. Quality of work life is viewed as a continuous process, in which the company utilizes all its resources and strives for awareness and understanding among its employees. General Motors' program includes a team concept and assessment centers for hiring.Quality of work life at Volvo involves a different approach. The corporate strategy is to develop production technology and work organizations toward craftsmanship and automation. Each Volvo plant has developed its own pattern of change and new ways of organizing work, including work groups. —Fuller, Stephen H. and Jonsson, Berth; *Personnel Jrnl,* Aug 1980, 59(8): pp. 632-638. Avail. ABI 80-15897

Quality of work, Life, Job enrichment, Work environment, General Motors-Detroit, Volvo-Sweden

Dynamic Systems and the Quality of Work Life (4)
In discussing the quality of work life, the actions in each of 3 sectors-management, union, and the workers themselves-affect the actions in the others. An automobile plant was studied, and data were gathered via 3 methods: participant observation, in-depth interviews, and a questionnaire distributed to all workers. A high percentage of the workers were classified as highly alienated from work, due to the repetition of the work which leads to boredom and monotony. The workers used many techniques, such as

games and entrepreneurial ventures, to lessen these effects. Over 40% of the workers indicated that they consumed alcohol at lunch time. Few took interest in the union activities, although most workers considered the union necessary. In regard to changes that would improve plant work life, 36.3% of the workers cited various managerial changes. The second most frequently cited need was environmental-changes to improve the quality of work life. A systems approach was developed to show the interrelationships among the variables important to workers on the assembly line. Certain "entry" points into the system would be most successful at effecting change. A start could be made by management taking action or impressing on the supervisors that the company does have an interest in the workers. The union could show workers that they were important at times other than elections and dues collection. Charts. —Runcie, John F.; *Personnel*, Nov/Dec 1980, 57(6): pp. 13-24. Avail. ABI 81-01754

Quality of work, Job satisfaction, Job attitudes, Employee attitude (PER), Work environment, Systems, Models, Labor relations, Organizational behavior, Studies

Elliot Lehman, Lewis Weinberg, CoChief Executive (5) Officers, Fel-Pro Inc.

The co-chief executive officers of Fel-Pro Inc. in Skokie, Ill., Elliot Lehman and Lewis C. Weinberg, operate their privately-held family business with an emphasis on the development and maintenance of strong labor-management relations. The $100 million firm markets automotive gaskets and other sealing products, along with a line of sealants, adhesives, and specialty lubricants to industry. Lehman and Weinberg, both of whom entered the business through marriage at the end of the Great Depression, believe that the profit element and the human element are intertwined. They provide a multitude of benefits for their employees and pay them well, but in return demand a high level of performance. Their management style fosters cooperation, teamwork, and an interest in quality and quantity from their 1, 500 employees. The commitment to their employees is evidenced in personal attention, recreational facilities, the plant itself, and the Employee Forum, which gives employees the opportunity to make their views known. As a result, the firm attracts a very high caliber of worker. —Anonymous; *Industry Week*, Oct 27, 1980, 207(2): pp. 53-55. Avail. ABI 80-22316

Case studies, Labor relations, Employee benefits, Job enrichment, Humanization of work

Equal Employment Opportunity and the Physical (6) Planning of the Work Place

Most corporations continually make changes in some part of their facilities, often without considering the effects on employment opportunities. It falls to those with equal employment opportunity (EEO) responsibilities to be aware of the many relationships between the physical work environment and employment opportunities and to work to guarantee that the physical alterations made in the work place help, rather than act as a barrier, to EEO attempts. Many of the EEO considerations in workplace design are associated with the fact that most women and minorities are in clerical or other low-level jobs from which it is difficult to rise. The physical arrangement and design within the working environment often exacerbate

the situation for such workers. Designs should avoid affectations that make employees uncomfortable or segregated. Concern should be given to the amount of space necessary to perform certain work and to eliminating distractions. Workplace planning is also needed in manufacturing facilities.
—Macleod, Jennifer S.; *EEO Today,* Summer 1981, 8(2): pp. 137-142. Avail. ABI 82-04365

   Affirmative action, Personnel policies, Facilities planning, Work environment, Office layout, Restrictions, Employment, Opportunity, Career advancement, Women, Minorities, Site selection

Ergonomics: Fitting the Work to the Worker   (7)

Ergonomics refers to a branch of industrial engineering that aims to humanize jobs by fitting the work to the worker. It is an inter-disciplinary approach consisting of engineering and the sciences of the mind and body. The information from ergonomics safeguards workers from undue overextention and strain and ensures better use of both human capabilities and abilities. According to experts in the field, if US industry adopted more human engineering into the design of manufacturing systems, American productivity could be improved.Material handling is one area where ergonomics has much to offer industry. Any type of manual material movement is often dangerous, costly, and relatively inefficient. However, injuries caused by manual material movement are not concentrated in industries with heavy labor-they tend to occur in light manufacturing plants, retail establishments, and in warehouses. One solution is for the workplace to become totally automated, but not all systems can be so mechanized. People often must be used as the kingpins, and they should be considered essential components of such a system. Data on body build and strength as well as other factors should be taken into consideration. For safety considerations, the workplace's design should try to avoid strain on employee's muscles, joints, ligaments, and respiratory and circulatory systems. Illustration. Diagram. —Anonymous; *Jrnl of American Insurance,* Winter 1979/1980, 55(4): pp. 8-12. Avail. ABI 80-10258

   Ergonomics, Work, Humanization of work, Job enrichment, Materials handling, Criteria, Equipment

The Female Manager - The Pressures and the Problems   (8)

Women are playing an increasing role in the workplace. In 1960, 31% of US married women were working, with the figure jumping to 44% in 1975. A similar trend is found in the UK, but the UK lags behind other European countries. Women have difficulty reaching senior management positions and this creates great pressures. The heart disease rate for Type A married working women is rising. Type A personalities are characterized by high achievement and competitiveness. Because there are internal conflicts about working and raising a family, working women appear to experience more stress and marital dissatisfaction than men. The following organizational policy changes are needed to acknowledge the reality of the dual-career managerial family and to help the female manager of the future: 1. more flexible workweeks for women, 2. paternity and maternity leaves, 3. day nursery facilities, and 4. changes in relocation policies. Table. Diagram.

References. —Cooper, Cary L. and Davidson, Marilyn J.; *Long Range Planning (UK),* Feb 1983, 16(1): pp. 10-14. Avail. ABI 83-10794

Women, Managers, Trends, Stress, Problems, Personnel policies, Changes, Statistical data, Career development planning

Focus on Human Factors When Managing Change (9)

Worker attitude and ability constitute the greatest single influence on office productivity. The workers operating the automated office systems of the future probably will have different characters from those in offices today. Technologies influence character, according to John Connell of the Office Research Technology Group. More and more people are being involved in the decision-making process by management partly to promote a sense of participation and partly to account for the changing character of office workers. There is greater support for a system from the workers if they are allowed to suggest changes. Management also needs to declare openly all proposed changes and the reasons for them. User education and training should be a priority. Special training materials and/or "hands-on" assistance should be expected from equipment vendors. Ergonomic considerations should have an important place in planning for changes in office automation. —Clapp, Robert V.; *Jrnl of Micrographics,* Feb 1983, 16(2): pp. 34-36. Avail. ABI 83-06179

Office automation, Changes, Management, Employee attitude (PER), Users, Training

Human Resource Accounting: Is Quality of Worklife (10) Profitable?

The aim of human resource accounting (HRA) is to identify, quantify, and report investments made in the workforce to tell companies what their employees are really costing them. Many corporations, such as General Motors, have adopted HRA. It can enhance management decision-making and profitability by showing whether there is enough human capability to reach organizational objectives, whether capabilities are properly handled, and whether personnel are being developed adequately. Investments in human resources are classed into 3 categories: 1. outlay costs to obtain, keep, and develop human assets, 2. replacement costs to replace talent, and 3. economic value to determine, for example, return on investments. HRA seeks to provide employees with the highest form of benefits and to provide a systematic means of guaranteeing opportunities and the full use of talent. It corrects shortcomings of conventional accounting, such as failure to budget funds for improving human resources. —LaBau, Marilyn L.; *Management World,* Jan 1982, 11(1): pp. 45-46. Avail. ABI 82-06699

Human resource accounting, Human resources, Quality of work, Personnel management

Humanising the Workplace as Squaring the Circle (11)

Since people spend much of their time in the workplace, they seek to make that portion of their lives more comfortable. The desire to do things more easily is basic. The struggle for humanization of the workplace has been an ongoing one with twin motivations-to increase productivity, and to increase human happiness. Human satisfaction with the workplace centers on such factors as good pay, good benefits, seniority, the chance to advance, and a sense that the work itself is productive and worthwhile. Physical conditions of the workplace are also important. Studies have revealed that few people consider their work challenging, exciting, or fulfilling, and life outside of work is considered a source of more rewards and less pressure. Increased productivity is no indicator of growing satisfaction at work, and there is also little evidence that work has become any less boring over the years. Improving and humanizing the workplace involves 3 efforts: 1. the pursuit of advanced technology on every possible level, 2. a new system of distributing societal resources, and 3. acknowledgement of new human value systems. References. –Macarov, D.; *International Jrnl of Manpower (UK)*, 1981, 2(3): pp. 6-14. Avail. MCB 82-12793

Quality of work, Work environment, History, Humanization of work, Job enrichment, Working, Studies, Job satisfaction

The Humanistic Messenger: A Consultant's Work in Humanizing an Organization   (12)

Technology, bureaucracy, non-relevant education, and the complexities of life have all but destroyed human qualities and human awareness in the workplace. Managers are often unaware of the humanistic issues facing them. A crucial step in regaining human awareness in the workplace, called consciousness revolution, is the process of providing feedback in the form of confrontation, with a consultant in the role of messenger/coach and the manager in the role of receiver/subject. Managers who work through the humanistic message usually develop such strategies as: 1. allowing people the freedom to make mistakes, 2. giving prime attention to capable people, and encouraging them to do better, 3. eliminating game-playing and put-downs, 4. employing conflict resolution techniques that move beyond avoidance and blame, and 5. developing a strong sense of, and responsibility for, personal ownership for problems, and helping others take responsibility for their own lives. References. –LeBaron, Melvin J.; *Southern Review of Public Administration*, Sep 1980, 4(2): pp. 147-165. Avail. ABI 80-23684

Humanization of work, Managers, Organizational, Clients, Competition, Communication, Teamwork, Social integration, Strategy

Humanizing the Work Place in Europe: An Overview of Six Countries   (13)

Despite the many benefits of a modern industrial society, there have been enormous human costs. These take the form of dull, boring, and dehumanizing jobs. The production systems developed many years ago are not meeting the needs of the work force, as seen by increasing industrial relations problems, high absenteeism, and turnover in selected industries, poorer quality products, failures to meet delivery dates, and other problems. During the last 10 years, a significant number of work humanization experiments were introduced throughout Europe. The 4 principles of humanization at work included and still include: 1. security, 2. equity, 3. individuation, and 4. democracy.In Denmark, the Danish Employers' Confederation and the Danish Federation of Trade Unions negotiated an agreement on cooperation which introduced the idea of employees having the opportunity to be decision-partners in the organization of their own work situations and of influencing the decision-making processes of their companies. In France, a national agency is devoted to improving work conditions. In the Netherlands, Philips Company has experimented with white-collar work humanization programs, resulting in increased productivity and job satisfaction. Finally, Italy, West Germany, and the UK have also made advances in humanization programs. —Cooper, Cary L.; *Personnel Jrnl,* Jun 1980, 59(6): pp. 488-491. Avail. ABI 80-12625

Humanization of work, Europe, Manycountries, Programs, Manycompanies, Denmark, France, Netherlands, Italy, Germany, UK

Humanizing the Workplace (14)

Examining one's organizational values from the view of "as if people mattered," was the theme of a week-long workshop which included 20 top US managers. An interview was conducted with A. V. Manwoanger a workshop participant, in which the principles espoused in the workshop were discussed. According to Manwoanger, employees have to seek representation to be heard in an organization built on a foundation typical of private enterprise-growth, permanence, and net profit. As a result of the workshop, shared expectations, values, and trust were found to be key factors. Three principles were used during the workshop: 1. In any relationship with another person, if one is not part of the solution, one is part of the problem, from the other person's perspective. 2. When something goes wrong, the other person is subtly assumed guilty until proven innocent. 3. By moving back from the situation and becoming an objective observer of one's view and the other person's, one can move closer to the other person's perspective. Humanizing the work place has to begin with each individual manager becoming aware of being part of the problem, employing the 3 principles, and being part of the solution from the other person's perspective. —Young, Benjamin I., Jr.; *Training & Development Jrnl,* Dec 1981, 35(12): pp. 86-90. Avail. ABI 82-01014

Personnel management, Humanization of work, Supervision

Improvement of Working Conditions and Environment: (15) A Peruvian Experiment with New Forms of Work Organization

A Peruvian experiment attempting to make work more human was reported. The experiment was conducted in a group of small and medium-sized urban undertakings in the "associate" or "self-management" sector. The experiment involved a number of activities carried out by the National Institute of Research and Action for Development with the objectives of: 1. making such undertakings more viable, 2. promoting systematic participation by workers in decision-making, 3. improving working conditions and environment, and 4. introducing new forms of work organization. The experiment involved the establishment of a number of production and work co-operatives. Generally speaking, the results of the experiment were positive. The project succeeded in mobilizing the shopfloor workers to identify the problems in the production process and to propose solutions involving greater participation and more democratic management. While the results are interesting, they do not provide an answer to the question of whether or not it is possible to really make industrial work more human. Table. References. —Neffa, Julio Cesar; *International Labour Review (Switzerland),* Jul/Aug 1981, 120(4): pp. 473-490. Avail. ABI 81-22742

Peru, Humanization of work, Quality of work, Organizational, Structure, Reorganization, Participatory management

Improving the Quality of Working Life: The Role of the (16) Management Services Officer

The management services officer clearly plays a vital role in the design of work and the setting of organizational parameters. The work study officer has traditionally been viewed as having a negative impact on the quality of working life. However, members of the profession of management services officers would clearly deny this image. A number of studies have been done to determine the role of the management services officer in improving the quality of working life. The overall results of such studies indicate the management services officer needs a great deal of positive support from the organization, with specific demands and expectations from clients, together with advanced training in the application of quality of work life approaches. Table. References. —Hibbert, Dena and Knibbs, John; *Jrnl of European Industrial Training (UK),* 1983, 7(1): pp. vii-viii. Avail. MCB 83-19301

Quality of work, Job satisfaction, Job evaluation, Work methods improvement, Productivity, Studies

Job Security: The Quality of Worklife Issue (17)

Although many organizations are increasingly beginning to look at what quality of worklife (QWL) means in the work environment, too often they ignore the most fundamental QWL issue - job security. QWL is not possible when workers can be dismissed for little reason and with little recourse. Management continues to invest more money in human resources through such programs as quality circles and other forms of job development, but as the relative size of the prime workforce declines, management must rethink the notion that people constitute just another commodity to be bought and sold at will. Otherwise, the long-term social and economic consequences of job insecurity will undermine the US economic system and political institutions. To strengthen QWL efforts and job security for US workers, at least 6 actions must be taken by US business organizations: 1. Reconcile the inconsistency between investment in human development and job insecurity. 2. Implement alternative work options. 3. Change traditional cost-cutting approaches. 4. Accept the fact that real changes are needed. 5. Do more long-range manpower planning. 6. Consider Japan's QWL efforts. —Metz, Edmund J.; *Managerial Planning,* Sep/Oct 1982, 31(2): pp. 4-9. Avail. ABI 82-26040

Employment security, Quality of work, Employee attitude (PER), Loyalty, Terminations, Human resources, Planning

Moving Beyond Assembly Lines (18)

Germans appear to be in the vanguard of other nations in modifying or eliminating the conventional assembly line. This was one of the preliminary findings of an American management and labor group that visited 3 German factories in early May. The tour was organized by the Work in America

Institute Inc. and included representatives from a number of companies. Germany has long had a large degree of labor-management cooperation on the shop floor and is, therefore, focusing on new types of work organization and the use of ergonomics, a biotechnological approach for designing the workplace to lessen physical and mental strain and to improve efficiency. The German government has funded work humanization projects since 1974. The major emphasis has been placed on enlarging typical assembly line jobs by adding more complex tasks, thus lengthening the work cycle. – Anonymous; *Business Week,* Jul 27, 1981, (2698)(Industrial Edition): pp. 87,90. Avail. ABI 81-17464

Humanization of work, Germany, Work environment, Ergonomics, Groups, Assembly lines, Teams

Occupational Safety and Health: A Report on Worker   (19) Perceptions

Quality of Employment Surveys conducted by the Institute for Social Research at the University of Michigan in 1969, 1972, and 1977 have gathered data on the characteristics of the worker and on the worker's subjective assessment of his worklife. In the period spanned by the surveys, work-injury rates have fallen despite the fact that respondents to these surveys have indicated that work-related injuries have increased. The workers perceive health problems of various kinds as due to workplace exposure, and these illnesses are not reflected in the government statistics. Another trend in the survey was the increase in work-related injuries to women. This is possibly due to inroads made by women into traditionally male occupations. Workers who felt that they were exposed to work hazards were less satisfied with their jobs. About a third of the workers surveyed indicated a willingness to forego a 10% pay increase for safer working conditions. Other studies have found a relationship between tenure and the probability of having an accident. Tenure was also found to be a factor in reporting a hazard to management, with fewer than 30% of employees with less than 3 months' tenure reporting. The studies found that workers want their unions to place as much emphasis on improving working conditions as on increasing wages. Tables. References. –Frenkel, Richard L.; Priest, W. Curtiss; and Ashford, Nicholas A.; *Monthly Labor Review,* Sep 1980, 103(9): pp. 11-14. Avail. ABI 80-20069

Occupational safety, Occupational hazards, Employee attitude (PER), Perceptions, Job satisfaction, Working conditions, Studies

Quality of Work Life and Manpower Planning   (20)

Quality of Work Life (QWL) programs are aimed at making workers feel better about their jobs. QWL programs benefit both employees and employers, as they generally result in lower absenteeism and improved quality of work. QWL programs impact manufacturing planning in numerous ways. For example, they tend to involve more people in the entire planning process. Manpower planning is also affected by QWL programs, as job characteristics tend to change, including those of management. The most significant effect on manpower planning is in the area of job descriptions for supervisors, managers, and manufacturing engineers.

Although some managers and engineers resist such change, others recognize an opportunity to make a bigger contribution, at a higher level, to improve their own QWL. General Motors' QWL is more than a program because it has also become a philosophy, a goal, and an ongoing process. QWL defines itself as it develops in given situations and in specific organizations. As QWL programs evolve, both company and individual expectations are likely to rise, and the program should adapt to such expectations. —Anonymous; *Production,* 1981, Ma(ufacturi(g PLANBOOK): pp. 90-93. Avail. ABI 81-12738

Quality of work, Workforce planning, Organization development, Improvements, General Motors-Detroit, Programs, Case studies

Quality of Work Life Among Public Administration Professors (21)

A study was conducted to examine the quality of work life of professors in public administration from a job satisfaction perspective. Sixty subjects were drawn from the national universe of public administration professors engaged in teaching, research, and service in state universities during the 1973-74 academic year. Subjects were asked to complete questionnaires that concerned quality of work life. Nine variables were examined: 1. age, 2. education, 3. salary, 4. academic rank, 5. number of years at present university, 6. work load, 7. participation in decisions, 8. size of the organizational unit, and 9. institutional location of the public administration unit.Data were subjected to a bivariate and/or multivariate analysis to assess their impact on professional role satisfaction. The results indicate that factors involving the immediate working environment are indeed important and distinct from personal background or movement in the profession. Participation in policy formation appears to have the greatest impact on satisfaction. Tables. References. —Putt, A. D. and Springer, J. F.; *International Jrnl of Public Administration,* 1980, 2(2): pp. 225-246. Avail. ABI 80-15269

Quality of life, Quality of work, Job satisfaction, Working conditions, Colleges & universities, Public administration, Educators, Studies

Quality of Work Life Issues for the 1980s (22)

An excerpt from Work in America-The Decade Ahead (Van Nostrand Reinhold, 1979) indicates that economic, sociological, technological, and psychological factors will be influencing the shape of the work environment in America during the 1980s. The critical issues include: 1. pay, 2. employee benefits, 3. job security, 4. alternative work schedules, 5. occupational stress, 6. participation, and 7. democracy in the workplace. Despite important changes in the attitudes of workers in America, some serious barriers remain to progressive changes. These include: 1. slow economic growth combined with inflation which reduces profit margins and incentives for capital investment, 2. apprehension over government regulation and enforcement of labor and civil-rights legislation, 3. public attack on the governance of corporation, 4. high unemployment, slowdown in productivity, and demands for interesting, productive jobs, and 5. rising wages, salaries, and benefits.

References. —Rosow, Jerome M.; *Training & Development Jrnl,* Mar 1981, 35(3): pp. 33-52. Avail. ABI 81-06856

Quality of work, Life, Work environment, Job satisfaction, Compensation, Employment security, Flexible hours, Participatory management, Employee attitude (PER), Expectations

Quality of Work Life: Labor's Love Found (23)

The quality of work life (QWL) concept is concerned with humanizing the workplace and striking a productive balance between people and technology. The emphasis is on employee participation, and outcome is measured in terms of improved productivity. QWL is a management philosophy that is people-oriented, democratic, participatory, and flexible. Its objective is to make both the job and the work environment meet as many employee needs as possible. QWL in the office represents a new frontier. Initially, QWL had its greatest effect in the factory. A survey of human resource programs designed to boost productivity revealed that lower costs and improved productivity were reported by more than 50% of the organizations that actively pursued human-resource programs. Improved employee morale was reported by 67% of the companies with 500 or more employees. While the survey revealed that QWL is weak, it is spreading. The quality circle is the fastest growing QWL technique. Graph. Wakin, Edward; *Today's Office,* Jul 1983, 18(2): pp. 34-40. Avail. ABI 83-21659

Quality of work, Organizational behavior, Trends, Management styles, Surveys, Quality circles, Human resources, Employee development (PER)

The Quality-of-Worklife Project at Bolivar: an (24) Assessment

At Harman International Industries, Inc., in Bolivar, Tennessee, the quality-of-worklife project is a cooperative change effort between the company and the United Auto Workers of America (UAW). The project is set up so that both parties can jointly determine and implement organizational change according to guidelines that are mutually agreed upon. The project's objectives are to improve employees' quality-of-worklife and enhance organizational effectiveness.The explicit internal goals were job security, job equity, worker humanization, and worker democracy. Since the implementation of the project, there have been a number of changes: 1. More jobs were created, with the hourly employment level rising 55%. 2. Accident rates decreased significantly. 3. Daily output per hourly-paid employee, adjusted for inflation, rose 23%. 4. Productivity has increased, and absences have declined. Table. References. —Macy, Barry A.; *Monthly Labor Review,* Jul 1980, 103(7): pp. 41-43. Avail. ABI 80-15330

Quality of work, Projects, Programs, Case studies, Statistical data, Work environment, Employment security, Health

Recent Developments in the Humanisation of Working (25) Conditions in Belgium

A retrospective analysis of employment and labor problems in Belgium results in 3 observations: 1. Government, employer, and trade union circles have always attached the most importance to the maintenance or pursuit of full employment, but there has never been a precise definition of a rate of unemployment. 2. Over the years the term "full employment" has taken on a wider and deeper significance. 3. Belgium has not experienced a movement to improve the quality of working life. In 1977 a real quality of working life program was begun by the Government. Under this program, the Ministry of Employment and Labor, which coordinates general policy, has been reinforced by the creation of: 1. the Fund for the Humanization of Working Conditions, which provides financial incentives, and 2. the Institute for the Improvement of Working Conditions, whose role is to encourage change. The structures, operating methods, and accomplishments of these 2 agencies are examined. Optimism is justified since recognition is increasing that refusal to innovate could paralyze the entire social system. References. – Pierre, Marcel; *International Labour Review (Switzerland),* May/Jun 1981, 120(3): pp. 279-290. Avail. ABI 81-18097

Belgium, Humanization of work, Working conditions, Funds, Quality of work, Programs

Spillover Versus Compensation: A Review of the   (26) Literature on the Relationship Between Work and Nonwork

Evidence is examined concerning the relationship between workers' experiences on and off the job. The debate over 2 rival hypotheses is of particular interest. The "spillover" hypothesis maintains that workers' experiences on the job carry over into the nonwork area, and possibly vice versa, so that a similarity develops in the patterning of work and nonwork life. The "compensation" hypothesis makes several arguments for a negative association between work and nonwork.Data from relevant studies support the concepts of spillover and compensation under different conditions, but generally offer more evidence of spillover than compensation. For example, support for spillover is reflected in the positive correlations between general types of activities engaged in at work and corresponding nonwork activities. Support is also evident in the positive correlations between subjective reactions to work and to leisure and family life. One important exception to this pattern of spillover is physical effort on the job. Table. References. – Staines, Graham L.; *Human Relations,* Feb 1980, 33(2): pp. 111-129. Avail. ABI 80-06979

Ergonomics, Lifestyles, Work, Psychological aspects, Social impact, Leisure time, Conformity, Studies, Job satisfaction, Job attitudes, Demography

Success Story: The Team Approach to Work   (27) Restructuring

It is possible to make startling improvements in productivity and quality of worklife by restructuring blue collar jobs in ways that permit incumbents to work in teams and give them more discretion, greater interaction with co-workers, and responsibility for a larger work area. Although success with restructuring blue collar jobs has been relatively rare, there is one instance of success at a Sherwin-Williams plant in Richmond, Kentucky.The Sherwin-Williams plant represented a significant change in managerial philosophy as it involved the company's first real experiment with job restructuring. The experiment had the full support of top management and was designed to make work more challenging and even more fun.The innovation at Richmond was successful because of the sociotechnical design elements, including plant design and layout, organization structure, job and· workflow design, and pay scheme, and the implementation factors involving employee selection, training, and actual team building. Some of the benefits of the innovation include reduction in workforce size, reduced absenteeism, increased productivity, and better team coordination. Charts. Table. References. —Poza, Ernesto J. and Markus, M. Lynne; *Organizational Dynamics,* Winter 1980, 8(3): pp. 2-25. Avail. ABI 80-06204

Case studies, Sherwin Williams-Cleveland, Organizational change, Plants (PROD), Design, Control systems, Organizational plans, Teamwork, Implementations, Humanization of work, Organization development

A Systematic Framework for Quality of Working Life Studies (28)

If the Quality of Working Life (QWL) is to be a distinct "school," it should have all the characteristics of a school, such as vocabulary, concepts, and methodology. A QWL framework here developed involves 5 broad components-topic areas which together make one way of defining the field of inquiry: 1. access to work, 2. aspects of job context, 3. perceptions, attitudes, and responses, 4. actors and their interrelationships, and 5. measurement. An immediate priority in the study of QWL is the need to develop a comprehensive synthesis, and the systems approach may prove helpful. QWL can be viewed as a subsystem of socioeconomic systems, and as such QWL can be said to be concerned with the study of the structure and processes of the dynamic field of work relations within a complex and interdependent environment of many systems. QWL students need to study the environmental systems, the elements of the structure, the process of adaptation of these structural elements to their environment, the accommodation and conflict generated by these processes, the work relations emerging from these responses, and the feedback mechanisms by which the open and dynamic system constantly adjusts. Charts. References. —Pettman, Barrie O.; Newton, Keith; and Leckie, Norman; *International Jrnl of Manpower (UK),* 1980, 1(2): pp. 20-24. Avail. MCB 81-15703

Quality of work, Humanization of work, Work environment, Job satisfaction

They Hear You ... But They're Not Listening (29)

Today's workers present significant challenges for employers. Management must contend with employees who now demand self-fulfillment beyond the traditional salary increases and promotions. The attitudes and rising expectations of young employees can create a block of internal communications. As a result, there is a need for a change from the traditional employer orientation to employee orientation. The following approaches to employee communications are offered as alternatives to the traditional employer oriented management: 1. human values orientation, 2. planning, 3. effective procedure for grievance, 4. responsive supervisors, 5. active listening, and 6. management involvement. These guidelines respond to the demands of young employees, rather than management, for more and better communication. A comprehensive communication program can produce increased productivity and improved internal relations. —Aiello, Robert J.; *Public Relations Jrnl,* Mar 1983, 39(3): pp. 18-21. Avail. ABI 83-08846

Internal, Communication, Job attitudes, Job satisfaction, Younger workers, Expectations, Problems, Employee attitude (PER), Guidelines

Who Cares About Job Design? Some Reflections on its (30) Present and Future

In the last 15 years, job design has emerged as a recognizable area of study of "the quality of working life". The likelihood that development of this study area will continue rests on the answers to 4 main questions: 1. Is there a consistent theory of job design? 2. Can management easily apply the techniques? 3. Will techniques dispersion take place? 4. Can redesigning jobs produce a good quality of working life? There is no general solution to job design since jobs must be designed to fit the needs of a certain plant at a certain time. The needs of the worker will be shaped during the process of participation in job design. A corps of change agents who can begin their training without waiting for the work design package to be completed can help management apply the techniques. This corps of change agents can also help in the dispersion of the techniques for improving the quality of working life. Finally, the answer to the question "Who Cares About Job Design?" depends on whether one believes the worker is entitled to any humane treatment he can get. This workplace quality of life includes pay, job mobility, and the amount and quality of leisure time created or allowed by the job. References. —Kirkman, Frank; *International Jrnl of Operations & Production Mgmt (UK),* 1981, 2(1): pp. 3-13. Avail. MCB 82-04951

Job, Design, Quality of work, Technology, Implementations, Effects, Behavior, Job satisfaction, Job enrichment, Employee attitude (PER), Organizational behavior

Why Quality of Work Life Doesn't Always Mean (31) Quality

The quality of work life (QWL) movement has made a great impact on US businesses, and techniques being promoted under that concept include Quality Circles, horizontal business teams, and productivity gains sharing. Goals of all QWL programs are: 1. involving workers in improving work life, 2. removing some controls, and 3. giving workers information and problem-solving skills. The experience with QWL programs has been mixed. For example, General Foods instituted participatory management programs at one of its plants. The program was a success, but other segments of the firm considered the project as an oddity and resented it. Northeastern Labor Management Center has set forth some ground rules for a successful QWL program. These rules include: 1. Be sure management is committed to QWL and is willing to see it through. 2. Train everyone extensively, for inadequate training is a prime cause of failure. 3. Use strategic planning in the implementation of a QWL program. 4. Since isolation and deterioration of programs are typical problems, plan for institutionalization and diffusion from the onset. —Cohen, Deborah Shaw; *Training,* Oct 1981, 18(10): pp. 54-60. Avail. ABI 81-24459

Quality of work, Participatory management, Programs, Success, Factors

Worksite Health Promotion Can Be Cost-Effective   (32)

Efforts to contain medical expenditures through worksite health promotion programs have drawn considerable attention. Most agree that comprehensive health-promotion programs are worthwhile, but for some managers, these programs may seem too costly when results may not be known for many years. There are risk-intervention programs that are highly cost-effective over the short term. Such programs include: 1. smoking cessation, 2. high blood pressure detection and control, 3. control of lipid levels, 4. weight control and fitness, and 5. stress management. The whole health promotion process starts with awareness. The commitment of upper management is essential. The programs should be publicized in a conspicuous but conservative manner. Health programs can be on-site with internal staff or on- or off-site with an outside staff. The health promotion programs conducted at Metropolitan Life Insurance Co. have achieved success rates that are quite acceptable. The company's cost-effective intervention programs have also proven to be result-effective. Table. – Brennan, Andrew J. J.; *Personnel Administrator,* Apr 1983, 28(4): pp. 39-42. Avail. ABI 83-10553

Health care, Programs, Costs, Risk, Reduction, Employee problems, Stress, Behavior modification

7 Myths About Quality of Working Life   (33)

Recent national surveys indicate a general decline in job satisfaction which is causing many managers to look to quality of working life programs for help. In order to successfully implement such a program, the manager needs to view it as a new way of thinking rather than as a series of techniques. Successful implementation will include: 1. incorporation of human emotions, intuition, and feelings, 2. the use of chance occurrences to suggest changes in routine, and 3. the introduction of phases to guide the organization through the preliminary stages of development. If the total approach is not used, 7 common myths may stand in the way of full development. The names coined to represent common misconceptions about the work force are: 1. the altruism myth, 2. the know-it-all myth, 3. the snapshot myth, 4. the instant gratification myth, 5. the cloning myth, 6. the typecasting myth, and 7. the department of "blank" myth. Generalizations represented by the 7 myths are inaccurate because quality of work life variables are highly interactive; one variable affects another. The attempt to formulate consistent generalizations with so many changing variables is difficult. Table. References. –Wacker, Gerald and Nadler, Gerald; *California Mgmt Review,* Spring 1980, 22(3): pp. 15-23. Avail. ABI 80-16896

Quality of work, Job satisfaction, Productivity, Job enrichment, Humanization of work, Programs, Problems

HUMANIZING THE TECHNOLOGICAL ENVIRONMENT

Computerisation-The Methods for Change   (34)

The increased use of computerized visual display units (VDUs) brings about changes in work organization. The changes have not always been smooth, due in part to poor design and the lack of employee involvement in the changes. Employee dissatisfaction and negative attitudes toward new technology can create unwanted stress and a lower performance quality. The introduction of VDUs to the workplace should be viewed first as a people problem, then as a technical problem. To avoid job dissatisfaction, care should be taken to meet employee needs in 4 areas: 1. physical comfort, 2. job security, 3. pay levels, and 4. social interaction. In addition, job satisfaction can be enhanced by achieving 5 more outcomes: 1. matching skill levels, 2. providing job variety and meaningfulness, 3. autonomy, 4. performance feedback, and 5. promotion. —Anonymous; *Work & People (Australia)*, 1981, 7(2): pp. 30-33. Avail. ABI 82-07662

Office automation, Technological change, Ergonomics, Job improvement, Job satisfaction, Job, Design, VDTs, Terminals (DP)

Easing Tensions Between Man and Machine   (35)

Ergonomics, the science of adapting machines to people, is currently preoccupied with making computers truly user-friendly for the workers that use them day after day. Many employees complain about eye problems, aching backs and necks, fatigue, and stress on the job. The video display terminal (VDT) makers are promising that ergonomics will solve all of these problems. Ergonomists are focusing on improving keyboard design, including layout of letters and symbols, standardizing across the breadth of each manufacturer's line, and they have sculpted the keys for an easy touch. Office worker unions in Germany and Sweden have persuaded their governments to enact ergonomic standards. In the US, the VDT health scares of the 1970s have resulted in greater concerns about this area. US manufacturers have been trying to prevent the implementation of national standards for VDT design. However, 11 states are currently considering laws that would control the design of VDTs. —McQuade, Walter; *Fortune*, Mar 19, 1984, 109(6): pp. 58-66. Avail. ABI 84-10303

Ergonomics, VDTs, Employee problems, Stress

Examining the 'Human' Aspects of Technology   (36)

Ergonomics research is more advanced in Europe than in the United States, and ergonomic requirements, either in the form of legislation or recommendations, much more stringent. One of the current issues in ergonomic investigation of the automated office is the effect on the spine of a worker who must sit continuously at a cathode ray tube (CRT) centered work station. Back problems have long been observed as a hazard in dedicated typing jobs, but researchers now suggest the problem will be aggravated for the CRT user, who will not move from the unnatural typing posture, even in the small ways traditionally necessary to change paper in the machine. Operators can avoid some of these problems by taking frequent breaks. In addition, some work-station design features can prevent fatigue. —Jones, Keith; *Mini-Micro Systems,* Aug 1981, 14(8): pp. 50,55,59. Avail. ABI 81-23946

CRTs, Personnel, Terminals (DP), Computer peripherals, Health hazards, Occupational hazards, Ergonomics, Working conditions

Frustration in the Workplace: Its Effect on Productivity (37)

For many people, frustration is a constant part of the work environment. The pressures of a demanding pace and the anxiety caused by machine failure at inopportune times can combine to make employees frustrated and angry, and thus, less productive and less efficient. Frustration has a direct impact on productivity, particularly if no relief is offered. Frustration lowers morale, causes absenteeism and turnover, and can result in work stoppages. Industry is looking to science to help reduce frustration in the workplace through humanizing the workplace and concentrating on the human factor when adopting new systems and ordering new equipment. Some workplace frustration can be addressed by replacing malfunctioning equipment with machines that are more dependable, easier to use, and more easily serviced. As makers of office systems try to provide the office of the future, they should address the frustration issue in the design, engineering, manufacturing, sales and service steps of their business. Office automation must be combined with ergonomics. Graphs. References. —Anonymous; *Jrnl of Micrographics,* Mar 1982, 15(3): pp. 16-21. Avail. ABI 82-08458

Job attitudes, Effects, Productivity, Work environment, Job satisfaction, Office automation

The Future: 1990's Office Will Need Human Focus (38)

Both managers and employees were recently asked to identify problems that could arise from expected changes in the office workplace, in a survey conducted by the Administrative Management Society Foundation (Willow Grove, Pennsylvania). The questions they raised were responded to by experts in human resources management and office automation. Increased automation can make work methods more flexible in at least 2 ways: 1. Machines will be able to take over more routine work and free employees for more creative tasks. 2. Automation will allow workers to perform their tasks away from their offices. Maintaining a human element in an automated office is a function of attitude. There must be an essential faith in the importance of people and an emphasis on automation as a support tool. In the job restructuring that is essential to automation, employees should be given responsibility and authority and be allowed to plan and implement their automated area. —Smith, Harold T.; *Association Mgmt,* Mar 1984, 36(3): pp. 193-202. Avail. ABI 84-11528

Office automation, Information systems, Effects, Internal public relations, Employee morale, Resistance

High Tech Anxiety (39)

The advent of the computer age has been distinguished by unprecedented efficiency and productivity, which is exactly what business needs to stay strong and vital. However, another palliative may be needed - one to placate growing fears that there may be health hazards associated with the increasing use of electronic office equipment. The controversy is focused on video display terminals (VDT). Workers are concerned that prolonged exposure to VDTs may cause radiation-related problems, psychological stress, musculoskeletal strain, and eyestrain. The way that management responds to the issue of side effects from high technology may affect the health and productivity of employees and organizations. Ergonomic studies, which evaluate the effects of technology on people, could help management identify and reduce the kinds of stress caused by office automation. As increasing numbers of workers use VDTs, management should watch for such signals as: 1. high levels of absenteeism, 2. excessive physical complaints, and 3. a high turnover. Flexibility in job and organizational design can help reduce occupational stress. —Herdman, Patricia C.; *Management Focus,* Jan/Feb 1983, 30(1): pp. 29-31. Avail. ABI 83-23545

VDTs, CRTs, Stress, Health hazards, Radiation, Working conditions, Ergonomics, Occupational safety

The Human Factor: A Mix of Quality, Efficiency (40)

New improvements in technology may result in inventions that strip a job of the elements that make the job worthwhile for the employees. A study has been performed to determine if this is true of operators of cordless (css1) switchboard systems. The study was designed to explore the physiological and behavioral correlation of operators' psychological well-being at work, to account for operator dissatisfaction and reduced efficiency, and determine whether the cordless switchroom reduced operators' work responsiveness. Factors of "well-being" and "competency" were distinguished in the mood self-ratings. The study indicated that cordless switchboard operators dislike their job because of the hardware and procedural constraints of the system which inhibit their skills. Remedial measures must consider the basic job design and equipment design trends. Graphs. —Brown, Ivan D.; Wastell, D. G.; Tredre, B.; Copeman, A. K.; and Collins, J.; *Telephony,* Mar 16, 1981, 200(11): pp. 20-22. Avail. ABI 81-08260

Telecommunications, Personnel, Technological change, Effects, Job satisfaction, Studies, Behavior, Efficiency, Psychological aspects

Humanized Computers: The Need for Them and the (41)
Substantial Pay-Off

High-ranking officials admit that the identification numbers which are a by-product of mass data processing systems are felt to be problematic by the public. It is perhaps appropriate to devote attention to the new industrial data pollution which is a function of the increase in the new data processing industry. The frustrations of computer systems which are inadequately designed for ease of human use can certainly cause severe psychological distress.As early as about 1970, Bell Labs in New Jersey conducted much research into a narrow but important aspect of the work environment of their many employees in the Bell Corporation. They found that the typical abstract numeric codes which were in common use as a result of early data processing traditions, dating back to electromechanical machines before the Second World War, were a significant barrier to employee productivity. Meaningful mnemonic codes were considered the easiest to work with, and alphanumeric and numeric codes were more difficult. It was illustrated that if the codes were "human engineered" in the direction of easy-to-remember codes which were related to whatever they represented, then people could improve their ability to learn, to remember, and to reproduce them correctly. Both employees and outsiders affected by the system, the general public, and employees of other institutions and firms should have certain rights to expect a reasonable standard of human engineering in computer systems. Appendix. References. Tables. Graph. —Gilb, Tom; *Computers & People,* May/Jun 1980, 29(5) ,6: pp. 7-12,19. Avail. ABI 80-11689

Computers, Codes, Policy, Data, Pollution, Humanization of work, Guidelines

The Implementation of New Technology: A Question of   (42)
Attitudes

A comparison of employment practices in the US, the UK, and Japan, indicates differences in the ease with which technology can be implemented and moves to new social arrangements made. US employees are highly individualistic and competitive, while Japanese employees have a strong sense of team performance, and in both countries, adult re-training is a high priority. In the UK, however, re-training and human resources skills do not have the same importance for management, in part because of the strong protectionist attitude toward particular jobs and a tendency for the worker to identify with the country as a whole, rather than with his or her own company. Lack of attention to human resources has caused UK productivity difficulties. Management is moving toward participation by employees, but this needs to be done carefully to avoid destroying confidence in management. An atmosphere of understanding and trust is important, and training and reward systems need to be made more responsive to individual workers. Several specific steps should be taken: 1. Organizations should adopt mechanisms for quicker responses to social and technological changes, identifying immediately where human resources systems are insufficiently flexible. 2. Incremental rather than large-scale social change should be instituted. 3. Senior management should take time from day-to-day problems in order to consider tomorrow's world and its needs. 4. Efforts should be made to understand the effects of such social changes as the growth in use of consultants and outside contractors. 5. Managers should be equipped with the skills to work with the political element of their management work. Tables. Chart. —Russell, John; *Industrial & Commercial Training (UK),* Mar 1981, 13(3): pp. 86-92. Avail. ABI 81-10544

UK, Productivity, Technology, Innovations, Implementations, Technological change, Employment practices, Personnel policies, Comparative analysis, US, Japan, Education, Employee attitude (PER), Motivation, Human resources

Macht Bueroarbeit krank? (Does Office Work Make   (43)
You Ill?)

Office jobs are generally considered to be safe, compared with many high-risk jobs in the production field, and complaints afflicting office staff have been dismissed as insignificant. However, a survey of some 1,500 office employees who used video screens, as well as another 300 typists, indicates most of the physical complaints stemming from such activities were caused

by not sitting comfortably. Insurance statistics for sickness benefit claims between the years 1975 and 1979 indicates while the number of shop floor workers insured rose by 2.5% compared to a rise of 4.9% for office workers, the total number of sickness benefits paid out to the former dropped by 14%, while those paid to the latter rose 12%. There was an enormous rise in the number of instances affecting the body's mobility, while the number of instances of serious illness showed a marked decrease. The survey also considers different professional groups; here the instances of illness were considerably lower in all the age brackets tested, but the worst affected group was office staff. The causes of this marked deterioration in working conditions are uncertain, and the reasons can only be elucidated by analysis of statistical material and the changes in working situations. Charts. Graphs.
—Cakir, Ahmet; *Buero & EDV (Germany)*, Nov 1981, pp. 8-9. Avail. ABI 82-08654

Offices, Clerical personnel, Absenteeism, Increases, Ergonomics, Illnesses, Working conditions, CRTs

Office Routine: The Automated Pink Collar   (44)

Although electronic aids are changing work routines in offices, not all changes may be for the better. Studies indicate that people's work lives must be considered in relation to the new equipment. If not, morale may decline, even though office workers' initial expectations for the new equipment may have been high. Studies also show that the promises of high productivity gains with advanced electronic equipment often prove to be elusive. In contemporary accounts of the office of the future, the focus is placed primarily on computing technologies for flexible text processing, scheduling, and communications. However, variations in the character of the offices and life within them is largely ignored. People often find new tasks that exploit the gains in productivity brought about by advancements in equipment. The efficiency standards some companies set up also can be counterproductive, further offsetting the promised productivity gains. The lesson to be gained is clear: technology alone cannot guarantee improved performance and higher morale in the office. Graphs. —Iacono, Suzanne and Kling, Rob; *IEEE Spectrum*, Jun 1984, 21(6): pp. 73-76. Avail. ABI 84-22694

Office automation, Technology, Support personnel, Job attitudes, Productivity

Social Choice in the Development of Advanced   (45)
Information Technology

The new information technology has greatly affected the nature of work performed by clerical, professional, and managerial personnel. Social criteria should be employed in the design and implementation of this technology because of the range and importance of its impact. Too often, introduction of this technology has resulted in employee alienation and defective problem-solving. These negative effects can be avoided through social policy. It is most likely that the industrial trend will be toward applying human development criteria to the design of office equipment. Before implementing a new technology, the firm should: 1. have explicit normative models to determine good, bad, and neutral human effects, 2. not approve a design until an organizational impact statement has been prepared and reviewed, and 3. develop a practical method of user involvement. A trial-

and-error period helps companies learn how to exercise social choice in systems design. References. —Walton, Richard E.; *Human Relations,* Dec 1982, 35(12): pp. 1073-1083. Avail. ABI 83-04223

Information, Technology, Human relations, Human resources, Work environment, Quality of work

Tackling the Problem of How Computers Affect (46) Employees

Thirty years ago computers were introduced to the world. Now commonplace in many offices, computers get the blame for eyestrain, headaches, cataracts, general fatigue, sore muscles and unknown dangers of radiation. Emmett J. McTeague of Aetna Life & Casualty Co., in Hartford, is now conducting a study on the effect computers have on people. McTeague's position as director in corporate administration is geared toward identifying problems and correcting them before they get out of hand. While McTeague contends computer technology itself is positive, the human factors are strongly negative. With highly advanced computer equipment, Aetna is especially interested in how expansion in this area will affect its own staff. Radiation dangers have been all but dismissed in most research, according to McTeague, and only one ophthalmologist has been found who believes the cathode ray in the computer could cause early cataract formation. Office furniture, McTeague finds, accounts for much of the fatigue factor. Outside consultants are assisting Aetna in remedying problems having to do with lighting and furniture. Psychological stress has been found by McTeague to be exaggerated at Aetna, though other companies have found it to be real. Also, efforts are being undertaken to aid users in feeling more comfortable toward computers. Dislocation will be a problem, McTeague contends, in that unskilled people will have a much harder time finding a job in the future. —Anonymous; *New England Business,* Feb 15, 1982, 4(3): pp. 38-40. Avail. ABI 82-08155

Computers, Occupational hazards, VDTs, Office automation, Case studies, Occupational safety, Aetna Life & Casualty-Hartford, Employee relations programs

Technostress (47)

Technostress is a psychological problem posed by machines. People's characters are being transformed by computers. Some experience only subtle changes, while others change more dramatically. The latter are individuals who have become technocentered. They let their relationship with the computer determine their relationship with everyone else. Becoming emotionally distant is a preliminary symptom of technostress. Technocentered individuals have lost perspective and are all-encompassed by their work. They are characterized by: 1. constantly striving to improve their work performance by pushing themselves and ignoring their own limits, 2. operating in terms of perfection, logic, and sequential thinking, and 3. losing track of time and considering socializing or staff meetings an annoyance. —Brod, Craig; *Computerworld,* Feb 13, 1984, 18(7): pp. In Depth 43-48. Avail. ABI 84-07628

Employee problems, Stress, Technological change, Psychological aspects

TechnoStress Lurks Inside Every Manager   (48)

"TechnoStress" is a label describing any of several problems that individuals experience in work or personal relations due to computers. US companies are losing between $50 billion and $75 billion a year in productivity because of job-related stress problems. Turnover in high-technology fields is estimated at 25% to 40%. As computers become more interactive and demand participation from users, more stress can be seen in those users. Even after people are comfortable with the computer, workstation stress, in the form of alleged radiation hazards, visual disturbances, and musculoskeletal difficulties, can cause job-related stress. Information processing managers are prime candidates for management stress because they bridge the gap between executives, users, and their information specialists. In addition to causing problems on the job, stress at work is often carried home. Chart. – McDonald, Thomas F.; *Data Mgmt,* Sep 1983, 21(9): pp. 10-14. Avail. ABI 83-25738

Technology, Impacts, Stress, Burnout, Data processing, Man machine interaction (DP), Ergonomics, Employee problems

Understanding the Real Causes of Accidents   (49)

There exists a need for an ergonomics (human factors) engineering approach to the problems of man at work, for a change in production schedule or methodology will surely interact at the man/machine/environment interface. Although indirect causes of accidents are significant, they may be exaggerated by relating them to a production schedule which may, in itself, contribute to the accident. It becomes increasingly evident that accidents involving human error are the result of a misplaced habit. Habits become automatic in the presence of normal stimuli, and the habit will manifest itself even if those stimuli are also present in situations where the usual response is neither safe nor desirable.Case studies illustrate the often obscure relationship between habit and error and the fact that occurrences often described as freak accidents or carelessness are, in actuality, results of lack of understanding of the relationship between man and his working environment. Given that accidents are costly in both manpower and money, their causes must be fully understood before they can be effectively prevented. –Jones, Donald F.; *Industrial Engineering,* Feb 1980, 12(2): pp. 38-41. Avail. ABI 80-04636

Industrial accidents, Ergonomics, Accidents, Performance, Stress, Case studies, Factors

Unrest in the Data-Entry Department: Time Running   (50)
Out?

Data-entry workers are often managed as if they are mere extensions of the keyboards they operate. Opportunities to move up in the corporation are few, and the path is often blocked. According to a study conducted by the National Institute of Occupational Safety and Health (NIOSH), the data-entry operator's job is more stressful than that of an air-traffic controller. Data entry can be easily monitored; the computer can literally record how many keystrokes a data-entry operator makes every minute of the day. Monitoring holds a power that often reminds operators of Big Brother. Some feel it is an attempt to treat operators as children. However, monitoring does provide objective performance records that are not disputable. Incentive programs that reward operators for hitting the most keys must also be examined. These programs can increase productivity, but also have risks: 1. There is danger in encouraging a system that penalizes those who do the hardest, most time-consuming work. 2. People do not always perform in one steady stream of excellence. Working conditions such as these can lead to: 1. low morale, 2. high turnover, and 3. unionization fights. The quality of the data-entry operator's job must be improved, and the mentality that led to these conditions must be altered. –Lasden, Martin; *Computer Decisions,* May 1983, 15(5): pp. 164-185. Avail. ABI 83-19478

Data entry, Operators, Employee problems, Productivity, Stress, Job satisfaction

White-Color Blues   (51)

Office work has grown from the intimate Victorian office at the turn of the century into an impersonal, highly structured organization. The number of clerical workers who are dissatisfied with their jobs is about the same now as for blue-collar workers according to an employee opinion poll conducted by Opinion Research Corporation. The US Bureau of Labor Statistics predicts a 24% growth in white-collar jobs by 1990. There is an increasing tendency toward more rigid work rules and also toward automation in the office. More rigid employment of work measurement analysis antagonizes workers, causing communications breakdowns. Managers believe a lack of promotional opportunities exists due to procedural constraints. Automation in the form of word processing and computers is a fast-rising force in the office. Technological innovations of the past caused office work to proliferate, not decrease. There is a lack of clear concept concerning the purpose of the office. –Thackray, John; *Management Today (UK),* Mar 1980, pp. 94-101. Avail. ABI 80-08812

Job attitudes, Employee attitude (PER), White collar workers, Productivity, Job satisfaction, Performance evaluation, Automation, Word processing

9 to 5 President Raps Office Automation, Says It   (52)
Deskills, Devalues Office Jobs

According to Karen Nussbaum, president of 9 to 5 National Association of Working Women, (9 to 5) since 1977, speaking in a recent interview, the major trend in office automation is to deskill, devalue, and downgrade office jobs. New technology certainly aids office workers, such as secretaries, when it eliminates the need for repetitive operations, but it actually enhances only a small number of jobs. Automation is having a definite impact on women office workers, as is seen in the high level of stress, particularly among those automated jobs. Resistance to automation is increasing among women, and female office workers who average 80 hours of work a week at home and on the job suffer more from stress than do men who average 50 hours of work a week at home and on the job. Future job displacement due to automation will also become an increasing problem. Before implementing automation, management needs to consult the workers about their needs. Management generally is reluctant to involve 9 to 5 in its plans for automation. –Anonymous; *Computerworld,* May 3, 1982, 16(18): pp. 53-54. Avail. ABI 82-12938

Office automation, Clerical personnel, Support personnel, Job attitudes

2

Scheduling for Effectiveness

PART-TIME EMPLOYMENT, JOB SHARING

Alternative Work Patterns Sweep Western Europe (53)

A survey of executives in 10 European countries, conducted by International Management, has revealed that alternative work patterns are enjoying significantly increased popularity in Europe. Alternative work schedules are being spurred by such factors as rising unemployment and increased worker demands for more leisure time. Firms in the Netherlands and Sweden have been the most experimental with new concepts, while those in Italy and Spain have not. Sixty percent of the organizations surveyed in all 10 nations have adopted the use of flexible working hours, and the 2 reasons cited most were greater independence and self-confidence on the part of employees, and a reduction in the accident rate during morning rush hour. Only about 35% of those surveyed express a desire for their workers to do their work at home, but many feel various factors, such as advent of cheap and efficient communications, will make the work-at-home alternative more desirable soon. The most popular alternative work pattern at present is part-time employment. Other alternatives cited are job sharing, shorter workweeks, alternative retirement plans, and sabbaticals. Problems cited include insufficient thought given to hidden costs, union opposition, and inadequate top management commitment. —Zippo, Mary; *Personnel,* Jan/Feb 1982, 59(1): pp. 34-37. Avail. ABI 82-05678

Europe, Flexible hours, Work hours, Work sharing, Part time employment

Changing Times: The Use of Reduced Work Time (54)
Options in the United States

Many employees are looking at their time as a precious commodity, and a study has shown that some employees are willing to take pay cuts of up to 10% if their time at work could be reduced in one of 5 ways. Job sharing is one option for reducing an employee's time at work. Job sharing works well if these rules are followed: 1. It should be voluntary. 2. The expectations of employer and employee should be clear from the beginning. 3. Job sharers should have parity with full-time employees. 4. Job sharing should be supported by the direct supervisor. A voluntary reduced work time (VRWT) plan as introduced in Santa Clara County, California, allows employees to request a reduction of hours and income of 2.5%, 5%, 10% or 20%. In a 6-month period, the county payroll was reduced $619,000. Reduced and restructured work time arrangements redistribute work and spread employment. Such arrangements also help balance work and other responsibilities. References. —Olmsted, Barney; *International Labour Review (Switzerland),* Jul/Aug 1983, 122(4): pp. 479-492. Avail. ABI 83-24798

Alternative, Work hours, Part time employment, Pilot projects, Work sharing, Schedules, Workforce planning, Employee attitude (PER)

Die Musse als Mass (Leisure as Measure) (55)

German employers, unions, and politicians are discussing the concept of job-sharing, and a parliamentary group has suggested testing various models to determine job-sharing's effect on the number of full-time jobs, social security, principles of employment law, and the level of skilled work. Traditional ways of work need to be reexamined in Germany because the labor market must accommodate the products of the baby boom of the 1950s and 1960s, along with the unprecedentedly high number of women entering the market. One study has indicated many German workers wanted earlier or staggered retirement, more opportunities for part-time work, and a long holiday of 2-6 months, while another indicates that 92.2% of the jobs investigated could be transformed into part-time jobs without difficulty, if a more flexible approach than mornings plus afternoons were adopted. Experience has shown job-sharing has no financial disadvantages, only improvements in productivity, low absenteeism, and flexibility. There are a number of procedures that should be followed if job sharing is to be introduced, but none are difficult. Variations on the traditional work pattern include: 1. the range of variation model, 2. the flexible working hours model, with mandatory and flexible days, 3. blocks systems, 4. unconventional part-time work, and 5. two-day weeks. —Derschka, Peter and Gottschall, Dietmar; *Manager Magazin (Germany),* Oct 1981, pp. 148-160. Avail. ABI 82-08650

Germany, Work sharing, Part time employment, Personnel policies, Workweeks, Flexible hours

Full-Timers vs. Part-Timers: How Different Are They? (56)

The size and nature of the part-time workforce have changed dramatically in recent years, with growing numbers of people seeking part-time work and greater numbers of employers increasing their use of part-timers. Researchers from the University of Wyoming recently studied the importance of various job characteristics to determine if there are significant differences in job attitudes between full-time and part-time employees. It was concluded that the differences between male and female full-time and part-time workers in the managerial/professional and blue-collar job categories are too insignificant to justify the belief that these workers seek radically different things from their jobs. The importance of accomplishment was rated very high by all part-time employees, even higher than for those working full-time. —Zippo, Mary; *Personnel,* May/Jun 1982, 59(3): pp. 48-49. Avail. ABI 82-15537

Part time employment, Full time, Employment, Job attitudes, Differences, Studies

How to Make Job Sharing Work (57)

Even before the UK government's recent decision to offer grants to employers who gave a half-time job to an unemployed person, the practice of job sharing was gaining in popularity. Job sharing is undeniably here to stay, whether used as a means of helping to reduce unemployment, of securing the services of those unwilling or unable to work full-time, or as a bridge into early retirement. Potential advantages of job sharing include: 1. reduced turnover, 2. increased efficiency, 3. greater continuity, and 4. higher productivity. In addition, proponents of the concept feel that 2 sharers can offer a wider range of skills and contacts. Implementation has affirmed some disadvantages to job sharing. These include: 1. It can create awkward divisions of responsibility and thus cause delays. 2. Sharers may not have the same commitment to the task as a full-time employee. 3. Increased time may have to be accorded communications from supervisors and managers to job sharers. 4. Additional costs may be incurred in administering a job sharing program. Despite its disadvantages, it is winning many advocates; it remains a viable alternative to the 40-hour week. —Syrett, Michel; *Personnel Mgmt (UK),* Oct 1982, 14(10): pp. 44-47. Avail. ABI 82-29221

Work sharing, UK, Unions, Unemployment, Problems, Work environment, Personnel management

Job Sharing - A Concept Whose Time Has Come (58)

Job sharing is the holding of one full-time position by at least 2 employees, who divide responsibilities, salary, and fringe benefits. Benefits to employers from job sharing include: 1. reduction of turnover, 2. reduction of absenteeism, and 3. reduction in overtime costs. To establish a job-sharing program, a coordinator must be appointed and a timetable developed; then, goals and objectives must be set, followed by design of a policy statement. Other important steps include: 1. instituting an employee screening process, and 2. communicating results to the organization. A successful job-sharing program must include well-written job descriptions. Employers must also tell team members whether they are equal, complementary, or unequal and mention any unusual hours or time requirements of a job. One operation that takes more time with job sharing is performance appraisal of the team. Chart. —Lee, Patricia; *Office Administration & Automation,* Apr 1984, 45(4): pp. 28-30,88. Avail. ABI 84-14648

Work sharing, Office automation, Planning, Programs, Effects

Job Sharing Is Winning Wider Support (59)

The concept of job sharing as a means of reducing unemployment is gradually gaining support from European governments. The idea behind job sharing is that if 10% of those now working decided to share their jobs with someone else, enough jobs would be created to reduce unemployment to zero. Some companies are developing job sharing schemes already. One company's approach was to offer 3 options: 1. current factory workers could volunteer to work as job sharers, 2. laid-off workers could return to work as job sharers only, and 3. job sharing openings would be made available for recent school-leavers. Job sharers could move into full-time positions later as they became available. All 3 options proved popular and successful. Although the amount of training time for new recruits doubled, absenteeism and turnover decreased markedly. Another company used job sharing to solve a different problem. During recent layoffs, senior workers were kept on, distorting the company's age profile so that in future years, the company would suffer problems from having a workforce primarily over the age of 50. The company chose not to risk losing essential skills by encouraging early retirement, but to encourage selected older workers to move to half-time work job sharing with a younger partner. Job sharing partners can also fill in for their absent colleagues without having to be paid overtime. –Clutterbuck, David; *International Mgmt (UK),* Oct 1982, 37(10): pp. 44 E-6,44 E-8. Avail. ABI 82-29512

Job, Sharing, Alternative, Work hours, Employment practices, UK, Unemployment

Job-Sharing: An Effective Problem-Solving Tool (60)

For many managers, job-sharing has been the answer to a particular company problem. The concept involves 2 or more people sharing the hours and responsibilities of one full-time position. Job-sharing can improve attendance, serve as an alternative to layoffs, and cut back on overtime pay. Other advantages of job-sharing include: 1. It increases the chances of keeping good employees. 2. It serves as a good way to ease employees into retirement. 3. It prevents a void when an employee takes off suddenly. Job-sharing can pose a cost savings, and it is applicable to professional as well as clerical jobs. However, it must be set up properly or it will not work. Not everyone is a candidate for job-sharing. Potential job-sharers should meet and interact before they establish an arrangement, as communication between job-sharers is vital. To be successful, agreements should never be standard but tailored to meet the individual needs of each position and job-sharing team. –Anonymous; *Effective Manager,* Jan 1982, 5(4): pp. 5-6. Avail. ABI 82-04251

Job, Sharing, Arrangements, Advantages

Job-Sharing: What's in It for the Employer? (61)

GEC Telecommunications has successfully implemented job sharing in which 2 part-time workers share one full-time job. While the costs involved are somewhat higher, the benefits - including lower absenteeism and greater productivity - outweigh them. The UK government hopes that job sharing will help ease unemployment. A Chief Executive survey of 9 nations' top management attitudes revealed little interest in job sharing. However, unless they accept it, they may eventually have expensive government measures forced on them. The UK's Department of Employment gives a L750 grant to companies for each job split into 2 part-time jobs. The part-time workers must meet certain criteria, such as being unemployed and receiving unemployment. The split job must offer at least 15 hours of work weekly and must be split for a whole year. Local authorities are enthusiastic about the program, but private industry is wary. The jobs best suited to job sharing include those with: 1. well-defined duties, 2. restricted training requirements,

3. no night work, and 4. limited preparation time. —Harvey, David; *Chief Executive (UK)*, May 1983, pp. 9-10. Avail. ABI 83-17930

UK, Case studies, Telecommunications industry, Work sharing

Part-Time Employment: Making the Future Work in Education   (62)

A study was conducted to investigate teachers' perceptions of the major costs and benefits associated with the introduction of permanent part-time work in the New South Wales, Australia, primary schools. The study suggests that the greater the range of employment opportunities available to the contemporary workforce, the higher the probability of spreading employment equitably across the workforce. Additionally, permanent part-time work represents an important work option which may assist in developing employment options more in touch with the needs of a post-industrial society. For the study, which used a stratified sample, the cost/benefit impacts upon primary schools were divided into the following areas: 1. teachers' working conditions, 2. supply and demand for teachers, 3. teaching and administration of schools, and 4. social relationships and interactions. The study employed an analytical survey approach, with primary data gathered from a questionnaire. Graph. Tables. References. — Wood, Jack M.; *Work & People (Australia)*, 1984, 10(1): pp. 6-14. Avail. ABI 84-24086

Part time employment, Australia, Work sharing, Surveys, Educators, Benefit cost analysis

Part-Time Work Will Increase, Bringing Change to Social Mores and Standards of Compensation   (63)

Since the 1960s, attitudes toward work have changed, many women have joined the workforce, and the number of part time jobs has increased almost 3 times as fast as full-time jobs. Much of the part-time market is filled by women and the elderly. Women's demands for job equity with men have been supported by job/pay equity and non-discrimination legislation. A recent trend toward more equal relations between the sexes will cause more men to reduce their working hours. These trends are expected to extend, and likely expand, into the 21st Century. Employers' attitudes toward part-time workers also are changing. Some employers still perceive part-time workers as economically unproductive, inconvenient, and requiring a longer pay-off time for training. However, as the rigidity of the 40-hour week breaks down, the potential for growth in the part-time workforce will expand. This increase will require new laws on employee rights and working conditions. References. —Barrett, Nancy S.; *Personnel Administrator*, Dec 1983, 28(12): pp. 94-98,104. Avail. ABI 84-01731

Part time employment, Trends, Job attitudes, Workforce planning, Personnel management, Wages & salaries, Women, Sex roles, Personnel policies

Part-Time Workers as Missing Persons in Organizational Research   (64)

Even though part-time employees presently account for 18% of the US labor force and their numbers are increasing, little empirical attention has been directed to the job attitudes and behaviors of part-time employees. Part-time and full-time employees differ, and personnel policies that do not reflect these differences are probably inadequate and may be dysfunctional to one group or the other. The literature suggests that part- and full-time workers differ in the number of hours of work, demographic characteristics, employment opportunities, and possibly in skill levels and abilities. Reported differential treatment appears to result from a priori managerial beliefs about part-time workers and work. Managers who employ part-time workers tend to view them positively, while managers who do not tend to have negative views of part-time workers. Systematic empirical research is needed to examine thoroughly the issue of part-time employees and any differences in their behaviors and job attitudes. Table. References. —Rotchford, Nancy L. and Roberts, Karlene H.; *Academy of Mgmt Review,* Apr 1982, 7(2): pp. 228-234. Avail. ABI 82-14382

Part time employment, Labor force, Job attitudes, Employee attitude (PER), Job satisfaction, Organizational behavior, Full time, Employees, Differences

Permanent Part-Time Professional Employment   (65)

Permanent part-time professional employment could be a significant solution to a number of work problems facing organizations in the next 10 years. Such employment is defined as long-term, high-talent positions for 35 or fewer hours per week. According to Cohen and Gadon (1978), women represent the largest share of permanent part-time (PPT) workers. PPT jobs are generally concentrated in the service industries, such as libraries, educational institutions, health care facilities, and other public agencies. PPT jobs usually have discrete job responsibilities that can be done in pieces by an individual, or they have predictable cycles of work demand. Permanent part-time jobs for professionals are usually initiated by a current employee and reviewed by the employer on an individual basis. Advantages to companies using PPT workers include: 1. greater flexibility in scheduling, 2. retention of valued employees, 3. greater employee energy, 4. an increased recruitment pool for the organization, and 5. increased employee satisfaction. Disadvantages to the employer include: 1. benefit and training costs, 2. administrative difficulties in scheduling, and 3. maintaining communication between PPT and full-time employees. Chart. References. —Zimmer, Barbara and Napier, Nancy; *Arizona Business,* Sep/Oct 1982, 29(6): pp. 3-8. Avail. ABI 83-00779

Permanent, Part time employment, Professional development, Employee development (PER), Human resources

Protective Legislation and Part-Time Employment in   (66)
Britain

The probable impact of a proposed European Community Directive on part-time employment in the UK is analyzed. The provisions of the Directive, which grants part-time workers several legal rights presently available to only full-time employees, are compared to the current state of British law in the area of regulating part-time work. The impact is investigated by testing models that identify the determinants of supply and demand for part-time employees. These tests indicate that existing regulations have affected the way in which part-time employees are utilized. However, there is no evidence that the existing partial protective legislation has reduced the level of part-time employment. The legal case for supporting the Directive is strong, but there is no evidence to suggest that part-time employment will be negatively affected by the consequent legislation upon enactment of the Directive. Graphs. Equations. Table. References. —Disney, R. and Szyszczak, E. M.; *British Jrnl of Industrial Relations (UK)*, Mar 1984, 22(1): pp. 78-100. Avail. Tieto 84-15008

Protective, Legislation, Part time employment, UK, Employment security, Sex discrimination, Economic models, Labor supply, Statistical analysis

What the Boom in Part-Time Work Means for Management (67)

Companies are depending more and more on part-time workers, most of them women. Many problems are involved, such as whether to let such workers unionize and how to compensate them. Studies have revealed a pervasive trend toward discrimination against part-time workers, although some countries, like Belgium, have adopted legal protections. Management benefits from part-timers in a variety of ways, such as lower costs, flexibility, higher productivity, and discouragement of unionization. In countries where these workers are protected by legislation, their compensation and benefits can exceed those of full-time workers. It appears that part-time work is a growing trend, despite allegations that it is just a product of economic stagnation that will disappear when recovery starts to spread. Managers and unions alike are beginning to acknowledge the changes in lifestyle and individual preference that make part-time work attractive to many workers. —Anonymous; *International Mgmt (UK)*, May 1984, 39(5) (European Edition): pp. 38-40. Avail. ABI 84-17812

Part time employment, Manycountries, Labor relations, Productivity, Advantages

Work Sharing Takes Off in the Netherlands (68)

The Dutch Ministry of Social Affairs has set up a program to encourage increased employment by work sharing, or splitting full-time jobs into part-time jobs. The program provides subsidies through which the employer who creates an extra job via work sharing can claim $960 for the first year, and employees who participate receive a supplement that partially restores lost wages for a year. Over 255 organizations have participated in the program during its first 6 months, and the government is actively pursuing a policy of work sharing for its employees. The pressure on the ministry from women's rights groups and some political parties to increase the availability of part-time employment has been joined by part-time workers themselves. The postal and telephone services both have many part-time workers. These organizations like having part-time workers because it enables them to maintain service at a reasonable cost. —Clutterbuck, David; *International Mgmt (UK)*, Sep 1981, 36(9): pp. 55-58. Avail. ABI 81-23532

Work sharing, Programs, Netherlands, Part time employment, Workforce planning, Case studies, Postal service

Worksharing and Factor Prices (69)

This paper focuses on one aspect of policy action designed to encourage worksharing. This involves changes in relative factor prices with the goal of inducing a redistribution of labor hours toward more employees working fewer average hours per employee. Factor prices include all the main categories of wage and non-wage labor payments, as well as the price of capital goods. Analysis of the effects of marginal employment subsidies on worksharing is also undertaken, with reference to the French solidarity contracts. The model used includes capital stock and worker productivity as endogenous inputs. Analysis shows that simple worksharing strategies do not provide simple solutions; indeed, under certain conditions, they can produce opposite results to those that were intended. However, the results do point to further examination of 2 types of policy measures: 1. the unconditional payment of marginal wage and/or non-wage subsidies, and 2. the complete removal of wage ceilings to statutory social welfare contributions. Graphs. Equations. References. Appendix. –Hart, Robert A.; *European Economic Review (Netherlands)*, Mar 1984, 24(2): pp. 165-188. Avail. ABI 84-23825

Work sharing, Economic models, Production functions (ECON), Production factors (ECON), Wages & salaries, Subsidies, Tax rates, Policy making, Implications

WORK AT HOME, TELECOMMUTING

Flexiplace: An Idea Whose Time Has Come (70)

The concept of flexiplace involves giving people greater options on where they work, including the possibility that they can work at home all or part of the time. There is a growing potential for these arrangements, especially for engineers. Flexiplace can reduce the volume of daily commuting, help save gasoline, reduce pollution and traffic congestion, and help lower accident rates. Flexiplace must be voluntary and tailored to fit particular needs and circumstances. Possible benefits and disadvantages are reviewed in the light of recent experience and prospective technological and economic trends. Most of the impetus for its wider use must come from the private sector. Pilot tests should be carried out to overcome possible objections. The nature of work equipment makes the concept more viable. For example, data and word processing equipment that results in printouts in central office locations can now be operated from homes and other distant locations, and the substitution of videoconferencing for travel is already an accepted method. References. –Schiff, Frank W.; *IEEE Transactions on Engineering Mgmt*, Feb 1983, EM) -30n1: pp. 26-30. Avail. ABI 83-10362

Flexible, Work, Site, Engineers, Electronic, Cottage industries

If You Worked Here, You'd Be Home Now (71)

Kathy Tunheim, a public relations manager at Honeywell Inc., spends most of her working week at a computer terminal in her home. Via the computer, she communicates with her boss and subordinates in the Minneapolis, Minnesota, headquarters of Honeywell. Jack Nilles of the University of Southern California Center for Future Research estimates that there are currently 30,000 people in the US working at home with company computers at least part time. Another 20,000 may be working closer to home because computers have encouraged companies to decentralize. Nilles says that productivity gains of 20% to 300% can be realized by workers who can choose their own time to work. Such flexible working conditions can also reduce staff turnover problems. Control Data Corp. has employed about 50 disabled persons who work from their homes. —Lewis, Mike; *Nation's Business,* Apr 1984, 72(4): pp. 50-52. Avail. ABI 84-14671

Honeywell-Minneapolis, Case studies, Computer industry, Cottage industries

Probing the Telecommuting Debate (72)

Telecommuting, where employees work in their homes using computer terminals, has not been adopted by any major company on a wide scale. Instead, it is evolving on an experimental, by-exception basis. With telecommuting, managers often worry about how to get and how to measure employee productivity. Similarly, employees are concerned over the possibility of stunted careers. Unions want to ban the "electronic cottage" altogether. Control Data Corp. (CDC) is a pioneer in telecommuting. The company set up a framework for its computer designers and programmers to work in their homes. CDC has experienced several payoffs, including: 1. the retention of experienced and valuable employees, 2. increased productivity, 3. the ability to tap talented personnel in a laborforce short on skilled workers, and 4. savings in facilities overhead. CDC also claims performance has improved and deadlines are met more frequently. The experiences of many other companies have been more problematical. — Lallande, Ann; *Business Computer Systems,* Apr 1984, 3(4): pp. 102-113. Avail. ABI 84-16724

Telecommunications, Cottage industries, Productivity, Programmers, Cost reduction, Advantages, Disadvantages

'So You Want to Work at Home, Eh?' (73)

Homework is a better term for work performed at home than telecommuting. Data processing (DP) personnel may find homework perfect for them, partly because DP output is measurable and primarily performed on an individual basis. While there are a variety of reasons why workers may want homework, managers and employees must decide if an employee has the temperament to work at home. Disadvantages to working at home include: 1. Employees give up the social and professional contacts with other employees. 2. Employees working at home save little or no money because the needed DP equipment raises electricity bills. Homework does allow flexibility, however, as well as more time to be spent with the family. Since managers cannot communicate face-to-face with the homeworking employee, they must trust the employee and be able to measure the work solely on output. Staff and management cooperation and communication are invaluable. —Barnes, Kate; *Infosystems,* Apr 1983, 30(4) (Part 1): pp. 90-92. Avail. ABI 83-14327

Cottage industries, Advantages, Disadvantages, Data processing, Personnel management

Sour Notes Still Soil a Sweet Idea (74)

The concept of work at home has many labels but few real practitioners. Called modern-day cottage industries, the electronic cottage, tele-commuting, alternate worksite, flexi-place, and HOMEWORK, the idea has prompted a few experiments, but no real trend toward a change is seen. Its proponents say that working at home is an ideal recruiting tool and one that allows women to stay on the job while raising a family. Company costs can be reduced because: 1. Fringe benefit packages are less expensive because stay-at-home workers do not need the same packages as those who come to the office. 2. Less office space is needed. 3. Productivity increases, sometimes as much as 300%. 4. Employee morale rises. Managers and supervisors unconvinced of the concept's utility mention the lack of feedback for a homeworker and the fewer opportunities for promotions. Household and neighborhood distractions are potentials for disruption of work. Insurance, legal, security, and service issues also must be considered. State regulatory agencies may pose problems. The lack of communication between employees is also a drawback. —Anonymous; *Modern Office Procedures*, Apr 1983, 28(4): pp. 46-52. Avail. ABI 83-11107

Electronic, Cottage industries, Homes, Terminals (DP), Case studies, Programs

Telecommuting: An Idea Beginning to Catch On (75)

Workers traditionally go to their work sites. However, the advent of telecommuting provides alternate work sites. Dataprocessing or word processing jobs and computer programming done outside the office via telecommuting provide employers such advantages as: 1. being able to use people who otherwise may be unable to work at an office, 2. controlling office-space costs, and 3. shifting computer workload timing. Besides the home, alternate telecommuting work sites include satellite offices and neighborhood work centers. The telecommuting approach involves such human resource management issues as: 1. selecting the right people to work with telecommuting arrangements, 2. identifying jobs that can be done off-site, and 3. training both off-site employees and managers of off-site employees. As applications of telecommuting increase, companies can evaluate the concept for a possible fit into their operations. Telecommuting provides viable new options for employment. In the future, most companies are likely to have up to 5% of the staff working off-site using telecommuting. —Gordon, Gil E.; *Office*, Feb 1984, 99(2): pp. 46-53. Avail. ABI 84-09572

Cottage industries, Trends, Employers, Advantages

Telecommuting: No Workplace Like Home (76)

Telecommuting usually involves workers performing job-related tasks at home and communicating with a central office via computer. Sharpened communications skills and clearer definitions of expectations in terms of productivity and quality of work are required of managers and workers in telecommuting situations. Employees who will benefit most from telecommuting, according to a study by Electronic Services Unlimited (ESU), are those with company experience who know their job well and enjoy working independently. Careful orientation of both those who work at home and those who continue to work in the office is important for the success of telecommuting. Telecommuting also provides opportunities for self-employment at a very reasonable cost. ESU predictions call for 5% of the workforce to be working at home within 3 years. —Woldenberg, Jeanne; *Words*, Jun/Jul 1984, 13(1): pp. 24-27. Avail. ABI 84-22431

Cottage industries, Computers, Personnel management, Compensation, Start up costs, Supervision

A Telecommuting Primer (77)

There has been little experience with telecommuting - the substitution of communications for travel so that all or part of a job can be performed at home. However, it is possible to establish some guidelines for telecommuting. Good candidates are jobs with characteristics, including: 1. project-orientation, 2. defined milestones, and 3. minimal need for equipment and space. The jobs best suited to telecommuting at many companies are word processing and computer programming. Good planning ability are important for successful telecommuters. Companies should conduct pilot tests before full-scale implementation. Concerns with telecommuting include: 1. communication of information, 2. productivity, and 3. promotion of employees. It is important to secure data in telecommuting environments by such means as dial-up capability. Other considerations include: 1. zoning of the employee's residence, 2. compensation of participants, and 3. tax issues for employees. —DeSanctis, Gerardine; *Datamation,* Oct 1983, 29(10): pp. 214-220. Avail. ABI 83-29764

Cottage industries, Telecommunications, Programs, Implementations, Guidelines

Working at Home Electronically (78)

Telecommuting - working at home using a microcomputer or terminal linked to the office - is attracting a growing number of professional workers, such as investment strategists and computer programmers. This type of job arrangement, however, is still at a tentative stage, practiced by only 20,000-30,000 people. It is limited mainly to professions involved in the production or transfer of information, and its progress is slowed by company and union resistance. Advantages include: 1. increased productivity, 2. time and energy savings, 3. more time with families, and 4. the freedom to choose a home away from city life. The disadvantages emerging from pilot programs show feelings of isolation among a few telecommuters and resentment among office colleagues who envy the freedom and convenience of telecommuting. Despite predictions that tomorrow's office will be the home, there are many opponents to telecommuting, primarily those concerned with the loss of control by labor unions and management. Unions base their objections on possible exploitation of home workers, and managements believe that workers cannot be trusted without direct supervision. —Jacobs, Sally; *New England Business,* May 21, 1984, 6(9): pp. 14-21. Avail. ABI 84-19418

Electronic, Cottage industries, Manycompanies, Manypeople, Microcomputers, Telecommunications

ALTERNATIVE WORK SCHEDULES

After Flexible Hours, Now It's Flexiyears (79)

A dozen West German companies are experimenting with the flexible working year wherein workers contract to work a certain number of hours a year and are free to choose when they work them. Preliminary results from those using flexible working years are positive. Most use weekly hours as the foundation of their work arrangements. At Beck-Feldmeier KG, a Munich store, a survey found that many workers wanted to work fewer hours. In conjunction with an effort to improve productivity, the company gradually let more workers become part-time and began letting them choose the number of hours and when they wanted to work. During slack seasons, they work less, and in rush periods, they accumulate more hours. The flexible work hours have attracted a large pool of qualified part-time workers. The benefits of this arrangement are: 1. lower personnel costs, 2. higher sales per man-hour, 3. lower absenteeism and turnover, and 4. more cost-effective use of employees. —Clutterbuck, David; *International Mgmt (UK)*, Mar 1982, 37(3): pp. 31-32, 36. Avail. ABI 82-09176

Flexible hours, Workforce planning, Germany, Personnel policies, Case studies

Alternate Workstyles: A Solution to Productivity Problems? (80)

Alternate workstyles have been in use for more than a decade, with both successful and unsuccessful results. Employees' values and needs, as well as the corporation's new needs, may be met by alternate workstyles. Alternate workstyles are widely varied. Some of the most commonly used forms include: 1. full flextime, 2. modified flextime, 3. permanent part-time, 4. short hours, 4. job sharing, 6. seasonal or project work, 7. work sharing, 8. flexiplace, and 9. the compressed workweek. Flextime is the most widely used alternate workstyle. While there are many advantages to alternate workstyles, problems do occur. Additional planning and scheduling is required. Coordination becomes an important issue, and supervisors' concerns involve monitoring the number of hours each employee puts in, how they will use a 10-hour day, and how employees will be scheduled to be certain all the company's needs are being met. At Prudential, for example, a half-hour overlap between shifts has helped to provide a smooth transition, while supervisors vary their hours in order to provide managerial support to all employees. —Schroeer, Susan G.; *Supervisory Mgmt*, Jul 1983, 28(7): pp. 24-30. Avail. ABI 83-19592

Productivity, Labor force, Workforce, Flexible hours, Part time employment, Work sharing, Work hours, Advantages, Problems, Employee benefits

Alternative Work Patterns - Is Productivity the Real Issue? (81)

Recent changes in working schedules are one of the important social and economic changes occurring in the workplace. The concept of alternative work patterns (AWP) is strongly supported in the US. Some of the common AWPs are: 1. flexible work hours, 2. job sharing, 3. permanent part-time employment, and 4. compressed work weeks. A survey was conducted of 214 companies to determine if AWPs had an effect on productivity, morale, turnover, and absenteeism. The survey had a response rate of 36%. The most frequently used AWP was flextime, followed by permanent part-time employment. A total of 139 instances of improvements were reported by the respondents. The most common improvements were reduced absenteeism and improved productivity. One or more improvements were noticed by 83% of the respondents. However, 64% of the respondents had no figures to back up AWP evaluations and no system to evaluate AWPs. This raises questions as to the validity of the comments that improvements had been made as a result of AWPs. Tables. References. —Burdetsky, Ben and Katzman, Marvin S.; *Work & People (Australia),* 1982, 8(2): pp. 31-34. Avail. ABI 83-08902

Flexible hours, Productivity, Surveys, Job improvement, Job attitudes, Work environment

Alternative Work Pattern Applications (82)

A survey was conducted to identify and qualify improvements organizations have experienced as a result of implementing alternative work patterns (AWPs) for their employees. AWP is any variation of the requirement that employees adhere to the same 5-day, 40-hour work week. AWP applications include flexible work hours, job sharing, permanent part-time employment, and the compressed work week. A sampling of survey results includes: 1. Of the 214 responding organizations, 63 reported 139 instances where AWP had brought about an improvement within their organizations. 2. Improvements cited included improved productivity, reduced absenteeism, reduced turnover, and improved morale. 3. In the majority of cases, however, no formal system existed to evaluate the success of AWP. 4. Flextime was the most frequently used AWP, followed by permanent part-time, compressed work week, and job sharing. Tables. References. —Burdetsky, Ben and Kaplan, Marvin; *Jrnl of Systems Mgmt,* Dec 1981, 32(12): pp. 6-9. Avail. ABI 82-01702

Flexible hours, Work sharing, Part time employment, Surveys, Effects, Absenteeism, Turnover, Productivity

Do Flexible Workhour Effects Decay over Time? Some (83) Warning Signs and Five Remedial Suggestions

Studies of flexible workhours or flexi-time (F-T) indicate that there are a broad range of positive short-term effects - as measured by attitudes and performance in business and public agencies. Such results have encouraged numerous applications of flexible workhours, but not enough thought has been given to the possible long-term effects of F-T. This review attempts to overcome the inadequacy of the literature somewhat, by presenting an opinion survey in one product division of a large corporation. The focus is on 4 items at 5 years of experience with F-T. The items permit a longitudinal comparison. The results may be useful in the same sense that trend analysis of public opinion emphasizes variation in the same items at several points in time. There are some warning signs that indicate the F-T program is decaying over time, such as an increase in perceived abuse of the system. A few suggestions that might be helpful in preventing the decay of the F-T program include: 1. monitoring, 2. re-emphasizing reciprocal obligations, 3. obtaining management, union, and employee support for supervisors who deal with F-T abuses, 4. training supervisors in planning, scheduling, and delegating, and 5. building trust. Tables. References. —Golembiewski, Robert T.; *Public Productivity Review,* Mar/Jun 1982, 6(1)-2: pp. 35-45. Avail. ABI 82-21336

Flexible hours, Long term, Effects, Surveys, Personnel policies, Attitudes, Problems, Productivity, Recommendations

Effect of Flexible Working Hours on Employee (84) Satisfaction and Performance: A Field Experiment

As part of a general trend to reexamine patterns of working times, a growing number of work organizations have introduced flexible working hours (flexitime) for their employees. Despite its widespread acceptance by many organizations, the actual impact of flexible working hours on employee morale and productivity has yet to be demonstrated. The effect of flexible working hours on employee satisfaction and performance was investigated in a field experiment conducted in a federal agency among 64 clerical employees who were randomly assigned to either flexible or fixed working hours for 6 months. Flexitime caused a significant increase in satisfaction but had negligible effects on performance, whether assessed by ratings or output. It can be concluded that flexible working hours may have more advantages than problems for work organizations as a way of improving the quality of working life, particularly as it is a system that is relatively inexpensive to introduce. References. —Orpen, Christopher; *Jrnl of Applied Psychology,* Feb 1981, 66(1): pp. 113-115. Avail. ABI 81-08359

Flexible hours, Effects, Satisfaction, Performance, Employee attitude (PER), Job satisfaction, Productivity, Studies, Government agencies

Effectively Managing Alternative Work Options   (85)

Recent surveys by the Bureau of Labor Statistics indicate that 12% of all US workers are involved in some kind of alternative work arrangement, such as permanent part-time employment, flextime, and job sharing. Supervisors have responsibilities in the areas of scheduling, coordination, communication, discipline, performance, and training. Supervisors should consider a number of key steps to help themselves manage in alternative work arrangements: 1. Candidates should be screened carefully for temperament and professional goals. 2. A viable work plan should be developed to help employees meet the appropriate goals. 3. Careful planning and coordination is needed to train employees working on different schedules. 4. Ongoing managerial support is needed. 5. Open communication at all levels is needed for flexible working arrangements to be effective. – Olsten, William; *Supervisory Mgmt,* Apr 1984, 29(4): pp. 10-15. Avail. ABI 84-13500

Supervisors, Workforce planning, Flexible hours, Personnel selection, Goal setting, Training

Effectiveness of the Twelve-Hour Shift   (86)

In 1981, the United Paperworkers International Union proposed to Temple-Eastex Inc., a Texas paper mill, the implementation of a 12-hour schedule in the woodyard department. Such schedules had already been implemented in the petrochemical industry, and the primary concern was that the new longer shifts not net employees any gain or loss in income. Other concerns were that employees favor the change and that there be no adverse impacts on safety and productivity. Employees liked the idea because it meant gas savings from fewer weekly trips to the mill and more time off during the week. The program was implemented on a 6-month trial period, at the end of which an evaluation was conducted. The overall consensus was that the 12-hour shifts were successful. Safety improved, production developed an upward trend, and overtime hours were lowered. Any company trying this arrangement should seek the ongoing cooperation of employees and prepare a thoroughly designed implementation plan to avoid confusion. Changes in procedures may be required in such areas as union contract language and whether or not supervisors want to change to the new timetable in concert with their workers. Tables. References. —Brinton, Robert D.; *Personnel Jrnl,* May 1983, 62(5): pp. 393-398. Avail. ABI 83-13585

Case studies, Paper industry, Pulp mills, Work hours, Safety, Occupational, Health, Absenteeism, Labor contracts, Working conditions

The Effects of Flextime (87)

Flextime (FT) is a system whereby workers are permitted to set their working hours within certain limits. Core time is the number of hours designated during which all employees must be on the job, while flexible time is work hours within which the employee may choose the starting and ending time of the workday.A recent survey of civil service employees found that an overwhelming percentage of the individuals favored implementing FT; managers were in favor of its adoption by 89%. Job attitude increased for 78% of the managers, and productivity increased for 70% of the managers. For 72% of non-managers, job attitude increased, and for 74% of non-managers, productivity increased. Research indicates that when a company adopts FT, both the top management and the employees react favorably to the system. FT emphasizes job satisfaction and tends to reduce the absenteeism of employees. FT does require a change in attitude for both managers and non-managers to realize that people can set their own work hours. Tables. References. —Bunger, Gerald E.; *Government Accountants Jrnl,* Winter 1979/1980, 28(4): pp. 52-57. Avail. AGA 80-06836

Flexible hours, Productivity, Job attitudes, Studies, Absenteeism, Questionnaires

Effects of Flexitime on Employee Attendance and (88) Performance: A Field Experiment

The effects of a flexitime program in a county welfare agency are assessed. The study attempts to remedy some methodological weaknesses of previous studies by: 1. employing a pre-intervention measure of each criterion for both the experimental and control group, 2. using "hard" criterion measures, 3. taking into account the nature of a task when performance measures are analyzed, and 4. attempting to increase the external validity of the findings reported by Schein et al. (1977). Results suggest that flexitime significantly reduces employees' unpaid absences. The positive impact of flexitime on short-term unpaid absenteeism, however, appears to be much stronger than on the long-term unpaid absenteeism. In addition, flexitime either had a positive impact on performance or, at a minimum, encouraged an increase in performance. However, the findings imply that the potential positive impact of flexitime on performance efficiency may not be constant across different tasks. Overall, results justify the argument that the flexitime program has a positive impact on attendance and performance among public-sector employees. Tables. References. —Kim, Jay S. and Campagna, Anthony F.; *Academy of Mgmt Jrnl,* Dec 1981, 24(4): pp. 729-741. Avail. ABI 82-04068

Flexible hours, Effects, Attendance, Absenteeism, Performance, Efficiency, Productivity, Organization development, Studies

Employee Responses to Flexible Work Schedules: An **(89)** Inter-Organization, Inter-System Comparison

A study was conducted to assess employee behavioral and effective responses to flexible working schedules. Employee differences in organizational attachment, attendance, performance, stress, off-job satisfaction, and job attitudes were compared by fixed versus flexible work schedules, and by the degree of work schedule flexibility. The variations on flexitime which were studied included a staggered-start work schedule, an optional-start time schedule, maintained for 2-week periods, and an optional-start time schedule with daily flexibility. Organizational attachment, attendance, performance, and job attitudes were significantly higher for flexitime workers than for fixed-schedule workers. However, no significant differences in employee behavioral and affective responses were noted across flexitime variations. The results indicate that the benefits of increasing degrees of flexibility may be dependent upon employee perceptions of the value of time and their ability to manage time effectively. Tables. References. —Pierce, Jon L. and Newstrom, John W.; *Jrnl of Mgmt,* Spring 1982, 8(1): pp. 9-25. Avail. ABI 83-00545

Flexible hours, Work hours, Sampling, Variance analysis, Behavior, Employee attitude (PER)

The Flexilife Future **(90)**

The traditional pattern of working life has consisted of 3 stages: preparing for work, working, and retirement, but this pattern may be slowly changing as the 20th century comes to a close. The concept of flexilife, still far from a reality, would allow individuals some choice as to when, and for how long, they would spend their time in the 3 stages of working life. Flexilife is a logical, large scale extension of the flexitime concept, which allows workers some choice as to when they perform their jobs in the course of the day, week, or month.More and more people are willing to forego some of the material benefits of working in return for more leisure and flexibility in their lifestyle. One idea of flexilife is to allow employees extended leaves for furthering their education. It is argued that young people might be better served if they had less education in the pre-employment years, with greater opportunities to acquire more education after work experience. Older people often prefer to work past the normal retirement age, and flexilife would include provisions for elder workers. Some elements of flexilife, such as the compressed work day or week and the work year contract, are already in use in various countries, and job sharing, to increase leisure time, is growing worldwide. —Willatt, Norris; *Management Today (UK),* Jun 1980, pp. 80-83,164-166. Avail. ABI 80-15469

Work, Planning, Ergonomics, Flexible hours, Working, Leaves of absence, Retirement

Flexitime and the Compressed Workweek for the Small **(91)** Firm: Some Employee Reactions

The results of the implementation of a flexitime and a compressed (10 hours per day, 4 day) workweek schedule in 3 small firms representing the retail, manufacturing, and service industries are reported. A pre-flexitime and compressed workweek questionnaire was administered and compared to a questionnaire administered 1 year after the implementation of both programs. The variables measured were preference, job attitudes, perceived productivity, personal life, and employee turnover. Results indicate that the employees of all 3 firms preferred flexitime and the compressed workweek. They reported feeling more favorable toward job, company, and co-workers. All employees indicated that flexitime had increased their performance at work, but only the retail and manufacturing groups felt there was an increase in productivity due to the compressed workweek. Finally, all 3 groups rated personal life more positive under both programs. Change in employee turnover was found to be insignificant in all 3 groups from the "pre" to the "post" periods. Tables. References. –Latona, Joseph C.; *American Jrnl of Small Business,* Winter 1981, 5(3): pp. 23-29. Avail. ABI 81-14497

Flexible hours, Workweeks, Small business, Employee attitude (PER), Retailing industry, Manufacturing, Service industries, Studies, Job attitudes

Flexitime in the United States: The Lessons of Experience (92)

Flexitime was introduced into the US in 1972. The basis of flexitime is to replace the traditionally fixed times at which an employee begins and ends work by allowing him/her a limited choice in selecting hours for each workday. This is accomplished by establishing a core period of several hours during the workday when all workers must be on the job, plus a flexible band of hours that allow them to add on to this core period enough hours to meet the required daily total. Flexitime offers employees and organizations a number of benefits that include: 1. increased employee morale, 2. reduced tardiness, 3. decreased absenteeism, 4. reduced turnover, 5. a cut in employee commuting time, and 6. increased productivity. Analysis of organizations' experiences with flexitime indicates that there are conditions that favor its successful implementation: 1. clear, appropriate objectives, 2. management support, 3. makeup of the workforce, 4. extent of flexibility permitted, and 5. flexitime installation strategy. Charts. –Peterson, Donald J.; *Personnel,* Jan/Feb 1980, 57(1): pp. 21-31. Avail. ABI 80-06376

Flexible hours, Advantages, Impacts, Absenteeism, Turnover, Job satisfaction, Productivity, Studies, Manycompanies

Flexitime in the Utilities Industry (93)

According to a survey conducted by J. Carroll Swart, professor of management at Ball State University, a great majority of utilities companies with flexitime schedules report good results in terms of increasing job satisfaction and reducing tardiness among their clerical staffs. Questionnaires sent out by Swart were completed by the vice-presidents of personnel/human resources at 125 gas and electric companies in the US. Of the 125 firms, 25 (20%) had flexitime schedules for their clerical staffs. Under flexitime, 25% experienced a somewhat higher quantity of work and higher quality of work; 72% had lower tardiness rates; 25% had reduced absenteeism; and 16.7% had somewhat lower overtime rates. All experienced improvement in clerical workers' job satisfaction, about 33% reported higher

efficiency, and most felt the flexitime program was effective. —Zippo, Mary;
Personnel, Mar/Apr 1984, 61(2): pp. 42-44. Avail. ABI 84-13622

   Utilities, Clerical personnel, Flexible hours, Surveys

Flexitime: The Kentucky Experiments   (94)

Since June 1977, the Kentucky Department of Personnel has completed 3
trials of flexible work scheduling-flexitime. At the end of the trials, data were
gathered from participating individuals and agencies by questionnaires
designed to measure effects upon productivity, absenteeism, morale, and
transportation. Nearly half of the employees said they were more productive
under flexitime, while the other half said they were completing about the
same amount of work. Nearly half of the respondents used less leave time
while the other half took the same number of leave hours during flexitime.
More than two-thirds of the division directors thought employee morale was
affected positively. None thought there was a negative effect. Most
respondents were pleased with and preferred the flexitime option. The
majority responded that flexitime did not affect their ability to carpool. Two-
thirds responded that transportation to and from work was easier or much
easier during flexitime. The majority said they spent less time commuting
and found parking either easier or the same. The flexitime option has been
extended as an agency option through the 1980-81 fiscal year. Tables.
Reference. —Craddock, Susanne; Lewis, Tom; and Rose, Jack; *Public Personnel Mgmt,*
Summer 1981, 10(2): pp. 244-252. Avail. ABI 82-02103

   State employees, Government employees, Kentucky, Flexible hours, Productivity,
   Absenteeism, Employee morale, Scheduling, Advantages, Statistical data

Flexiyear Schedules in Germany   (95)

The difficulty of predicting how many hours an employee will work in a
given year, and the demands for increases and decreases in production over
a year's time, provide a rationale for allocating work time on a yearly basis.
Flexiyear experiments in West Germany have resulted in full-time
employees being able to work fewer hours, part-time employees gaining
options to work more, and temporary employees working on a monthly basis
at one-twelfth of yearly salary. One insurance company went to a flexiyear
system in 3 steps: 1. changing many full-time jobs to part-time, 2. keeping
track of employees' hours on a monthly basis, and 3. allowing employees
flexible daily and weekly hours. The establishment of a flexiyear system by
a German trade company involved: 1. determining customer flow for time
periods, 2. contracting employee hours on a yearly basis, 3. setting a number
of monthly hours for each employee, and 4. scheduling specific days and
hours of work. References. —Teriet, Bernhard; *Personnel Jrnl,* Jun 1982, 61(6): pp. 428-
429. Avail. ABI 82-15882

   Germany, Flexible hours, Annual, Work hours, Preferences, Schedules, Personnel policies

Flexiyear: The Ultimate in Flexitime?   (96)

In the past few years, the use of flexitime has led some companies in West
Germany and Austria to believe that flexiyear is a logical evolution of the
flexitime concept. Flexitime facilitates employee productivity as well as
lowered absenteeism and turnover. Among those companies having

experimented with flexiyear is Beck-Feldmeier KG (Munich, Germany). The Beck department store introduced its flexiyear plan in 1978 to accommodate staffing needs and employees' working hour preferences. Employees decide how many hours they want to work at 6-month intervals. Although an employee's actual working hours may vary each month, the employee's monthly paycheck is the same. This flexiyear system has benefited Beck by: 1. upgrading staff quality by tapping available part-time labor, 2. decreasing personnel cost, and 3. increasing sales per manhour. Although the program cannot always meet employees' working time preferences, it has been successful. The flexiyear concept also enhances a company's ability to plan labor needs. —Zippo, Mary and Greenberg, Karen; *Personnel,* Nov/Dec 1982, 59(6): pp. 45-47. Avail. ABI 83-02714

Flexible hours, Human resources, Personnel management

Flextime Scheduling: A Survey (97)

Flextime allows workers some discretion in what times of the day they will work, just so long as all employees work during certain core hours. In Germany, where it originated, a full 25% of the workforce already uses flextime. Increasingly, US firms are adopting it. It increases productivity, boosts morale, and results in lower turnover. Among the problems associated with flextime are that workers will get second jobs and flood the labor market, and that some workers may abuse the privilege. A survey was done of 15 companies' managers where flextime is used to elicit their views on the benefits of such scheduling. All respondents stated that tardiness had decreased. Two-thirds found lower absenteeism, the remainder found it to be the same. Eighty-six percent said that the need for supervision was lower or the same as before flextime. All found employee morale to be higher due to flextime. All found maintenance costs to be no higher. Eighty six percent saw an increase in productivity. Tables. References. —McGrath, Diane; *Industrial Mgmt,* Nov/Dec 1980, 22(6): pp. 1-4. Avail. ABI 81-04090

Flexible hours, Scheduling, Advantages, Surveys, Flexibility, Employee morale

Flex-Time: Short-Term Benefits; Long-Term ...? (98)

Much field research now alleges to demonstrate that flexible work hours can improve organizational performance, employee satisfaction and productivity, and management/employee relations, but the research depends on subjective measures and ignores important dimensions or organizational behavior. In an experiment at the US Social Security Administration, "flex-time" elicited generally favorable subjective evaluations, but objective indicators of performance and employee commitment produced mixed results. There were also some signs of declining supervisor/employee rapport. The analysis suggests several points of caution to guide future research: 1. Flex-time may augment the intrinsic rewards of work already enjoyed by white collar employees, while refocusing on the relative attractiveness of domestic life for blue-collar workers. 2. The gains illustrated in prior research may reflect a "Hawthorne" effect. 3. Future research must encompass the effects of the complete work environment. 4. Managers who rely on poorly conceived field research to test flex-time will have long-term problems. Tables. References. —Rainey, Glenn W.,

Jr. and Wolf, Lawrence; *Public Administration Review,* Jan/Feb 1981, 41(1): pp. 52-63. Avail. ASPA 81-06731

Flexible hours, Social Security Administration-US, Experiments, Results, Supervisors, Employees, Job satisfaction, Performance, Impacts

Flextime: The Way of the Future? (99)

According to many of today's human resource managers, working uniform hours is out-of-date. The modern method is to allow employees to select their own hours under a concept known as flextime. Under flextime, all employees are present under the mid-day core period, but starting and ending times are ranges rather than points. Rather than beginning work at 8 AM, employees may opt for starting times anywhere between 7 and 9, and the same type of flexibility is employed for the end of the work day. The system allows employees to schedule many non-work appointments, but the most important impact may be in the improvement of labor-management relations. The growing number of working women and changing life styles have given rise to the adoption of flextime. Flextime schedules have become important employment factors for firms that employ a substantial number of women and older persons who often find the standard work schedule too rigid. There are potentially some serious disadvantages from the adoption of flextime. Assembly-line operations do not generally lend themselves to it, and in firms that have less-than-complete employer control, there can be problems in customer and supplier relations. The biggest problem with flextime is that it may establish a precedent for loosening employer control of employee work standards. Charts. —Foegen, J. H. and Curry, Talmer E., Jr.; *Administrative Mgmt,* Sep 1980, 41(9): pp. 26-29,55-56. Avail. ABI 80-18534

Flexible hours, Scheduling, Employee attitude (PER), Job attitudes, Employee benefits, Costs, Quality of work, Work environment

The Four-Day, Ten-Hour Workweek (100)

The Police division of Henrico County, Virginia, had a morale problem among the uniformed officers, along with a subsequently high turnover rate, excessive use of sick time, and an increase in absenteeism. Complaints of officers included their 7-day, 8-hour work schedule and the variation of work on their "beats". A committee was set up to address the problem. A decision was made to adopt a 4-10 workweek, i.e., 4 consecutive workdays of 10 hours each would be worked. Prior to implementing the schedule, the officers affected were surveyed, and about 82% were in favor of the new workweek. A follow-up survey was done after 3 months on the schedule, and the reaction remained generally positive. A benefit of the 4-10 work schedule is the significant increase in productivity and efficiency. Felony arrests increased 42.5%, misdemeanor arrests increased 69.5%, and drunk driving arrests increased 75.4%. The use of sick leave has also decreased. —Crowder, Robert H., Jr.; *Personnel Jrnl,* Jan 1982, 61(1): pp. 26,27. Avail. ABI 82-03238

Short, Workweeks, Work, Schedules, Police, Case studies, Improvements, Productivity, Employee morale

The Impact of a Four-Day Workweek on Employees (101)

In order to boost productivity, improve job satisfaction, reduce absenteeism, etc. many employers are trying the 4-day, 40-hour workweek (4-40). A study was performed in which employee satisfaction, absenteeism, and leisure time were investigated before, during, and after implementation of 4-40. The results of the job satisfaction measures for all 3 time periods show that internal work motivation and general satisfaction were higher during the 4-40 implementation period than before or after, when it was about the same. During 4-40, absentee rates significantly decreased, but after the program was terminated, absenteeism rates exceeded what they had been before the program went into effect. Thus it may be preferrable not to try 4-40 at all than to try it for a short time and withdraw it. Employees may see this as a punishment and increase their absences, or they may have resented not being consulted in the matter of withdrawal. Tables. References. —Millard, Cheedle W.; Lockwood, Diane L.; and Luthans, Fred; *MSU Business Topics,* Spring 1980, 28(2): pp. 31-37. Avail. ABI 80-11196

Workweeks, Work hours, Job satisfaction, Job attitudes, Work, Schedules, Studies, Statistical analysis, Absenteeism

The Impact of Flexitime on Employee Attitudes (102)

In Europe, and to a lesser degree in the US, there has been a tendency to abolish fixed working hours and to adapt hours to individual desires and needs. One technique is to follow a flexible work pattern entitled flexitime, flex-time or flexible hours. In order to examine this idea, data were collected from 2 companies in Central Ohio. The participating employees were placed into one of 2 groups: fixed-hour and flexitime. The examination of flexitime did not support the traditional idea of flexitime consequences for work satisfaction or leisure satisfaction. However, employees working under a flexitime schedule reported certain other improvements, such as easier travel and parking, a smaller amount of interrole conflict, an increased feeling of being in control in the work setting, and more opportunity for leisure activities. The most surprising finding dealt with the lack of significant differences between the flexitime groups and the fixed-hour groups on work satisfaction measures. Table. References. —Hicks, William D. and Klimoski, Richard J.; *Academy of Mgmt Jrnl,* Jun 1981, 24(2): pp. 333-341. Avail. ABI 81-14524

Flexible hours, Job attitudes, Studies, Employee attitude (PER), Advantages, Multivariate analysis, Job satisfaction

More Managers Allow Varied Work Schedules/Better (103) Productivity, Use of Resources Among Reasons for Flexible Schedules

There is a new atmosphere in the data processing (DP) workplace that recognizes and accommodates workers' needs and places a premium on trust, responsibility, and flexibility. A recent mail survey by Computerworld of 203 DP managers indicated that 54% offer alternative work schedules. The 109 who offer flexible work schedules feel that staff productivity improved because of it. Most of these managers feel their sense of control has remained constant. "Flex time" was the most commonly mentioned option. The respondents indicated several reasons for using alternative work schedules, including: 1. to give workers flexibility and increase productivity, 2. to use computer resources better, 3. to reduce backlogs with a limited staff, 4. to attract and retain qualified personnel, and 5. because of budget cuts or to cut overtime. Most of those who use scheduling options are pleased with them and expect to continue using them in the future. —Zientara, Marguerite; *Computerworld,* Jun 20, 1983, 17(25): pp. 1,11. Avail. ABI 83-18479

Flexible hours, Data processing, Surveys, Productivity, Work hours

New Work Schedules for a Changing Office   (104)

Because of demographic, social, and workforce changes, the traditional 5-day, 40-hour workweek is being replaced by new kinds of work schedules. Three categories of new work schedules are: 1. compressed workweeks, 2. flexitime, and 3. part-time. Compressed workweeks reallocate work in different ways, such as four 10-hour days, but do not usually give the worker greater control over working hours. Flexitime allows employees to choose their working hours within management guidelines. Varieties of flexitime include: 1. flexitour, in which employees may vary their schedules from period to period, 2. variable day, in which a given number of hours are worked by the end of a certain period, and 3. gliding time, in which start/end times vary daily. Part-time includes: 1. job sharing, 2. work sharing, and 3. phased retirement. The obstacles to flexitime include choosing the jobs for which the concept is appropriate. Part-time work has obstacles, such as career-path difficulties, while the problems with compressed time include increased fatigue and labor and union laws about overtime pay. Graph. — Rosow, Jerome M.; *Administrative Mgmt,* Feb 1982, 43(2): pp. 48-50,64-65. Avail. ABI 82-06327

Part time employment, Flexible hours, Workweeks, Work, Schedules, Advantages, Disadvantages

New Work Systems   (105)

The current increased emphasis on quality of work life (QWL) has led to a number of variations on the traditional 9-to-5 work day. Attempts are being made to accommodate workers because of a changed labor force, changing attitudes about work itself, and the problem of decline in job satisfaction among US workers. The new work systems being adopted include: 1. flextime whereby workers can alter their working hours as long as they put in the required number of hours weekly, 2. job-sharing whereby 2 or more persons share the same job, 3. permanent part-time work, 4. the compressed work week wherein 40 hours are worked in 4 days instead of 5, 5. work sharing, which, unlike job-sharing, is a short-term measure designed to keep experienced workers during a slowdown, and 6. work during nights or on weekends only. All these options have their advantages and some disadvantages, and they all demand special training for participants. — Mundale, Susan; *Training,* Apr 1981, 18(4): pp. 45,48,50. Avail. ABI 81-09248

Flexible hours, Work sharing, Part time employment, Alternative, Work, Systems, Trends

New Workplace Techniques: Can They Benefit Your Firm? (106)

There are a number of new workplace techniques, some of which are truly new and some only new in the professional setting. Those techniques include: 1. flexible scheduling, under which employees choose starting and quitting times, 2. job sharing, in which two people share a full time job, 3. permanent part-time jobs, 4. task system, 5. home offices linked by computer terminals, 6. sabbaticals, 7. cumulative earned leave, and 8. phased retirement. The technology making these new work techniques possible stems from the communications revolution which allows office workers to work wherever they are, and from new techniques such as the paperless office, the electronic briefcase, intelligent telephones, and robots which give workers time to be allocated in innovative ways. The new workplace techniques do prompt some concerns: 1. productivity and the cost of new equipment, 2. worker displacement, 3. performance evaluation of unseen employees, 4. security and privacy, and 5. employee motivation. References. —Cheatham, Carole B.; *Woman CPA,* Apr 1983, 45(2): pp. 3-6. Avail. ABI 83-15295

Alternative, Work hours, Cottage industries, Office automation, Implications

No More 9 to 5? (107)

More companies are departing from the traditional 9 to 5 workday. The trend is toward alternative schedules, which include a variety of approaches, such as: 1. flexitime, in which employees set their own schedules within certain limits, 2. compressed workweeks, composed of fewer but longer workdays, and 3. work-at-home arrangements. The new arrangements almost always result in improved productivity. They also usually reduce absenteeism and tardiness. A feeling of trust is conveyed by the increased responsibility and freedom. Turnover is reduced because the employees are happier. Potential problems in these alternative arrangements include communication and coordination problems and employee abuse of the system. Several applications of alternative work schedules are discussed. — Kull, David; *Computer Decisions,* Jun 1982, 14(6): pp. 160-178. Avail. ABI 82-16652

Flexible hours, Manycompanies, Work, Scheduling, Personnel management

The Organizationally Dysfunctional Consequences of (108) Flexible Work Hours: A General Overview

Most research on flexible work hours has been inadequate in conception, and the innovation may have some important dysfunctional consequences for organizations that adopt it. The existing body of research on flex-time has 4 problems associated with it: 1. Much of it relies on subjective survey questions. 2. There has been a lack of effort to link flex-time to theoretical constructs concerning organizational behavior through psychometric scales. 3. Objective measures of key behavioral dimensions are rarely used or reported. 4. The adoption of variable work hour systems is rarely accompanied by comprehensive planning and organizational development. The dysfunctional consequences of flex-time can be grouped under 4 headings: 1. employee attitudes, 2. employee and organizational performance, 3. management-employee relations, and 4. unanticipated costs of implementation. These dysfunctional consequences can be avoided if management has the capability and the willingness to acquire sophisticated information on flex-time and uses it with responsibility and intelligence. References. —Rainey, Glenn W., Jr. and Wolf, Lawrence; *Public Personnel Mgmt,* Summer 1982, 11(2): pp. 165-175. Avail. ABI 82-20280

> Flexible hours, Organizational, Impacts, Employee attitude (PER), Personnel management, Personnel policies

Punch Out the Time Clocks (109)

In many firms, the time clock has become a thing of the past, as a myriad of demographic, social, and economic trends have transformed the world of work and reinforced the new ideas of time management. There are 5 forms of new work schedules or job designs that have great potential for the 1980s: 1. flexitime, in which employees choose their starting and quitting times within limits set by management, 2. permanent part-time, which works well at high-level professional and managerial positions, 3. job sharing, in which 2 or more part-timers share one job, 4. compressed workweeks, in which a full week's worth of work is accomplished in less than 5 days, and 5. work sharing, an alternative to layoffs in which the entire workforce of a company works reduced hours for reduced pay. All the new ways of working offer certain common advantages: they cost little or nothing to install, they require no changes in technology or plant, or any organizational restructuring, and they help improve productivity. These methods must be carefully implemented, since there are obstacles. Graphs. References. —Rosow, Jerome M. and Zager, Robert; *Harvard Business Review,* Mar/Apr 1983, 61(2): pp. 12-30. Avail. ABI 83-08661

> Flexible hours, Part time employment, Workweeks, Work sharing, Work, Schedules, Programs, Unemployment insurance, Manycompanies, Unions

Putting 9 to 5 up on the Shelf (110)

Surveys were sent to 3,000 executives, primarily personnel managers in manufacturing companies, to assess attitudes toward, and implementation of, alternative work patterns. There were 896 responses from 10 Western European countries. Almost 60% of the respondents have implemented flexible working hours, although many variations exist in the systems used. Reasons for using flexible schedules include improved employee morale and fewer traffic accidents during rush-hours, although such problems as inadequate staffing and abuses of the system exist. Almost 70% of the firms have employed part-time workers, generally because of employee preference and cyclical business volumes. About 1/6 of the firms surveyed have tried home workers. This is seen as a trend of the future, particularly as cheap, efficient communications technology increases. Job sharing has attracted a significant following, particularly in Sweden. Rationales for its use include: 1. easing unemployment, 2. placing those just out of school in jobs, and 3. coping with slack production. About 6.8% of the firms offer sabbaticals. The use of alternative work patterns is meant to respond to the needs of employers and employees, although practical, administrative, and attitudinal problems must be addressed in implementation. Tables. —Arbose, Jules R.; *International Mgmt (UK),* Oct 1981, 36(10): pp. 16-20. Avail. ABI 81-25483

Flexible hours, Europe, Part time employment, Retirement, Work sharing

Shift Work and Flexible Schedules: Are They Compatible? (111)

The steady rise of shift work in Western industrial society has been accompanied by a growing concern about the effects of this type of working arrangement on the individual workers. Health factors and worker output are of some importance, but the disruption of family, social, and leisure activity is the primary concern. Normal day workers have been aided in this area by flexible working schedules, often called "flextime", but such a system has generally been viewed as incompatible with shift work schedules. Three distinct approaches to more flexible scheduling in shift work systems are reviewed: 1. Rearrangement of shift schedules involves manipulation of 4 parameters-length of shift, shift changeover times, number and type of shifts worked, and number and type of rest days. 2. Personal flexibility schemes stem from the practice of flexible change-over times between workers who relieve each other. 3. The flexible-time manning and work year contract approach suggests expanding the reference period for workers from the week to the year and preplanning the number of hours in a year to be worked by each employee. Two studies of chemical companies, one with 1000 shift workers and one with 120, show some of the mechanics of the work year contract concept in practice. Tables. References. —Young, W. McEwan; *International Labour Review (Switzerland),* Jan/Feb 1980, 119(1): pp. 1-17. Avail. ABI 80-07471

Shifts, Flexible hours, Scheduling, Workforce planning, Contracts, Case studies

Shift Work Has Complex Effects on Lifestyles and Work Habits (112)

Different work shifts have different effects on a worker's health, attitudes, and performance. A number of studies have demonstrated these differences. A general review of the literature on shift work is offered. Although the differences were small, one study showed that the night shift has the lowest output while the afternoon shift has the highest. It appears, based on a few studies, that quality of production is also negatively related to shift work. The absenteeism rates of day and night workers are not significantly different, but when shift work is introduced, many workers suffer disturbances in their social and familial relationships. Fixed shift schedules offer more advantages than do rotating shift schedules. Rapid rotation is best if a rotating shift schedule is necessary, since it facilitates social life. —Gannon, Martin J.; Norland, Douglas L.; and Robeson, Franklin E.; *Personnel Administrator,* May 1983, 28(5): pp. 93-97. Avail. ABI 83-13914

Rotating, Fixed, Shifts, Productivity, Work hours, Workweeks, Quality of life, Studies, Employee attitude (PER)

Shift Work Related to Job Attitudes, Social   (113)
Participation and Withdrawal Behavior: A Study of
Nurses and Industrial Workers

A study was done to investigate the relationship between shift schedules and mental health, job satisfaction, social participation, organizational commitment, anticipated turnover, absenteeism, and tardiness. Measures were obtained for each variable by using several different methods. The subjects were 440 nurses in two hospitals and 383 rank-and-file workers in a manufacturing organization. The results provide support for the model which projected that workers on fixed schedules would be better off than workers on rotating work schedules in terms of mental health, job satisfaction, organizational commitment, and social participation. Workers on fixed shift schedules were shown to be lower on anticipated turnover, absenteeism, and tardiness than workers on rotating shift schedules. Tables. References. —Jamal, Muhammad; *Personnel Psychology,* Autumn 1981, 34(3): pp. 535-547. Avail. ABI 81-23855

Shifts, Effects, Job attitudes, Behavior, Job satisfaction, Correlation analysis, Social, Participation, Employee problems, Employee turnover, Absenteeism, Organizational behavior, Occupational, Psychology, Studies

Shiftwork - The Personal Aspects   (114)

In 1976, it was estimated that 15% of the Australian workforce was involved in shiftwork. About 66% of the shiftworkers have no trouble adapting their schedules to the requirements of shiftwork. The effects of shiftwork stem from the body's circadian cycles, which are biological rhythms based on a day/night cycle. A study of 150 employees in a Victoria, Australia, manufacturing plant was undertaken via questionnaire to determine how a shiftworker compares to a day worker in regard to health, social, and family life. The shiftworkers were divided into 2 groups: continuous roster and 15-day roster workers. The day workers formed the control. Of the 3 groups, 15-day shiftworkers scored higher than day workers and continuous roster workers on an overall scale measuring the effects of work on sexual, social, anxiety, and health problems. This may be influenced by their age, and the length of time they had done shiftwork. Workers cite money and time off as the main advantages of shiftwork. A more rapidly changing shift structure would alleviate some of the problems. Tables. Graphs. References. — Hannaford, Marie; *Work & People (Australia),* 1982, 8(1): pp. 3-11. Avail. ABI 83-01446

Shifts, Work hours, Workforce, Job attitudes, Employee attitude (PER), Australia, Studies, Job satisfaction

Should Your Firm Consider the Flexitime Alternative?   (115)

Flexitime, a system which has enjoyed increasing popularity, allows employees a degree of freedom and responsibility in determining their working hours and consists of core time, when employees must be at work, and flexible time, when they can vary arrival and departure times. It has been introduced in all major industries in response to such motivations as employee relations, and the desire to conserve energy and use public transportation effectively. Management views it as an investment in human resources, and unions are beginning to view it with more satisfaction and approval. The success rate for flexitime programs is high, 92-97% as revealed in recent studies, and it appears to improve employee morale. Costs to employers are small, because it usually does not involve expanding the duration of building operation. Studies indicate that it contributes to organizational effectiveness, and productivity is improved. Successful flexitime programs must be well planned, and what problems arise are usually due to poor supervision or coverage. Charts. References. —McCarthy, Maureen; *Industrial Engineering,* Jan 1981, 13(1): pp. 49-50,55-57,89. Avail. ABI 81-02555

Flexible hours, Work hours, Labor relations, Productivity, Job satisfaction, Advantages

Taking a Look at Flexitime (116)
By allowing people to restructure their work hours, flexitime helps reduce absenteeism, tardiness, and turnover and increase job satisfaction, morale, and productivity. While the concept of flexitime has gained considerable management and employee support, a company's needs and objectives must be carefully evaluated before flexible work hours are allowed. There are both advantages and disadvantages to flexitime. Before implementing flexitime, a company should know the conditions favoring its adoption. There are a number of steps that can be taken to ensure the successful installation of a flexitime program, including: 1. obtaining top management's support, 2. involving employees at all levels, and 3. setting clear, appropriate goals. —Morgan, Philip I. and Baker, H. Kent; *Supervisory Mgmt,* Feb 1984, 29(2): pp. 37-43. Avail. ABI 84-07175

Flexible hours, Personnel policies, Supervisors, Guidelines

Toward a Conceptual Clarification of Employee (117)
Responses to Flexible Working Hours: A Work
Adjustment Approach
A work adjustment model is used to consider how employee responses are linked to flexible working time. A framework and rationale explain how and why flexible working hours can contribute to work adjustment and, as a result, affect employees' attitudes and behaviors. Two basic work schedules are used to define flexible working hours: 1. flexitime, under which an employee sets the time to start daily work and, sometimes, break and lunch times, and 2. variable working hours, under which an employee is free to set the required hours of work within a specified period, e.g., per day, week, or month. Evidence has developed that flexible working hours result in: 1. increased employee job satisfaction; 2. improved job performance, and 3. a decrease in withdrawal behavior, i.e., tardiness, absenteeism, and turnover. These results occur under conditions whereby the abilities of the employee and the ability requirements of the work environment are in harmony, and where the needs of the employee are met by the work environment. Job satisfaction and tenure are also likely to follow. Flexible working hours are discussed in terms of body rhythms, stress, worker autonomy, time, commitment, job involvement and absenteeism, as well as the possible drawbacks to implementing such a system. Chart. References. —Pierce, Jon L. and Newstrom, John W.; *Jrnl of Mgmt,* Fall 1980, 6(2): pp. 117-134. Avail. ABI 81-26077

Flexible hours, Effects, Employee attitude (PER), Job satisfaction, Stress, Performance, Models

Union and Employer Policies on Alternative Work **(118)**
Patterns
The Human Resources Section of the Australian Department of Productivity
conducted a survey recently of trades unions and employer associations. The
survey examined formulated policies concerning the introduction of new
working patterns or modifications of traditional arrangements. Union
respondents experienced an overall membership increase and an increasing
number of women members. Employers reported a number of employment
changes generally reflecting trends of male/female participation in the
Australian labor force. Employer associations had fewer formalized policies
than did the unions, which is due in part to a different emphasis within
employer associations. The problems in developing policies perceived by
employer associations included: 1. union acceptance, 2. nature of the
industry, and 3. membership consensus problems. Unions saw problems such
as members' resistance to change. Areas where progress has been made
include: 1. compressed work week/fortnight, 2. shorter working hours, and
3. flexitime in public service areas. Tables. References. Appendix. —Hogan,
Ann and Milton, Peter; *Work & People (Australia),* 1980, 6(1): pp. 8-14. Avail. ABI 80-23471
Australia, Surveys, Unions, Employers, Policies, Work, Pattern, Work hours, Flexible hours,
Part time employment, Overtime, Shifts, Government

An Update of Nonstandard Work Schedules **(119)**
The 40-hour, 5-day work week is the current standard work schedule, but
there are 4 significant nonstandard schedules: 1. part-time schedules, defined
as work of 30 or less hours per week, 2. staggered hours, which require 40
hours per week, with various groups having different, assigned start/end
times, 3. flextime, which require 40 hours per week, but allow individuals or
groups to select their own start/end times provided core periods are covered,
and 4. shorter workweeks which usually require 40 hours per week in less
than 5 days. Changes in the workweek could result from desires for: 1.
reduced unemployment, 2. more leisure time and more autonomy, and 3.
more productivity, improved recruiting, and greater retention.Arizona State
University conducted a survey in 1979 comparing Arizona with national
work schedule practices, differentiating between the manufacturing and
nonmanufacturing sectors. The results show nonmanufacturers using part-
time and staggered schedules extensively. Except for staggered hours,
nonstandard work schedules are used for less than 25% of the work force in
both sectors. All employers agree on the major advantages and
disadvantages of the nonstandard work schedules. Employees express the
most acceptance of flextime or shorter work weeks which are least likely to
be implemented by employers for business considerations. Employers
offering varied work schedules may gain recruiting and retention benefits.
Tables. References. —Bohlander, George W.; Werther, William B., Jr.; and Wolfe, Michael
N.; *Arizona Business,* Feb 1980, 27(2): pp. 16-24. Avail. ABI 80-07295
Work hours, Schedules, Surveys, Arizona, Flexible hours, Part time employment,
Advantages, Disadvantages, Attitude surveys, Short, Workweeks

Updating Four-Day Week (120)

The Work in American Institute has cited 7 issues or critical factors that will impact quality of worklife and productivity. These include alternative work schedules. A reduced workweek, including the 4-day, 40-hour workweek, has received much attention. A recent study by Robert E. Allen and Douglas K. Hawes found that a high percentage of employees favored the 4-40 plan. Another study by Cheedle W. Millard, Diane L. Lockwood, and Fred Luthans found that the 4-40 plan significantly improved employee satisfaction and reduced absenteeism. In March 1981, Senator William L. Armstrong introduced S 398 which amended the Walsh-Healy act which required that all employees who worked over 40 hours per week had to be paid overtime. The bill is still pending in Congress. References. —Kovarik, Joseph P. and Zawacki, Robert A.; *Personnel Administrator,* Jan 1983, 28(1): pp. 19-20. Avail. ABI 83-03774

Flexible hours, Personnel administration, Personnel management, Surveys, Job satisfaction, Employee attitude (PER)

What Is Happening to Flexitime, Flexitour, Gliding (121) Time, the Variable Day? And Permanent Part-Time Employment? And the Four-Day Week?

Flexitime and permanent part-time make fundamental changes in how workers relate to the workplace and to their employers. Flexitime makes it possible for employees to choose their own hours, within management's constraints, giving the employee autonomy, self-management, and the ability to make decisions. The success rate for flexitime is very high, and flexitime is almost certain to improve employee morale. The odds are good that productivity will be increased and costs reduced by flexitime. Permanent part-time allows women to retain their roles at home while pursuing a career, and it allows men the time to be active parents. It can solve scheduling problems and labor cost and quality for businesses. These kinds of alternative work schedules are needed because: 1. The US labor force is experiencing a period of revolutionary change. 2. Job satisfaction is declining. 3. Traditional work schedules cause problems for a third of all workers, and their schedules interfere with family life. 4. The ideology of American industrial relations is about to change. 5. Productivity growth in the last several years in American business is the second worst among all industrialized nations. 6. Businesses are ranked near the bottom in opinion polls for respect that people have for institutions. Many concepts have to be understood and acted upon for alternative work schedules to achieve full potential. References. —Nollen, Stanley D.; *Across the Board,* Apr 1980, 17(4): pp. 6-21. Avail. ABI 80-08077

Flexible hours, Work hours, Work, Scheduling, Productivity, Employee morale, Part time employment

Why Flexitime Is Spreading (122)

This spring, under the auspices of the White House Conference on Families Business Task Force and the Conference Board, around 200 corporate personnel executives will meet to share what they are doing to promote flexible schedules. Flexitime has proved to those who use it to be almost as beneficial to the corporation as to the family. Currently, 12%-16% of all US firms offer flexitime. Flexitime is an alternative to the standard 8-hour, 5-day, 9-5 work schedule. Flexitime evolved in response to the needs of married women workers. Although certain "core" hours are required, free choice of working time is allowed for the remainder of the working day. Corporations using flexitime have found that it pays off by providing: 1. higher productivity, 2. lower turnover, and 3. better employee morale. Organized labor encourages flexitime in collective bargaining. Setting up flexitime entails little cost, but careful planning is vital, as is acceptance of it by front-line supervisors. —Anonymous; *Business Week,* Feb 23, 1981, 2676) (Industrial Edition): pp. 46J,46N-46O. Avail. ABI 81-05441

Flexible hours, Work hours, Personnel policies, Manycompanies

Why Rotating Shifts Sharply Reduce Productivity   (123)

Working a frequently rotating shift will affect key mental processes, such as motivation, alertness, and judgment, and may cause health, family, and work problems. The resulting loss of efficiency and productivity is due to an artificially produced stress which causes body rhythms to be forced out of phase. Internal body clocks, which lock in and correct many body activities such as hormone secretions, will reverse most day-night time body functions in about 24 to 30 days. If a worker is assigned to a 7-day rotating shift, his body will never adjust as his body clock will be set adrift.Rotating shift workers occasionally have periods of sleep loss, which also affects their productivity. There are now available innovations which aid in the study of individual biological rhythms, but as yet, these have not been applied in recent studies of rotating shift work. However, once management accepts the limitations imposed on workers by biology, perhaps they will recognize such valid solutions as rotating people within fixed shifts, which would eliminate the inefficiency while promoting a sense of unity and organization. —Fly, Ralph D.; *Supervisory Mgmt,* Jan 1980, 25(1): pp. 16-21. Avail. ABI 80-03566

Scheduling, Rotating, Shifts, Impacts, Productivity, Stress

The 12-Hour Work Day: Differing Employee Reactions   (124)

In recent years, there has been an increasing interest in the area of nontraditional work scheduling. A field study was conducted to examine the reactions of 671 non-exempt employees to utilizing a "compressed work schedule" (12-hour shifts) for staffing a continuous process plant which operated 24-hours a day/7-days a week. The 12-hour shifts were fixed with changes at noon and midnight. It was hypothesized that the employees who had actually worked the 12-hour schedule would be more positive towards it than those who had never worked it. It was also hypothesized that those employees working the noon to midnight shift would be less out of synchronization with physiological and social rhythms and would react more positively than employees who worked the midnight to noon shift. Results supported both hypotheses. Tables. References. —Breaugh, James A.; *Personnel Psychology,* Summer 1983, 36(2): pp. 277-288. Avail. ABI 83-18086

Shifts, Schedules, Work hours, Employee attitude (PER), Studies, Statistical data

The 7-Day Workweek: Time for a Second Look   (125)

It has been suggested that people should consider working only half-days, but every day - for example, from 7:00 a.m. until noon. Although the suggestion may sound crazy to some, it is not terribly unusual in the context of the changing workforce and many other experiments with unusual working hours. As the labor force changes, chances of acceptance increase. It is possible that going to work for 7 half-days a week could be accepted if the proper groundwork were laid. Making such a drastic change may seem difficult in view of the fact that today's younger workers appear interested in having extra time off. However, some workers might prefer the 7-day work schedule, as individualization of work schedules has become more common. The 7-day workweek would not be possible or desirable everywhere. Still, in line with the trend toward more individual choice in the workplace, it deserves serious consideration by managers interested in willing, productive employee cooperation. References. —Foegen, J. H.; *Enterprise,* Autumn 1982, 2(1): pp. 11-13. Avail. ABI 83-06743

Work hours, Flexible hours, Work sharing, Manycompanies, Workforce, Shifts

3

Career Development

PLANNING FOR CAREER ADVANCEMENT

Bicycle Management (126)

Given the fact that few can rise to the top of a company, it follows that most careers will stop somewhere along the route to the top, making most individuals both boss and subordinate at the same time. "Bicycle management" is a management philosophy taught in Germany in which this boss/subordinate role is likened to riding a bicycle. The individual has his head "down and bowed" in respect to superiors, while at the same time, his feet are "churning over subordinates" repeatedly.If an individual finds himself in an organization where the bicycle management concept prevails, he has 3 options opent to him: 1. If the individual does not mind that sort of atmosphere, then no problem really exists. 2. If the individual does not like the situation, he can discuss the problem with his boss in the hope of ameliorating the problem and coming to a better meeting of the minds. 3. If the atmosphere is unbearable, the individual must seek a position in a firm where bicycle management does not exist. In a bicycle management situation, it is difficult for the individual to make meaningful contributions, and much job stress usually exists. —Delaney, William A.; *Supervisory Mgmt,* Apr 1980, 25(4): pp. 15-19. Avail. ABI 80-07338

Management, Corporate management, Career advancement, Supervisors, Employee morale, Employee, Relations, Job attitudes

Career Development Through Employee Training (127)

Reassessments of employee training priorities are becoming necessary because of bottom-line economics, the rapid-paced import and export of technology, and desires for growth and staying power. Employees are disliking the jobs they perform because they are the only jobs they know, resulting in job boredom, poor attitudes, absenteeism, lost productivity, and high turnover rates. The philosophy of employee training should include continuing employee education at all job levels. Developing personal careers within the company should be the objective. The future growth and success of every organization will be proportional to the employees' growth and development.The 2 immediate payoffs of internal employee training are reduction of employee turnover and improvement of productivity. To keep employees, a company needs to provide opportunities for job satisfaction and personal growth. Problems in communications and training begin with the new hire and go through to all levels of management. Failure to recognize employee communications and training problems, plus a failure to correct them, will cost more than implementing a solution. Priorities need to be identified before initiating employee-training, career-development programs. Career development within the company will begin a new era in the 1980s of higher education. Tables. —Boylen, Mary E.; *Public Relations Jrnl,* Mar 1980, 36(3): pp. 26-30,51. Avail. ABI 80-08251

Career advancement, Career development planning, Training, Education, Employee attitude (PER), Job attitudes

Career Development: What Organizations Are Doing About It (128)

Insecurity and uncertainty in the workplace can result in economic loss to the organization and severe stress to the employees. The occurrence of illness resulting from the adverse effects of stress is increasing as business becomes more complex and demanding. To determine what steps are being taken by management to help employees deal with business-related and personal stress, a survey was conducted which involved 118 of the Fortune 500 companies. There were 3 purposes for the survey: 1. identification of people in the organization responsible for administrating and providing services for career development, 2. analyzing the scope of career development services, and 3. ascertaining top management's commitment to career development and the extent to which this concept is integrated with corporate personnel practices.The results of the survey showed that career development in the corporation is more a management function than an auxiliary one, and that career development programs are offered in a majority of organizations, but often only to a small portion of the workforce. The organization's long-range interests will be served if career development services are recognized as a way of increasing productivity. Turnover rates could be reduced significantly if management made it possible for employees to grow through career development programs. Charts. —Griffith, Albert R.; *Personnel,* Mar/Apr 1980, 57(2): pp. 63-69. Avail. ABI 80-10211

Career advancement, Career development planning, Programs, Surveys, Personnel management, Affirmative action, Job enrichment

Career Development: The Ultimate Incentive (129)

Workers want more from their jobs than a paycheck and a few fringe benefits. Increasingly, their loyalty to their organizations depends more upon the degree to which their employers satisfy new wants. Successful managers are the ones who adapt to a changing environment. It is now necessary for managers to concern themselves with changing worker goals; without such attention, higher employee turnover and lower productivity will ensue. Today's better educated, more demanding workforce will lose its commitment to an organization if accommodations are not made to them. These accommodations should take the form of a career development (CD) program. CD is a planned program designed to match individual and organizational needs. Examples of CD programs include recruitment policies that encourage a full exchange of information between the applicant and the company. CD allows for the changes in individuals as their work roles overlap with their family and social roles. A management climate continuum was set forth, and appropriate CD program actions were related to this continuum. This CD perspective acknowledges the increasing parity between management and labor. Tables. —Kent, William E. and Otte, Fred L.; *Advanced Mgmt Jrnl,* Spring 1982, 47(2): pp. 8-16. Avail. ABI 82-12903

Career development planning, Incentives, Work environment, Job satisfaction

Career-Life Planning and Development Management (130)

Career-life planning provides some focus on what people want from work. Career-life planning is a systematic effort by the organization to design jobs according to the aptitudes, abilities, and objectives of employees. Career-life planning is based on organizational adaptability in the face of several assumptions about organizational and human behavior.Career-life planning methods typically begin with problem recognition and end with changes in structure and processes. Job redesign, as a planning technique, means an increase in employee involvement with the entire job, and this results in the employee exercising more variability and taking more responsibility.There are some significant problems with career-life planning programs, such as: 1. widespread employee dissatisfaction with work and life, and 2. inability of organizations to always change the amount of control that employees have over career choices through devices such as job redesign, model career patterns, broadened authority patterns, and variable rewards. Charts. References. —Klingner, Donald E.; *Public Personnel Mgmt,* Nov/Dec 1979, 8(6): pp. 382-390. Avail. ABI 80-02488

Career development planning, Human resources, Management, Employee development (PER), Organizational behavior, Training, Programs, Job satisfaction

Getting Employees to Analyze Their Ambitions (131)

SmithKline Corp, Philadelphia, Pennsylvania, holds career planning workshops every 3 months to help employees examine their goals in life. The employees range from clerks to managers and are in all age groups. They come together to examine their priorities in life, their ambitions, and their weaknesses. They then explore the options and opportunities open to them and set personal and career goals for themselves. They are then encouraged to develop strategies for achieving these goals even if it means leaving the company.More than 500 employees have attended the workshops since they were introduced 8 years ago. The company was among the first US companies to institute such a program. The company feels the program is important because it helps workers be more productive and to relate their personal goals and career plans to corporate objectives and future requirements. All of the workshops are held during normal working hours, and any employee may attend with the approval of his or her supervisor. — Tavernier, Gerard; *International Mgmt (UK),* Jun 1980, 35(6): pp. 47-50. Avail. ABI 80-13658

Smith Kline-Philadelphia, Case studies, Career development planning, Workshops, Job attitudes

How to Change Careers   (132)

In a study of 91 professional and managerial men who changed careers between the ages of 35 and 53, most of the men indicated that their reason for changing was to obtain more meaningful work, find a better fit of values and work, or find a chance for greater achievement. Most people can manage to make a career change despite the economy if they have the willingness and ability to take risks. Once a person is prepared to take risks, he or she is ready to plan a career change. The first step in planning a career change is self-assessment. This involves writing down a work history, isolating skills and knowledge, or listing important achievements and noting the kinds of skills involved. The second step is to translate the list of skills into an occupational goal. It is often helpful in this step to enlist the aid of friends or others of similar background who are changing careers. The third step is often the most difficult, making the decision to change. Once the decision is made, the final step is locating the person or organization that has the desired position. It is important to be prepared to do the necessary investigating to locate the position that fulfills one's individual requirements. —Robbins, Paula I.; *Advanced Mgmt Jrnl,* Summer 1980, 45(3): pp. 46-57. Avail. ABI 80-17223

Careers, Changes, Occupational mobility, Career development planning, Job hunting, Self, Evaluation

How to Know When It's Time to Change Jobs   (133)

There is a systematic procedure available for assessing the attractiveness of a person's current job. In order to foster systematic thinking about one's current job there are 3 important questions to consider: 1. Why do people work? 2. What causes people to be satisfied with their jobs? 3. How do people decide if their job is attractive? Whatever a person's situation, he/she should try to recognize the needs that he/she is trying to satisfy through the job. There are many specific things that determine how satisfied people are with their jobs, but the important point is that people are satisfied if their needs are being met. A decision to stay in or leave a job should be based on how well a person thinks the job will satisfy his/her needs in the future. A rational decision-maker will compare alternatives and select the alternatives that performs best on some measure. There are 3 different approaches that can be used in decision-making: 1. making trade-offs, 2. using minimum acceptable criteria, and 3. using a dominant criterion. Charts. —Ferratt, Thomas W. and Starke, Frederick A.; *Jrnl of Systems Mgmt,* Jul 1981, 32(7): pp. 6-11. Avail. ABI 81-19856

Job satisfaction, Factors, Job attitudes, Career development planning, Job evaluation, Job, Changes

Job Posting: A Way to Unlock Employee Talent   (134)

A firm's future growth depends largely on its ability to make the best use of its existing employees. However, as a company and its workforce grows, it may become difficult to determine which employees are qualified for promotion. The leading cause of employee turnover is the lack of readily identifiable career opportunities within a company. In an effort to lower turnover and its related costs, many employers are improving in-house career opportunities through job posting. Job posting involves posting in-house job opportunities on bulletin boards or in company publications and giving employees the first right to compete for job vacancies within the company. Job posting is also an integrated approach to internal staffing and career development at many company levels. Job posting should be a formal companywide policy that covers: 1. employee skills inventory, 2. guidelines, 3. posting, 4. bidding, 5. screening, and 6. selection. –Anonymous; *Small Business Report,* Nov 1983, 8(11): pp. 52-54. Avail. ABI 83-32169

Job, Posting, Small business, Personnel policies, Promotions (MAN), Recruitment, Career advancement, Personnel selection

Management Development in the 1980s (135)

America's "new workers" look to a job as more than just compensation. They desire self-fulfillment and expression through their work. A distribution manager must train individuals to do the job at hand but also develop them for expanded future responsibilities. This requires: 1. comprehensive job interviews, job descriptions, and attainable goals, 2. formal and informal job training, based on a plan of action for general and particular skills development, and 3. an annual performance assessment based on a skills profile or concurrent rating to pinpoint weaknesses. Managers must assist in employee career development and be prepared to promote them when they are ready. Further, management must be open to communications and ideas from all levels which will increase productivity. Day-to-day open dialogue between management and employees is recommended to identify problems, seek solutions, and discuss overall corporate performance. The distribution manager should be committed to human resource development. –Harrington, Lisa H.; *Traffic Mgmt,* Feb 1983, 22(2): pp. 26-30. Avail. ABI 83-07869

Distribution, Managers, Programs, Career development planning, Management development, Case studies, Management training

A Model of Intra-Organizational Mobility (136)

A model is presented to integrate research on the mobility of personnel upward, downward, and laterally through an organization. The model is based on 9 propositions as they affect mobility: 1. vacancies, 2. organizational character, 3. work force environment, 4. job movement criteria, 5. interaction of existing variables, 6. mobility experience, 7. individual expectations, 8. satisfaction levels, and 9. the interrelation of expectations and realities on work behavior. The model may enable a systematic collection of empirical evidence on mobility within organizations, thereby permitting more informed human resources planning, recruitment, training, and professional development. Diagram. References. –Anderson, John C.; Milkovich, George T.; and Tsui, Anne; *Academy of Mgmt Review,* Oct 1981, 6(4): pp. 529-538. Avail. ABI 82-00030

Mobility, Occupational mobility, Career advancement, Personnel management, Organizational behavior, Models, Criteria, Promotions (MAN)

Toward a More Creative You: The Actualizing Climate (137)

Since environment and work climate have a significant bearing on employee attitudes toward a company and job performance, creation of an actualizing climate is of great concern to management. Sources of worker discontent include production goals set by others, standardization of operating techniques, routinizing of detailed operations, etc.Organization actualization builds and extends the principles of organization development (OD). Employees in any organization experience great need for both personal and professional growth, and psychological contact fostered with employees can nurture this growth.To design a climate that will encourage self-development, certain attitudes concerning employee growth must exist. These include: 1. Growth results from experience. 2. Growth is both an intellectual and emotional process. 3. Growth is unique and individual. 4. Growth is an evolutionary process. In the actualizing organization, the climate recognizes the right of individuals to make mistakes, has an atmosphere of trust, is one of acceptance and respect, is nonthreatening psychologically, emphasizes the personal nature of growth, etc. —McAlindon, Harold R.; *Supervisory Mgmt,* Apr 1980, 25(4): pp. 35-40. Avail. ABI 80-07341

Career advancement, Career development planning, Employee attitude (PER), Job attitudes, Working conditions, Personal, Growth

The Trauma of Promotion: High Anxiety   (138)

Job performance is often seriously hindered when the response to promotion, or the possibility of it, is increased anxiety and emotional stress. The current economic upswing ensures the opening of new management positions in most industries, bringing the prospect of promotions to more people. Those adjusted to taking risks will better cope with increased authority. Other necessary qualities are the ability to learn and to perform, self-confidence, and objectivity. The choice of persons for promotion often has less to do with technical excellence than with leadership potential. Selections based solely on past technical performance are often disappointing. Especially problem-charged reasons for promotion are rewards for specific performance, those promotions intended to force one to take responsibility to resolve a complex problem, and personal favoritism. Abiding by a well-planned career strategy and maintaining tactful negotiations with superiors offer the best defenses against promotion trauma. —Miles, Mary; *Computer Decisions,* Jul 1984, 16(9): pp. 88-102. Avail. ABI 84-25908

Promotions (MAN), Anxieties, Career advancement, Employee problems, Career development planning

Up Is Not the Only Way   (139)

Now that technical obsolescence is a reality, career development is a necessity. Increasingly, managers are being held responsible for helping subordinates cope with, adapt to, and plan for change. As such, managers need to point out the choice of career goals which exist.Most people are interested in moving up and many consider upward mobility the only acceptable and rewarding way to develop a career. A manager can assist employees by discussing positions at the next higher level or by organizing resource material to help them make plans.There are other ways in which employees can develop their careers: 1. moving across, which involves a change in function and/or title without necessarily undergoing a change in status or salary, 2. moving downward, to free oneself from time-consuming positions to develop through outside interests, 3. exploring, which involves researching, interviewing, and testing out ideas and opportunities to make an eventual decision about another field, 4. staying put and developing existing opportunities, and 5. moving out. —Kaye, Beverly L.; *Supervisory Mgmt,* Feb 1980, 25(2): pp. 2-9. Avail. ABI 80-05286

Personnel management, Career development planning, Horizontal, Promotions (MAN), Career advancement, Supervision

What's New in Career Development (140)

Companies often have to change organizational policies, procedures, and culture to encourage career development. Organizations that are unable to offer traditional promotion opportunities should shift away from the advancement-oriented view of careers and emphasize career development at the same organizational level or within the present job. The increasing number of dual-career couples and the external mobility of workers are particular problems for the organization. Career development methods available to smaller firms include job enrichment, through temporary secondments or interchanges with other firms, and sabbaticals. Assessment centers are useful in promotional decision making and employee development. Benefits of career planning include a greater sense of personal responsibility for career development and increased awareness of available opportunities. Employee involvement in career decision making is enhanced by lifeskills teaching, counseling, and career development workshops. References. —Williams, Richard; *Personnel Mgmt (UK),* March 1984, 16(3): pp. 31-33. Avail. ABI 84-10533

Career development planning, Personnel management, Personnel policies, Dual career couples, Mobility, Life, Skills, Development

You Want Me to Do What? (141)

For a long time, career development was seen as the job of the personnel department, used for new employees or an occasional employee concerned about his or her future with the organization. The philosophy was that if an employee worked hard and showed promise, he or she would move up in the organization and retire with a pension. Now the importance of career development is being realized. Managers need to play an integral role in individualized career coaching, as they are closest to the employee. The managers themselves need to be coached as they may not have the knowledge to guide their employees. Not everyone is cut out to be a manager, and a company should realize that and allow advancement only to those who truly want it. Once managers feel competent in career guidance, they should practice it. A successful program will see greater productivity, reduced turnover, and an increase in employee development. References. Tables. —Jones, Pamela R.; Kaye, Beverly; and Taylor, Hugh R.; *Training & Development Jrnl,* Jul 1981, 35(7): pp. 56-62. Avail. ABI 81-16798

Career development planning, Managers, Supervisors, Employee counseling, Human resources, Development, Responsibilities

CONFLICTS BETWEEN CAREER AND PERSONAL GOALS

The Bottom Line on Day Care   (142)

Joseph Wexelbaum, the president of Red Rope Industries, Bristol, Pennsylvania, solved the problems of excessive employee turnover and absenteeism by opening an innovative free child care center for his company's working mothers. Red Rope Industries began the child care center in 1972, converting space in the plant cafeteria and hiring an experienced day care director and staff. The company did not qualify for federal funding for the center, but did qualify for a 50% credit against its state corporate income taxes through the Neighborhood Assistance Act. Over 10% of its employees needed quality day care for infants and preschoolers, therefore, Abt Associates Inc., Cambridge, Massachusetts, decided to participate in the founding of a cooperative day care center. The Abt Associates' center also began in 1972, with some employees donating time each week in the center, and the company subsidizing part of the costs. Abt still provides some subsidy to the center, which is now open to the nearby business community. —Fooner, Andrea; *Inc.,* May 1981, 3(5): pp. 94-102. Avail. ABI 81-10339

> Corporate, Day care, Day care centers, Employees, Working mothers, Absenteeism, Reduction, Employee turnover, Case studies

Career and Family: The Juggling Act of the '80s   (143)

Balancing the needs of one's career, family, and personal life can result in an unending series of commitment choices and conflicts. Executive and spousal needs vary with the age and sex of the executive, the degree of professional success, career stage and generation, and the attitudes and priorities of each partner. Getting married is perceived as a must for male executives and being single may be a greater advantage for female executives. Business travel can add extra stress to a marriage because it usually accompanies the age and career stage at which the executive is usually needed most at home. Relocating is a major trauma. Studies indicate that the number of executives willing to relocate for career reasons is declining. Younger middle managers are shifting in attitude from strong traditional roles of executive-breadwinner/spouse-homemaker marriages toward more equal participation in both professional and family-oriented responsibilities. —Wakin, Edward; *Today's Office,* Aug 1983, 18(3): pp. 42-52. Avail. ABI 83-23112

> Family, Relations, Social change, Lifestyles, Careers, Travel, Problems

Companies Start to Meet Executive Mothers Halfway   (144)

Many executives who become mothers return to their old work routines soon after childbirth, but there are others who have wanted to modify their schedules. Now, some employers have begun to make special arrangements for these women. There are a number of major corporations today that approve part-time employment or other special accommodations for large numbers of corporate mothers. Changing demographics have stimulated corporate change. Women increasingly have postponed childbearing until they have achieved enough job status to make their bosses willing to accommodate them. Companies acknowledge that they agree to the new arrangements to retain valued employees. Although the curtailment of work schedules often means a career setback, most women agree that working a modified schedule is better than quitting. Banks and financial companies seemingly find it easier to adapt to part-time executives than many other businesses. Employers who oblige their women executives in this way seem content. —Anonymous; *Business Week,* Oct 17, 1983, (2812): pp. 191,195. Avail. ABI 83-28295

Personnel policies, Executives, Working mothers, Women, Part time employment

Conflicts Between Work and Family Life (145)

Results from the Quality of Employment Survey, conducted for the US Dept. of Labor, indicate that a substantial minority of workers living in families experienced conflict between work and family life. While work-family conflict seemed heightened among parents, compared with other couples, women did not report more conflict than men. Those who reported "some" or "a lot" of interference between their work and family life cited excessive work time, schedule conflicts, and fatigue and irritability as reasons for the conflict. Job characteristics as potential sources of such conflicts were: 1. number of hours worked, 2. frequent overtime, 3. work schedules, and 4. physically or psychologically demanding work.Workers reporting work-family conflict also reported significantly lower satisfaction with both jobs and family life, and lower contentment with life in general. Work-family conflicts can be costly both to individuals and to companies. The survey results suggest that such effects should be studied, together with other factors, when policies regarding working conditions are considered. Tables. References. —Pleck, Joseph H.; Staines, Graham L.; and Lang, Linda; *Monthly Labor Review,* Mar 1980, 103(3): pp. 29-32. Avail. ABI 80-07843

Working conditions, Work, Family, Conflicts, Surveys, Job attitudes, Job satisfaction, Statistical analysis

Coping with Dual-Career Couples (146)

Often, good employees are lost with little forewarning when their spouses take irresistible job offers in distant cities. Two-earner families represented about 65% of workers in 1983. More women are now at work and more women are entering traditionally male-dominated fields. Two-career couples are distinguished from 2-income families in that both spouses have long-term commitments to their careers. The career goals of such couples include personal growth and achievement and increasing responsibility. The decision of whether to accept one spouse's job opportunity is usually joint. Spouse-referral and relocation services exist, some sponsored by regional consortia of corporations. The 2-career couple sees itself as an economic unit and must be dealt with accordingly. Relocation and placement programs are valuable recruiting tools. Organizations must face the concerns of these couples if they are to attract and keep top achievers. —Miles, Mary; *Computer Decisions,* Jul 1984, 16(9): pp. 257-260. Avail. ABI 84-25918

Dual career couples, Organizational, Impacts, Problems

Divorce: The Price of Success? (147)

For executives climbing the corporate ladder, as well as those already at the top, the stresses and strains of sustaining both a marriage and a career are not new. Both roles are demanding, and favoring one often leaves the other neglected and wanting. Divorce, once damaging to a successful career, is now commonplace and is not as large a career roadblock. However, divorce is not only difficult on a personal level, it is also a strain for the corporation. While acceptance of divorce is still difficult for some corporations, others are beginning to realize that their demands on employees are often the very cause of it.Women too, have found that divorce can be the result of a career-oriented life. Some career bound divorcees remarry, but tend to maintain a cautious optimism about blending career and marriage the second time around. —Jacobs, Bruce A.; *Industry Week,* Jun 23, 1980, 205(6): pp. 76-82. Avail. ABI 80-13246

Divorce, Effects, Career advancement, Executives, Success, Stress, Marriage, Manypeople

Does It Matter If His Wife Works? (148)

Economic and behavioral theory and research predict that the job performance of married men is affected by two-earner household status. Two-earner household proliferation can be expected to intensify an already conspicuous trend towards a more leisure oriented workforce. Companies are paying for their unwillingness to accommodate the preferences of their employees through lower productivity and higher turnover. In a study based on 283 one-earner and two-earner families over a five year period it was found that two-earner families tend to work fewer average annual hours, take longer or more frequent vacations, spend less time commuting to work and change jobs more readily. The study results vindicate the theory that greater income security invites men to seek more leisure time at the expense of time spent working and decreases the role of financial rewards as a career determinant. Tables. Graphs. References. —Mooney, Marta; *Personnel Administrator,* Jan 1981, 26(1): pp. 43-49. Avail. ABI 81-03112

Effects, Dual career couples, Job, Performance, Husbands, Men, Work hours, White collar workers, Blue collar workers, Occupational mobility, Training, Studies

The Dual Career Couple: A Challenge to Personnel in the Eighties (149)

The dual career couple is becoming more common on the US corporate scene and causing a variety of problems that can result in the loss of productive employees for an organization. The dual-career couple presents a new sort of working family unit in which both members are following their own careers and actively supporting their spouse's career development. Companies which employ one or more members of a dual-career family are faced with new problems in human resources management. Employee recruitment and selection is greatly affected by dual-career considerations. Dual-career families do not view an individual offer alone, which challenges the traditional recruitment and selection techniques that emphasize the individual. Policies against nepotism may also cause problems for dual-career couples employed by the same firm. Transfer to a new location may present a crucial career decision for dual-career couples. Scheduling and training and development are other areas affected by the trend toward dual-career couples. If companies wish to recruit and retain these employees they will have to address their special needs, seek to meet the development needs of both members, and review personnel policies. Table. References. —Gilmore, Carol B. and Fannin, William R.; *Business Horizons,* May/June 1982, 25(3): pp. 36-41. Avail. ABI 82-14226

Dual career couples, Personnel policies, Transfers of employees, Nepotism, Recruitment, Personnel management, Scheduling, Training

Dual Career Couples: A Corporate Personnel Dilemma (150)

Today's increasing number of dual career couples will cause organizations to rethink and revise many current personnel policies and practices. Companies appear to be quite divided on their willingness to hire husband-wife teams. Many problems are inherent in the hiring of such couples: 1. Recruiters are at a disadvantage because some questions require answers by both, rather than just one, members of the team. 2. Scheduling problems may arise because time constraints are particularly strict for the dual career couple, especially when children are involved. 3. It may be difficult to design a benefits package for this group because there may be considerable overlap in the benefits covering each member. 4. Conflict of interest is an issue. Other factors that must be weighed are career development, "deadwood" within the organization, and the future of the image of the corporate wife. Dual career couples have "caught society by surprise", and coping mechanisms are not yet fully developed. —Weaver, Cindi and Smith, Linda Couchman; *Texas Business Executive,* Summer 1980, 6(1): pp. 28-31. Avail. ABI 81-09225

Dual career couples, Lifestyles, Nepotism, Policy, Hiring, Recruitment, Personnel selection, Career advancement, Roles

Dual Careers: Impact on Individuals, Families, Organizations (151)

During 1982 and 1983, Resource:Careers (Cleveland, Ohio), a career development and referral service, surveyed 167 organizations and 784 partners in dual-career couples on issues related to career and family. The dual-career couples indicated a need for programs to help them in making changes. Their concerns related to child care, time and stress management, and maternity/paternity leave. Resource:Careers has developed an action plan for organizations, individuals, and couples. A needs analysis should be conducted in each organization to determine employees' career and dual-career concerns. Progressive organizations that develop policies more linked to the changing needs of the workforce will have an advantage in recruiting and retaining good employees. Alternative work schedules, such as flextime and shared jobs, and flexible benefits, would be valuable to dual-career couples. Tables. —Miller, Claire A. Scott; *NABW Jrnl (National Assn of Bank Women),* Mar/Apr 1984, 60(3): pp. 4-9. Avail. ABI 84-10848

Dual career couples, Surveys, Personnel management, Recruitment, Employee benefits, Career development planning

Dual-Career Couples: The Organizational Response   (152)
As the number of dual-career couples increases, companies who fail to address the particular problems of this group of employees will lose many effective workers. This review tests 4 hypotheses with regard to this group: 1. Corporations with a high proportion of female employees will have more problems related to dual-career couples. 2. Firms with a high proportion of female-exempt employees will have more problems related to dual-career couples. 3. Firms with more female employees will institute more initiatives to ameliorate associated problems of dual-career couples. 4. Firms with higher proportions of female-exempt workers will be more apt to engage in activities which will ameliorate problems of dual-career couples. A survey was conducted to test the hypotheses, and a sampling of results includes: 1. The most common ameliorative action taken by companies was the absence of restrictions against hiring both husband and wife. 2. Firms with high proportions of female and female-exempt workers were more likely to institute flexible work hours. 3. Of the respondents, 22% practiced couple counselling, but the frequency was unrelated to the number of female and female-exempt employees. 4. Job sharing and child-care assistance were not provided to any meaningful extent. Tables. References. –Kopelman, Richard E.; Rosensweig, Lyn; and Lally, Laura H.; *Personnel Administrator,* Sep 1982, 27(9): pp. 73-78. Avail. ABI 82-22532
  Dual career couples, Surveys, Females, Human resources, Corporate, Practices

Dual-Career Couples - A Corporate Challenge   (153)
At least 4 factors are contributing to the trend of employee resistance to relocation: 1. the changing role of women in the family and workforce, 2. the increase in dual-career marriages, 3. changing values, particularly the decline of the "company man" syndrome, and 4. economic factors. In an effort to address the problem of relocation and dual-career couples, more corporations are offering spouse employment assistance. Companies are helping spouses with resume preparation, setting up interviews with other companies, finding employment agencies, and sometimes hiring the spouse, as corporate rules to prevent nepotism are relaxed. In some cities, large corporations work together to share information through a spouse-employment network. In some cases, couples are opting for "commuter marriages"; both people keep their careers, but live in different locations during the week and commute to their mutual home on weekends. Additional solutions are being considered as more companies examine the problem, and more employees should be attracted by that concern. References. –Sekas, Maria Helene; *Personnel Administrator,* Apr 1984, 29(4): pp. 37-45. Avail. ABI 84-14635
  Dual career couples, Relocation, Women, Roles, Changes, Values, Costs, Trends, Personnel policies

The Effects of Employer-Sponsored Child Care on (154) Employee Absenteeism, Turnover, Productivity, Recruitment or Job Satisfaction: What Is Claimed and What Is Known

An evaluation is conducted of the evidence supporting claims that employer-sponsored child care programs improve employee work behaviors and attitudes. A presentation is made of: 1. the explanation of the logic behind expectations for success, 2. the description of testimony for employer-sponsored child care, and 3. critiques of empirical studies. It appears that well-planned evaluations with proper controls have not been undertaken. Documentation was equivocal concerning whether women workers of child-bearing age were absent from work more than men or quit more frequently than men. Greater absences among women could be due to factors other than child care, such as: 1. lower attachment to work, 2. lower need for wages in 2-income households, or 3. holding poorly paid and low prestige jobs. Credible research does not support assertions that employer-sponsored child care reduces workers' absenteeism or tardiness. References. —Miller, Thomas I.; *Personnel Psychology,* Summer 1984, 37(2): pp. 277-289. Avail. ABI 84-20340

Child care, Corporate, Sponsors, Effects, Absenteeism, Employee turnover, Female employees, Job satisfaction, Day care centers, Employee problems

The Effects of Marriage and a Working Wife on (155) Occupational and Wage Attainment

In examining a national random sample of mature male managerial, professional, and blue-collar workers, the positive impact of being married and the negative impact of having a working wife on both occupational status and wage attainment were observed most strongly for the professional and managerial subsamples. These results are consistent with both a conformance-to-social expectations and wife-as-career resource arguments, but not as consistent with either human capital/market-signalling or distributive justice assertions. The impact of particular organizational tenure, education, and socioeconomic origins on both forms of attainment tended to be stronger for managers than for professionals, and, in turn, than for the blue-collar respondents. These results are consistent with the different need for control, given the uncertainty of evaluation and performance and importance of the positions, and the varying mechanisms for accomplishing control. Professional control is achieved more by extraorganizational mechanisms, while managerial control is achieved through background certification, and tenure, which are associated with compliance to the normative structure. Tables. References. —Pfeffer, Jeffrey and Ross, Jerry; *Administrative Science Qtrly,* Mar 1982, 27(1): pp. 66-80. Avail. ABI 82-10017

Dual career couples, Marriage, Effects, Men, Job status, Wages & salaries, Studies, Regression analysis, Statistical analysis

Executive Dilemma: Work Vs. Family (156)

Because of the impact of family-related stress on executive performance, many leading US companies have sought help from the famed Menninger Foundation, Topeka, Kansas. The Menninger Foundation has been useful in opening up perspectives formerly unfamiliar to executives. Annually, about 200 executives participate in Menninger mental health seminars. Seminar attendees are composed of executives with personal problems or executives who supervise those with personal problems. Executive problems arise from: 1. normal life cycles, 2. job transfers, and 3. corporate pressures that require conforming to an executive image. The Menninger seminars do not solve all of an executive's problems. However, the program does help the executive to understand and become aware of personal problems which, in turn, helps the executive to bring work and the family into a more tolerable balance. Graph. —Adkins, Lynn; *Dun's Review,* Nov 1980, 116(5): pp. 120-122. Avail. ABI 80-24011

Family, Job, Stress, Transfers of employees, Planning, Lifestyles

Executive Marriages: The Hidden Stresses (157)

Several factors contribute to sexual impotence in male executives: 1. fear, 2. anxiety, 3. physical tiredness, 4. the fact that men who achieve top positions do so in their time of life now described as the "executive menopause," and 5. a tendency to be uncommunicative. Furthermore, the women executives who marry tend to be selected for their "presentability" rather than their qualities of understanding. Thus, the support an impotent executive needs may not be available. There is usually a pattern in impotent executives: depression because of work problems or other pressures is followed by anxiety about being able to cope, which is followed by sexual problems, possibly impotence. Therapy usually involves talking through the problem with the couple, and may involve drugs, such as anti-depressants. Some analysts contend that the feminist movement has contributed to male feelings of sexual inadequacy. Career women tend to view a husband's failure in business as a sign of impotence. Resentment for whatever reason can lead to withholding sexual attention by either marriage partner. Another reaction to executive menopause is for the man to take up with a younger woman to prove his virility. —Underwood, Lynn; *Chief Executive (UK),* Mar 1982, pp. 19-22. Avail. ABI 82-12695

UK, Executives, Stress, Marriage, Couples, Stress, Sexual, Problems, Dual career couples, Wives, Husbands, Chief executive officer

How Employers Can Help (158)

Although it is not yet widely apparent, employers are quietly bending the rules to ease the strain on working couples. Business is slowly responding to the reality of the 2-income family. Working couples are asking for help with: 1. day care, 2. flexible hours so that parents can share parental duties, 3. adjustments in fringe benefits so that insurance benefits do not overlap but vacations do, and 4. job-placement services to help spouses find new jobs when their mates are transferred. The willingness of the employer to make concessions often depends on an employee's seniority or talents. The US lags far behind Europe in family benefits offered by employers. In countries with strong trade-union support or welfare-state programs, maternity leaves are for years instead of months. —Eisenberg, Richard; *Money,* Nov 1980, 9(11): pp. 89-92. Avail. Money 80-23296

Dual career couples, Relocating personnel, Flexible hours, Day care centers, Employee benefits

Impact of Dual Career Couples on Employers: Problems and Solutions (159)

Employers encounter an increasing number of difficulties as dual career and dual worker families enter the workforce. Problems may be divided into 3 categories: 1. hiring procedures including legislation and interview procedures, 2. working conditions including the number of hours spent working, business travel, and geographic mobility, and 3. personal considerations including child care, work-related stress, and marital stress. Some of the solutions proposed include: 1. offering child care as an option in employee benefits programs, 2. offering employee assistance programs fostering proactive and positive support for dual career lifestyles, 3. having work-related discussion groups to deal with the stress problem, 4. experimenting with new forms of work hours and alternative work styles, 5. improving the training of recruiters and interviewers, 6. consulting the employee about family ramifications of job-related travel, and 7. providing more training moves and career tracks within a limited geographical area. References. —Stringer-Moore, Donna M.; *Public Personnel Mgmt,* Winter 1981, 10(4): pp. 393-401. Avail. ABI 82-03981

Dual career couples, Impacts, Hiring, Employment, Procedures, Recruitment, Working conditions, Problems, Stress, Child care

Impact of Occupational Demands on Nonwork Experiences (160)

The relationship between occupational demands and nonwork experiences is examined for 127 senior administrators of correctional institutions. The general hypothesis underlying the research is that greater occupational demands will have an adverse effect on workers' nonwork experiences. These adverse effects will be more pronounced in areas closest to the work-family connection and less so in other areas. Eighteen occupational demands, including complexity, ambiguity, overload, responsibility for people, and role conflict, were evaluated. Dependent variables included negative-feeling states, marital and life satisfaction, satisfaction with home and family life, social participation, social support, psychosomatic symptoms, life style, and physical health. Regression analyses indicate that the occupational demands for administrators of correctional institutions have negative effects on nonwork experiences and that effects are more pronounced in work-and-family-related areas than in other areas, as predicted by the hypothesis. These conclusions constitute both a reproduction and an extension of earlier research. Earlier research is discussed, suggestions for further research are given, and implications for stress management are discussed. Charts. References. —Burke, Ronald J. and Weir, Tamara; *Group & Organization Studies,* Dec 1981, 6(4): pp. 472-485. Avail. ABI 82-02649

Organizational behavior, Occupational, Stress, Work environment, Effects, Non-, Work, Experience, Family, Satisfaction, Regression analysis

The Measurement of Mothers' Work Attitudes (161)

The number of mothers in employment has increased considerably in recent years. Statistics indicate that nearly half of all women with dependent children are now in paid employment. These women work in both paid jobs and in an unpaid capacity inside the home. However, the existing measures of job attitude do not consider the dual commitment to child-care and employment roles. There is also no measure of the stress produced by coping with the demands of both roles. A study was conducted to develop 3 scales which cover the mother's attitude to employment and domestic work roles, and the strain which may be generated by their interaction. The scales were developed through a questionnaire investigation preceded by less formal inquiries. The subjects were 185 working class women, of British origin, who were living with their husbands and had children under the age of 14. The scales were shown to be acceptable to working-class mothers with young children, and their psychometric properties were good. The scales have high internal consistency, seem to tap different constructs, are intercorrelated as required by their definition, and are associated with other measures as anticipated. Table. Appendix. References. —Parry, Glenys and Warr, Peter; *Jrnl of Occupational Psychology (UK),* Dec 1980, 53(4): pp. 245-252. Avail. ABI 81-02510

Working mothers, Work, Attitudes, Job attitudes, Blue collar workers, UK, Studies, Measurement, Life, Satisfaction, Women

Midcareer Mothers: A New Challenge for Employers (162)

A new generation of young, well-educated, career-oriented women who entered the labor market at an unprecedented rate are now having children once their careers are well established. This relatively new trend raises important implications for decision makers involved in hiring, retaining, and promoting qualified women who elect to become mothers in midcareer. The potential interruption at midcareer has not routinely been handled by organizations. Codetermination is necessary between employers and their employees; this entails some advance planning with the prospective mother, maintenance of professional ties during her absence, some semblance of a maternity leave program, and some flexibility after the child is born to strike a balance that is mutually satisfactory. —Alden, Alison; *EEO Today,* Summer 1982, 9(2): pp. 172-183. Avail. ABI 82-20005

Working mothers, Careers, Affirmative action, Policy, Children, Career development planning

Personal Loss and Professional Survival: Balancing (163) Divorce and Your Career

Divorce is the most common personal trauma to affect association executives, and learning how to balance the pain of the divorce with the demands of work is not an easy task. Many executives are initially comforted by throwing themselves into their work, putting in 50 and 60 hours of work per week. However, their job performance and their personal lives will not improve until they realize they need more than work, and until they face and deal with the divorce rather than try to escape it. Others have found their job performance suffers due to depression, lack of motivation or illness. Yet, this reaction to divorce seems healthier than over-work because these people are at least facing the pain. The ideal reaction is a balanced one; going to work every day provides some escape, but going home each night and dealing with the problems is also necessary. By forcing oneself to maintain a routine work schedule, the new home life will settle down sooner. —Hoffer, William; *Association Mgmt,* Jan 1982, 34(1): pp. 64-68. Avail. ABI 82-03854

Associations, Executives, Divorce, Stress, Personal, Problems

Two Paycheck Power   (164)

Two-paycheck families are now the norm rather than the exception. There are advantages to this situation in times of inflation and recession, but there are also logistical and power problems. Most couples manage nicely, but they complain that they are changing more quickly than the institutions with which they have to live.Most institutions are not responding to the difference the second paycheck makes in the availability of people, in the way people feel about work, and in the similar ways men and women behave on the job. The system continues to work against sex equality at home and at work. Most sizable business enterprises are run by men and operated at the bench and office machine level by women. The balance between home and work is further hampered by the standard schedule, the unspoken assumption that people are willing to relocate, expected separation of home and work, and peak effort during child rearing years. We need to redesign our jobs around people and to consider such moves as granting parental leaves. —Bird, Caroline; *Vital Speeches,* Jan 15, 1980, 46(7): pp. 202-205. Avail. ABI 80-04245

Changes, Dual career couples, Social change, Attitudes, Work, Family, Sex discrimination

Two-Career Couples: Asking for Trouble?   (165)

About 4.7 million of the 2-paycheck families in the US today are 2-career families, and some employers are viewing 2 careers within the same family as one too many, citing a number of special problems that come about. Critics of the trend cite such problems as more difficult relocation and recruiting, and they note that children may well be neglected in a situation where both parents are on career tracks. However, the trend toward 2-career families appears to be irreversible, so companies have no choice but to accommodate the special needs of such families. For example, firms that relocate employees are also providing informal employment assistance to career-oriented spouses who must also move to new jobs. Special companies are being formed to aid in the complexities of such a move, an example being the Employment Management Association (Wellesley, Massachusetts), which is building a national spouse-referral service for its members. Some examples of 2-career families are provided to illustrate the problems that occur, their solutions, and the views of their career-oriented members. —Johnson, Greg; *Industry Week,* Dec 13, 1982, 215(6): pp. 42-48. Avail. ABI 83-01840

Dual career couples, Relocating personnel, Couples, Professional recruitment, Transfers of employees, Executives

U.S. and European Executives Begin to Think Alike   (166)

The attitudes of European and American executives on the value of their home and corporate lives are beginning to converge. Managers are showing increasing resistance to job changes that affect their lifestyles. Europeans seem more willing to place their home life before their work. American managers seem to have higher life's ambitions than their European counterparts. They are also more optimistic about achieving their ambitions. German and Danish executives reported they receive more satisfaction from their careers than their home lives. Italian, Swiss, and UK managers favored their home lives. A majority (61.7%) of European executives reported that they would attend an important corporate function at the expense of an important family event. As the importance of family and lifestyle choices increases, employers may be called upon to help their executives manage resulting conflicts and stress. Graphs. —Anonymous; *International Mgmt (UK),* Mar 1983, 38(3) (European Edition): pp. 58-60. Avail. ABI 83-12065

Manycountries, Executives, Attitudes, Surveys, Family, Life, Job satisfaction, Stress, European, Managers

When Family Stress Affects Worker Productivity   (167)

A model is presented which shows 4 different types of situations involving family stress and productivity: 1. high productivity/low stress, 2. high productivity/high stress, 3. low productivity/low stress, and 4. low productivity/high stress. Placing various employees on the model can be helpful in determining how best to supervise each. Even with an understanding of family-related stress, the supervisor is still left with the problem of what to do about employees experiencing it at high levels. In instances where poor performance has become a problem, a supervisor should be understanding but remember that the stress is affecting the person's performance. The supervisor should also: 1. be available to the highly stressed employee, 2. use techniques of active listening to gain information and help the employee, 3. stick to the agenda at meetings with the employees, 4. monitor the time spent meeting with the employee, and 5. prepare documentation. Chart. Graph. —Ross, John K. and Halatin, Ted; *Supervisory Mgmt,* Jul 1982, 27(7): pp. 2-8. Avail. ABI 82-19126

Family, Stress, Job, Productivity, Supervision, Guidelines

When Working Women Become Pregnant   (168)

According to Bureau of Labor Statistics, women made up 53% of the workforce by the end of 1982. Forty-six percent of mothers with children under age 3 are working. Women and corporations must deal with the issues of maternity leave and the division of time between family and career. Some women executives say employers fear that women who take advantage of maternity leave will not return to work. Pregnancy does seem to slow down career advancement for at least as long as the period of maternity leave, and some women are given less responsibility when they return to work. Women are making efforts to combine motherhood and career by taking their infants to the office, switching to part-time work, joining more flexible companies, and depending on husbands and child care services. At GenRad Inc. (Concord, Massachusetts), women are entitled to disability payments, usually for about 8 weeks. —Adams, Jane Meredith; *New England Business,* Feb 20, 1984, 6(3): pp. 18-21. Avail. ABI 84-08568

Working mothers, Maternity benefits, Pregnancy, Career advancement, Personnel policies

The Work Alibi: When It's Harder to Go Home (169)

Although work may contribute to an executive's unsatisfactory family life in some cases, in many others, it becomes an alibi that executives use to cover up much more important worries. Those worries involve: 1. incorrect assumptions about the time and skills necessary to maintain personal relationships, 2. an excessive fear of confronting conflicts in marriage, 3. legitimate distractions for avoiding communication, such as work and children, and 4. the tomorrow attitude, whereby people postpone paying attention to their private lives. Potential solutions to the executive's problem include: 1. avoid the tomorrow attitude, and develop creative and appealing ways of being with one's family, 2. deal with conflicts by continuing a dialogue on an everyday basis and giving feedback and by dealing with persistent and deeper problems, 3. become authentic by getting rid of excessive fears and unconscious fantasies, and 4. abandon the assumptions that personal relationships are too complex and difficult to handle, that having a good private life is easy, and that it is too difficult to change. Charts. References. −Bartolome, Fernando; *Harvard Business Review,* Mar/Apr 1983, 61(2): pp. 66-74. Avail. ABI 83-08664

Time management, Personal, Life, Family, Problems, Work hours, Marriage, Job satisfaction, Executives, Lifestyles

Work and Families: What Is the Employer's Responsibility? (170)

There is increasing sentiment that companies or employers should aid employees in dealing with their personal and family problems. Any company developing a program needs a framework within which it can direct its efforts, plan and implement effective programs, and measure results. An assessment must be done, and when it is complete and management has agreed to sponsor a program, a service plan must be developed. A service or program plan delineates the problems that need to be considered and identifies the types of services that could remedy those problems. Such a plan also discusses the constraints and parameters in which the program must work and outlines the services that will be offered. Some of the major types of programs that have been offered by employers include: referral programs, flexible work schedules, flexible benefits, service programs, employee assistance programs, and child care. Increasingly, employers are realizing that family-oriented benefits help improve absenteeism and turnover rates and increase productivity. References. −McCroskey, Jacquelyn; *Personnel Jrnl,* Jan 1982, 61(1): pp. 30-38. Avail. ABI 82-03239

Employee benefits, Family, Child care, Day care, Flexible hours, Employee counseling, Fringe benefits, Trends

Work and Family Life Must Be Integrated (171)

Because of the changes that men and women are experiencing at home and in the workplace, people are recognizing that a new integration of work and family roles is needed. There are 2 myths that have operated successfully in the 20th century: 1. Competition is central to survival. 2. Work life is separate from family life. However, new considerations are changing the laborforce, therefore, organizations are facing a new breed of workers who do not accept these myths. A specified procedure for analyzing the impact of each personnel policy on the personal lives of employees and their families would help eliminate outmoded and punitive policies that are based on erroneous assumptions. Organizations can lessen the probability of future conflicts by implementing thoughtful recruiting methods which include: 1. selective recruiting aimed at achieving a good fit, 2. realistic job previews given to both the employee and spouse, and 3. organizational assistance in finding employment for the spouse. Companies should examine their policies concerning transfer, travel, and time commitments because of the impact these factors have on families. Organizations can plan and implement strategies needed for a successful work/family integration. —Hunsaker, Johanna S.; *Personnel Administrator,* Apr 1983, 28(4): pp. 87-91. Avail. ABI 83-10560

Integration, Family, Work, Labor force, Changes, Dual career couples, Social responsibility, Personnel policies, Recruitment

Work Demands on Administrators and Spouse Well-Being (172)

An investigation is made of the relationship of work demands experienced by 85 male senior administrators of correctional institutions and the well-being of their spouses. Data were collected through questionnaires completed independently by the husbands and their wives. Eighteen occupational demands were listed on the questionnaires.Wives whose husbands reported greater occupational demands reported: 1. less marital and life satisfaction, 2. decreased social participation, and 3. increased psychosomatic symptoms and negative feeling states. In no case was wives' well-being enhanced as a function of increased occupational demands on husbands. Job demands thus had an influence beyond the workplace and into the lives of their spouses. The interaction between work and nonwork experiences for the quality of individuals' lives and the interdependence of husband and wife in this regard require further research. Tables. References. —Burke, Ronald J.; Weir, Tamara; and DuWors, Richard E., Jr.; *Human Relations,* Apr 1980, 33(4): pp. 253-278. Avail. ABI 80-11000

Managers, Correctional institutions, Job, Stress, Effects, Quality of life, Marriage, Wives, Studies

EASING EMPLOYEE RELOCATION PROBLEMS

America's New Immobile Society (173)

America's celebrated "mobile society" is becoming stationary, and dealing with the impact of this change will be one of the top challenges of the 1980s for US industry. Companies will be confronted with major problems in recruiting, training, motivating, and promoting employees, particularly managers and professionals, who will now remain in one spot for long periods. In addition, declining mobility will decentralize the US economy as companies construct new, electronically-linked plants near untapped labor sources, to the increasing detriment of the cities. International Business Machines (IBM) serves as an example of the mobility changes. Frequent moves with IBM have been legend, but the firm is cutting the percentage of its 200,000-person work force that it moves each year to less than 3%, from 5% in the mid-1970s. The company plans to reduce the number further next year. However, the immobility trend may mean that companies will gain a new depth of experience in their ranks. Chart. —Anonymous; *Business Week,* Jul 27, 1981, (2698)(Industrial Edition): pp. 58-62. Avail. ABI 81-17453

Decreasing, Mobility, Trends, Relocating personnel, Costs, Manycompanies, Transfers of employees, Personnel policies

Audit Considerations for Employee Relocation Plans   (174)

Many companies will incur significant costs in transferring and relocating employees in 1984, despite the decline in mortgage interest rates. Relocation policies usually provide for: 1. reimbursement of moving expenses, 2. disposition of employees' real estate, 3. acquisition of real estate at the new location, and 4. a relocation allowance. Corporate relocation policies have varying features. Auditors should obtain copies of all corporate-policy statements regarding employee transfers to gain an understanding of the typical relocation expenses and allowances provided to all employees of the corporation. The entire administrative and budgeting functions must be reviewed by the auditor, and the review must go beyond a cursory review of variances. The annual corporate audit plan of companies involved in employee transfers should include reviews of corporation relocation policies and compliance therewith. Specific concerns should focus on: 1. compliance with corporate policy for expense reimbursements to transferees, 2. adequacy of documentation of the transactions, 3. appropriate recognition of payments in excess of appraised values, and 4. compliance with all Internal Revenue Service regulations. Chart. References. —Lemieux, Richard N.; *Internal Auditor,* Apr 1984, 41(2): pp. 38-42. Avail. ABI 84-16298

Internal auditing, Auditing procedures, Relocating personnel, Real estate, Reimbursement, Corporate, Policy, Transfers of employees

The Career Prospects of Married Women   (175)

To determine the extent to which companies provide career assistance to wives of relocating male managers, 24 replies from questionnaires sent to UK firms were analyzed. Eighteen of the respondents expected their managers to relocate, and 17 provided no help to the managers' wives in finding new work. At companies where relocating is voluntary, only 4 companies provided any assistance. Most respondents cited concern for children's education as the main reason managers refused to relocate. When relocating, the male manager's wife usually makes all the moving arrangements and must deal with relocation's disruptive effect on her career. Further research is needed to determine the full effect of relocation. Such research should include a survey of managers' spouses to determine how necessary relocation is and how to provide more assistance for spouses. Tables. References. —Marsh, Jacqui and Cooper, Cary L.; *Leadership & Organization Development Jrnl (UK),* 1983, 4(1): pp. 13-16. Avail. MCB 84-04488

Career development planning, Wives, Relocating personnel, Surveys, UK, Dual career couples

The Changing Work Force: Dual-Career Couples and   (176)
Relocation

The problem of relocation for dual-career couples is becoming more common as more women enter the workforce in higher level positions. The economic issue seems to cause the most concern among these couples, which include: 1. cost of living in the new area, 2. cost of housing in the new area, and 3. employment conditions in the new area. It would be difficult for dual-career couples to maintain their standard of living if the relocated spouse has to quit working or take a lower paying position. Some companies are beginning to help by offering assistance to the spouse in job hunting, helping the spouse to prepare and distribute resumes, reimbursing all or part of the spouse's salary while the spouse searches for a job, or covering the expense of sending the spouse on job hunting trips. Innovative relocation programs that consider the special problems of dual-career couples can be viewed as investments in the quality of a firm's human resources. Chart. Table. References. —Mathews, Patricia A.; *Personnel Administrator,* Apr 1984, 29(4): pp. 55-62. Avail. ABI 84-14637

Dual career couples, Relocating personnel, Economic conditions, Advantages, Disadvantages, Costs

Coping with the Culture Shock of an Overseas Posting   (177)

The Centre for International Briefing in the UK is helping businesspeople and their families adjust to the challenges of overseas assignments. The Centre offers week-long residential courses on cross-cultural adjustment. As more companies and organizations recognize the effects of culture shock, the Centre becomes more successful. It can cost a company $36,000 for the failed relocation of an employee. Relocations that do not work out in part hinge upon the wife's adjustment to the move. The Centre prepares wives for the change in environment. For women, the problems of relocation can be more acute than for their working husbands. Many have to give up careers. Also, family stress can increase when the cultural mores of parental authority are challenged. —Hill, Roy; *International Mgmt (UK),* Mar 1983, 38(3) (European Edition): pp. 81-85. Avail. ABI 83-12071

Culture shock, Transfers of employees, Wives, Problems, Expatriate employees, Host country, Manycountries, Multinational corporations

Corporate Women-Now Eager to Accept Transfers   (178)

Contrary to the situation in the past, the corporate woman manager is now eager to accept transfers, realizing and savoring the impetus such moves make to progress up the corporate ladder. Society itself now views a woman's relocation as proof of commitment to her career, and ambition is no longer regarded as an admission of lack of femininity. For women near the top, the relocation may be symbolic of many years of effort to achieve an elevated position within the firm. Furthermore, there is an implicit understanding by women that some career paths, especially those in sales and marketing, involve mining.Some women managers regard the excitement of moving with its new places and people as an asset rather than a liability, but marriage remains the most complicating factor in a projected move. Women that turn down relocations do so most often out of concern for its debilitating effects on marriage and family members. Single women, however, almost never turn down relocations that are involved with promotions, and in general, women appear to be playing the corporate game by traditional rules. — Anonymous; *Business Week,* May 26, 1980, (2638): pp. 153,156. Avail. ABI 80-10446

   Women, Managers, Transfers of employees, Transfers, Career advancement, Promotions (MAN)

The Current State of Corporate Relocation (179)

Results of a recent survey by the Employee Relocation Council (ERC) (Washington, DC), show that more companies are providing relocation assistance to experienced recruits. The survey indicated that real-estate assistance is usually offered on a selective or negotiated basis, rather than as standard assistance to all new hires. Merrill Lynch Relocation Management Inc. (MLRM) surveyed 611 Fortune 1000 companies and reports: 1. that 96% of respondents provide some assistance in helping employees dispose of their current homes, 2. nearly 56% of the respondents in 1981 used a relocation firm or bank to buy the transferee's home, and 3. at least 9 out of 10 companies provided reimbursements to renters. Even when a valued employee looks forward to relocation, the personal and financial uncertainties involved can cause problems that affect a person's productivity and morale. An employer can make relocation easier through counseling on relocation services, lifestyle, finances, and spouse assistance. Checklists. —Debats, Karen E.; *Personnel Jrnl,* Sep 1982, 61(9): pp. 664-670. Avail. ABI 82-23876

   Relocating personnel, Transfers of employees, Personnel policies, Recruitment, Employee benefits, Surveys

Dealing with the Costs of Employee Relocation (180)

Normal relocation of an employee involves many expenses, including costs of disposing of the employee's present home, the possible loss on the house sale, and a host of costs related to relocation itself. Companies offer a variety of plans to help reduce the employees' expenses, but few are aware of the sometimes hidden costs involved. A relocation company can save the typical firm 25% or more of total relocation costs. It can also provide substantial nondollar benefits stemming from the relocation service's full-time expertise and its ability to solve house-buying problems for the employee. Recent years' climbing mortgage costs can be a devastating financial blow for the employee, which can be dealt with by employers' offering to pay the interest rate difference. The housing cost difference between the 2 areas, determined by recently available indices on housing and living costs, can be handled through a supplementary allowance for the transferee. Second mortgages priced below the prevailing market rate and unsecured loans might also be utilized to aid the employee. —Bell, Theodore D.; *Financial Executive,* Aug 1980, 48(8): pp. 16-20. Avail. ABI 80-16253

   Relocating personnel, Transfers of employees, Costs, Real estate, Problems, Mortgages, Housing, Interest rates

The Dilemma of Compensation Policy on Domestic Relocation   (181)

No uniform, well-developed procedures appear to exist involving compensation practices in the area of domestic relocation. The impacts of inflation, higher taxes, and differing property values are examined. A questionnaire was mailed to 326 randomly selected, Fortune 500 companies. Analysis indicates there are no uniform policies, with only 35% of the 153 responding companies indicating they have a policy to maintain equal levels of discretionary income for a transferred employee. Specific company policies examined include: 1. cost of living adjustments, 2. premium pay, 3. educational allowance, 4. taxes, 5. commuting costs, 6. general reimbursement policies, 7. miscellaneous moving expenses, and 8. real estate considerations. There seems to be a great deal of variety in domestic relocation policies, with the result often being that the employee must bear the financial and emotional consequences. Tables. —Mills, Lavelle and Rachel, Frank M.; *Compensation Review,* Fourth Quarter 1983, 15(4): pp. 44-52. Avail. ABI 83-31384

Relocating personnel, Cost of living differentials, Personnel policies, Compensation, Surveys, Moving expenses, Reimbursement, Transfers of employees, Statistical data

Do Managers on the Move Get Anywhere?   (182)

A study of managerial careers was undertaken to shed light on the subject of mobility and its effect on managers' careers. Over 1,000 managers up to the level of vice-president in 3 major US corporations answered questionnaires. The results indicate that: 1. Most managers believe that they always move upward. 2. Thirty-five percent of 6,332 career moves studied involved relocation before mid-career. 3. Managers seldom change corporate allegiances. Career mobility is highest at the beginning of a managerial career and decreases gradually over its span. According to their own estimates, mobile managers: 1. are more exposed to top management, 2. follow in the footsteps of mobile managers, and 3. are motivated by fear of stagnation and impatience. Mobile managers do not fare better monetarily and are less satisfied than their immobile counterparts with salary and advancement. The disadvantages of mobility are often not acknowledged by mobile managers. Graphs. References. —Veiga, John F.; *Harvard Business Review,* Mar/Apr 1981, 59(2): pp. 20-38. Avail. ABI 81-07071

Managers, Career advancement, Mobility, Lateral transfers (PER), Promotions (MAN), Demotions, Relocating personnel, Occupational mobility, Job satisfaction, Compensation, Career development planning, Surveys, Studies

The Effect of Working Couple Status on the Decision to Offer Geographic Transfer   (183)

This study assesses the issue of geographic mobility of working couples from the perspective of the employer. A national sample of 425 US managers were asked to make a simulated decision of geographic transfer involving a member of a family in which both partners worked. A differentiation was made among a dual-career, a dual-earner, and a single-career couple. The overall purpose was to examine the effect of dual-career status on organizational decisions to transfer one member of such a couple. Primary findings were: 1. Being a member of the dual-career couple had a significant negative effect on the decision. 2. The effect was moderated by some characteristics of both the decision maker and the organization. It appears that being a member of a dual-career couple decreased the chances of being offered a geographic transfer, with managers perceiving such people as less suited to geographic moves. This situation can have an adverse effect on career progressions. Tables. Chart. References. —Le Louarn, Jean-Yves and DeCotiis, Thomas A.; *Human Relations,* Nov 1983, 36(11): pp. 1031-1043. Avail. ABI 84-02170

Dual career couples, Personnel policies, Transfers of employees, Studies, Occupational mobility, Organizational behavior, Statistical analysis

Employee Relocation Trends (184)

Despite the difficulties of an uncertain economy and the real estate market, most corporations have maintained or increased their relocation of personnel. US firms relocate more than 250,000 employees a year, and about 80% of the companies experience some difficulty with employees' resistance to moving. Such resistance is often based on both financial and family considerations. In 1982, the average cost of moving a 4-person family 1,000 miles was $40,000, but costs frequently run as high as $100,000. Hidden costs include the emotional impact of the situation, which often leads to losses in productivity and psychological dissatisfaction. To counter the problems associated with employee relocation, many companies retain relocation management firms to assess the company's relocation policies both qualitatively and quantitatively. A home sale assistance program, which offers the transferred employee the guaranteed sale of the home at current market value, is especially helpful. Graph. Chart. —Kunisch, Robert D.; *Corporate Design,* Jan/Feb 1983, 2(1) pp 15-16. Avail. ABI 83 11068

Relocating personnel, Trends, Costs, Transfers of employees, Policies

Employee Relocation: Expanded Responsibilities for the (185)
Personnel Department

Corporations spend an estimated $30,000 to $60,000 for each transferring employee, depending on the relocation benefits offered. These costs result from: 1. sale of the employee's current home and purchase of a new one, 2. shipping household goods, 3. temporary living and travel expenses, 4. company administration costs, 5. tax assistance, and 6. diminished productivity during the relocation phase. Most companies place the responsibility for helping transferring employees with the personnel department, as relocation assistance is considered part of the employee's benefit package. The personnel department's role includes: 1. discussing financial concerns with employees and helping them handle these concerns, 2. developing effective two-way communication, 3. providing personal counseling, 4. interpreting and implementing relocation policy, and 5. helping establish the family in the new home and community. Tables. — Moore, John M.; *Personnel,* Sep/Oct 1981, 58(5): pp. 62-69. Avail. ABI 81-25050

Personnel, Departments, Roles, Relocating personnel, Transfers of employees, Assistance, Employee benefits

Employee Relocation: It's a Whole New Ballgame   (186)

An employee's decision to make a relocation is significantly affected by increasing economic pressures. The Employee Transfer Corporation (ETC) conducted a survey which found that employees were less willing to transfer in 1979 than in 1978, due to increasing costs involved in transferring. Although corporations are attempting to ease the financial burdens associated with relocation, the family's attitude toward the move should be considered by the corporation, according to the ETC survey.There are various compensation policies for expenses incurred by the employees during relocation. With mortgage interest payments continuing to rise, many firms may find it necessary to initiate emergency loan programs or to make funds for mortgages available to employees. A trend is now emerging to reimburse the difference in interest rates between the old and new mortgage. Those firms who reported having a formal relocation policy have the following provisions in their typical relocation plans: 1. Only salaried employees are covered. 2. Payments are made for differentials in mortgage rates for a 3-year period. 3. An offset is paid to employees covering the tax liability on these payments. Relocation policies and practices are currently being reviewed and revised by organizations and include real estate sales assistance, tax assistance programs, and miscellaneous allowances. —Zippo, Mary; *Personnel,* Mar/Apr 1980, 57(2): pp. 70-73. Avail. ABI 80-10212

Relocating personnel, Transfers of employees, Economic impact, Housing, Interest rates, Inflation, Reimbursement, Family, Attitudes

Exploring the Male Mobility Myth   (187)

There is a new explanation for the mobility of the American male executive. He no longer unthinkingly accepts the customary values of the corporate establishment, because he selects his job changes according to his personal lifestyle and his perception of professional versus employer rewards. This conflicts with the myth that the American male executive will move anywhere, anytime, to achieve corporate success.A company must identify and deal with the executive's many goals. The company should continually communicate career development plans to its managers, and reevaluate managerial job content and organization relations and structure. By better understanding the realities that lie behind the male mobility myth, an organization can better handle and develop key individuals. A number of factors considered by a male executive evaluating a career move are discussed. Charts. Graphs. —Schwarzkopf, Ed A. and Miller, Edwin L.; *Business Horizons,* Jun 1980, 23(3): pp. 38-44. Avail. ABI 80-13392

Mobility, Relocating personnel, Transfers of employees, Job, Changes, Priorities, Guidelines

Five Steps to Set Employee Relocations on the Right   (188)
Track

Many relocations become difficult and uncomfortable procedures due to mishandled employer-employee communications. However, some simple techniques applied by personnel administrators can relieve much of the difficulty for both the organization and proposed transferee. Management must recognize that employee and family relocation can be highly disruptive and costly to all parties concerned, as well as being a broadening, rewarding experience. Management can increase the probability of transfer acceptance by establishing 5 general conditions for breaking the news of a proposed transfer during a series of interviews: 1. provide information regarding the transfer during the first interview, 2. the stress of the transferred employee should be acknowledged during this interview, 3. during the second interview, a safe environment should be provided, 4. help the employee separate facts from assumptions to bring anticipation of events closer to reality and to create alternatives, and 5. share relocation experience and concerns to provide a sense of group and commonality. The transfer administrator should be both patient and timely, and should instill confidence that the company and employee are in the move together, to the benefit of both. Chart. —Raymond, Ronald, Jr. and Eliot, Stephen; *Personnel Administrator,* Nov 1981, 26(11): pp. 43-47. Avail. ABI 81-26301

Relocating personnel, Transfers of employees, Personnel policies, Guidelines, Procedures, Employee, Acceptance, Interviews

Getting Employees to Relocate ... When They Won't   (189)

Employees have become increasingly resistant to relocation due to changing values, the changing role of women, dual career families, and economic constraints. In addition a company must consider the high cost of relocation which can run from $15,000 to $30,000. Service firms, which act as a liaison between employer and employee, can provide expertise in all areas related to corporate relocation. Services offered by these firms include: 1. home sale assistance, 2. new location counseling and homefinding, and 3. moving and storage. According to National Personnel Associates, non-salary relocation benefits are being sought more frequently by today's potential management candidates. Employers are offering a variety of relocation benefits, and middle and lower level employees are also eligible for such benefits. It is currently being debated as to whether the government should assist in relocation expenses. To cut down on the relocation costs, employers are attempting to hire within a central commuting area and reducing the number of candidates brought in for interviews. Chart. —Guillet, Denise R.; *Administrative Mgmt,* Oct 1980, 41(10): pp. 43-44,70-74. Avail. ABI 80-20495

Relocating personnel, Transfers of employees, Incentives, Mobility, Costs, Cost control

The Going Gets Lusher for Employees Who Move   (190)

Most corporations still like to keep their executives moving, but in recent years executives have become more resistant to relocation. It is now estimated that 80% of employees refuse their first transfer assignment, and the most likely to resist are executives between 25 and 45 whose personal goals depend more on lifestyle than on work. Resistance has also been influenced by the rise of dual-career couples, and this trend is growing particularly among the people that top management most wants to keep. Another factor in relocation resistance is the dramatic increase in home mortgage rates.To help lessen the financial burden of buying another house, many companies are adopting the mortgage interest differential (MID) to cover additional costs. The difference between the old mortgage rate and the new one is multiplied by the old mortgage balance, and the result is usually paid out over a short term, such as 3 years. The MID is costly to the employer and may be inequitable to people who have low balances or who are buying their first home. In addition to MID's, some companies are offering cost-of-living differentials as an inducement to relocate, but the most common incentive is a raise or a bonus. All of these benefits have escalated costs for companies who need to move executives. —Morrison, Ann M.; *Fortune,* Jun 16, 1980, 101(12): pp. 159-173. Avail. ABI 80-12354

Transfers of employees, Relocating personnel, Policies, Moving expenses, Housing, Cost of living adjustments (PER)

Have Spouse, Will Travel (if You Find Us Both a Job)   (191)

A few US companies are using transplacement as a means of getting married managers to accept a move. This involves finding the spouse of the relocated manager a job comparable to the one he or she had at the old location. This issue is becoming of growing importance with the increase in the number of 2-career families. However, some companies have cut down on relocations, due in large part to the cost involved. Such companies as Union Pacific are informally offering transplacement services, and transplacement is also being used as a recruiting tool by some firms. One group of consultants, Challenger, Gray & Christmas, Inc., offers training to relocated spouses in how to get a job in their new locale. Other corporations try to find new jobs for both spouses if they both work for the company and one is transferred. —Bickerstaffe, George; *International Mgmt (UK),* Mar 1982, 37(3): pp. 21-22,26. Avail. ABI 82-09173

Relocating personnel, Transfers of employees, Mobility, Dual career couples, Problems

How Companies Reimburse for Transfer Expenses   (192)

To determine to what degree companies in the US and Canada pay for the moving expenses of employees, a survey questionnaire was sent to the Administrative Management Society (AMS) Committee of 500, a survey group composed of representatives from AMS chapters throughout North America. Usable returns were received from 302 respondents. Of the 302 respondents, 222 indicated that their companies reimburse employees for relocation to another city. Some 80 firms did not do so. Of the companies reimbursing employees, 88.6% have a formal moving policy. Further, 88.7% of the firms with a reimbursement plan said that they pay for moving expenses only when the company initiates the move. Other findings included: 1. 96.4% of the companies with a reimbursement plan pay moving expenses for transferred employees. 2. About 39% pay expenses for new employees who are hired for jobs which require them to relocate. 3. More than 1/2 of the companies pay the moving expenses of selected new employees. Tables. —Thomas, Edward G.; *Management World,* Nov 1980, 9(11): pp. 15-17. Avail. ABI 80-23939

Relocating personnel, Transfers of employees, Reimbursement, Moving expenses, Surveys

How Compromise Can Handle the Complexities of   (193)
Relocation

In order for the cost of relocation not to become excessive, all of the costs of a move must be determined and provided for in advance. Personnel directors concerned with the expenses of relocation may want to consider the value of a relocation company to take the corporation out of the house-buying and house-hunting business. Relocation companies purchase the homes of transferred employees, help them find new ones, and manage the moving of their household goods. The relocation company can handle these tasks faster than the typical employer, which means an overall savings to the company. Helping the employee to find a suitable new home is as important as taking his old home off his hands. The employee should ideally be counseled on where to look and what to expect to pay. The personnel director should also be concerned with minimizing any payment of cost differentials to the employee; this can be done by obtaining current figures on local costs, so that the corporation does not have to guess as to the expenses. Tables. – Mack, James G.; *Personnel Administrator,* Sep 1980, 25(9): pp. 59-61. Avail. ABI 80-17876

Relocating personnel, Transfers of employees, Costs, Homeowners, Assistance, Services

How Relocation Abroad Affects Expatriates' Family Life (194)

Overseas living may have a number of effects on an expatriate family. There are some strengthening factors such as: 1. greater involvement in family activities, 2. greater concern for one another, and 3. company entertainment that includes the entire family. However, just as there are advantages in living abroad, there are a number of factors that can be disruptive to a family: 1. loneliness for the spouse, 2. boredom, 3. communications problems, 3. living conditions that contribute to mental and physical sickness, and 4. anxiety and stress caused by separation of loved ones. An overseas move can be very stressful if one family member is opposed to it. There are a number of tips for both husbands and wives to help them and their families adjust to an overseas move. It is a good idea for both parties to identify the stressors that living abroad may cause and to take an objective and positive view of living abroad. –Howard, Cecil G.; *Personnel Administrator,* Nov 1980, 25(11): pp. 71-78. Avail. ABI 80-21708

Expatriate employees, Impacts, Family, Marriage, Wives, Husbands, Stress

Insurers Easing Relocation Trauma (195)

An increasing number of insurance companies are assuming more of the financial burden of employees being relocated. A number of large insurers have made changes designed to ease potentially traumatic economic and social tolls of moving families around the country. For example, Mutual of New York will subsidize a relocated employee for the difference between his new mortgage rate and a base rate of 10% and has also turned to the services of an outside relocation service to smooth the process of selling employee homes and finding new ones.Prudential has also changed its format and established a national rate of 9.5% for the first 6 months of 1980 for the mortgages it provides, a change from the previous policy of offering mortgages at 1.5% below the current area market rate where the employee relocates.Resistance among employees to relocating has increased since mortgage rates began skyrocketing, and Equitable goes so far as to help employees adjust to new communities through introductions to clubs, churches, and school groups. —Katz, David M.; *National Underwriter (Property/ Casualty),* Feb 29, 1980, 84(9): pp. 1,5-6. Avail. ABI 80-07050

> Relocating personnel, Transfers of employees, Costs, Insurance companies, Home loans, Promotions (MAN)

Job-Transfer Survivors (196)

Corporations are continuing to reshuffle and relocate their employees, while paying little attention to the human problems that are associated with such relocations. An analysis of the situation affirms that even though most workers go along with company-mandated moves, there is an undercurrent of resistance that may be increasing. Companies will be negotiating in the future with more dual-career couples who pose greater obstacles to relocations. In general, the practice of moving star employees to groom them for top positions continues. A study of the subject by Catalyst (New York) reveals that although some companies such as International Business Machines Corp. set limits on how many times a worker is moved, firms in general provide too little information about the new job and the new location, in addition to other communication inadequacies. It is evident that if firms want to keep relocating workers, and move will have to be advantageous for both parties, not just for the company. Stress associated with moving and its effect on the family unit will have to be accorded more attention. —Haight, Gretchen Griffin; *Across the Board,* Dec 1983, 20(11): pp. 20-26. Avail. ABI 84-03743

> Transfers of employees, Relocating personnel, Problems, Employee attitude (PER), Personnel management, Personnel policies, Psychological aspects, Organizational behavior

Motivating Managers to Move On (197)

The mobility of labor has attracted more attention in the UK in recent years in terms of movement between separate locations within the same company. This phenomenon has resulted in some very real problems which affect the lives of many families. These problems have affected those who must follow the transfered employee and the executives who are responsible for career planning and management development.In the financial sector of the UK economy, there are banks, insurance companies, and building societies which have a proliferation of branches in nearly every town and city. These branches cannot generally be staffed with local managerial talent. Although mobility is encouraged by companies, there is a real threat to the employees' living standards in the area of housing and general economics. The fact of dual-career couples has added complexity to mobility problems. The question of international mobility is even more complex. Management has the responsibility to be sure that personnel relocate for the right reasons, such as greater prospects, more job interest, greater responsibilities and experience. References. —Rozier, Bernard; *Personnel Mgmt (UK),* May 1980, 12(5): pp. 30-33. Avail. ABI 80-13303

> Mobility, Motivation, Transfers, Transfers of employees, Clauses, Employment contracts, Standard of living, Dual career couples, Relocating personnel, UK

Moving Up and Away: What You Need to Consider in a Transfer (198)

Because of the many problems involved in transfers, many companies have developed policies that compensate the transferee for the basic relocation costs incurred in the move. Others go further by: 1. offering to purchase the transferee's present home at a fair market value, 2. counseling him on the new location, 3. assisting him in locating a suitable new home, and 4. managing the moving of household goods. Some things that the employer can do to help the transferee include the important considerations of cost of housing and cost of living. If the person is being transferred to an area where buying a comparable home is considerably more expensive, the employer can offer to pay the transferee a supplementary allowance based on the differential. Another problem is often increased mortgage rates. To handle this problem, employers can offer to: 1. pay the full rate differential on the old mortgage balance, 2. pay the rate differential on the new mortgage, or 3. pay the rate differential only if the interest rate is more than 10%. Finally, if the transferee is moving to an area with a higher cost of living, the employer might offer a cost of living allowance. —Mack, James G.; *Management World,* Nov 1980, 9(11): pp. 12-14. Avail. ABI 80-23938

Relocating personnel, Transfers of employees, Employee benefits, Housing, Costs, Allowances, Mortgages, Interest rates, Differentials, Cost of living adjustments (PER)

The Other Side of Relocation-Relocating the Spouse (199)

In a relocation situation, the importance of dealing with the spouse is apparent because non-working spouses are more involved in job change decisions, and dual career marriages are on the rise. It has become desirable to test the spouse's desire to make the change and to keep the communication channels open for both the candidate and the spouse. Although each relocation is different, these guidelines might prove helpful: 1. Know what the husband and wife want. 2. Invite the couple to visit the community. 3. After the relocation offer has been accepted, help bridge the move. 4. Make the transition to the community as easy as possible. An important part of the relocating process is tending to the spouse as well as the candidate, and any aid to the total move assists in making the transition a smooth one for the candidate and his family. References. —Cardwell, James W.; *Personnel Administrator,* Sep 1980, 25(9): pp. 53-56. Avail. ABI 80-17875

Transfers of employees, Relocating personnel, Dual career couples, Family, Decision making, Priorities

Personal Support Services in Corporate Relocation Programs (200)

There exist some very particular personal needs and concerns as they apply to the primary type of transferee today: the managerial or professional level person transferred within the continental US at company request. Some of the most important considerations that bear on the decision to relocate are nonmonetary in nature and include family approval and career impact. To ease the stress of relocation, companies should supply information about the employee's own career and the new community. Early communication with the employee's spouse is also important. Undoubtedly, as the number of transfer refusals increase and the high cost of relocation also increases, policies which penalize the non-mobile employee need reexamination. Employees need to have a clear picture of the consequences of refusal, and special attention must be paid to erroneous assumptions. For those employees accepting such relocation, some helpful aids have been on-site relocation assistants, community support, and the use of the case management system. References. —Levenson, Myra K. and Hollmann, Robert W.; *Personnel Administrator,* Sep 1980, 25(9): pp. 45-51. Avail. ABI 80-17874

Family, Personal, Support, Services, Relocating personnel, Transfers of employees, Communication, Counseling, Workshops, Cases, Management, Systems, Personnel management

Preventing Family Distress During Relocation: (201)
Initiatives for Human Resource Managers

Relocation often causes stress for the employee and family. People may deal with the stress caused by relocation by drinking, extramarital affairs, or using drugs. Children often react to relocation by getting into trouble at home and in the community. The reaction of the spouse can affect how the children react. A recent study found that the wives of successful executives have 3 coping mechanisms. The first is the wife's ability to fit into the corporate lifestyle. This suggests a close identification with her husband's employment. The 2nd mechanism involves the wife relying on extrafamily relationships to meet intrapersonal needs. The wife's ability to rely on internal resources to meet personal needs is the 3rd mechanism. Educational literature that explains the events pertaining to the relocation helps to reduce stress. Children are helped by introductory letters about school; they may sometimes be assigned another classmate to show them around. Clubs like Welcome Wagon try to help the wife get to know the new community. All of these efforts are greatly needed. Table. —Gullotta, Thomas P. and Donohue, Kevin C.; *Personnel Administrator,* Dec 1982, 27(12): pp. 37-43. Avail. ABI 83-01410

Relocating personnel, Transfers of employees, Human resources, Family, Personnel management, Employee morale, Adjustments, Stress

Relocating Women Managers: Can Your Company   (202)
Meet Their Needs?

While today's women managers recognize relocation as a means to professional advancement, they have other priorities that businesses must consider if they are to convince their women executives to make a move. Accordingly, many corporations are tempting their managers with a list of relocation benefits addressed to their lifestyles and financial needs. The most difficult problem for companies in this area involves dual-career couples. During the 1980s, as current employment trends continue, the number of women managers who make the decision to relocate will increase significantly. In formulating relocation policies, corporate administrators should address several areas. 1. Since many single women transferees will be renting, corporations need to liberalize their relocation benefits for nonhomeowners. 2. In cases of divorced women with children, their needs include educational, recreational, and day care information. 3.

Communication of relocation should be emphasized, and companies should recognize that managers, male and female, no longer automatically feel that relocation comes first. —Firestone, R. Darlene; *Advanced Mgmt Jrnl,* Spring 1981, 46(2): pp. 40-46. Avail. ABI 81-12942

Women, Managers, Relocating personnel, Transfers of employees, Dual career couples, Relocation, Policy, Employee benefits

Relocation: Changing Attitudes and Company Policies   (203)

In an environment of rising costs of living and housing, more 2-career families, and the stress of family relocation, more employees are thinking harder about accepting requests to transfer. In addition, the costs of relocation to the corporation have also increased. Employee Transfer Corporation (ETC), a Chicago, Illinois, relocation firm reports that, for 4 straight years, there has been a decrease in the number of transferred employees who would be willing to relocate again. Relocation policies need to be part of the overall personnel policies of the organization. Pointers for companies include: 1. Know employees' attitudes concerning relocation. 2. Screen proposed relocation candidates. 3. Develop career paths. 4. Develop corporate human resource development policies. 5. Analyze policy changes. 6. Modify recruitment strategies. A basic relocation package includes such items as tax assistance, house hunting assistance, shipment of household goods, etc. New policy areas include: 1. cost-of-living allowances, 2. mortgage interest differential allowances, 3. shared appreciation mortgages, and 4. property management. —Magnus, Margaret and Dodd, John; *Personnel Jrnl,* Jul 1981, 60(7): pp. 538-545,548. Avail. ABI 81-16977

Relocating personnel, Transfers of employees, Relocation, Policy, Dual career couples, Personnel policies, Cost of living differentials, Stress, Reduction

Relocation: Getting More for the Dollars You Spend   (204)

Various findings are reported from a nationwide study involving more than 70 major firms and conducted by Catalyst, a nonprofit organization studying relationships between workplace and family. The study focused on corporate relocation practices using questionnaires, group discussions, and in-depth interviews with relocation and personnel managers, relocated employees, and relocation companies. The success or failure of relocation is directly affected by personal and family issues. Many corporations are now helping transferees by: 1. providing information on the new location via information packets, with literature from several local organizations, 2. using area consultation services to help the family fit into the new community, and 3. offering home-finding services. Some companies provide a "Newcomer's Club" made up of other recent transferees to orient the new families to the new community. Other companies are offering employment assistance to the relocated spouse. Many employers agree that the services offered to help in the relocation are cost-effective in the long run. Charts. References. —Johnson, Arlene A.; *Personnel Administrator,* Apr 1984, 29(4): pp. 29-35,136. Avail. ABI 84-14634

Relocating personnel, Costs, Employee benefits, Stress, Personnel policies, Transfers of employees

Relocation in an Unsettled Economy (205)

Conditions in the housing industry are strongly impacting the manner in which corporations have conventionally done business, particularly concerning promotion and relocation. These pressing problems for corporate relocation administrators and their transferees may not be completely solvable, but there are some ways to help cope during these difficult economic times: 1. Avoid or postpone transfers whenever possible, particularly lateral moves or ones not involving key personnel. 2. Make some policy changes and improvements that will lessen risks, costs, and other possible sacrifices that transferees and their families foresee in moving. 3. Improve communication techniques to get feedback on present policies, to determine what changes would be appropriate and to improve employee relations by expressing company concern and discussing relocation issues. When transfers cannot be avoided, certain steps should be taken: 1. Change the way of determining mortgage interest differential reimbursements to a formula based on 125% of the old mortgage balance. 2. Share equally with employees any loan origination fees or discount points greater than 2%. 3. Reimburse employees for mortgage prepayment and other refinancing costs when interest rates decline. 4. Increase the miscellaneous expense allowance at the new location to one month's salary or a minimum of $2,500. 5. Cover employee interim living expenses for at least 30 days. –Kunisch, Robert D.; *Personnel Administrator,* Sep 1980, 25(9): pp. 25-28. Avail. ABI 80-17871

Relocating personnel, Transfers of employees, Homeowners, Costs, Cost reduction, Mortgages, Interest rates, Problems

Relocation Policies: Boom and Bust (206)

There are 3 important issues associated with the relocation process today: 1. basic issues associated with the relocation process regardless of economic conditions, 2. broad economic issues that impact the willingness of employee and company to bear costs of relocation, and 3. issues a company must consider when developing or evaluating relocation policies. Costs incurred in a relocation range from moving and storage of household goods and personal effects to reimbursement for added tax liability. Who pays for the costs of a transfer depends on the history of the company's reimbursement, competitor practices, the length of time the employee has been with the firm, etc. A critical economic factor in relocation, in addition to other costs, is the changing real estate situation. Companies are beginning to pay mortgage interest rate differentials to aid against the impact of rising mortgage rates. Further, some have discovered that in areas with cost of living differences, they need to pay cost of living allowances to employees moving into higher cost areas. Some employers are also including programs to assist the transferred employee's spouse in locating employment. Graphs. –Gardiner, Charles V. and Rich, Kenneth L.; *Personnel Administrator,* Sep 1980, 25(9): pp. 37-42,64,104-105. Avail. ABI 80-17873

Relocating personnel, Transfers of employees, Policy, Costs, Cost control, Reimbursement, Homeowners, Real estate, Economic conditions, Fair market value, Houses, Interest rates, Mortgages

Relocation Policies (207)

A survey on corporate relocation policies indicated that 43 of the 45 respondents have policies covering permanent transfers, and 21 of the 43 have policies on short-term transfers. Recent economic conditions have brought modifications of these policies, with about half of the respondents reporting that their policies have undergone some change. All permanent relocation policies described by respondents reimburse employees for 3 major moving expense items: househunting trips, temporary living expenses, and shipment of household goods. Overall, the survey shows that most companies do try to relieve employees of the major monetary costs of relocation. However, few respondents have taken such steps as pre-moving counseling to prepare employees and their families for the emotional problems and social realities of such a move. Tables. —Levine, Hermine Zagat; *Personnel,* Nov/Dec 1983, 60(6): pp. 4-11. Avail. ABI 84-03842

Relocating personnel, Surveys, Transfers of employees, Personnel policies, Costs

Relocation Policy Update: Innovations and Changes for the '80s (208)

Emerging social and economic trends, such as 2-career marriages, changing lifestyle preferences, diminishing corporate loyalty, high mortgage rates, and soaring housing costs, have dramatically affected relocation patterns in recent years and have made employees resistant to transfer. This relatively new and still evolving situation has affected the relocation environment and presented new challenges for relocation policy planners. Companies still need to entice people to move, particularly to higher-cost areas, in a way that is cost-effective to the employee and the firm. Relocation attempts to fill critical openings in a company, ensure the management development process, and fill manpower needs. The basic relocation package has consisted of purchase of old home, shipping of household goods, and temporary living allowance. Proposed policy changes should be carefully evaluated. A creative relocation policy might include such features as mortgage interest differential, direct mortgage assistance, cost of living allowance tied to interest rates on the new and old mortgage, term loans, greater salary assistance, and career assistance for the spouse. —Moore, John M.; *Personnel Administrator,* Dec 1981, 26(12): pp. 39-42. Avail. ABI 82-00441

Transfers of employees, Resistance, Relocating personnel, Personnel policies, Assistance, Mortgages, Interest rates, Differentials, Allowances, Cost of living

Relocation Strategies: Part II (209)

Given the fact that the costs of relocating employees have skyrocketed, how employee relocation is handled is important to a company's overall success. Many firms have undertaken relocation assistance programs that address total cost-of-living differentials in the new location. Many relocating workers are renters rather than homeowners, and they, too, experience a cost-of-living impact. Thus, companies have instituted renter relocation assistance programs that provide quarterly payments to take care of the annual differential in rents. In addition, it is usual for companies to have career-path plans for employees working their way up the corporate ladder. However, career path plans of the past are no longer effective unless cost-of-living differences among locations are taken into account. Companies must take care not to lose valuable employees who wish to remain in lower cost areas because they have built up quite an investment in such workers. There is also the current trend of treating new hires just about the same as longer term employees when it comes to relocation assistance, contrary to the situation that used to prevail. —Milbrandt, Gaylord F.; *Personnel Jrnl,* Aug 1981, 60(8): pp. 644-646. Avail. ABI 81-18786

> Relocating personnel, Transfers of employees, Cost of living differentials, Workforce planning, Career development planning, Personnel policies

Relocation Trends-Moving into the '80s   (210)

The relocation challenge of the '80s will be to address fully the problems of moving employees to high cost areas, especially when the change is from a moderate or low cost area to a high cost area. Data from an annual relocation trends survey (1977 through 1980) indicate that the number of corporate moves has increased in each of those years, in spite of considerable increases in relocation costs. Some of the cost increases are attributable to inflation, but much is a result of more liberal relocation policy coverage in the areas of household goods, travel, temporary living, househunting, and real estate related expenses. Some other relocation policy areas experiencing such changes include: 1. tax reimbursement, 2. miscellaneous allowance, and 3. cost of living allowances. Costs are one of the most immediate concerns to any corporation, and unfortunately, in the area of relocation, dramatic increases will be occurring which are beyond the control of a skilled professional relocation manager. As a result, the effect of the relocation cost increases will probably be that many companies reduce the number of moves. Graphs. Tables. —Collie, H. Cris and DiDomenico, Peter J.; *Personnel Administrator,* Sep 1980, 25(9): pp. 31-35,66-68. Avail. ABI 80-17872

> Relocating personnel, Transfers of employees, Policy, Trends, Costs, Reimbursement, Homeowners, Assistance

Relocation: Why More Employees Are Saying No   (211)

An increasing number of middle managers and executives are turning down promotions that involve relocating. These middle managers and executives believe that they will lose out, both financially and emotionally, because relocation in the 1980s means having to deal with the rising cost of living. Another factor is social uncertainty for the employee and his family. Families are impacted by a relocation, although more on subsequent transfers than by the first. The spouse may have career problems or coping problems with a relocation. Raising the acceptance level of relocation and ensuring a smooth transition period requires a sharp corporate sensitivity to the employee's and his family's personal needs. Organizations can also develop a climate in which employee turndowns are not perceived as disloyal, but rather as a result of a conflict between loyalty to the family and loyalty to the firm. —Anonymous; *Personnel,* Jan/Feb 1981, 58(1): pp. 40-43. Avail. ABI 81-06781

> Relocating personnel, Employees, Decisions, Rejections, Executives, Impacts, Family, Careers, Acceptance, Suggestions

Relocations Without Pain (212)

In planning employee relocation policies, the major question to be answered concerns what benefits the employee and the company will derive from relocation. Much of the question revolves around whether the cost/benefits support a decision to proceed with a move. Areas of concern for a relocation policy include: 1. selling the candidate, 2. accommodation, 3. financial assistance, 4. removal of household goods and personal effects, and 5. travelling to the new location. The relocation policy should also contain a section on expense pay-back in the event that transferred employees leave a company's employ before completing their designated period of service. However, if an employee is released with cause, or laid off, he would not be expected to pay back these costs. Well-planned provisions will make employees and their families happier, and they will therefore be more productive. –Duncan, H. James; *CA Magazine (Canada),* Jan 1981, 114(1): pp. 72-74. Avail. ABI 81-04676

Relocating personnel, Transfers of employees, Policy, Housing, Moving expenses

The Role Relocation Plays in Management Planning (213)

Relocation has been identified as an integral component of the management development process. Relocation, as a management development tool, broadens the experience of high potential managers and permits internal development of management talent to meet executive staffing needs as often as possible. A strategic relocation policy increases morale, improves productivity, broadens developmental experiences, and places the right people in strategically important positions. A survey conducted by Robie Ingram Associates for Merrill Lynch Relocation Management found that most companies prefer to relocate insiders rather than hire outsiders. It also found a trend toward lateral moves within a company in order to increase expertise. The growing resistance to transfer has led some companies to establish new relocation guidelines, such as limiting the number of transfers within a given period of time. Flexible benefit plans enable employees to select the relocation benefits that fit their particular needs. Financial aid is a vital factor in all relocation efforts. The corporate commitment to relocation is demonstrated by the flexible relocation policies available. – Moore, John M.; *Personnel Administrator,* Dec 1982, 27(12): pp. 31-34. Avail. ABI 83-01409

Relocation, Personnel management, Executives, Human resources, Transfers of employees, Relocating personnel

Spouse Relocation: A Creative Approach to Recruitment (214) and Employee Transfer

The relocation process is more complicated when dealing with 2-career families. Many relocation offers are not accepted because the spouse has a career and does not want to give it up. Usually, a raise will not offset the spouse's lost earning ability. The need for effective support for the career-oriented spouse in providing for dual relocation is recognized by many organizations. A successful spouse relocation program must include: 1. A full assessment of the spouse in terms of background, experience, education, and skills. 2. Preparation and printing of a resume. 3. Developing a marketing strategy. 4. A follow-up to provide encouragement to the spouse. The company may benefit from this program by speeding up the relocation process, filling vacancies more quickly, and being able to place high-potential managers in areas where they are critically needed. —Driessnack, Carl H.; *Personnel Administrator*, Dec 1982, 27(12): pp. 59-65. Avail. ABI 83-01413

> Relocating personnel, Transfers of employees, Career advancement, Couples, Husbands, Wives, Human resources

Starting to Treat Relocation Blues (215)

As relocation expenses rise and employees resist the idea of moving, many companies are buying transfer "insurance" from a new kind of organization that is symptomatic of the immobile 1980s: the relocation-counseling service. Probably the oldest and biggest of the new relocation "shrink tanks" is Transition Inc., of Wilton, Connecticut, founded by psychologists Stephen V. Eliot and Ronald J. Raymond Jr. Relocation counselors attempt to help transferring families assess their deep feelings about pulling up roots. In addition, employers want to ensure that transferees do not regret moving and then function badly in the new location. Transition clients generally attend 3 or more group workshops. The purposes of the workshops are: 1. to help them determine if they really want to move, and 2. to help them deal with mounting stresses just before the move takes place. Nida Training & Development Group, San Rafael, California, teaches companies to do their own relocation counseling. —Anonymous; *Business Week,* Aug 24, 1981, (2702) (Industrial Edition): pp. 90 N,P. Avail. ABI 81-19412

> Relocating personnel, Psychological aspects, Transfers of employees, Stress

Study Shows Relocation Resistance Reversing (216)

A nationwide survey of transferred employees found that 84.9% would be willing to transfer again, compared to 76.3% in 1980. Many things affect the willingness to transfer, including: 1. family considerations, 2. the kinds of relocation benefits, and 3. feelings about the new community and the one left behind. The study uncovered some trends about transferees. They tend to have more education and are well off economically; a third are 41 years or older; they tend to be stable family people. The survey also covered the importance of such topics as: 1. house expenses in the new area, 2. the feelings of the spouse, 3. relocation policies, and 4. living expenses. Comparative statistics are given. —Blomquist, Ceil; *Personnel Administrator*, Dec 1982, 27(12): pp. 55-56. Avail. ABI 83-01412

> Relocating personnel, Transfers of employees, Human resources, Employee attitude (PER), Employee morale, Career advancement

Sweetening the Pot to Lure Transfers (217)

The combination of high mortgage costs, the unavailability of money, and tight housing is causing people to refuse job opportunities that they would have sought 5 years ago. There is a greater reluctance on the part of many to relocate. Corporations have been forced to make costly arrangements to attract valued personnel to the cities and jobs where they are needed most. Mortgage "differentials" appear to be the tool most widely used at present. Additionally, companies are often including reimbursement of all moving and travel expenses, real estate fees, and even up-front bonuses of 2-3 months' salary to cover other expenses. Many of the financial deals that result are for "new hires," and some of the companies are uncomfortable that they are offering outsiders things that they will not offer current personnel. With today's economic reality, flexibility may prove to be necessary. —Anonymous; *Industry Week,* May 12, 1980, 205(3): pp. 34-36. Avail. ABI 80-10606

Transfers of employees, Relocating personnel, Employee benefits, Fringe benefits

Transfer Woes Grow, But Executives Still Go   (218)

In spite of higher mortgage rates and the doubling of the cost of the average move to $30,000, most executives relocate when asked by their companies, according to the president of a New York consulting firm. Reasons executives are more willing to relocate than lower level colleagues include: 1. pending promotions, 2. greater company identification, and 3. more experience with corporate moves. Spouses more easily accept living apart during the week; they often find the arrangement enhances their careers. Many executives hesitate to transfer due to high mortgage rates, and many companies have postponed transfers recently due to relocation costs. Because of the mortgage rates, many companies are offering a mortgage-rate differential allowance as part of their relocation packages. It is possible that companies will restrict future relocations only to promotions. Possible new relocation benefits include: 1. a new car and car insurance, 2. psychological counseling for transferees and family, and 3. mortgage-protection insurance. —Anonymous; *Industry Week,* Nov 30, 1981, 211(5): pp. 98-99,102. Avail. ABI 82-00671

Transfers of employees, Relocating personnel, Dual career couples, Problems, Relocation, Advantages, Trends

Urban Geographic Factors and Location Satisfaction   (219)
Following a Personnel Transfer

Recently transferred employees of 6 Canadian firms were surveyed to determine the factors which contribute to satisfaction with a new geographic location. Transferred employees' spouses were also surveyed. Respondents indicated their satisfaction with their new locations in comparison to their previous locations on the basis of: 1. a variety of urban characteristics, 2. their prior familiarity with their new locations, 3. additional compensation resulting from the transfers, and 4. spouses' work situations. The major determinants of satisfaction with a new location were found to be prior familiarity and increased compensation. On the basis of urban characteristics, satisfaction was greatest when relocation involved moving to a city which had a high growth rate and a healthy economy. A significant determinant of satisfaction for spouses, but not for the employees themselves, was whether or not spouses had lost or gained employment as a result of the transfer. Tables. References. —Carruthers, Norman E. and Pinder, Craig C.; *Academy of Mgmt Jrnl,* Sep 1983, 26(3): pp. 520-526. Avail. ABI 83-24921

Transfers of employees, Geographic, Satisfaction, Impacts, Mobility, Regression analysis, Studies, Relocating personnel

What Mortgage Rates Are Doing to Executive Mobility (220)

Increasingly, mid-level and top executives are refusing job offers or promotions that would require relocation. Their reasons include: 1. unprecedentedly high mortgage rates, 2. the increased importance of lifestyle, and 3. the 2-career family. It is possible that the difficulty in moving key executives will damage an organization's ability to meet its goals. Mortgage assistance is the top inducement to relocation according to chief executive officers of 500 firms surveyed by the Thomas-Mangum executive search firm (Los Angeles, California). More emphasis is being placed on other parts of the executive's lifestyle, such as family and community involvement. Executives also seek attractive environments with such attributes as clean air and good schools. The new 2-career family wants career growth for both partners. Salary considerations are still significant in relocation decisions, but mortgage issues have gained greater prominence. Chart. —Mangum, William T.; *Administrative Mgmt,* Feb 1982, 43(2): pp. 59-60,86-87. Avail. ABI 82-06330

Executives, Mobility, Employee attitude (PER), Resistance, Relocating personnel, Lifestyles, Dual career couples, Mortgages, Interest rates

When Moving Up the Ladder Means Moving Out of (221) Town

An employee's entire family will be affected by the decision to accept a transfer, so each member should be involved in making the decision. The financial, professional, and personal effects must be considered. The family must first understand the new job responsibilities, career potential, and fringe benefits. Schools, recreational facilities, community lifestyle, and neighborhood are also major considerations. If the decision to relocate is made, several guidelines can be helpful: 1. Develop a sensitivity to the transition process of relocation. 2. Involve family members in the housing search. 3. Take time off during the household move. 4. Prepare an outline of corporate jargon, titles, and names. 5. Review your travel schedule immediately after the move. 6. Encourage your family to visit your place of work. 7. Attend seminars on the effects of relocation on the employee and family. 8. Give yourself and your family time to feel at home. —Prah, D. W.; *Supervisory Mgmt,* Jul 1983, 28(7): pp. 18-22. Avail. ABI 83-19591

Relocating personnel, Transfers of employees, Dual career couples, Guidelines, Career advancement

Why Managers Won't Move On (222)

Last year Canadian employers in both the private and the public sectors relocated between 40,000 and 45,000 employees. Companies relocate personnel as a reflection of changing economic conditions, to expand and restructure their operations, to put the right person in the right place, and to develop and train the top managers of the future by rotating them through a series of operational areas. However, now the transfer process has become more difficult and costly. Relocation appears to be costing companies between $22,000 and $40,000 per employee transferred. Generous financial provisions reflect a growing uneasiness among employees to relocate. Many people are unwilling to relocate because of the financial and psychological costs. However, statistics are unavailable as to how many executives are actually refusing to move. Companies are offering a number of incentives to entice employees to relocate, such as cost-of-living differentials, home purchase plans, and job-finding assistance for the spouse. —Weiner, Andrew; *Canadian Business (Canada),* Mar 1981, 54(3): pp. 54-62. Avail. ABI 81-06695

Canada, Executives, Relocating personnel, Transfers of employees, Rejections, Attitudes, Surveys, Effects, Wives, Cost of living differentials, Housing

10th Annual Relocation Survey Examines New Topics (223)

According to the Merrill Lynch Relocation Management Inc.'s (MLRM) annual Study of Corporate Relocation Policy, the majority of the 611 major corporations surveyed indicated that relocated employees who leave a company within a year of being transferred do not have to pay back any of the related expenses. Additionally, 12% of the companies surveyed noted that they would offer to move an employee back to the original location, or to another location, if the move did not work out. It appears that corporations are adapting their relocation policies to encourage employee transfers. Corporations are devising new relocation strategies to respond to employees' increasing demand for more meaningful and fulfilling jobs and improved quality of work life. Responding to the needs of dual-career marriages, 25% of the respondents indicated that they now provide job assistance to spouses. Most companies also provide some assistance in disposing of their employees' homes. Corporations are developing human resource plans which balance corporate needs with those of the employees. Graph. — Anonymous; *United States Banker,* Aug 1982, 93(8): pp. 16,18. Avail. ABI 82-21911

Consulting firms, Relocating personnel, Transfers of employees, Surveys

4

Job Satisfaction

Absenteeism, Job Involvement, and Job Satisfaction in an Organizational Setting   (224)

Using a sample of state government employees, measures of job satisfaction, job involvement, and absenteeism were gathered. Zero-order correlation results indicated that both job satisfaction and job involvement were inversely related to absenteeism, but job involvement was more consistently related to absence behavior. However, partial correlation coefficients for the satisfaction-absence (job involvement held constant) and involvement-absence (job satisfaction held constant) relationships revealed that although job involvement was related to absenteeism, job satisfaction was not. It appeared that the variance in the relationship between absenteeism and job satisfaction was accounted for by the mediating influence of job involvement. It is suggested that future studies of attitude-absence relationships use multiple measures of these variables designed to reveal possible complexities in these relationships. Tables. References. —Cheloha, Randall S. and Farr, James L.; *Jrnl of Applied Psychology*, Aug 1980, 65(4): pp. 467-473. Avail. ABI 80-15793

Studies, Organizational, Psychology, Job satisfaction, Correlations, Absenteeism, Employee, Behavior

Absenteeism When Workers Have a Voice: The Case of Employee Ownership   (225)

Steers and Rhodes (1978) constructed a model that isolated the causes of both voluntary and involuntary absenteeism. Voluntary absenteeism was seen as a function of job satisfaction and pressure to attend work, while involuntary absenteeism was regarded as a function of individual characteristics that determine the ability to come to work. Steers and Rhodes model was used to predict and explain patterns of absenteeism in an organization that had converted from corporate ownership to employee ownership through divestiture. The focus of the study was the prediction of voluntary absenteeism. The subjects were 112 nonsupervisory workers. Absenteeism data were obtained from personnel records; information about individual characteristics, the job situation, job satisfaction, and financial and organizational commitment was obtained from a questionnaire. The results indicated that absenteeism is affected primarily by organizational and financial commitment, but job satisfaction was not found to be a prediction of absenteeism. Tables. Graphs. References. —Hammer, Tove Helland; Landau, Jacqueline C.; and Stern, Robert N.; *Jrnl of Applied Psychology,* Oct 1981, 66(5): pp. 561-573. Avail. ABI 81-25569

Voluntary, Absenteeism, Employee, Ownership, Business ownership, Job satisfaction, Attendance, Behavior, Studies

The Alchemy of Career Changes (226)

Changing expectations and values of executives promise to revolutionize work in the 1980s, according to Daniel Yankelovich, president of the social research firm of Yankelovich, Skelly & White, Inc. The materialistic and authoritative tendency of most corporations flies in the face of the new set of values and beliefs of young executives who are no longer willing to tolerate the stress and anxiety that accompany corporate life. The increase in 2-career families and the new opportunities created by modern technologies put second careers within the reach of most Americans. Some people are leaving their first careers for entirely new and different ones and others work at 2 careers simultaneously. Hobbies can become new full-time career options. Small business ownership offers the individual the advantage of having a secure job with the capability of reducing hours as needed. The number of people following these multi-career opportunities is astounding. According to the 1970 census, nearly 1/3 of the entire US work force had changed occupations between 1965 and 1970. —Sager, Leon B. and Kipling, Richard E.; *Business Horizons,* Aug 1980, 23(4): pp. 23-30. Avail. ABI 80-16471

Job satisfaction, Careers, Changes, Mobility, Lifestyles

All About Job Satisfaction (227)

Job satisfaction is an indication of how individuals feel about their job when their expectations are compared to what is actually received from different facets of the work situation. When an individual expresses satisfaction with the situation as a whole, there is little that can be done to improve the work environment. On the other hand, when satisfaction refers to an individual's feelings towards specific aspects of the job, the manager is better able to improve the work environment by eliminating those facets that are causing dissatisfaction. Before doing so, it is necessary for the manager to know what situations and conditions affect overall job satisfaction. The relationship between job satisfaction and behavior has been studied and reveals that the consequences of dissatisfaction with any factor may not be the same as the consequences of dissatisfaction with another factor. It is also found that job satisfaction affects life satisfaction more than life satisfaction influences job satisfaction. —Milbourn, Gene, Jr. and Francis, G. James; *Supervisory Mgmt,* Aug 1981, 26(8): pp. 35-43. Avail. ABI 81-18939

Job satisfaction, Employee attitude (PER), Work environment, Job, Characteristics, Rankings

Allowing Productivity to Happen (228)

In an era in which productivity is as important as it is today, many firms are suppressing one of the most natural sources of productivity increases-self-responsibility. Productivity itself is a "function of responsibility freely accepted," and to achieve it, managers must support people in doing their individual jobs.Factors contributing to an unworkable job environment are: 1. suppression of emotion, 2. supervisors who do not make jobs clear, 3. repetition of unacknowledged mistakes, and 4. jobs that become too spread out.There are 4 steps managers can take to support employees in getting their jobs done and to create an environment conducive to more productive work: 1. allow emotions to be expressed freely. 2. Make clear performance measurements and the purpose for each job. 3. Set agreements within which employees can operate with some discretion. 4. Acknowledge mistakes as well as contributions. −Harvey, Frederick W.; *Supervisory Mgmt,* Jun 1980, 25(6): pp. 21-25. Avail. ABI 80-11060

Productivity, Job satisfaction, Work environment, Personnel management, Guidelines

Are Job Enrichment Programs Really Worth It?   (229)

The concept of "job enrichment" began with the theories of Frederick Hertzberg more than 20 years ago and has been tried since then by several large corporations. Job enrichment involves restructuring a job to give employees greater freedom and responsibility, a variety of tasks, and an increased opportunity for achievement and recognition. Job enrichment is only effective if: 1. workers want a challenge and support the program, 2. job boredom is the problem and it is uncomplicated by other issues such as pay and working conditions, 3. job restructuring is substantial, and 4. enrichment is undertaken along with an effort to improve policies regarding pay, job security, and working conditions. The purpose of a job enrichment program is to improve employee attitudes, productivity, and, thus, profits. −Anonymous; *Effective Manager,* Jan 1981, 4(4): pp. 1-3. Avail. ABI 81-03939

Job enrichment, Programs, Job satisfaction

Are U.S. Organizational Concepts and Measures   (230)
Transferable to Another Culture? An Empirical
Investigation

A multivariate cross-cultural approach is illustrated for exploring the meaning of 2 attitudinal concepts-job involvement and job satisfaction-and their correlates across 2 cultures, the US and India. A total of 267 white collar workers were randomly chosen from 12 banks in the midwestern US, and 307 similar workers were similarly chosen from 9 banks in the central and southern parts of India. In both cultures, identical questionnaires were administered by the same researcher. Judged by factor analysis results, it can be concluded that both measures of job involvement and job satisfaction are equally applicable to the 2 cultures. For job involvement, tenure on the job was an important predictor, and for job satisfaction, job variety and job stress were the predictors common to both cultures. The test models indicated no differences in the predictors for job satisfaction in the 2 cultures, and only age seemed to predict job involvement differentially in the 2 cultures. Tables. References. −Sekaran, Uma; *Academy of Mgmt Jrnl,* Jun 1981, 24(2): pp. 409-417. Avail. ABI 81-14530

Cross cultural, Studies, Job satisfaction, Job attitudes, India, Banking, Personnel, White collar workers, Statistical analysis

Attitudinal Congruence and Similarity as Related to (231)
Interpersonal Evaluations in Manager-Subordinate
Dyads

Recently, applied researchers have become increasingly interested in the interpersonal relationships within manager-subordinate dyads. Both actual similarity and perceptual congruence examined from the view of both the manager and subordinate are of particular interest.Students from 2 large midwestern universities were asked to participate in a study if they presently worked and reported to an immediate manager. Data were collected from 194 students having positions in different organizations throughout northern Ohio. In addition, the immediate manager of each of these subjects was involved, resulting in 194 separate manager-subordinate dyads. The more cognizant a manager was of a subordinate's work-related attitudes, the more positively the subordinate was evaluated by that manager. In addition, the more congruently the subordinate saw the manager's attitudes, the more satisfied the subordinate was with supervision received from the manager. Although person-person congruence has been examined, future experimental work is needed to start examining the relative contributions of worker-organization, worker-job, and person-person perceptual congruence to employee satisfaction and performance. Tables. References. —Wexley, Kenneth N.; Alexander, Ralph A.; Greenawalt, James P.; and Couch, Michael A.; *Academy of Mgmt Jrnl,* Jun 1980, 23(2): pp. 320-330. Avail. ABI 80-12752

Job attitudes, Managers, Subordinates, Performance, Job satisfaction, Performance evaluation, Studies, Perceptions, Correlation analysis

Audit of Personnel Management (232)

Where employees derive personal satisfaction from their jobs, morale and performance improve, fewer personnel problems are reported, and the workforce is better adjusted overall. It is management's responsibility to provide creative, constructive, and productive reactions among workers. The management of workday affairs with regard for the needs of people does not place additional burdens on busy supervisors, but it does require systematic, purposeful, and effective performance of responsibilities by those involved with personnel management. In the process of auditing a personnel management function, a personnel questionnaire was created by a company to determine how employees rated their position, workload, working conditions, supervision, performance appraisals, training, and incentive awards. Interviews with employees showed that morale, motivation, and attitudes left much to be desired. Personnel management requires 2 characteristics to be effective: 1. improvement of line officials as personnel managers, and 2. improved staff-line relationships between personnel departments and organizational elements. —Weinbach, Lawrence P.; *Internal Auditor,* Jun 1983, 40(3): pp. 23-25. Avail. ABI 83-16736

Auditing, Personnel administration, Employee problems, Job satisfaction, Guidelines

The Availability and Helpfulness of Socialization Practices (233)

Through socialization, newcomers to an organization come to understand expectations of their roles and behaviors. However, little is known about the impact of socialization on employee attitudes. An exploratory study was conducted to assess the availability, effectiveness, and impact of organizational socialization practices. Recently employed business school graduates were surveyed about their employers' socialization activities, including formal orientations, buddy systems, supervisory support, peer interactions, and social/recreational activities with co-workers. Respondents also completed job satisfaction and organizational commitment questionnaires. While generally available, formal orientations were found to have little effect in socializing new workers and enhancing their job satisfaction. Peer interactions, buddy systems, and supervisory support were found to be the most effective means of organizational socialization in that they result in the highest levels of job satisfaction and organizational commitment. Tables. References. —Louis, Meryl R.; Posner, Barry Z.; and Powell, Gary N.; *Personnel Psychology,* Winter 1983, 36(4): pp. 857-866. Avail. ABI 84-03967

New employees, Social customs, Orientations, Employee attitude (PER), Studies, Organizational behavior, Statistical analysis, Employee development (PER), Job satisfaction

Background, Personality, Job Characteristics, and Satisfaction with Work in a National Sample (234)

For many years, job satisfaction has held a prominent place in the organizational psychology literature. Correlates of job satisfaction are reported in this research, using data from a 1977 national survey of 3,288 adult Canadians; general alienation, feelings of internal versus external locus of control, and interpersonal trust were measured in that survey, along with numerous biographic and job characteristic variables. The present research follows Hulin and Blood (1968) in treating response to working conditions as tempered by personality dispositions which are general in nature and mostly independent of work conditions. The results show that personality and job characteristics have strong, independent relationships with a multidimensional job satisfaction index. Personal alienation and internal-external control had large correlations with the index when job characteristics and personal background were controlled. All variables taken together explain 30% of the variance in job satisfaction. The reciprocal nature of cause and effect in the relationship between personality and job satisfaction is discussed in view of other recent analyses of panel data on response to work. Tables. References. —King, Michael; Murray, Michael A.; and Atkinson, Tom; *Human Relations,* Feb 1982, 35(2): pp. 119-133. Avail. ABI 82-10064

Personality, Job, Characteristics, Effects, Job satisfaction, Correlations, Studies, Variables, Organizational behavior

Bringing Some Clarity to Role Ambiguity Research (235)

A theoretical view of role ambiguity and role conflict deals with unclear differences between a person's organizational position and personal, behavioral consequences. In this context, ambiguity refers to the relative unpredictability of the outcomes of a person's behavior. However, empirical research on role ambiguity has been multi-faceted, and has confounded role ambiguity with job dissatisfaction and formalization. Information inadequacy is stressed. An integrative model, consistent with expectancy theory, is offered to direct future research on role ambiguity. The model stresses 4 points: 1. The consequences of the behavior of those working through others are more ambiguous than those of people whose outcomes are not mediated by others. 2. Delay of definitive feedback increases experienced ambiguity. 3. Those who find behavior consequences unpredictable will have more stress than those with more predictable behavioral consequences. 4. Only those outcomes deemed important will lead to stress. The model emphasizes unpredictability, rather than deficiency in information, as critical for understanding role ambiguity and its impact on organizational behavior. Chart. References. –Pearce, Jone L.; *Academy of Mgmt Review,* Oct 1981, 6(4): pp. 665-674. Avail. ABI 82-00044

Roles, Conflict, Job satisfaction, Models, Organization theory, Organizational behavior

Causal Inferences Between Leader Reward Behaviour (236) and Subordinate Performance, Absenteeism, and Work Satisfaction

A longitudinal field study, using corrected cross-lag correlations, was conducted to investigate the causal inference relationships between perceived leader reward behavior and subordinate performance, absenteeism, and work satisfaction. The subjects were 128 employees in a controller's department of a mechandising organization. Data were obtained by means of questionnaires, productivity, and attendance records at 2 time-periods, about 3 months apart. Measures were obtained for: 1. leader reward behavior, 2. punitive leader behavior, 3. performance, 4. absenteeism, and 5. job satisfaction. The results of the study indicated the following: 1. Perceived positive leader reward behavior serves as a source of causation for subordinate performance and work satisfaction. 2. Perceived punitive leader behavior acts as a source of causation for subordinate work dissatisfaction. 3. Subordinate performance and absenteeism serve as sources of causation for perceived punitive leader behavior. Tables. Equations. References. – Szilagyi, Andrew D.; *Jrnl of Occupational Psychology (UK),* Sep 1980, 53(3): pp. 195-204. Avail. ABI 80-21268

Studies, Occupational, Psychology, Leadership, Behavior, Absenteeism, Personnel management, Subordinates, Performance, Job satisfaction

Chairmen of the Bored (237)

Managerial boredom is one of the best-kept secrets in the business world. It occurs for several reasons: 1. too little to do, 2. repeating the same task over and over again, and 3. frustrated ambition. Boredom results when these complaints are combined with excessive amounts of spare time. Managers who are short of time may simply never have noticed their own symptoms. When a break in activity occurs, they often come to the realization that their job is boring. A number of new management techniques are being tried to alleviate the problem. Job rotation moves an employee from one department to another. Job redesign is also being used. It involves giving the employee something more or different to do. For employees in companies that do not try such techniques, they should try them themselves. They should look for projects that are different enough to be interesting, but are still in accord with corporate purposes. They should also exercise or initiate more contact with their colleagues. —Kiechel, Walter, III; *Fortune,* Mar 5, 1984, 109(5): pp. 175-176. Avail. ABI 84-09895

Corporate officers, Job satisfaction, Job attitudes, Employee problems, Job enrichment, Job rotation

Changes in Social Density: Relationships with Functional Interaction and Perceptions of Job Characteristics, Role Stress, and Work Satisfaction (238)

Research investigated the relationships among social density changes, functional interaction, and perceptions of job characteristics, role stress, and work satisfaction of 96 professional employees in a petroleum-related company. The social density change occurred as a result of the physical movement of the employees to a new building. Data were obtained from questionnaire measures, measurements of physical space, and functional interaction. The results indicated that the employees who experienced a social density increase reported significantly less role stress and job autonomy, but significantly greater job feedback, friendship opportunities, and work satisfaction. The results of the study challenge the widely held belief that work-force social density increases will have dysfunctional effects on individual behavior and attitudes. Tables. References. —Szilagyi, Andrew D. and Holland, Winford E.; *Jrnl of Applied Psychology,* Feb 1980, 65(1): pp. 28-33. Avail. ABI 80-04317

Employee attitude (PER), Employee, Behavior, Work environment, Social, Density, Changes, Increases, Effects, Job satisfaction, Stress, Studies

Changing Employee Values in America (239)

Lifestyles of the 1980's have diverged from the conformity of previous years. Between 1950 and 1981, 240,000 employees in 188 companies participated in surveys geared to documenting the changing values of employees. Human resource planners need to understand the transition and be prepared to capitalize by instituting innovative changes in job design and organizational structures. Among the general categories covered were: 1. perceptions of the company, 2. job satisfaction and several extrinsic factors, such as job security, pay rates, and fringe benefits, 3. advancement opportunities and promotions, 4. company communications, and 5. ability of top management. Each of these categories are tabulated for individual components. Implications drawn from the surveys' findings are that management would be well advised to: 1. increase delegation, 2. support more interactive communication, 3. involve the employee in the total picture, and 4. offer realistic company previews. Tables. —O'Neill, Harry W.; *Employee Relations Law Jrnl,* Summer 1981, 7(1): pp. 21-35. Avail. ABI 81-22370

Employee attitude (PER), Attitude surveys, Employee, Ratings, Companies, Job satisfaction, Employment security, Wage rates, Employee benefits, Promotions (MAN), Internal, Communication, Information, Sources, Labor relations

The Commitment and Job Tenure of New Employees: (240)
Some Evidence of Postdecisional Justification

By questioning 108 Master of Business Administration (MBA) graduates about job choices and their subsequent attitudes concerning those choices, and by examining turnover data, the effects of self-justification after initial commitment were studied. Those who made their job choice volitionally (from a number of offers and free of external constraints) and who viewed the choice as irrevocable proved to be more satisfied and committed to the job than others. Self-justification, after the initial commitment, appeared to strengthen the commitment. Prospective and retrospective processes appear to shape attitudes and behaviors. The social information process during the initial employment period can help an individual realign previous expectations and can act to bind an individual more tightly with the employing firm. Tables. References. –O'Reilly, Charles A., III and Caldwell, David F.; *Administrative Science Qtrly,* Dec 1981, 26(4): pp. 597-616. Avail. ABI 82-03841

New employees, Commitments, Tenure, Job satisfaction, Employee turnover, Job, Choices, Decision making, Behavior, Statistical analysis, Organizational behavior

Commitment to Organization and Profession: A Review   (241)

Within an organizational context, 2 major centers of commitment exist for employees-the employing organization and the profession or professional field of interest. It has frequently been presumed that commitment processes in organizations generate desirable results, such as employee job satisfaction. However, job satisfaction alone is not an adequate measure of performance, and must be combined with other effectiveness measures, such as: 1. efficiency in carrying out task assignments, 2. adaptation to alterations in task requirements, 3. avoidance of conflict that impedes task progress, 4. satisfaction with job aspects, and 5. achievement of task goals. These measures were used with 107 industrially-employed scientists and engineers, and results indicate that commitment to profession is unrelated to overall effectiveness. In addition, employees who are highly committed to their organization are likely to be relatively ineffective performers. Some important managerial implications include: 1. Commitment to profession does not preclude commitment to organization. 2. Conflict between the attainment of professional and organizational goals will most likely happen with cosmopolitan employees. 3. In a dynamic, changing environment, an organizational commitment can be linked with dysfunctional results. 4. The usefulness of organizational and professional commitment is questionable in a dynamic organization. Table. References. –Rotondi, Thomas; *Jrnl of General Mgmt (UK),* Autumn 1980, 6(1): pp. 15-21. Avail. ABI 80-23464

Organizational, Professional, Commitments, Effectiveness, Studies, Efficiency, Adaptation, Conflicts, Job satisfaction, Goals, Integration, Job improvement

A Comparison of the Predictive Power of Subtractive   (242)
and Multiplicative Models of Job Satisfaction and
Performance

In 6 samples, multiple regression was used to compare subtractive and multiplicative contingency models to each other and to non-contingency models. Life Style and Organization Structure measures were the independent variables studied. Dependent variables included the Job Descriptive Index, other job attitude measures, and performance measures. In the combined samples, an additive model was most predictive for 6 dependent variables. The congruence model-a contingency model-was most predictive for only 2 variables. Organization structure was predictive for the other dependent variables. A significant model emerged for all dependent variables. It is apparent that, especially as sample size decreases, contingency models have the least predictive power compared to others studied. The application of contingency models to the study of job satisfaction is unsatisfactory. Alternative approaches yield the highest predictive levels. Tables. References. –Norton, S. D. and Di Marco, N.; *Jrnl of Mgmt Studies (UK),* Oct 1980, 17(3): pp. 303-315. Avail. ABI 81-03854

Job satisfaction, Performance, Contingencies, Models, Studies, Lifestyles, Job attitudes, Statistical analysis, Organizational, Structure

A Comparison of the Relationships Between (243) Subordinates' Perceptions of Supervisory Behavior and Measures of Subordinates' Job Satisfaction for Male and Female Leaders

Reviews by Terborg (1977) and Schein (1978) have emphasized the absence of consistent results in tests of the predictions of a sex-role congruency hypothesis concerning the relationships between leader behavior and subordinate work-related attitudes. The sex-role congruency hypothesis was tested with a large sample of 2,432, while controlling for subordinate demographics, job type, and role stress perceptions. It was hypothesized that considerate supervisory behavior by female leaders will be more positively correlated with subordinates' satisfaction than will considerate supervisory behavior by male leaders. Further, initiating structure behavior by male leaders will be more positively correlated with subordinates' satisfaction than initiating structure behavior by female leaders. Results did not provide support for the sex-role congruency hypothesis as it pertains to leaders' consideration or initiating structure. Male and female leaders' consideration were both strongly, positively correlated with male and female subordinates' satisfaction with supervision in all subgroups for all job classifications. Tables. References. –Petty, M. M. and Bruning, Nealia S.; *Academy of Mgmt Jrnl,* Dec 1980, 23(4): pp. 717-725. Avail. ABI 81-00758

Leadership, Behavior, Job satisfaction, Sex roles, Statistical analysis, Job, Classification, Organizational behavior

A Contingency Approach to Organization Development (244) Based on Differentiated Roles

Research is reported exploring similarities and differences between health-care administrators and health-care professionals regarding their perceptions of climate, role stress, functional influence, job satisfaction, and the relationships between these variables. As a logical extension of the principle of individual differences, it is suggested that there exist differentiated groups within organizations that may necessitate customized interventions.

Administrators and professionals are 2 such groups represented in most organizations. Focusing on job satisfaction as the dependent variable in a health-care organization, the researchers found that a contingency perspective is warranted. Overall, the theory predicted accurately and significantly in 65 of a possible 136 relationships for the professionals and in only 44 of the relationships for the administrators. This result indicates that differential-intervention strategies should be used for the 2 groups, even in the identical organization. Tables. References. —LaVan, Helen; Welsch, Harold P.; and Full, James M.; *Group & Organization Studies,* Jun 1981, 6(2): pp. 176-189. Avail. ABI 81-16784

Organization development, Contingencies, Theory, Job satisfaction, Roles, Conflict, Organizational, Climates, Hospitals, Health facilities, Medical personnel, Managers, Studies

A Cross-Lagged Regression Test of the Relationships (245) Between Job Tension and Employee Satisfaction

Research into organizational causes and consequences of job stress has suggested a causal relationship between job tension and employee satisfaction. A study was conducted to clarify the causal relationships between job-related tension and employee satisfaction. Longitudinal data were obtained from 129 nursing department employees. Subjects completed questionnaires designed to measure job tension and job satisfaction. The results indicate that job tension and overall satisfaction are reciprocally caused. Consideration of specific facets of satisfaction points to differing causal influences. For the nurses studied, dissatisfaction with work and with physicians precedes job tension, while dissatisfaction with supervision and with pay results from job tension. Tables. References. —Bateman, Thomas S. and Strasser, Stephen; *Jrnl of Applied Psychology,* Aug 1983, 68(3): pp. 439-445. Avail. ABI 83-23432

Tension, Job satisfaction, Regression analysis, Stress, Supervision, Work environment, Personnel management

Cultural Orientations and Individual Reactions to (246) Organizations: A Study of Employees of Japanese-Owned Firms

A study was conducted to examine the cultural differences in the reactions of persons to work organizations. An examination was made of 28 organizations that were Japanese-owned establishments in southern California. Subjects were divided into 3 national origin groups: 1. Japanese citizens, 2. Japanese-Americans, and 3. American citizens with no Japanese ancestry. Data were obtained from interviews with chief executives, an analysis of company data, and self-administered questionnaires. The results indicated that: 1. Japanese and Japanese-American employees were more likely to value paternalistic company behavior. 2. There were no differences among national origin groups in the extent of personal ties with co-workers. 3. There were lower levels of work satisfaction among the Japanese and Japanese-Americans. A model of personal ties and work satisfaction was developed which allowed effects to vary across national origin categories.

Tables. References. —Lincoln, James R.; Hanada, Mitsuyo; and Olson, Jon; *Administrative Science Qtrly,* Mar 1981, 26(1): pp. 93-115. Avail. ABI 81-10826

Organization theory, Organizational, Structure, Vertical, Horizontal, Differentiation, Japan, Formal organization, Job, Orientations, Organizational behavior, Cultural, Differences, Employee attitude (PER), Job satisfaction, Models, Correlations, Paternalism, Regression analysis

The Desire for an Enriched Job as a Moderator of the   (247) Enrichment-Satisfaction Relationship

Previous research has examined 3 kinds of moderators of the enrichment-satisfaction relationship: urban-rural influences, work values, and growth need strength. A recent review has suggested that none of the variables tested provides evidence for consistent moderating effect. The present study was conducted in an attempt to show that these factors do have a moderating effect on enrichment-satisfaction.The subjects were 3053 workers in 53 companies throughout the US. The subjects were asked to complete questionnaires regarding attitudes toward one's specific job, the company, and work in general, and demographics. The results indicated that the desire for an enriched job was a significant moderator of the enrichment-satisfaction relationship. A person's desire for job enrichment was found to be a much better moderator than indirect estimates inferred from urban-rural influences or work values. Tables. Figure. References. —Cherrington, David J. and England, J. Lynn; *Organizational Behavior & Human Performance,* Feb 1980, 25(1): pp. 139-159. Avail. ABI 80-04118

Satisfaction, Job satisfaction, Job enrichment, Variables, Workers, Surveys, Correlation analysis, Regression analysis, Variance analysis, Studies

Determinants and Behavioral Consequences of Pay   (248) Satisfaction: A Comparison of Two Models

Dissatisfaction with pay influences the following: 1. performance, 2. work stoppages, 3. absenteeism, 4. turnover, and 5. job dissatisfaction. Not all results are negative, because dissatisfaction may lead to increased performance or turnover, both positive responses. An organization must comprehend both the determinants and consequences of pay satisfaction to facilitate positive rather than negative organizational consequences. Models of determinants of pay satisfaction proposed by Lawler and by Dyer and Theriault are examined. The basic proposition of Lawler's model explains only a moderate amount of pay satisfaction, and therefore, an improved conceptualization of Lawler's proposition is proposed. Dyer and Theriault add pay administration variables to Lawler's model, and this expanded model is found to account for more pay satisfaction variance and to better predict consequences of pay dissatisfaction. Tables. Equations. Appendix. References. Weiner, Nan; *Personnel Psychology,* Winter 1980, 33(4): pp. 741-757. Avail. ABI 81-03122

Wages & salaries, Job satisfaction, Performance, Organizational behavior, Job attitudes, Absenteeism, Statistical analysis

Did Job Satisfaction Really Drop During the 1970's? (249)

While it has been widely asserted that discontent in the American workforce is increasing, most credible research has indicated high and essentially stable levels of job satisfaction. However, Staines and Quinn (1979) using data derived from the 1977 Quality of Employment Survey, presented evidence of a significant drop in the national job satisfaction level. These data are reviewed and contrasted with data from similar surveys of the same era. Generally, the pattern of decline reported by Staines and Quinn is not confirmed in the other surveys. The Staines and Quinn report may be implausible for several reasons, including: 1. The announced decline is inconsistent with a long history of prior research showing high and essentially stable levels of job satisfaction. 2. A parallel decline in overall life satisfaction registered in the employment series is not replicated in 2 independent tests. Tables. References. —Chelte, Anthony F.; Wright, James; and Tausky, Curt; *Monthly Labor Review,* Nov 1982, 105(11): pp. 33-36. Avail. ABI 83-01917

Job satisfaction, Quality of work, Surveys, Quality of life, Trends

Die Fuehrung praegt den Arbeitswillen (Management (250) Determines Will to Work)

A manager must motivate his staff and must determine whether an apparently lazy or uninterested staff member lacks ability or training, has satisfactory relationships with colleagues, and/or is content in the working environment. The authoritarian style of management creates distrust, does not stimulate communication, may seek to disguise inadequate work knowledge and lack of human understanding, and can create a bad atmosphere, leading to high absenteeism and resignations. The cooperative style achieves better understanding and more sense of purpose and responsibility. A survey of employees' priorities for their job environments reveals differences between management's judgments of what staff consider important and what staff actually consider important. It was found that: 1. job security, always ranked high, was rated more important in 1981 than in 1976. 2. Several needs rank higher than material rewards; they are ignored by managers at their peril. 3. Priorities reflect conditions created by management. 4. Management needs to understand the psychology of its staff and bring together the individual's needs and the constraints of business life. Table. —Fiedler, Hans; *Fortschrittliche Betriebsfuehrung und Industrial Engineering (Germany),* Aug 1981, 30(4): pp. 315-318. Avail. ABI 82-01590

Personnel management, Motivation, Employee attitude (PER), Job satisfaction, Factors, Studies, Germany

Disgruntled Employees (251)

Employee disgruntlement is the cause of some of the most prevalent conditions that cripple today's organization, including disasters in the workforce. Disgruntlement may be manifested through insubordination, hostility, pilfering, and sabotage, resulting in property destruction, absenteeism, or increased turnover. A major cause of employee dissatisfaction is poor management. The real problem often remains undetected while management reacts by punishing the guilty party and dispensing warnings to the rest of the employees. However, there are ways to keep track of employee well-being before disgruntlement occurs. Attitude and morale surveys can reveal the cause of discontent. Disgruntlement can be prevented by ensuring that employees have a safe, challenging, rewarding workplace. Rules must be established and enforced and employees should participate in rule-making and standard-setting. —Miles, Mary; *Computer Decisions,* Oct 1983, 15(11): pp. 210,214. Avail. ABI 83-29325

Employee problems, Job satisfaction, Employee morale

Do We Really Need Job Enrichment? (252)

Statistics have indicated the ever-increasing dissatisfaction of workers with their jobs. Behavioral psychologists, armed with such statistics, have developed techniques that they claim will enrich even the most boring jobs. However, in the mad rush to modernize job techniques, managers may be guilty of blindly accepting and overgeneralizing about the value of job enrichment. Recent studies indicate that the key job enrichment assumption, that the workers are not satisfied with their jobs, may not be true. A report from the University of Michigan's Institute of Social Research based on interviews with 2,010 workers concluded that boring jobs attract those workers temperamentally suited to them. Other erroneous premises of job enrichment include the idea that the best method of satisfying workers is to redesign their jobs and that such job enrichment schemes will automatically lead to increased productivity. Recent experience contradicts these premises. —Jenkins, Kenneth; *Management World,* Jan 1981, 10(1): pp. 39-40. Avail. ABI 81-04603

Job enrichment, Studies, Job satisfaction

Early Warning Signals-Growing Discontent among Managers (253)

A clear and consistent pattern of downturns in managerial attitudes has been determined by a national survey conducted by Opinion Research Corporation. Due in part to the strides made by hourly workers, many managers now feel that they no longer have many of the prerogatives that once were theirs alone. Attitude information was gathered on numerous subjects such as job satisfaction, work environment satisfaction, and communications effectiveness. In all areas of the study, managerial attitudes showed declining levels of satisfaction, which, in several cases, were in direct contradiction to those indications of clerical and hourly workers.Middle management feels that top management is both excessively controlling and increasingly ignoring them. To eliminate some of this deterioration, top-management must be willing to delegate some of its decision making authority. More timely and complete disclosure of information to middle managers would facilitate reaching organizational goals and restore to middle management their identification as an important part of the management team. Graphs. References. —Cooper, Michael R.; Gelfond, Peter A.; and Foley, Patricia M.; *Business,* Jan/Feb 1980, 30(1): pp. 2-12. Avail. ABI 80-04016

Middle management, Job attitudes, Job satisfaction, Employee attitude (PER), Trends, Surveys, Ratings

The Effect of Employee Physical Fitness on Job Performance   (254)

Private industry's investment in employee fitness programs is based on the widespread assumption that the fit employee has better morale, more self-esteem, and out-performs the sedentary employee. Although active individuals do report feelings of better health, improved work performance, and more positive work attitudes, there is no documented evidence that improved employee fitness and increased job performance are related. A study was conducted to determine if increased fitness was related to improved job performance. The subjects were commercial real estate investment brokers who were basically sedentary. The training groups participated in a monitored aerobics training program. The results indicated that while the subjects improved in physical fitness, there was no significant improvement in job performance or satisfaction. Tables. References. – Edwards, Sandra E. and Gettman, Larry R.; *Personnel Administrator,* Nov 1980, 25(11): pp. 41-44,61. Avail. ABI 80-21703

Employees, Performance, Physical fitness, Exercise, Impacts, Studies, Job satisfaction, Effectiveness

The Effect of Job Dissatisfaction on the Decision to Start a Business   (255)

A study was made to determine if dissatisfaction with a previous job was what pushed entrepreneurs into starting their own businesses. The Job Description Index (JDI) which tests employee satisfaction with his work, his perception of supervision, pay, and promotional opportunities, and attitudes toward co-workers, was administered to entrepreneurs, managers that had changed organizations, and managers that had recently been promoted within their organization.Entrepreneurs were most dissatisfied with promotional opportunities. They were also highly dissatisfied with the work itself at their former place of employment. When this combined with unsatisfactory supervision and co-workers, and unless a satisfactory promotion was imminent, it resulted in the push to start one's own business. In general, entrepreneurs were more dissatisfied than the other 2 groups with all aspects of their previous job, except for pay. Transferred managers' scores more closely resembled those of promoted managers, except where promotional opportunities were concerned. Recently promoted managers viewed promotional chances much higher than the other 2 groups. Tables. References. –Brockhaus, Robert H.; *Jrnl of Small Business Mgmt,* Jan 1980, 18(1): pp. 37-43. Avail. ABI 80-07002

Job satisfaction, Effects, Decision making, Small business, Start up, Decisions, Studies

Effects of an Organizational Control System on Managerial Satisfaction and Performance   (256)

Organizational theorists have long realized that, for an organization to function and be effective, the resources and efforts of the participants must be directed toward a common goal. Previous research on goal setting and feedback is put in the context of an organizational control system to explore the issue. Using a sample of 100 managers, the independent impacts of 3 components of a control system (goal setting, measurement, and corrective actions) on managerial satisfaction and performance were examined. The general hypothesis examined was that various aspects of an organizational control system, when functioning correctly, would independently contribute to increased managerial performance and positive job attitudes. Results indicated that aspects of the 3 components of the control model were independently related to performance. Although a number of significant bivariate correlations between job satisfaction and control-system variables were evident, no strong independent associations were found. Chart. Tables. References. —Anderson, John C. and O'Reilly, Charles A., III; *Human Relations,* Jun 1981, 34(6): pp. 491-501. Avail. ABI 81-20702

Organizational, Control systems, Effects, Managers, Performance, Job attitudes, Job satisfaction, Studies, Goal setting, Performance appraisal, Feedback

Effects of Changes in Job Characteristics on Some (257) Theory-Specific Attitudinal Outcomes: Results from a Naturally Occurring Quasi-Experiment

Current research on antecedents of employees' positive response to enriched jobs has been substantially affected by the job characteristics model of work motivation proposed and validated by Hackman and Oldham (1975, 76). These studies and others have gathered considerable correlational evidence for a consistent pattern of relationships between motivational characteristics of jobs and attitudes and behaviors of job holders.In an effort to reduce utility costs, a manufacturing organization adopted a planned change from a 5- to a 4-day work week. Changes in characteristics of jobs in the organization which resulted from the shortened work week were introduced without accounting for the motivational consequences of the new schedule. "Expectation levels" and organizational policies pertaining to the reward system were changed when the 4-day work week was implemented. The total design of the planned change resembled that of a quasi-experiment, allowing examination of the causal impact of changes in core job dimensions on employee attitudinal outcomes. Measures of core job dimensions and outcome variables were collected before and after the new system. Results indicated that the group characterized by an increase in the motivational properties of their jobs had corresponding alterations in theory-specific attitudinal outcomes. Tables. References. —Bhagat, Rabi S. and Chassie, Marilyn B.; *Human Relations,* May 1980, 33(5): pp. 297-313. Avail. ABI 80-12255

Effects, Changes, Job, Characteristics, Attitudes, Job enrichment, Job attitudes, Employee attitude (PER), Job satisfaction, Motivation, Studies

The Effects of Congruency Between Perceived and (258) Desired Job Attributes upon Job Satisfaction

A study was conducted to investigate whether job satisfaction is more strongly associated with congruency between desired and perceived job attributes than with job attributes alone. The subjects were a cluster sample of 1383 employees in metropolitan Adelaide, Australia. They completed questionnaires either by themselves or in a structured interview in their homes. Measurement was made of: 1. job attributes, 2. desired job attributes or work values, 3. job satisfaction, and 4. demographic and personal variables.The results indicated support for the congruency hypothesis for the attributes of skill-utilization and variety but not for influence, pressure, or social interaction. The findings suggest that specific work values or desired job attributes only affect the job attribute-satisfaction relationship for certain attributes. Congruency between perceived and desired job attributes appears to be a much weaker predictor of job satisfaction than perceived attributes alone. Figure. Tables. References. –O'Brien, Gordon E. and Dowling, Peter; *Jrnl of Occupational Psychology (UK)*, Jun 1980, 53(2): pp. 121-130. Avail. ABI 80-14554

Job satisfaction, Studies, Perceptions, Job, Job attitudes

Effects of Higher Order Need Strength on the Job (259) Performance-Job Satisfaction Relationship

A study was conducted to examine the moderating effects of employee higher order need strength (HONS) on the relationship between job performance and job satisfaction. Data was obtained from a sample of 123 non-supervisory employees (mostly salespeople) in a large retail-drug organization. Subjects responded to a questionnaire administered by the researcher. The questionnaire was designed to measure job satisfaction and higher order need strength, while job performance was measured by independent supervisory ratings. Moderated regression and subgroup analyses were performed on the data.The results provided support for the moderating role of HONS. It is noted that job performance is positively related to intrinsic as well as extrinsic sources of job satisfaction for strong HONS individuals. However, no such relation was found for persons with weak HONS. The results suggest that the relationship between job performance and certain extrinsic sources of job satisfaction should not be treated as uniformly positive for all individuals. Graphs. Tables. References. –Abdel-Halim, Ahmed A.; *Personnel Psychology*, Summer 1980, 33(2): pp. 335-347. Avail. ABI 80-13881

Job, Performance, Job satisfaction, Measures, Statistical analysis, Relations

Effects of Person-Job Compatibility on Managerial (260) Reactions to Role Ambiguity

Research was conducted to examine the moderating effects on the need for achievement and locus of control and job scope characteristics, both independently and jointly, on managers' affective responses to role ambiguity. Data were obtained from a sample of 89 middle-lower managerial personnel in a large heavy-equipment manufacturing firm in the Midwest. Respondents were asked to complete questionnaires that pertained to role ambiguity, need for achievement, locus of control, job scope characteristics, job satisfaction, job involvement, and propensity to leave. The data were subjected to moderated regression and subgroup, joint-moderator analyses. The results support the hypothesized moderating effects of personality and job characteristics. The results indicate that managers with either low need for achievement or external locus of control who work on unenriched, low-scope jobs respond most negatively to role ambiguity, while this relation does not occur for managers with high need for achievement or internal locus of control who work on enriched, high-scope jobs. Graphs.

Tables. References. —Abdel-Halim, Ahmed A.; *Organizational Behavior & Human Performance,* Oct 1980, 26(2): pp. 193-211. Avail. ABI 80-19750

Personality, Characteristics, Roles, Job, Stress, Managers, Job satisfaction, Studies

Effects of Role Stress-Job Design-Technology (261)
Interaction on Employee Work Satisfaction

An attempt was made to examine the potential influence of organizational technology on the interaction between each of 3 role variables-role conflict, ambiguity, and overload-and job design characteristics in determining the level of employee satisfaction with work. The general hypothesis investigated is that role stress variables, job design characteristics, and organizational technology will interact such that individuals on simple, low-scope jobs in long-linked technology and individuals on complex, high-scope jobs in mediating technology will be less satisfied with their work under high rather than low levels of role stress. Data were collected from 2 samples: 1. a manufacturing sample consisting of 89 managerial and staff personnel working in production and other related units of a large, heavy equipment manufacturing firm, and 2. a banking sample including 81 managerial and nonmanagerial personnel chosen from 5 small to medium-size banks. Results support the hypothesis that employees on simple, low-scope jobs in long-linked technology and on complex, high-scope jobs in mediating technology are most vulnerable to the adverse effects of role stress. Tables. Graphs. References. —Abdel-Halim, Ahmed A.; *Academy of Mgmt Jrnl,* Jun 1981, 24(2): pp. 260-273. Avail. ABI 81-14519

Job satisfaction, Job attitudes, Roles, Stress, Job, Design, Characteristics, Variance analysis, Technology

Event and Agent: Toward a Structural Theory of Job (262)
Satisfaction

A study was conducted to evaluate a theory of job satisfaction, based on the logic of facet theory as presented by Guttman. The logical and methodological criticisms of Schneider and Locke are used as the starting point. Their categories, event and agent, are used as two domain facets for construction of a model. The radex structure was hypothesized as a formulation of job satisfaction variables representing the psychological phenomenon. The subjects were 104 employees from 8 different industrial organizations in Israel. Subjects were interviewed and asked to rate: 1. their job satisfaction with respect to 11 job factors, and 2. their conception of influence upon these job factors. The intercorrelation matrix of job satisfaction was subjected to a Guttman Smallest Space Analysis. The empirical space was interpreted for each facet both individually and jointly. The results show that when job satisfaction is defined by two domain facets, the radex structure is confirmed. Table. Figure. References. —Ben-Porat, A.; *Personnel Psychology,* Autumn 1981, 34(3): pp. 523-534. Avail. ABI 81-23854

Job satisfaction, Theory, Variables, Matrix, Correlation analysis, Organizational behavior, Studies

An Examination of the Independent and Joint (263)
Contributions of Organizational Commitment and Job
Satisfaction on Employee Intentions to Quit

Organizational commitment and job satisfaction have independent and joint effects on variables important to the employee withdrawal process. A study of these relationships were studied via a survey of 175 evening students at an urban university who were employed full-time. These participants voluntarily completed questionnaires. Regression analysis was used to analyze the results of the study. Organizational commitment was found to be more closely related to intention to quit than job satisfaction. Even so, job satisfaction in itself can make an independent contribution to the prediction of a person's intention to quit. It may be that progressively increasing job satisfaction leads to greater organizational commitment and increasing dissatisfaction leads to reduced commitment. Organization development (OD) practitioners should use tactics such as team building and job enlargement to improve both commitment and satisfaction. Tables. References. —Peters, Lawrence H.; Bhagat, Rabi S.; and O'Connor, Edward J.; *Group & Organization Studies,* Mar 1981, 6(1): pp. 73-82. Avail. ABI 81-18062

Organizational, Commitments, Job satisfaction, Effects, Employee, Voluntary, Terminations, Studies, Employee turnover

Exchange Variables as Predictors of Job Satisfaction, (264)
Job Commitment, and Turnover: The Impact of
Rewards, Costs, Alternatives, and Investments

The point of this research is to explore the ability of an investment model to predict job satisfaction, job commitment, and job turnover. Two studies are carried out which show that the model can explain these circumstances. Job reward and cost values are used to predict job satisfaction. Reward and cost values, alternative value, and investment size are predictors of job commitment. In studying job commitment and turnover, 2 variables must be considered in addition to job satisfaction, even though they are not related to the quality of the work experience: investment size and alternative value. Study one, a business analog experiment, indicates that job commitment and turnover are allied. Study 2, a survey of industrial workers, shows that job commitment correlates more closely with turnover than does job satisfaction. These results agree with the investment model. Heretofore, job satisfaction has been the principal predictor of turnover, but in this study, job commitment replaces it. Equations. Tables. References. —Farrell, Daniel and Rusbult, Caryl E.; *Organizational Behavior & Human Performance,* Aug 1981, 28(1): pp. 78-95. Avail. ABI 81-26266

Job satisfaction, Employee turnover, Job, Commitments, Job attitudes, Predictions, Investment, Models, Studies

Exit, Voice, Loyalty, and Neglect as Responses to Job (265)
Dissatisfaction: A Multidimensional Scaling Study

It is suggested that workers' responses to job dissatisfaction fall into 4 categories (exit, voice, loyalty, and neglect), which characterize a diverse group of more specific behaviors, including turnover, absenteeism, lateness, requesting a transfer, and talking to a supervisor. Exit refers to voluntary separation from the job, voice refers to attempts to change objectionable job factors, loyalty refers to remaining with the firm despite dissatisfaction, and neglect refers to lax behavior as a result of dissatisfaction. A multidimensional scaling analysis (MDS) was developed to collect data from panels of expert and non-expert subjects. Data collected by the MDS support the hypothesis. However, the model does not address all the possible responses to job dissatisfaction. For example, it does not consider psychological responses, such as pathological acceptance of job dissatisfaction. Tables. Chart. References. —Farrell, Dan; *Academy of Mgmt Jrnl,* Dec 1983, 26(4): pp. 596-607. Avail. ABI 84-01704

Job satisfaction, Organizational behavior, Employee turnover, Studies, Statistical analysis

Explaining Racial Differences in Job Satisfaction: A Reexamination of the Data (266)

M. K. Moch (1980) attempted to assess the degree to which a variety of structural, cultural, social, and social-psychological factors could explain racial differences in job satisfaction and concluded that the data did not support any traditional explanations of high job satisfaction among Mexican Americans and low satisfaction displayed by blacks. This conclusion may be too pessimistic. A substantial part of the variance in job satisfaction associated with race was also associated with the mediating structural, cultural, social, and social-psychological factors, consistent with their hypothesized mediating role. The structural factors, including organizational level and racial composition of the work group, were associated most strongly with both race and job satisfaction. These factors appear to be quite important in accounting for racial differences in job satisfaction and warrant further research. Figure. Table. References. —Konar, Ellen; *Jrnl of Applied Psychology,* Aug 1981, 66(4): pp. 522-524. Avail. ABI 81-19447

Races, Differences, Job satisfaction, Factors, Studies

Exploring the Meaning of "Good" Management (267)

Managers are rewarded for increased productivity achieved by reducing absenteeism and turn-over and a variety of other means. To managers, good management is activity which brings about increases in productivity. This, however, is a short-term approach. A philosopher's view of good management would include metaphysical, epistemological, and ethical viewpoints. The scholar's view of good management attempts to include a balance between the needs of the individual and the needs of society. Alternative perspectives and their respective risks and benefits are examined. If worker satisfaction were paramount in managers' minds, it would contribute to low productivity, narcissism, and "groupthink" among the workers. References. —Koprowski, Eugene J.; *Academy of Mgmt Review,* Jul 1981, 6(3): pp. 459-467. Avail. ABI 81-19668

Management, Theory, Management science, Job satisfaction, Employee, Productivity

The Foreman: Is His Job as Bad as They Say? (268)

The foreman's job has changed over the years, and it is now considered to be one of the most stress- and strained-filled in industry. A study was undertaken in the Mid-South to determine how foremen felt about certain aspects of their job. Questionnaires were given to 208 foremen; 133 were returned. The 36 questions concerned aspects of the job which many experts consider to be major problem areas. Areas of low concern to respondents included: 1. informal relationships, 2. treatment of subordinates, 3. job importance, 4. job title, 5. relationship with management, 6. relationship with the hourly worker, 7. freedom to make decisions, 8. community image, and 9. job promotion. Areas of high concern were: 1. shift work, 2. job security, 3. problem solving, 4. unity of command, 5. monetary compensation, 6. feelings of importance, 7. work aspirations for their sons, 8. participative management, 9. managerial understanding, 10. provision of information, and 11. structural effects. The results of this study showed that not all foremen suffer from the same kinds of work-related problems. Less than 1/3 of a composite list of problem areas had 20% or more unfavorable responses, while 2/3 had 50% or more favorable responses. —Schoenfeldt, Roger C.; *Supervision,* Nov 1981, 43(11): pp. 12-14,17. Avail. ABI 81-25448

Foremen, First line, Supervisors, Job satisfaction, Surveys, Studies

Handling Gripes and Grievances (269)

Leadership, one key aspect of the manager's tasks, is the ability to influence the behavior of others in a desired direction. Attitude and willingness to assist employees goes a long way toward helping a manager become an effective leader. Handling employee gripes early, and properly, can prevent them from becoming grievances. A manager must recognize situations which need improvement and then correct them. Causes of employee dissatisfactions include: 1. the work, 2. poor supervision, 3. inadequate communication, and 4. other employees. Employee discipline should involve efforts to try to save by counseling and nonpunitive procedures before starting formal disciplinary action is started. Initial steps in a positive discipline system are verbal reminder and written reminder, followed by a formal hearing if the reminders did not produce the desired change. If a company has a union, do not make any settlement outside of the labor agreement or on the basis of what is fair. —Himes, Gary K.; *Supervision,* Feb 1981, 43(2): pp. 3-6. Avail. ABI 81-05066

Supervisors, Employee, Job satisfaction, Grievances, Discipline (PER), Guidelines, Hearings, Personnel management

Hierarchical Position in the Work Organization and Job (270) Satisfaction: A Failure to Replicate

Many studies of the relationship between position in the work organization and job satisfaction generally have shown job satisfaction to increase as the worker rose in the organizational hierarchy. A recent analysis of 4 separate national samples of job satisfaction and position in the work organization was made in an attempt to assess the stability of findings of a 1974 study that reported that family income, supervision and occupational prestige were positive correlates of job satisfaction among whites only. Data used for the analysis were from the National Opinion Research Center's Annual General Social Surveys, 1972-1978. The analyses used were the same as in the 1974 survey. The 1974 survey could not be satisfactorily replicated as: 1. data could not be generalized to other years, 2. findings were at marginal levels of statistical significance, and 3. early 1974 economical and social conditions had a different impact on work attitudes of those at different hierarchy levels, thus enhancing a weak association between position of authority and job satisfaction. The stability of such findings as those from the 1974 study should routinely be assessed on comparable survey data sets. Chart. References. —Ebling, Jon S. and King, Michael; *Human Relations,* Jul 1981, 34(7): pp. 567-572. Avail. ABI 81-22138

Organizational, Hierarchies, Prestige, Income, Age, Effects, Job satisfaction, Studies, Correlations, Organizational behavior

The High Achiever's Job Satisfaction (271)

A major problem for both high achievers and the organization is how to keep high achievers reasonably satisfied, stimulated, and productive at a level at least comparable to their past performance. The individual manager's philosophy, experience, and work environment determine how he will approach and handle achievement and self-fulfillment. Outside of the usual factors which influence interest and satisfaction with the job, there is one of major significance-the learning/growth curve. This factor represents the new or incremental knowledge, skills, perceptions, abilities, attributes, and experience which are still left to be learned. Continued learning/growth enhances the job and helps the high achiever avoid boredom and dissatisfaction. Graph. —Ginsburg, Sigmund G.; *Personnel Administrator,* Jan 1981, 26(1): pp. 78-81. Avail. ABI 81-03117

Job satisfaction, Motivation, Learning curves (PER), Job enrichment, Executives

How Will You Cope with Workers of the '80s? (272)

Evidence is mounting that low productivity in US industries is linked not to workers, but to managers. Thus, today's managers must understand the workers of today - their wants and desires and their motivation. As a result of changing social trends, the employee of the 1980s tends to be better educated, more involved with family considerations, and more likely to reject traditional work ethics in favor of personal work values. Modern workers want participation in their work and personal satisfaction from their careers. Because of high-stress working conditions, these employees are more subject to job burnout and personal problems. Many employee-related problems are in part the result of poor management. There are a number of ways managers can deal more effectively with new-breed workers, including: 1. develop a people-oriented style of management, with emphasis on participation rather than power, 2. use flextime, part-time scheduling, or the 4-day workweek, 3. trust the employees, 4. improve communication, and 5. be receptive to new management methods and systems. Taking a new approach to management can improve employee relations and boost productivity. —Packer, James S.; *Association Mgmt,* Jul 1983, 35(7): pp. 126-129. Avail. ABI 83-20667

Associations, Labor force, Education, Social, Trends, Values, Work ethic, Job satisfaction, Stress, Burnout

Impact of Employee Participation in Pay Plan   (273)
Development

Participative decision making was studied in the formation of a base pay
plan for a small manufacturer of tool and die equipment in central Ohio. An
employee committee was established which was further divided into 4
standing committees. A survey questionnaire was distributed to all
employees, and 85% were completed. A new wage plan was developed in
which hourly wages were increased by $ .50/hour. Both attitude and
behavior were measured. Both job and pay satisfaction increased
measurably. The conclusion was supported that employee participation in
pay decisions leads to positive reactions. Even though the raises were not
large, the employees felt that their pay was equitable. They experienced a
feeling of job satisfaction, trusted management more, and were unlikely to
terminate employment. The analysis indicates that these changes could be
due to participation. Understanding and commitment also rose. Tables.
References. —Jenkins, G. Douglas, Jr. and Lawler, Edward E., III; *Organizational Behavior
& Human Performance,* Aug 1981, 28(1): pp. 111-128. Avail. ABI 81-26268

> Participatory management, Employee, Participation, Design, Pay structure, Compensation
> plans, Effects, Employee attitude (PER), Job satisfaction, Studies

The Impact of Extra-Work Variables on Behavior in   (274)
Work Environments

The impact of the external environment on behavior in work organizations
is starting to receive more attention in the literature. Results of this effort can
have significant managerial implications. Sufficient and well articulated
theory is currently available to guide research on the effect of the external
environment on key work variables, such as pay satisfaction, voluntary
turnover, and employee attendance. Attitudes toward pay, along with other
aspects of job satisfaction, have been examined extensively. There is a long
history of research on the subject of employee turnover, as well. Employee
attendance has been the subject of numerous studies. The theories postulated
in these areas should be integrated to help provide directions for future
research. References. —Dreher, George F.; *Academy of Mgmt Review,* Apr 1982, 7(2): pp.
300-304. Avail. ABI 82-14390

> External, Variables, Effects, Job satisfaction, Wages & salaries, Perceptions, Employee
> turnover, Absenteeism, Organizational behavior

The Impact of Goal Change on Prominent Perceptions   (275)
and Behaviors of Employees

The influence of goal change on individual perceptions and behavioral
outcomes of individuals within organizations is examined. Hypothesized
relationships include: 1. Goal diversion and goal displacement are inversely
related to worker satisfaction. 2. Goal diversion and goal displacement are
inversely related to organizational commitment. 3. Worker satisfaction and
organizational commitment are inversely related to employee turnover. 4.
Organizational commitment is more strongly related to absenteeism than is
satisfaction. The investigation demonstrates that organizational commitment
has more of an influence on employee turnover than do employee

perceptions of general satisfaction. Goal displacement is found to be significantly related to satisfaction and organizational commitment. The model that posits actual paths from goal change to satisfaction and organizational commitment and then to turnover appears to be supported to some degree. Tables. Charts. References. –Abelson, Michael A.; *Jrnl of Mgmt,* Spring/Summer 1983, 9(1): pp. 65-79. Avail. ABI 83-20146

Organizational behavior, Goals, Changes, Job satisfaction, Organizational, Commitments, Absenteeism, Studies

In the Image of the CEO (276)

Employees' view of top management impact on employee work attitudes more directly than any other factor. After an original research study 2 years ago, Richard Ruch confirmed, during a second study, just how potent and influential top management's role can be in shaping employee work attitudes. Views of top management impact attitudes more strongly than does that of supervisory management, salary, fringe benefits, job training, co-worker relations, and company policies and procedures. A new approach to employee communication, based on reality, is needed. A communications audit should be done, using personal in-depth interviews of a cross section of the employees, with the added dimensions of questionnaires and systematic review and analysis of internal records. Employees want to know that top management considers employees as important as sales and profit, and that management is competent and has knowledge, care, and respect for employees. A variety of print, visual, art or other innovative sources of communications should be used, with a high level of quality. Charts. Goodman, Ronald and Ruch, Richard S.; *Public Relations Jrnl,* Feb 1981, 37(2): pp. 14 15,18 19. Avail. ABI 81-08067

Workers, Perceptions, Chief executive officer, Image, Effects, Job attitudes, Job satisfaction, Organizational behavior, Employee, Communication

Increasing People-Productivity (277)

A primary reason behind productivity and performance problems in most companies is the lack of commitment to people as the company's most important resource. Managers must: 1. learn the more subtle aspects of productivity and human behavior, 2. recognize early signs of employee problems and connect the symptoms with the cause, 3. become comfortable with face-to-face discussions of problems, and consequently deal more honestly and effectively with subordinates, and 4. learn skills for communication and motivation. In addition, research points to the positive effects of employee participation on performance. As a result of these changes in managerial performance, the company can expect such benefits as: 1. decreased turnover, 2. increased safety, 3. increased pride in work and less destructive criticism and complaining, 4. higher productivity per employee and more willingness to take on difficult tasks, 5. enhanced company image as a socially responsible organization, and 6. cost savings and increased overall profits related to all of the above. Chart. References.

—Vandervelde, Maryanne; *Jrnl of Contemporary Business,* Aug 1981, 10(2): pp. 19-31. Avail. ABI 81-23110

Employee, Productivity, Human capital, Managers, Training, Programs, Performance evaluation, Employee problems, Feedback, Participatory management, Job satisfaction

Indian Bank Employees' Perceptions of Jobs: (278) Implications for Job Designers

The Job Diagnostic Survey (JDS), developed by Hackman and Oldham, is the most popular instrument used to test theoretical models and to further instrument refinement. The JDS delineates 5 core job dimensions: 1. skill variety, 2. task identity, 3. task significance, 4. autonomy, and 5. feedback. A study was conducted to determine if the JDS is culture-bound or whether it can be employed as a valid instrument to tap the theorized core job dimensions in the Indian organizational settings. Research was done in 2 phases: 1. a questionnaire was administered to 255 white-collar workers in 3 large banks in Bombay, in 1975, and 2. an expanded questionnaire was completed by 1,135 white collar workers in 12 banks, in 3 metropolitan cities in India. The results of the study indicate that employees surveyed perceive their jobs along a single dimension of job complexity. The question remains as to whether this one-dimensional perception is characteristic of only the Indian bank employees or whether this is a general phenomenon occurring in all Indian organizations. Tables. References. —Sekaran, Uma; *ASCI Jrnl of Mgmt (India),* Sep 1980, 10(1): pp. 1-7. Avail. ABI 81-18200

India, Banking, Employee attitude (PER), White collar workers, Job satisfaction, Job attitudes, Studies

Individual Differences and Task Design: A Laboratory (279) Experiment

The idea that individual differences play an important role in determining workers' reactions to the scope of their jobs became prominent with the work of Turner and Lawrence (1965) and Hulin and Blood (1968). Hackman and Lawler's (1971) monograph later changed the focus of individual differences from the sociological level to the psychological or individual level and led to the exposition of a formal theory of job design (Hackman and Oldham, 1976). This task characteristics model has served a significant heuristic role for researchers since it provided a theoretical impetus for a large body of "moderator research" in task design. It is appropriate to assess this moderator literature and report the findings of an experimental test of the task characteristics model which attempted to overcome shortcomings of previous research.A laboratory experiment tested the moderating impact of Protestant Ethic, Growth Need Strength, Need for Achievement, and Arousal-Seeking Tendency on task design relationships. Objective task scope was manipulated by assigning 190 college students to a simple or a complex electronic assembly task. None of the individual differences variables significantly moderated the objective scope-satisfaction relationship, but need for achievement did moderate the perceived scope-satisfaction relationship. Examination of the interaction terms, however, revealed that the moderating effects were contrary to those hypothesized. Tables.

References. —Ganster, Daniel C.; *Organizational Behavior & Human Performance,* Aug 1980, 26(1): pp. 131-148. Avail. ABI 80-14130
Task, Job, Design, Workers, Behavior, Studies, Job attitudes, Job satisfaction

Individual Differences as a Moderator of the Job (280) Quality-Job Satisfaction Relationship: Evidence from a National Sample

The validity of the individual differences as a moderator hypothesis, which proposes that the relationship between job quality and job satisfaction varies as a function of important individual differences, was investigated with data obtained from a national sample of full-time male workers. Five individual differences variables were studied: worker anomies, current urban/rural residence, residence at age 16, educational attainment, and ethnic identity. Results of moderated regressional analysis suggested that the moderator hypothesis is valid for worker anomie, educational level, and former residence. It was not found so for the simple population index. For the ethnic identity moderator, the relationship between job quality and job satisfaction was: 1. positive for workers of Nordic extraction, 2. progressively less positive for workers of Anglo-Germanic and Latin Catholic roots, and 3. inverse for workers of East European backgrounds. It is concluded that the moderator hypothesis is descriptively valid, but the small magnitudes of the significant differences restrict the practical utility of the moderator hypothesis. Tables. Graphs. Map. References. —Vecchio, Robert P.; *Organizational Behavior & Human Performance,* Dec 1980, 26(3): pp. 305-325. Avail. ABI 80-23961
Individual, Job, Quality, Job satisfaction, Studies, Organizational behavior

Individuals and the Organization (281)

The survival of our society as we know it depends on the recognition and understanding of the crisis that exists between people and organizations. In this society, work is accomplished through organizations made up of individuals seeking to satisfy various needs through their participation in the organization. A more educated work force, extensive welfare programs, technological developments, and the changing nature of work itself have all contributed to changes in the expectations of the work force. New organizations are necessary. In these alternative organizations, people exercise discretion and act on their own decisions in decentralized locations. A self-maintaining group is the fundamental building block of the organization. It takes responsibility for the product it produces. The members of the team must possess operating, maintenance, planning, evaluation, and social skills in order to maintain the team. Implementation of alternative organizational forms promises help in overcoming the crisis between the individual and his needs and an outdated organization. References. —Davis, Louis E.; *California Mgmt Review,* Spring 1980, 22(3): pp. 5-14. Avail. ABI 80-16895
Organizational, Design, Organization theory, Social change, Labor force, Workforce, Unemployment, Economic impact, Environmental impact, Job enrichment, Job satisfaction

An Integrated Model of Perceived Job Characteristics (282)

A study was undertaken to clarify the mechanisms through which perceived job characteristics influence job satisfaction. The central theme of the effort has been that job characteristics do not act independently of one another, but act instead as interrelated components. The model separates perceived job characteristics into 2 components, an information and an action component, which are both related to role clarity and challenge. The model was fitted to data from samples of shop, office, and management personnel. Successive iterations of a path analysis technique indicated that the action and information components, through intervening psychological states of challenge and role clarity, explained substantial variance in global job satisfaction. The results showed that challenge was the primary determinant of job satisfaction. However, the impact of role clarity varied among the 3 samples and appeared to be a necessary precondition for perceived challenge. Tables. Figures. References. —Walsh, Jeffrey T.; Taber, Thomas D.; and Beehr, Terry A.; *Organizational Behavior & Human Performance,* Apr 1980, 25(2): pp. 252-267. Avail. ABI 80-09155

Job, Characteristics, Job satisfaction, Work, Design, Models, Statistical analysis, Roles, Job attitudes, Studies

Interpreting Employee Needs: Assuming vs. (283) Understanding

A case study at a sawmill in the Midwest revealed that production supervisors had difficulty in identifying their employees' likes and dislikes. A questionnaire administered to both employees and supervisors affirmed the lack of understanding. Analysis of the questionnaire answers revealed that the 3 most significant sources of employee dissatisfaction were: 1. inadequate compensation, 2. monotonous work, and 3. poor recognition. A brainstorming session was then conducted and resulted in a number of positive suggestions by supervisors, including: 1. rotating or alternating jobs, 2. giving frequent and concrete production feedback, 3. asking for employee suggestions at small meetings, 4. improving physical working conditions, and 5. demonstrating a willingness to accept some mistakes. The case study demonstrated that: 1. Supervisors must not "guess" or "assume" employee feelings. 2. Open communications with employees are mandatory. 3. Employees must be involved in the planning process. Charts. —Hoh, Andrew K.; *Supervisory Mgmt,* Apr 1980, 25(4): pp. 29-34. Avail. ABI 80-07340

Job attitudes, Employee attitude (PER), Supervisors, Managers, Attitudes, Supervisors, Job satisfaction, Incentives, Studies

Inter-Relationships Between Organizational (284) Commitment and Job Characteristics, Job Satisfaction, Professional Behavior, and Organizational Climate

Commitment to the organization is an important behavioral element that can be used to assess employees' strength of attachment. It is important to keep employees highly committed, particularly in non-profit firms where salary scales may be less competitive than in industrial firms. Research on organizational commitment can be centered around 2 points: 1. determination of the degree of commitment of organizational members, and 2. identification of variables that can result in increased organizational commitment. These variables can be grouped into 5 categories: 1. demographic characteristics, 2. job satisfaction, 3. job characteristics, 4.

professional behavior, and 5. organizational climate. Results from a study at a health care institution indicate that role conflict and role ambiguity are damaging to commitment. A participative climate, power, teamwork, reading professional journals, satisfaction with work and promotion opportunities, age, tenure, and length of professional employment are positively related to organizational commitment. Chart. References. —Welsch, Harold P. and LaVan, Helen; *Human Relations,* Dec 1981, 34(12): pp. 1079-1089. Avail. ABI 82-02784

> Employee, Organizational, Commitments, Job satisfaction, Job, Characteristics, Organizational behavior, Studies, Correlation analysis

Job Choice: The Impact of Intrinsic and Extrinsic   (285) Factors on Subsequent Satisfaction and Commitment

One hundred and eight recent Master's of Business Administration graduates were surveyed right after becoming employed and again 6 months later. It was hypothesized that subjects who made job selections on intrinsic bases would be more satisfied and committed than those who made the decision based on extrinsic factors. Results indicated both intrinsic and extrinsic decision factors to be positively related to subsequent satisfaction and commitment. Further, canonical correlation analysis illustrated an extrinsic job element, salary, to be positively related to future tenure intention and negatively related to job satisfaction. These findings suggest that job satisfaction and commitment may be associated with both the intrinsic and extrinsic factors considered when the original job choice is determined. The study was supportive of previous findings on decision making and commitment, but further research and theory building is needed to integrate the process of job choice into a more comprehensive model of organizational commitment and job satisfaction. Tables. References. —O'Reilly, Charles A, III and Caldwell, David F.; *Jrnl of Applied Psychology,* Oct 1980, 65(5): pp. 559-565. Avail. ABI 80-21736

> Job, Choices, Job satisfaction, Factors, Statistical analysis, Job attitudes

Job Context and Job Content: A Conceptual Perspective   (286)

Four sets of possible explanations for seemingly contradictory research findings for the moderating effect of job context satisfaction on job-content/worker-response relationships are explored: 1. chance occurrence, 2. sample distribution artifacts, 3. common method variance, and 4. a series of alternative conceptual explanations. A series of conceptual explanations for the moderating role of contextual satisfaction in the job-content/worker-response relationship is offered. The process by which context satisfaction operates is explored, and the absorption/distraction phenomenon are examined. Among other findings, the analysis shows that context-satisfaction level influences the level of worker absorption/distraction with the task. This level, inturn, moderates the job-satisfaction/worker-response relationship. Chart. References. —Dunham, Randall B.; Pierce, Jon L.; and Newstrom, John W.; *Jrnl of Mgmt,* Fall/Winter 1983, 9(2): pp. 187-202. Avail. ABI 83-32163

> Job attitudes, Job improvement, Job classification, Job satisfaction, Studies, Organizational behavior, Perceptions, Work environment

Job Design in Perspective (287)

The classical approach to designing jobs was seen as a way to improve productivity and standardization and was based on experiences of: 1. increased labor effectiveness, 2. lower production costs, and 3. greater predictability of system performance. Then, during the neo-classical era (i.e., 1940s-50s), a radically different perspective to the design of jobs was begun, and job enlargement and job enrichment became the themes for the modern perspective on designing work. Today, evidence indicates that employee attitudes are strongly associated with job design characteristics. Thus, job design and redesign cannot be approached without considering the physical and psychological context in which the job is imbedded. Since job design has evolved as an issue of importance, many questions concerning it have been answered. However, in answering these questions, more unanswered questions have come about. Although good operational guidelines for practitioners may still be some years away, the study of job design has become one of the most popular areas of inquiry in organization behavior. Tables. —Pierce, Jon L.; *Personnel Administrator,* Dec 1980, 25(12): pp. 67-74. Avail. ABI 81-00209

Job, Design, Job enrichment, Job satisfaction, Motivation, Employee attitude (PER), Theory

Job Dissatisfaction: A Social Disease (288)

Job dissatisfaction is a social disease whose causes and implications extend beyond the confines of the modern factory. Far too often the organization and its management have been labeled the sole cause of worker dissatisfaction. On the contrary, the root of the problem may be a combination of problems stemming from the organization and various social forces. These social forces include: 1. the psychology of industry, 2. arrogance, 3. mass education, 4. status, 5. human rights, 6. mass media, 7. increased leisure time, and 8. an American tradition of dissatisfaction. Job dissatisfaction is a complex problem. If it is viewed solely as an organizational issue, then management must carry the burden for its resolution. If its source is viewed as a co-contributorship between society and the organization, the problem resolution becomes much more complicated. To confront the issue of societal dissatisfaction requires reversing numerous social trends, many of which would be impossible or impractical to change. References. —McKenna, Jack F. and Oritt, Paul L.; *Business & Society,* Winter 1981/Spring 1982, 20(2) /v21n1: pp. 32-39. Avail. ABI 82-26943

Job satisfaction, Social impact, Social research, Workforce, Organizational behavior

Job Enrichment as a Means of Achieving Job (289)
Satisfaction

The belief that a positive correlation exists between job satisfaction and employee motivation makes job satisfaction a concern to managers at all levels. Historical development shows that in the early 1960s, Frederick Herzberg's research regarding hygiene and motivator factors led to the concept of job enrichment.Job enrichment strives to provide the worker with a job which meets 3 criteria: 1. The worker can identify a series of tasks or activities which result in a definable product or service. 2. As much decision-making control as possible over how to carry out the complete piece of work is delegated to the worker. 3. The work itself gives direct feedback to the worker on how well the job is done.To initiate job enrichment in an organization: 1. Decide on a class of jobs to be enriched. 2. Brainstorm possible job changes. 3. Remove non-feasible ideas and suggestions involving hygiene factors. 4. Introduce the changes decided upon. 5. Analyze productivity rates to check results. Basic theory and practice indicate that many jobs can be enriched, thus increasing job satisfaction. Graph. References. —Dolecheck, M. M.; *Northeast Louisiana Business Review,* Spring/Summer 1980, pp. 10-16. Avail. ABI 80-15618

Job enrichment, Job satisfaction, Motivation, Working conditions, Learning curves (PER), Volvo-Sweden

Job Enrichment Through Symbol Management (290)

Many organizations throughout the world are involved in job enrichment projects. Generally speaking, job enrichment has been found to decrease absenteeism and turnover and to increase job satisfaction and performance. Recently, however, certain questions have arisen concerning the theoretical basis and practical value of job enrichment. It has been suggested that workers do not perceive their jobs objectively, but are influenced by the interpretations of others regarding how enriched their jobs are. Objectively increasing the variety of tasks assigned to someone may have little effect unless the job holders perceive it, and such perceptions are often socially influenced. Managers have a great influence in job perceptions, sending symbolic messages about jobs in some very subtle ways. Through his language, patterns of activity, and the environment for interaction, a manager can positively or negatively influence job perceptions. Charts. References. —Moberg, Dennis J.; *California Mgmt Review,* Winter 1981, 24(2): pp. 24-30. Avail. ABI 82-07275

Job enrichment, Symbols, Management, Job satisfaction, Organizational behavior

Job Matching Brings Out the Best in Employees (291)

Employees who are carefully and appropriately matched to their jobs are satisfied and productive. Skilled job-matching requires effective employee recruitment and management. Use of the preferred skills model in problem-solving aids managers in identifying employees' specific and preferred skills. The model can also help managers to: 1. identify needs and create employment policies, 2. implement policies, 3. manage and administer implemented policies, and 4. market and sell policies at all levels. Further, the model specifically describes characteristics of: 1. creators and developers, 2. implementors, 3. managers, and 4. marketers and promoters. The model may be applied, in terms of employee identification, when recruiting and hiring. The model is also useful in delegating, forming work teams, and in career pathing. An accurate self-scoring guide, based on the model, aids managers and employees in assessing preferred skills and working styles.

Charts. References. —Coil, Ann; *Personnel Jrnl,* Jan 1984, 63(1): pp. 54-60. Avail. ABI 84-05404

> Job satisfaction, Personnel selection, Human resources, Employee evaluations, Job evaluation, Employee, Skills, Models

Job Satisfaction and Life Satisfaction: An Empirical   (292)
Evaluation of Their Interrelationship

A number of research studies have tended to support the positive relationship between job satisfaction and life satisfaction. However, the studies have failed to provide a decisive description of the interrelationship between job satisfaction and life satisfaction, which suggests that the empirical models may be misspecified. A study was done to empirically test the job satisfaction-life satisfaction relationship in an effort to better identify an appropriate model. The subjects were 129 employees of an auto parts manufacturer. Subjects were asked to complete a survey that measured life satisfaction and job satisfaction. The results of the study indicated that life satisfaction and job satisfaction should be considered to be jointly determined. Models which suggest that job satisfaction is a component of life satisfaction or vice versa require some reconsideration. Tables. Equations. References. —Keon, Thomas L. and McDonald, Bill; *Human Relations,* Mar 1982, 35(3): pp. 167-180. Avail. ABI 82-12665

> Job satisfaction, Job attitudes, Happiness, Empirical, Studies, Research, Surveys, Statistical analysis

Job Satisfaction: A Review of Progress and a   (293)
Management Viewpoint

During the 1970s teams from the British Civil Service Department started Job Satisfaction (JS) projects around the UK. JS is characterized by a climate of free communication with everyone giving input to problem-solving. In practice, JS may be accomplished by reducing tedious work, improving staff morale, introducing participatory management, or effecting changes in attitude. Implementation of JS plans are discussed. The changes and by-products of implementing a JS plan include benefits to both staff and unions-individually and collectively. A job that is satisfying to one individual may be a nightmare for another person. JS plans need to be highly flexible so they can be adapted to a variety of situations. —Shroff, Marie; *Management Services in Government (UK),* Aug 1981, 36(3): pp. 129-136. Avail. ABI 81-23405

> Management styles, Civil service, Job satisfaction, Personnel management

Job Satisfaction in the United States in the 1970s   (294)

Job satisfaction among US workers is examined. Since antecedents of global job satisfaction are largely unknown, its usefulness is limited, although for purposes of comparison with facet-specific satisfaction, data gathered with the global measure are of interest. Data can be used from 7 recent nationwide surveys to extend through 1978 the earlier evidence for 1958-73 by Quinn, Staines, and McCollough (1974) on global job satisfaction in the USA. This opportunity became available through the inclusion of the most commonly used global measure of job satisfaction for each year from 1972-1978 on the General Social Surveys. The General Social Surveys were developed as a data diffusion project and a program of social indicators research. Inclusion in the survey of demographic questions made it possible to furnish information on alterations in job satisfaction among segments of the US population.Job satisfaction among American workers was examined for 1972-1978 with a sample comprised of 7 independently drawn yearly national surveys. There were no substantial changes in overall levels of job satisfaction through 1978. In addition, a number of correlates of job satisfaction were still unchanged. Blacks were less job satisfied than whites, and no sex differences in job satisfaction existed. A positive association is emerging between job satisfaction and education, age, income, and occupation. Tables. References. —Weaver, Charles N.; *Jrnl of Applied Psychology,* Jun 1980, 65(3): pp. 364-367. Avail. ABI 80-12551

Job satisfaction, Factors, Attitude surveys, Statistical analysis, Studies, Variables

Job Switching in Autonomous Work Groups: An (295) Exploratory Study in a Pennsylvania Coal Mine

Increasing focus and concern has been directed in the past 10 years to the preservation of diminishing resources and to the amelioration of the high personal and social costs of unsatisfying work. Evidence indicates that one way to reach these goals is through the systematic redesign of jobs and the workplace. One technique of job design gaining much acceptance is associated with the use of the internally-led, self-regulating, autonomous work group.A 13-month field survey of a Pennsylvania coal mine explored the phenomenon of job-switching behavior and tried to isolate some of the important variables related to job switching in autonomous work groups. Age and job status were found to be strong determinants of job switching. In addition, job switching correlated negatively with job satisfaction and positively with absenteeism, feedback, task identity, and hazard. Although social and psychological variables have been found to be principal causes of behavior in other work systems, additional significant forces seem to be at work in the mine. The research sample was composed of 54 miners, and data for the analysis were collected by onsite observation and questionnaires. Tables. Figures. References. —Blumberg, Melvin; *Academy of Mgmt Jrnl,* Jun 1980, 23(2): pp. 287-306. Avail. ABI 80-12750

Job, Changes, Design, Switching, Behavior, Studies, Experiments, Job attitudes, Education, Job satisfaction, Seniority, Age, Status, Job classification

Job-Restructuring Plan Adds to Satisfaction of (296) Monsanto Employees

The management of Monsanto Co. (St. Louis, Missouri) began studying work redesign methodologies in response to problems in their central accounts payable department. Work effectiveness, a methodology developed by the management consulting firm Roy W. Walters & Associates, was selected, and a task force was formed to apply it to the department. Analysis included personal interviews and data gathered from a Job Diagnostic Survey (JDS). JDS measures a position's core job dimensions: 1. skill variety, 2. task identity, 3. task significance, 4. autonomy, and 5. feedback. Based on the results, the 3 sections of invoice processing, discrepancy, and inquiry were replaced with natural work units in support of particular vendors. The redesigned "vendor-account analysts" have full responsibility for processing invoices. The restructuring resulted in a strengthening of the core job dimensions and in greater employee satisfaction, as well as improved in-house and vendor service. —Anonymous; *Office,* Mar 1981, 93(3): pp. 63-64,68,74. Avail. ABI 81-08552

> Job, Structure, Changes, Job satisfaction, Case studies, Accounts payable, Departments, Monsanto-St Louis, Work, Effectiveness, Programs, Characteristics, Organizational change

## Leader Behavior and Subordinate Motivation						(297)

A study was conducted to examine the impact of managerial behavior on the key motivational constructs of expectancy, effort, and performance of subordinates. The subjects were 231 editors-subordinates, and 15 assistant managers employed in the production department of a large information processing organization. Editors were asked to complete questionnaires containing satisfaction measures, a role ambiguity measure, a self-rating of effort, a self-rating of overall performance, perceptions of supervisor mediated performance and ratings of supervisor behavior. The results of the study indicated support for the role of supervisor behaviors in influencing effort expenditure, the perception of organizational contingencies, and most facets of job satisfaction. Results also showed that supervisor behaviors were related to job performance as well. Therefore, supervisors who are explicit in their expectations, consistent in their demands, and supportive of their employees are more likely to have a satisfied work force. Tables. References. —Klimoski, Richard J. and Hayes, Noreen J.; *Personnel Psychology,* Autumn 1980, 33(3): pp. 543-555. Avail. ABI 80-21899

> Supervisors, Leadership, Behavior, Impacts, Subordinates, Motivation, Job satisfaction, Worker codetermination, Performance standards, Performance evaluation, Goal setting, Studies

## Listening to the Workers Produces Results						(298)

Norwegian bicycle manufacturer Jonas Oglaend has put participation theory into practice on the shop floor. The result has been a revolution in attitudes among both workers and managers. Workers at the bicycle factory have developed their own form of shop-floor democracy. To make such participation successful, the firm's managers never accept an occurring problem as they see it, but as the workers see it. The benefit to management under the new team organization has been a 20% increase in productivity. Oglaend found that the changes had to be instituted from the bottom up, while encouragement for them had to come from the top down. Following a union agreement, the form of the new work organization was tested on one of the plant's three bicycle lines.In sum, the process has taught both workers and management the same fundamental lesson. Management learned that what they think is secondary to what the workers think. And the workers learned that what the individual thinks is not as important as what the group thinks. —Arbose, Jules; *International Mgmt (UK),* Feb 1980, 35(2): pp. 40-41,44k. Avail. ABI 80-05701

> Participatory management, Worker codetermination, Case studies, Job attitudes, Employee attitude (PER), Job satisfaction, Quality, Productivity

Managers and Their Organizations: An Interactive (299)
Approach to Multidimensional Job Satisfaction

An attempt was made to examine the interaction of the individual attributes of education and age and the organizational characteristic of management position on the level of job satisfaction. To achieve a broader base for analysis, the tests of the hypotheses were repeated across 3 organizations, one each dealing with retail, banking, and insurance activities. A total of 1, 158 managers from the 3 organizations were given the Minnesota Satisfaction Questionnaire. A factorial nested analysis of variance was used to test hypotheses. Independent variables were age, education, and hierarchical level, and the dependent variables were 4 specific job satisfaction factor scores plus a global dimension. The results indicated that the structural attribute of hierarchical level has the most significant pervasive impact on managers' job satisfaction and that, when individual attributes do have significant impact, it is most often within the top level of management. The results also showed a very strong relationship between satisfaction with personal progress and development and overall job satisfaction. Tables. References. Appendix. —Bergmann, Thomas J.; *Jrnl of Occupational Psychology (UK)*, 1981, 54(4): pp. 275-288. Avail. ABI 82-03942

Managers, Job satisfaction, Age, Education, Upper, Management, Middle management, Job attitudes, Hypotheses, Tests, Studies, Management development, Compensation

Managing Dissatisfaction (300)

The challenge for management is to structure systems that identify dissatisfaction, analyze why it is there, and then furnish positive channels for translating dissatisfaction into increased productivity. The dissatisfied employee may be likely to choose one of several options: increased work effort, sabotage, departure from the organization, or apathy. Since dissatisfaction can become a very destructive force in an organization, it is necessary for management to develop a responsive management support system. An appropriate support system might include: 1. clearly defining responsibilities and desired results, 2. understanding and being able to describe what contributes to performance, 3. developing and training employees to improve performance, 4. understanding the environment within which the employee is working, and 5. developing active career counseling and placement programs. An important consideration is a mismatch between individual and job, as people frequently outgrow their jobs. However, turnover can be a positive factor if managed appropriately. Tables. —Baird, Lloyd; *Personnel,* May/Jun 1981, 58(3): pp. 12-21. Avail. ABI 81-15651

Job satisfaction, Productivity, Performance, Rewards, Personnel policies, Personnel management, Management, Support, Systems

The Moderating Effect of Work Context Satisfactions (301)
on the Curvilinear Relationship Between Job Scope and
Affective Response

The quality of the conterson's job affects the curvilinear relationship between job scope and psychological response. The moderating effect of work context satisfaction through the use of moderated regression analysis is examined. Data were obtained in 4 independent samples using the Job Diagnostic Survey (JDS). No statistically significant interactions with context satisfactions were found in 2 samples from a federal agency. 2. Significant interactions with only the linear job scope term were found in one research and development (R & D) organization (B). 3. Significant interactions with the curvilinear job scope term were found in another R & D organization (A). 4. The significant interactions, in each case, involved a different contextual satisfaction-supervisory satisfaction in R & D Organization A and social satisfaction in R & D Organization B. 5. The significant interactions involved only one affective response variable-growth satisfaction. Tables. References. —Champoux, Joseph E.; *Human Relations,* Jun 6, 1981, 34(6): pp. 503-515. Avail. ABI 81-20703

Job satisfaction, Motivation, Job attitudes, Job, Scope, Compensation, Employment security, Studies, Regression analysis

A New Look at Job Satisfaction in the Small Firm (302)

It has been widely accepted that job satisfaction is greater in a small firm than in a large one. The smaller firm has been seen as being especially superior in offering satisfying social relations, more varied and interesting work roles, and opportunities for identifying with the enterprise as a whole. Some of the previous literature concerning firm size and job satisfaction is reviewed. A critical examination was made of the above view. Workers in both small and large firms in the printing and electronics industries were interviewed. The interviews were carried out in the worker's home or other nonwork venue. Each respondent was requested to say what he thought was most important about a job, and each respondent was given a list of 14 items. Another set of questions concerned physical fatigue and boredom with the job. A final set of questions concerned levels of material rewards. It was found that job satisfaction was related to work environment and also nonwork influences such as family life-cycle position. When factors such as specific characteristics of the industry and age and marital status are taken into account, the size of the firm is not, in itself, an important factor in explaining levels of job satisfaction. Tables. References. —Stanworth, John and Curran, James; *Human Relations,* May 1981, 34(5): pp. 343-365. Avail. ABI 81-20388

Job satisfaction, Printing industry, Electronics industry, Work environment, Size of enterprise, Comparative studies, Job attitudes

Not Eyeball to Eyeball - Managers: More Discontent (303) Than Execs Think

A survey conducted for Industry Week by Research & Forecasts Inc. (New York) has revealed that top management is not seeing eye to eye with middle management on many issues, including career opportunities, loyalty, salary, and advancement. Middle managers have discovered they are as expendable as hourly workers despite education, long hours, and hard work. As a result, the traditional virtues of middle managers - "organization men" - are changing to ensure their survival. A sampling of survey findings includes: 1. About 42% of middle managers surveyed expect to leave their current job in the next 5 years. 2. While 38% of chief executive officers plan to use money as the primary incentive to retain middle managers, only 13% of the latter are primarily concerned with money. 3. Only 22% of middle managers consider opportunities for advancement good at their companies. Graphs. – Anonymous; *Industry Week*, Mar 19, 1984, 220(6): pp. 15-16. Avail. ABI 84-11643

Middle management, Job attitudes, Job satisfaction, Surveys, Chief executive officer

A Note on Some New Scales for Measuring Aspects of (304) Psychological Well-Being at Work

Scales for measuring aspects of psychological well-being at work have been developed by Warr et al. (1979), and Cook and Wall (1980). Factors upon which adequacy depends that have not been tested are: 1. equivalent psychometric characteristics across samples, and 2. an accumulation of descriptive statistics. This research attempts to provide evidence relevant to the aforementioned factors for 5 particular scales, which are: 1. perceived intrinsic job characteristics, 2. higher order need strength, 3. job satisfaction, 4. trust at work, and 5. organizational commitment. The scales, with the exception of the organizational commitment scale, performed in a psychometrically reliable fashion for all subsamples. Four of the scales were reasonably factorially independent, with job satisfaction displaying some overlap. Two organization-specific samples indicated construct validity. These findings suggest that these scales may have a general applicability, although their psychometric performance should be tested in different situations and a data bank compiled. Tables. References. –Clegg, Chris W. and Wall, Toby D.; *Jrnl of Occupational Psychology (UK)*, 1981, 54(3): pp. 221-225. Avail. ABI 81-23712

Job satisfaction, Organizational behavior, Statistical analysis, Psychological aspects, Measurement, Scale

O.D. also Stands for Organizational Deception (305)

In recent years, most large companies have devoted some effort to organizational development (OD) in order to help motivate its employees, to improve company productivity and efficiency, and to ensure meaningful careers for its personnel. Organizational deception, another kind of OD, cuts to the heart of the work environment shortcomings in many companies. Organizational deception can take many forms and can negate the well-intentioned directives of top management by preventing vital information about employee dissatisfaction from ever reaching them. The organizational rift that often develops between top and bottom occurs because self-interests, particularly of middle managers, have become more important than collective interests to many. Understanding what is actually occurring is the first step in alleviating organizational deception. Four case studies outline some typical types of organizational deception. References. –Werner, Gerald C.; *Manage*, Apr 1981, 33(2): pp. 2-5. Avail. ABI 81-11307

Organization development, Organizational behavior, Job satisfaction, Employee morale, Upper, Management, Failure, Performance appraisal, Reviews, Exit interviews (PER)

On Improving Employee Job Satisfaction: A Case Study (306)

In order to eliminate employee dissatisfaction and friction in a hospital dietary department, the department was reorganized and a schedule developed to ensure a balanced workload. The department was partitioned into 2 separate departments-Food Services and Nutritional Services-and new titles and job descriptions were assigned to supervisors.A functional analysis of the department's subsystems was performed, using data obtained from job descriptions, employee schedules, and interviews with supervisors. Schedules were developed and modified for supervisory and then non-supervisory employees, with employee involvement and feedback. The main result of the analysis was the discovery of a major amount of overlap on supervisory time; implementation of the adjusted schedules relieved the duplication and provided for necessary improvements in supervisor performance. Charts. Table. References. –Levary, Reuven R. and Dean, Burton V.; *Industrial Mgmt,* May/Jun 1980, 22(3): pp. 17-24. Avail. ABI 80-13713

Job satisfaction, Job attitudes, Workloads, Case studies, Reorganization, Personnel, Scheduling, Statistical data

On the Dubious Wisdom of Expecting Job Satisfaction to Correlate with Performance (307)

Previous research by organizational researchers on correlating job satisfaction to job performance has been unsuccessful. The reason for this failure is the complex relationship between attitude and behavior. Attitude theorists have recognized these complexities and have identified 3 concepts to consider in improving observed correlations. In the concept of consistency, a clear definition must be established as to what behavior is consistent with what attitude. A second concept is behavioral criteria, and the criteria for what type of behavior constitutes a positive or negative reaction must be defined. Generally, those criteria that require repeat observations are more reliable. The specificity of attitude measures must also be considered. The more specifically defined the question or attitude, the more reliable the results. Further research is necessary concerning the job satisfaction/job performance relationship using the 3 concepts, which may help clarify the inconsistent results of past studies. References. –Fisher, Cynthia D.; *Academy of Mgmt Review,* Oct 1980, 5(4): pp. 607-612. Avail. ABI 80-22568

Job satisfaction, Performance, Job attitudes, Organizational, Research, Organizational behavior

Organic Structure, Satisfaction, and Personality (308)

A study was conducted to examine the variation in satisfaction across a sample of employees whose work groups differ in structure along an organistic-mechanistic dimension. The basic research question involves how the personal satisfaction that an organization member derives from his/her work is related to the structure of the group he/she works in.The subjects were 93 persons in 24 groups in research and development divisions of 2 firms. Data was obtained regarding: 1. organicity, 2. satisfaction, 3. personality traits, and 4. innovativeness of task. The results show that organic structure in small work groups is positively associated with the satisfaction of higher-order needs, but that mechanistic structure is associated with their frustration. It was observed that employees with strong traits aspiring to dominance, autonomy, and achievement respond more positively to organic structure and more negatively to mechanistic structure than people with weaker traits. Tables. References. —Meadows, Ian S. G.; *Human Relations,* Jun 1980, 33(6): pp. 383-392. Avail. ABI 80-14048

Organizational behavior, Organizational, Structure, Job satisfaction, Small, Work, Groups, Studies, Personality, Satisfaction

Organisation und menschliche Beduerfnisse (309)
(Organization and Human Needs)

In many instances, efforts to meet human needs within organizations create new needs. In turn, these new needs bring about new organizational efforts in a vicious circle that is ultimately detrimental to achievement. Human needs are hard to define and satisfy in the workplace. A structure that is too well organized brings about its own conflicts. Human needs exist in the general areas of: 1. job/work content, 2. social relationships/teamwork, and 3. leadership. A case example of the restructuring of a data processing department illustrates the difficulty of satisfying all these need areas. It is assumed that people can adjust to most conditions and gain mental stability. In practice, however, lack of satisfaction will lead to certain negative compensation mechanisms being set in motion, e.g., regression, fantasies, and defensive reactions. An unsatisfactory organizational structure creates its own needs that are the inverse of normal needs. Such regressive needs require a yet higher degree of organization, which goes directly against recommended democratic and progressive forms of leadership. The successful firm will strive to satisfy the true human needs of its workers. Chart. References. —Forster, Werner A.; *Zeitschrift fuer Organisation (Germany),* Jan 1981, (1): pp. 9-13. Avail. ABI 81-22912

Employee, Needs, Job satisfaction, Work environment, Supervision, Organization theory

The Orientation to Work Controversy and the Social (310)
Construction of Work Value Systems

The orientation to work controversy centers on the dangers in using the social action frame of reference as an explanation of workers' attitudes, particularly as this relates to the tendency to minimize the importance of what are traditionally viewed as the structural factors in social life. Research was conducted to determine the extent to which the social action frame of reference is resistant to socialization processes for those situations encountered as part of the biographical history of the individual participant. The subjects for the study were 50 trainees attending the Skillcentre at Granton in Edinburgh. Subjects were interviewed, and data was obtained on the attitudes of the subjects relative to work situations that had been unfavorable and those expected to be favorable. The results indicated support for the importance of changing social situations as an influence on orientations to work, which suggests that dynamic orientation has greater explanatory and predictive value than the fixed orientation perspective. Tables. References. —Russell, Kevin J.; *Jrnl of Mgmt Studies (UK),* May 1980, 17(2): pp. 164-184. Avail. ABI 80-18325

Work, Value, Systems, Job attitudes, Priorities, Job satisfaction, Factors, Studies

Overall Job Satisfaction: Is It a Linear Function of Facet Satisfaction? (311)

Both linear and nonlinear models for combining satisfaction with specific job facets to arrive at overall job satisfaction are investigated. The specific models investigated are the compensatory, conjunctive, and disjunctive models presented by Einhorn (1970), used by Aldag and Brief (1978), and reviewed by Ogilvie and Schmitt (1979). The database was formed from the responses of 233 legal secretaries who were sent questionnaires at their places of employment throughout a midwestern state. Results marginally support the hypothesis that overall job satisfaction is a linear function of satisfaction with various job facets. The linear compensatory model of combining facets performs about as well as, or better than, the nonlinear models investigated. Tentative empirical support was found for the belief that an operational measure of overall job satisfaction can be developed by combining satisfactions with specific job facets. Tables. References. –Ferratt, Thomas W.; *Human Relations,* Jun 1981, 34(6): pp. 463-473. Avail. ABI 81-20701

Job satisfaction, Job attitudes, Evaluation, Measurement, Statistical analysis, Studies

A Partial Test of the Social Information Processing Model of Job Attitudes (312)

A study was conducted to examine the relative effects of social context and job characteristics on the determination of attitude and need statements. The study represents a partial examination of the social information processing perspective developed by Salancik and Pfeffer (1978).Data were obtained from 113 engineers working in two semiconductor design and manufacturing corporations. The Job Diagnostic Survey in its short form was used to assess the dimensions of the jobs, while measures of individual needs were obtained from the Manifest Needs Questionnaire. Attitudes toward the job and the organization were also measured along with work-group effects. The results provided support for a social information processing approach to analyzing attitudes and other personal constructs in work organizations. The results suggest the necessity of considering simultaneously job dimensions, social influences, and behaviors in explaining job attitudes. Figure. Tables. Appendix. References. –Pfeffer, Jeffrey; *Human Relations,* Jul 1980, 33(7): pp. 457-476. Avail. ABI 80-15398

Job attitudes, Job satisfaction, Employee attitude (PER), Social, Information processing, Models, Factors

A Path Analytic Model of Human Capital and Organizational Job Characteristics on Female Job Satisfaction (313)

In evaluating traditional job characteristics found in standard job satisfaction material, 4 human variables were cited as having strong influence on certain organizational career characteristics: 1. marital status, 2. formal education, 3. alternative work information, and 4. length of service. The 7 job characteristics influenced by the aforementioned variables are: 1. relationship with co-workers, 2. pay scale, 3. promotion, 4. job communications, 5. equal treatment, 6. centralization, and 7. routinization.

In turn, these variables have a strong impact on job satisfaction. This theory has particular significance in evaluating job satisfaction among female workers. Moreover, an increase in co-worker integration and reduced routinization were found to increase a worker's satisfaction. Figures. Tables. References. –Martin, Thomas N.; *Human Relations,* Nov 1981, 34(11): pp. 975-988. Avail. ABI 82-01378

Path, Analysis, Models, Human capital, Women, Job satisfaction, Female employees, Organizational behavior, Economic theory

A Path-Analytic Study of the Consequences of Role (314) Conflict and Ambiguity

Since the pioneering work of Jacobson, Charters, and Lieberman on the use of the role concept in the study of complex organizations, there has been a growing literature examining the relationship between role perceptions and work-related attitudes and behavior. Particularly, considerable attention has been centered on the negative outcome of such role-related phenomena as role conflict and ambiguity. For example, both role conflict and ambiguity have been linked to job dissatisfaction, job-induced tension, lower organizational commitment, and propensity to leave an organization. An attempt was made to reinvestigate the consequences of role conflict and ambiguity on tension, job satisfaction, and propensity to leave an organization through the use of path analysis. A Veterans Administration Medical Center was the object of examination, and the survey population was made up of 460 nursing staff members, from whom 202 usable questionnaires were obtained and analyzed. Results clearly confirm the importance of role perceptions in understanding job-related attitudes. Chart. Table. References. –Bedeian, Arthur G. and Armenakis, Achilles A.; *Academy of Mgmt Jrnl,* Jun 1981, 24(2). pp. 417-424. Avail. ABI 81-14531

Roles, Conflict, Organizational behavior, Job attitudes, Job satisfaction, Models, Statistical analysis

Perceived Job Characteristics and Job Satisfaction: An (315) Examination of Reciprocal Causation

Theoretical and empirical relationships between individuals' views of job characteristics and job satisfaction have been given considerable attention in the literature. By selecting a sample that included work environments that differed significantly on job attributes and workgroup structure variables, the researcher can test hypotheses about job satisfaction and job characteristics. Five subsamples consisting of nonsupervisory personnel from 6 organizations were employed. The following assumptions were tested: 1. Satisfaction with job/task events and perceptions of job challenge, autonomy, and importance are direct, reciprocal causes of each other, 2. Job perceptions are also caused directly by situation attributes, although perceptual distortions resulting for individual dispositions must be considered. 3. Job satisfaction is also cognitively consistent with individual dispositions, although these individual dispositions are usually different from those linked with job perceptions. 4. Individuals depend on job perceptions and not situational attributes for information in developing job satisfaction attitudes. A nonrecursive, structural equation analysis, combined with tests of logical consistency, lend credence to the assumptions. The results can be used to suggest changes in current perspectives about perceptual/affective dichotomies and unidirectional causal models and moderator models that link job perceptions to job satisfaction. Chart. Tables. Equations. References. —James, Lawrence R. and Jones, Allan P.; *Personnel Psychology,* Spring 1980, 33(1): pp. 97-135. Avail. ABI 80-08762

Perceptions, Job, Characteristics, Job satisfaction, Causality, Studies, Variables, Correlations, Regression analysis

Perceived Task Characteristics and Employee Productivity and Satisfaction   (316)

The effects of employee perceptions of task attributes on long-run productivity and degrees of job and personal satisfaction were investigated. A sample of 100 randomly selected employees of a manufacturing firm were surveyed regarding: 1. the task attributes of autonomy, variety, and feedback, 2. their degrees of job and personal satisfaction, and 3. their growth need strengths. Productivity was measured by averaging each employee's daily output over a one-year period. Perceived task attributes were found to be positively related to productivity and job satisfaction; however, no relationship was found between task characteristics and personal, overall satisfaction. Growth need strength was found to positively moderate the relationship between task perception and job satisfaction in both subgroup and moderated regression analyses, although it was not found to moderate the task-productivity or the task-personal satisfaction relationships. Tables. References. —Griffin, Ricky W.; *Human Relations,* Oct 1982, 35(10): pp. 927-938. Avail. ABI 83-00683

Job satisfaction, Employee attitude (PER), Task analysis, Productivity, Models

Perceptual Measures of Task Characteristics: The Biasing Effects of Differing Frames of Reference and Job Attitudes   (317)

Much research has been concerned with the effect of task characteristics on job satisfaction and performance. More recently, however, criticisms have been launched against job design literature, criticisms that ask questions about the validity of previous findings. In an effort to deal partially with these questions and based on evidence about the importance of frame of reference and informational influence as determinants of questionnaire responses, an investigation of sources of systematic variations in perceptions of task characteristics by employees holding identical jobs is revealing. It can be hypothesized that variance in task characteristics assessed by the Job Diagnostic Survey (JDS), a perceptual measure, will vary according to an individual's frame of reference. Responses were obtained from 98 country public health nurses, (PHNs) who were in the same job classification. The small sample size and cross-sectional nature of the examination make the conclusions tentative. Individuals studied appear to perceive similar task dimensions differently, and these systematic differences seem to come from the job holders' overall satisfaction with the job. More satisfied workers reported the task as being more motivating. Tables. References. —O'Reilly,

Charles A., Jr.; Parlette, G. Nicholas; and Bloom, Joan R.; *Academy of Mgmt Jrnl,* Mar 1980, 23(1): pp. 118-131. Avail. ABI 80-06282
Task, Job, Characteristics, Perceptions, Job attitudes, Task analysis, Design, Job satisfaction

Performance and Satisfaction in an Industrial Sales (318) Force: An Examination of Their Antecedents and Simultaneity

While both managers and salespeople relate performance with job satisfaction, little is understood about the nature of this relationship. In general, 4 possibilities exist: 1. Satisfaction causes performance. 2. Performance causes satisfaction. 3. The 2 variables are related reciprocally. 4. The variables are not causally related at all. An attempt is made to discover the true relationship between performance and satisfaction in an industrial sales force.A new methodology, structural equations with measurement error, that allows one to test each of the 4 possibilities is used. Previous approaches were not well suited to determine if the performance/satisfaction relation is spurious or simultaneous in nature. Results showed that the performance/satisfaction relation partially depends upon the degree to which individuals evaluate outcomes associated with the job. The greater the value placed on job outcomes, the higher the level of satisfaction with the attainment of subsequent rewards. Tables. Figure. References. Appendix. – Bagozzi, Richard P.; *Jrnl of Marketing,* Spring 1980, 44(2): pp. 65-77. Avail. ABI 80-10691
Performance, Job satisfaction, Industrial, Salespeople, Studies, Statistical analysis, Job attitudes, Self image, Motivation

The Personalising Behaviour of Managers . . . Or, How (319) They Look After Themselves

A group of 49 managers employed in a large iron and steel works were studied to investigate the ways they look after themselves. Issues of concern to them were identified as well as ways used to counteract these areas of concern. Several "personalizing responses," activities designed to attain or maintain an adequate quality of working life, were identified: 1. personal redefinition of job and work circumstances, 2. personal and collective restructuring, 3. restructuring and redefining work/non-work relationships, 4. seeking to change jobs within the organization, and 5. seeking to move to another organization. These responses are adopted to try to achieve an acceptable balance among the individual manager's needs, the needs of the family, social life, and the pressure from within the organization. The impact of situations at work and at home produces need satisfactions and need dissatisfactions, the latter acting as cues for personalizing behavior aimed at reducing the dissatisfactions. Tables. Graph. References. –Knibbs, John; *Personnel Review (UK),* 1982, 11(4): pp. 24-30. Avail. ABI 83-08512
Work environment, Organizational behavior, Studies, Managers, Attitudes, Working conditions, Job satisfaction, Job enrichment, Group dynamics, Job, Changes, Promotions (MAN), Employee problems

Personnel Assessment from the Perspective of the   (320)
Theory of Work Adjustment

At the heart of the Theory of Work Adjustment is the concept of interaction between individual and work environment, the health of which can be denoted by "correspondence." The work environment serves various organizational needs, and the individual has various needs such as those for recognition, fringe benefits, and accomplishment. Work adjustment is indicated by the individual's satisfaction and the satisfaction of the organization with the individual, and from the combination, tenure can be predicted. The organization's satisfaction with the individual (satisfactoriness) is predicted from correspondence between the individual's skills and the needs of the environment; satisfaction, a sine qua non of satisfactoriness, is predicted by correspondence of the reinforcer system to the individual's needs. Job performance should not be the criterion of personnel assessment, but rather it should be the capability to perform the job, which makes proper determination of skill requirements crucial. Traditional problems with content validity can be alleviated to some extent by use of practical rather than theoretical validity, but content validity is necessary for the assessment procedure. Skills and skill requirements can be described as abilities, but abilities can assess only the potential for skills, not possession of those skills. There is no substitute for skill assessment. —Dawis, Rene V.; *Public Personnel Mgmt,* 1980, 9(4): pp. 268-273. Avail. ABI 81-04000

Personnel, Assessments, Employee evaluations, Theory, Work environment, Job satisfaction, Skills, Requirements, Job, Performance, Performance evaluation, Procedures, Validation, Personnel management

A Picture Is Worth a Thousand Words   (321)

The components by which job satisfaction is measured consist of 6 indices including: 1. overall job satisfaction, 2. income security, 3. job prestige, 4. fairness of compensation, 5. agent-company relations, and 6. agent-manager relations. The responses to surveys from both US and Canadian agents were plotted on graphs. Over a decade, trends in job satisfaction among US agents reveal a slipping in job satisfaction across all areas. This information was obvious when graphs were compared. The most significant declines, occurring in 1978, were in income security and fairness of compensation areas. Among Canadian English-speaking agents, the 1980 scores were the lowest since the 1970 initiation of the survey. The only exception was in job prestige, which showed a slight increase. The most dramatic decline occurred in 1980 in the area of fairness of compensation. The 1980 survey scores for Canadian French-speaking agents were the lowest since 1970 in the areas of: 1. fairness of compensation, 2. agent-company relations, and 3. agent-manager relations. These graphs can help show managers what their agents feel about their jobs, their income, and their managers. Graphs. —Murray, Dorothy F.; *Managers Magazine,* Jan 1982, 57(1): pp. 14-16. Avail. ABI 82-02730

Insurance agents & brokers, Job satisfaction, Canada, Trends, Life insurance

Privacy at Work: Architectural Correlates of Job (322) Satisfaction and Job Performance

Research on the role of the physical setting in interpersonal behavior in organizations has been particularly uncommon, although social and environmental psychologists have developed theories that could apply. Social and environmental psychology can be applied to work settings. The role of privacy in job satisfaction and job performance is one area where such psychology can be utilized. Privacy can be defined in 2 ways: 1. as a psychological state, and 2. as a physical feature of the environment. In other words, privacy is architectural or psychological.Questionnaires were sent out to about 150 administrative employees of the State of Tennessee, with 85 participating in the study. In a second study, a small group of clerical workers were assessed, and a third examination included both clerical employees and people in complex jobs in a wide range or workspaces. It was illustrated that architectural privacy was consistently linked with psychological privacy. People who rated their workspaces as private tended to report less noise, distraction, and crowding problems than those in less private environments. However, practically no relationship was discovered between architectural accessibility and social interaction among co-workers. In conclusion, architectural and psychological privacy are associated, and both types of privacy are related to satisfaction with workspaces and job satisfaction. Tables. References. —Sundstrom, Eric; Burt, Robert E.; and Kamp, Douglas; *Academy of Mgmt Jrnl,* Mar 1980, 23(1): pp. 101-117. Avail. ABI 80-06281

   Privacy, Office layout, Work stations, Job satisfaction, Performance, Studies, Statistical analysis, Noise

Profile of the Public Personnel Administrator (323)

At the 1982 International Personnel Management Association conference, a 5-page questionnaire on attitudes, values, and beliefs was distributed to 681 participants, with 379 responding. Respondents were predominantly male, white, over 40 years of age, and held middle- to top-management jobs. Respondents who were over 40 years of age more frequently responded as being very satisfied with their jobs, compared with those under 40. Top and middle managers reported generally higher levels of job satisfaction than those at lower professional levels. Some 66% reported experiencing some job-related stress, and 63% said that burnout is a critical problem for their profession. The majority strongly favored broader appointment power for appointing authorities, as opposed to the historically independent civil service commission. Performance appraisal systems continue to be viewed as valuable methods, but when linked to merit pay, the validity and value of the method for improving performance is said to diminish. Tables. References. —Ross, Joyce D. and Pugh, Darrell L.; *Public Personnel Mgmt,* Fall 1983, 12(3): pp. 232-243. Avail. ABI 83-31763

   Personnel, Managers, Profiles, Job satisfaction, Responsibilities, Problems, Personnel management, Public sector, Job attitudes, Collective bargaining, Affirmative action, Surveys

The Project Manager: Kingpin in Personnel Motivation (324)

Data processing people seem to increasingly enjoy their jobs as their career progresses-until the time that they become project managers. At this time, neither the organization nor the manager are prepared for the job. The job dissatisfaction experienced by these managers has been analyzed in a study. Job motivation appears to come from skill variety, task identity, task significance, autonomy, and feedback. However, the principal cause of reduced job satisfaction for project managers is the way their firms have implemented the matrix organization. Surveys have also revealed that people in the computer field have low social need strength, and this fact applies also to project managers. Also revealed was a significant difference in job satisfaction between people who became project managers as a third or fourth step supervisor, and those whose first supervisory job was project management. The reasons for such findings appear to be: 1. Conflict management requires a more experienced manager. 2. Low social need strength people need more formal preparation for project management. Since the project manager is "kingpin" of data processing personnel motivation, the firm must be certain that the project manager himself receives the necessary behavioral/communications training and careful nurturing so he can do his job well. Exhibits. —Couger, J. Daniel; *Computerworld,* Sep 1, 1981, 15(35a): pp. 49-52,54-55. Avail. ABI 81-20442

Project management, Managers, Motivation, Models, Job satisfaction, Organizational behavior

Race Differences in Job Satisfaction: A Reappraisal   (325)

Earlier research has indicated that job satisfaction is a major determinant of labor market mobility. An analysis was conducted to determine what can account for the observed race differences in the individual's feelings about the job as a whole. Data were taken from the 1966, 1969, and 1971 National Longitudinal Surveys of Mature Men. A number of measures of job satisfaction were constructed. The results of the analysis indicated that the sign of the racial differential in job satisfaction cannot be predicted a priori. Although blacks do earn lower full wages than whites and should be less satisfied, discrimination may have caused blacks to be satisfied with less. In the case of older men, this direct effect of race on job satisfaction is dominant and becomes increasingly important as times goes on. Tables. References. — Bartel, Ann P.; *Jrnl of Human Resources,* Spring 1981, 16(2): pp. 294-303. Avail. ABI 81-13676

Job satisfaction, Job attitudes, Blacks, Minorities, Statistical analysis, Measurement

Racial Differences in Job Satisfaction: Testing Four   (326)
Common Explanations

Various researchers have reported differential employee satisfaction by race. It is possible that documenting these differences may be less important than determining why they occur. However, little empirical work has been conducted to determine the causes for racial differences in employee's job satisfaction. It seems appropriate then to attempt to identify and measure structural, cultural, social and social psychological explanations for differential employee satisfaction by race.Data were gathered from 466 employees in 5 departments of an assembly and packaging plant located in the South. The following factors are included in regressions of employee satisfaction on race: 1. racial composition of the employees' work group and organization level, 2. the importance the employee places on interpersonal relations, on intrinsic rewards, and on extrinsic rewards, and 3. the employee's social integration and perceived relative deprivation. Measures of the dependent and mediating variables were obtained from the Michigan Organization Assessment Package. Race variables accounted for 21% of the variance in satisfaction exceeding that accounted for by the other factors. The other factors, however, accounted for only 4% of the variance in satisfaction beyond that accounted for by race. Other explanations must be examined to explain job satisfaction by race. Table. References. –Moch, Michael K.; *Jrnl of Applied Psychology,* Jun 1980, 65(3): pp. 299-306. Avail. ABI 80-12542

Job satisfaction, Races, Studies, Variables, Cultural, Factors, Statistical analysis

Ready, Set and No Place to Go (327)

A recently-completed survey of more than 1,300 M.I.T. graduates from the 1950s has revealed a surprising amount of dissatisfaction among mid-career, technically-trained employees at all levels of the corporate pyramid. The survey reveals that this dissatisfaction can be traced to a common factor: the failure of most firms to recognize that despite their common educational backgrounds, these technically-trained employees are not alike. These employees are treated as if they all have the same aspirations and the same attitudes toward their work. If companies want to overcome the dissatisfaction that appears to be increasing among such technically trained employees, organizations must design job assignments that accommodate varying work orientations as well as the individual employee's particular talents. There are 6 kinds of potential to be considered: 1. high-potential, technically-oriented employees, 2. average-potential, technically-oriented employees, 3. high-potential, people-oriented employees, 4. average-potential, people-oriented employees, 5. high-potential, non-work oriented employees, and 6. average potential, nonwork oriented employees. Each type must be handled in terms specific to that description. Finally, in approaching the problems of job satisfaction among mid-career, technically trained employees, it is important to remember that mid-career is not an isolated point in an individual's life. References. –Bailyn, Lotte; *Wharton Magazine,* Winter 1980, 4(2): pp. 58-63. Avail. ABI 80-02847

Technical, Managers, Executives, Engineers, Career advancement, Career development planning, Surveys, Job attitudes, Job satisfaction, Mobility, Incentives, Job enrichment, Studies

Regional Differences in Attitudes Toward Work (328)

Data from 7 US national surveys taken between 1955 and 1980 were recently analyzed, as were responses to 5 surveys conducted by the National Opinion Research Center, to judge whether there was any basis in fact to the stereotype of the Southern worker as being lazy and shiftless. The questions asked of respondents dealt with: 1. job satisfaction, 2. importance of luck versus hard work, 3. desire to work versus need for money, and 4. the importance of various job characteristics. The responses of southern workers and workers from other regions were subjected to multiple classification analysis to do away with the effects of regional differences in sex, occupation, race, and age. Little difference was found in the responses of Southern and non-Southern workers, and what variances were found tended to refute the stereotype. In fact, questions testing the desire to work and the importance of hard work received a slightly larger proportion of work-oriented responses from Southern workers. Southerners gave more positive responses to questions on work enjoyment and job satisfaction. Tables. References. – Glenn, Norval D. and Weaver, Charles N.; *Texas Business Review,* Nov/Dec 1982, 56(6): pp. 263-266. Avail. ABI 83-01006

Regional, Differences, Workers, Job attitudes, Stereotypes, Surveys, Job satisfaction

The Relationship Between Work and Nonwork   (329)
Domains: A Review of Empirical Research

The relationship between work and nonwork aspects of life is not well understood despite extensive study and debate. With some important exceptions, the interdependence of work and society has received little attention in modern times. Conceptualization of the relationship between work and nonwork domains of life begins with separating each of the domains into 2 components: 1. objective aspects or structures, and 2. subjective aspects or reactions. Relationships between components within each domain, between reactions in the 2 domains, and between structures in the 2 domains have been extensively studied and documented. Focus is directed at the relationships which have received less attention, those between social structures in one domain and individual reactions in another. Studies of the relationship between work structure and nonwork reactions have covered overall life satisfaction, work as a central life interest, social participation, political behavior, leisure behavior, and family characteristics. Studies of nonwork structures and reaction to work have covered workers' demographic characteristics, community characteristics, state of health, and participation in nonwork activity. Correlation was found in both sets of relationships, but the direction of causality is unclear and it could not be determined whether the influence was direct or indirect. Chart. References. –Near, Janet P.; Rice, Robert W.; and Hunt, Raymond G.; *Academy of Mgmt Review,* Jul 1980, 5(3): pp. 415-429. Avail. ABI 80-16516

Working conditions, Living conditions, Correlations, Behavior, Attitudes, Job attitudes, Life, Satisfaction, Job satisfaction, Demography, Family, Variables, Work, Leisure time

The Relationship of Values and Job Satisfaction: Do   (330)
Birds of a Feather Work Well Together?

It is not personality differences which stop or limit communication, but basic value differences. Research was conducted to ascertain the correlation between the way a subordinate's values match those of his or her superior and that subordinate's job satisfaction. Respondents were asked to rank items in 2 lists of values and then to rank adjectives describing job satisfaction. The assumption that a relatively close match between the values of the subordinate and the superior would produce higher job satisfaction on the part of the subordinate was not borne out. Several work groups, however, did show a high correlation between job satisfaction and either instrumental or terminal value match. Results suggested that compensation is not the only and perhaps not the most important factor in satisfaction on the job. Work content was shown to be unimportant in at least some firms. Whether a group was service- or production-oriented made little difference.

The amount of prestige associated with their jobs may be a factor in job satisfaction among supervisors. Charts. —Brown, Martha A.; *Personnel,* Nov/Dec 1980, 57(6): pp. 66-73. Avail. ABI 81-01763

Values, Job satisfaction, Communication, Superiors, Subordinates, Studies

Relationships Among Individual, Task Design, and (331) Leader Behavior Variables

The most widely accepted contemporary view on task design is Hackman and Oldham's job characteristics theory (1976). However, researchers are beginning to realize that additional variables must be considered when trying to explain the individual's work environment. Griffin (1979) has presented a model integrating individual, task design, and leader behavior variables into a single framework. An empirical test of this model is therefore appropriate. The model was examined for 171 employees of a large manufacturing firm. Correlational analyses found significant relationships among variables and facets of satisfaction, but not productivity. Cross-lagged correlational analysis also gave some support for the model in terms of both satisfaction and productivity. Further research would need to include a reformulation and refinement of the model, including: 1. The complex network of individual, task design, and leader behavior variables must be stated with more precision. 2. The exact linkages between variable combinations and facets of satisfaction, as well as other potential outcome variables, should be more completely developed and described. Chart. Tables. References. —Griffin, Ricky W.; *Academy of Mgmt Jrnl,* Dec 1980, 23(4): pp. 665-683. Avail. ABI 81-00755

Task, Design, Job, Characteristics, Leadership, Organizational behavior, Models, Statistical analysis, Job satisfaction, Productivity

Relationships of Personality to Perceptual and (332) Behavioral Responses in Stimulating and Nonstimulating Tasks

Recently, task design has been increasingly emphasized as a way to furnish positive task stimulation for workers. Agreement exists that not everyone reacts positively to the "enriched" tasks, but a considerable amount of disagreement exists over what these individual differences might be. An examination of introverted and extroverted individuals and individuals who have a high and a low degree of neuroticism as they performed stimulating or nonstimulating tasks or as they differed in their perceptions with respect to expectancy and motivating characteritics of objective tasks is worthwhile.A sample of 96 undergraduate students was used. All students took the Eysenck Personality Inventory and were categorized. Half were randomly assigned to task groups. The intent was to test the interaction effects of task stimulation and extroversion on worker satisfaction and performance. Further, the role of extroversion and neuroticism dimensions of personality on expectancy and task perceptions of workers was studied. In combination with other findings, the task-extroversion interaction hypothesis was supported for worker satisfaction, but not for performance.

Tables. References. —Kim, Jay S.; *Academy of Mgmt Jrnl,* Jun 1980, 23(2): pp. 307-319. Avail. ABI 80-12751

Personality, Job satisfaction, Performance, Task, Job, Design, Studies, Perceptions, Behavior, Statistical analysis

The Relative Contribution of Perceived Skill-Utilization   (333)
and Other Perceived Job Attributes to the Prediction of
Job Satisfaction: A Cross-Validation Study

The importance of skill-utilization for predicting job satisfaction has been underestimated or neglected in most job satisfaction research despite the early work of Kornhauser, who claimed that the main determinant of the mental health of North American industrial workers was the amount of opportunity they had to use their skills and abilities on their jobs. A cross-validation study was performed to examine the relative contribution of perceived skill-utilization and other job attributes to the prediction of job satisfaction. The subjects were 1383 persons currently employed in an Australian metropolitan area. Subjects completed questionnaires that measured job attributes, job satisfaction, and demographic and personal variables. A simple multiple regression analysis indicated that job satisfaction was significantly predicted by the perceived job attributes of skill-utilization, influence, variety, pressure, and interaction. Skill-utilization was found to be the strongest predictor of job satisfaction. Tables. Equations. References. —O'Brien, Gordon E.; *Human Relations,* Mar 1982, 35(3): pp. 219-237. Avail. ABI 82-12668

Job satisfaction, Skills, Australia, Surveys, Regression analysis, Samples, Job, Characteristics, Organizational behavior

The Role of Environmental and Behavioral Uncertainty   (334)
as a Mediator of Situation-Performance Relationships

Some of the most important elements that have been suggested to affect an individual's job satisfaction and job performance are the uncertainties one feels about the surrounding environment and the uncertainties about the consequences of his behavior. Further, there are at least 3 primary sets of variables that affect performance and satisfaction for which a reduction in uncertainty may function as a mediating psychological explanation. In a simulated job environment, the causes and consequences of environmental and behavioral uncertainties were studied. Employees worked with a structuring and considerate leader on a structured or unstructured task and with or without a goal. The structuring leader and structured task resulted in more certainty than the considerate leader or the unstructured task. Goal setting had no effect, and the same independent variables and increased certainty resulted in higher performance. It was illustrated that the effects of task structure and leadership style on unertainty can be separated. Finally, the structure of the task has its primary effect on environmental uncertainty, and the structuring of the leader has its significant impact on behavioral uncertainty. Figures. Tables. Graph. References. —Weed, Stanley E. and Mitchell, Terence R.; *Academy of Mgmt Jrnl,* Mar 1980, 23(1): pp. 38-60. Avail. ABI 80-06278

Job, Environment, Behavior, Uncertainty, Performance, Job satisfaction, Job attitudes, Studies, Employees, Goals, Goal setting, Task, Structure

Role Perceptions, Satisfaction, and Performance: (335) Moderating Effects of Self-Esteem and Organizational Level

A study was conducted among 161 hospital professional and support personnel to examine what effects a person's self-esteem and position level in an organization might have on role ambiguity and role conflict. Both ambiguity and conflict tend to lessen employee satisfaction and performance, but high self-esteem tends to mitigate the undesirable effects of role ambiguity on job satisfaction. High self-esteem also ameliorates the effects of role conflict on job performance for employees at lower levels of an organization. The study findings support the theory that ability (whether objectively defined as work experience or subjectively defined as self-esteem) is important for employees facing role ambiguity or conflict problems. It is suggested that enhancing an employee's self-esteem, usually a long-term process, does contribute to a person's sense of personal worth and competence. Tables. References. —Mossholder, Keven W.; Bedeian, Arthur G.; and Armenakis, Achilles A.; *Organizational Behavior & Human Performance,* Oct 1981, 28(2): pp. 224-234. Avail. ABI 81-26277

Organizational behavior, Roles, Perceptions, Conflict, Job satisfaction, Performance, Self image, Organizational, Level

Self-Esteem and Causal Attributions for Job (336) Satisfaction and Dissatisfaction

Drawing from the Graduate School of Business Administration at Tel Aviv University, 110 male students were selected as subjects. A Hebrew translation of the Coopersmith Self-Esteem Inventory was used to measure self-esteem. The purpose of the examination was to apply attribution theory to predict how individuals explain the causal factors that produce their job satisfaction and dissatisfaction. Previous research has indicated that incidents of job dissatisfaction are more likely to result from external agents than are incidents of job satisfaction. It was hypothesized, following balance theory, that self-esteem would interact with whether an incident was one of satisfaction or dissatisfaction in determining the extent to which causality of the incident was attributed to the self or to outside forces. Repeated-measures analysis of variance suggested that the hypothesized interaction between satisfaction-dissatisfaction and self-esteem was significant.In one important aspect, the findings are seemingly at variance with the theory of self-consistency motivation. The finding that the high self-esteem and low self-esteem subjects were significantly more internal in their attributions for satisfying than for dissatisfying incidents is contrary to the presumption that dissatisfaction is more self-consistent than satisfaction for this group and that attributions should, therefore, have been more internal. Tables. References. —Adler, Seymour; *Jrnl of Applied Psychology,* Jun 1980, 65(3): pp. 327-332. Avail. ABI 80-12545

Job satisfaction, Self image, Variance analysis, Causality, Motivation, Studies

Structural Relationships, Job Characteristics, and (337)
Worker Satisfaction and Performance

Historically, most approaches to problems associated with over-simplified, boring work have focused exclusively on the worker and work content. The structural organization has been ignored by the "one person-one task" approach to job redesign. Research was conducted into the role of job characteristics as mediating variables between the organization's structural context and the attitudes and behaviors of its individual employees. Three structural relationships of the network of task positions within the organization were investigated: 1. the task position's centrality, 2. the degree to which it is critical to the workflow, and 3. the transaction alternatives available to a task position. Results indicated significant relationships between these measures and job characteristics. The hypothesis that job characteristics mediate the relationship between structure and individual responses was proven. Tables. References. —Brass, Daniel J.; *Administrative Science Qtrly*, Sep 1981, 26(3): pp. 331-348. Avail. ABI 81-21433

Job, Characteristics, Job satisfaction, Performance, Organizational, Structure, Job attitudes, Task, Organizational behavior

Taking a New Route to Job Satisfaction (338)

The recession, which led General Motors Corporation (GM) to lay off 138, 000 workers, made it difficult to improve the quality of employees' jobs and keep them interested in their work. According to GM, the Quality of Work Life (QWL) program has immunity to the traumas of the recession. The QWL process uses teams of employees who try to solve problems themselves and has the intention of letting hourly workers make a real contribution to the organization and to the development of their own jobs. The QWL program has made employee transfers within plants easier after the layoffs. The United Auto Workers (UAW) is committed to the QWL concept and actually urged its introduction during the 1973 contract negotiations. Every GM plant has been exposed to the QWL process in the last decade. GM's top executives support each plant in its work toward QWL, but do not try to impose the process. Some new GM plants are built around the QWL process. —Hill, Roy; *International Mgmt (UK)*, Sep 1980, 35(9): pp. 49-51. Avail. ABI 80-20389

General Motors-Detroit, Case studies, Job satisfaction, Quality of work, Life, Job attitudes, Labor relations

Using the Life Cycle to Anticipate Satisfaction at Work (339)

It is hypothesized that there are important nonlinear life cycle influences upon job and organizational satisfaction. Five common life-cycle stages are identified from the literature: 1. reality shock, 2. socialization and growth, 3. mid-career crisis, 4. acceptance, and 5. preretirement. The first, third, and fifth stages are expected to reveal declines in job and organizational satisfaction due to personal and job-related disappointments and crises that typically occur during these periods of life. The second and fourth stages are expected to reveal increases in satisfaction due to the pleasant life experiences that frequently occur during these periods. Cross-sectional rather than longitudinal data are utilized, necessitating controls for time-dependent variables. The tentative findings indicate that a close match appears to exist between the hedonic states suggested by the life-cycle literature and the levels of satisfaction for various age groups. Equation. Graph. Tables. References. –Kets de Vries, Manfred F. R.; Miller, Danny; Toulouse, Jean-Marie; Friesen, Peter H.; Boisvert, Maurice; and Theriault, Roland; *Jrnl of Forecasting (UK),* Apr-Jun 1984, 3(2): pp. 161-172. Avail. ABI 84-23774

Life, Cycles, Job satisfaction, Studies, Hypotheses, Regression analysis

Using the People/Problem Management Dichotomy (340)

One cause of dissatisfaction in the workplace is employees' preference for people management and problem-solving activities. While most organizations assess some combination of an individual's knowledge, skills, and experience, it is difficult to pinpoint significant attitudes and values. Being able to classify jobs in a way that highlights characteristics not usually included in job descriptions would be valuable. Research has shown that employees whose job content fits with their preferences are more satisfied and committed to their work than employees whose preferences do not fit. Those whose jobs had fewer people management activities than they desired were the least satisfied with their jobs. Employees who experience more people management than they prefer do not express dissatisfaction equal to that expressed by employees with less people management than they prefer. Effective organizational career development must provide opportunities for employees to hold jobs which fit with their preferences for people management and problem management activities. Charts. References. – Gordon, Judith R.; *Personnel Administrator,* Mar 1983, 28(3): pp. 51-57. Avail. ABI 83-08359

Recruitment, Hiring, Personnel selection, Criteria, Employee turnover, Job descriptions, Job classification, Problem solving, Promotions (MAN), Management development, Job satisfaction

Why John and Mary Won't Work (341)

Social scientists and bosses indicate that worker attitudes and performance have seriously deteriorated over the past decade. For some researchers, the problem is that changes in the composition of the work force and the values that Americans bring to the work place have resulted in a new work contract. These values and beliefs are so significantly different from the previous perspective that they promise to transform the character of work in America in the '80s. The unwritten contract that exists in workers' minds asks for new answers to 2 questions: 1. What does my job require me to do? 2. What is my reward for doing that job well? Their own responses suggest that they are motivated to work hard when: 1. Their tasks are interesting, varied, and involve some challenge, learning, and responsibility. 2. They have enough information, support, and authority to accomplish the job. 3. They help make decisions that affect their jobs because bosses recognize that they know their jobs best. 4. They understand how their own work fits into the larger picture. 5. They see rewards linked to performance and understand how employees move forward. 6. They are treated as individuals who are personally important to the organization. –Frederick, Sharon; *Inc.,* Apr 1981, 3(4): pp. 70-78. Avail. ABI 81-08843

Job satisfaction, Job attitudes, Work ethic, Changes

Worker Alienation as a Moderator of the Job Quality-   (342)
Job Satisfaction Relationship: The Case of Racial
Differences

The question of whether individual differences variables moderate the relationships between job attributes and employee attitudinal reactions has resulted in a significant amount of empirical research. To pursue the issue, 2,569 full-time male workers were surveyed by the National Opinion Research Center as part of the General Social Surveys conducted during 1972 to 1977. Results reaffirmed previously established significant main effect differences between blacks and whites on measures of job satisfaction, occupational attainment, and educational attainment. In addition, there were found to be significant differences in the manner in which these variables are related for blacks relative to whites. Inversely directed relationships between age and job prestige and between education and job satisfaction were suggestive of the operation of different labor market processes for blacks and whites. Evidence, therefore, was found that the moderator hypothesis is descriptively valid, but additional complexities must be considered before firm conclusions are drawn. Table. Graph. References. —Vecchio, Robert P.; *Academy of Mgmt Jrnl,* Sep 1980, 23(3): pp. 479-486. Avail. ABI 80-19895

Races, Workers, Alienation, Quality of work, Job satisfaction, Studies

OCCUPATION-SPECIFIC STUDIES

ACPA Members Rate Jobs High in Motivation   (343)

A recent survey of the Association of Computer Programmers and Analysts (ACPA) has revealed 3 differences from the national norm for personnel who are not professional society members: 1. ACPA members perceive their jobs containing more key components for motivation. 2. They participate more in goal setting. 3. Their need for social interaction is lower. ACPA members placed more importance than the national norm on core job dimensions: 1. skill variety, 2. task identity, 3. task significance, 4. autonomy, and 5. feedback.Programmer/analysts appear to have a greater need for growth than other professionals such as engineers and accountants, and this group tends to experience feedback problems. While ACPA members revealed a low need for social interaction, this condition would not affect a person in a rather cloistered job. But this attitude may be a prime cause for feedback problems as it would interfere with interface among other individuals performing their jobs in close proximity. The results of the survey make it clear that the special needs of computer personnel necessitate suitable management approaches that differ from those accorded other company employees. Table. Graph. —Couger, J. Daniel; *Computerworld,* Dec. 3, 1979, 13(49): pp. 31-32. Avail. ABI 80-00829

Surveys, Data processing, Personnel, Motivation, Needs, Job satisfaction

Admen Look at Both Sides   (344)

Business-to-business advertising is more stable and less glamorous than consumer advertising, but the job satisfactions and opportunities are just as great. There are trend setters in industrial advertising which are comparable to highly visible consumer advertising; the current trend setters are electronics accounts. There are numerous restrictions on consumer advertising, such as approval committees, which are absent in industrial advertising, leading perhaps to greater creativity in the industrial field. Consumer advertising using multimedia campaigns unquestionably has a greater budget than industrial advertising although industrial companies often have the higher profit ratios. Consumer advertising is generally better paying than industrial advertising and is usually more fun than trade advertising, according to Frank Scott at Warr, Foote & Rose, who handles both types of advertising for Picnic Foods. Some advantages in having industrial clients are: 1. good working relationships, 2. tendency to remain with the same agency, and 3. potentially higher ethical standards. The speed of measuring results is a big advantage of consumer advertising. –Holland, Brenda; *Advertising Age,* Jun 8, 1981, 52(24): pp. S-12,S-15. Avail. ABI 81-14081

Business, Industrial, Advertising, Careers, Job satisfaction

Antecedents of Employee Satisfaction in a Hospital (345) Environment

Employee satisfaction in hospitals relates closely to job design and has a significant impact on turnover, productivity, and absence. Contemporary job enrichment and job redesign efforts are directed at giving the worker more responsibility, making the work intrinsically worthwhile, and providing workers with feedback.One recent study of hospital personnel revealed that work satisfaction and job scope, or job characteristics, were positively related, particularly at higher occupational levels. In redesigning jobs, a careful diagnosis and the use of a theory as a guide are crucial. How job changes can be integrated into the total organization, whether the people whose jobs will change are ready for the change, and the receptivity of the organizational climate to the change, must be considered. In implementing the changes, 3 factors help assure success: 1. commitment of management and unions to the changes, 2. a continuing evaluation of the project, and 3. anticipating potential problems. Graphs. Table. References. –Bechtold, Stephen E.; Szilagyi, Andrew D.; and Sims, Henry P.; *Health Care Mgmt Review,* Winter 1980, 5(1): pp. 77-88. Avail. ABI 80-04725

Hospitals, Job satisfaction, Studies, Job, Design, Job descriptions, Characteristics

Coal Industry Resurgence Attracts Variety of New (346) Workers

The coal industry is attracting workers who are younger and have more years of education. Mining companies report no shortage of job applicants, though mining is one of the most hazardous occupations in the US. Survey evidence and results of interviews with coal mine company officials indicate: 1. Miners fared much better than other blue-collar workers in a sample of occupations focusing on average job stress. 2. Interviews with coal miners report a high incidence of job satisfaction. 3. High salary level was most frequently cited as the major consideration in the decision to work in coal mining, according to the results of a survey of United Mine Workers of America members. The next largest group stated that enjoyment of coal mining was the reason for their decision. More women are also being employed by the coal mining industry. Employment growth is expected, in the coming decade, for the bituminous coal industry. There should be no significant problems in recruiting workers. However, shortages may result in some areas and in some occupations, due to the uneven geographic pattern of growth for the coal industry. Tables. References. —Wool, Harold; *Monthly Labor Review,* Jan 1981, 104(1): pp. 3-8. Avail. ABI 81-04288

> Coal industry, Coal mining, Employment, Labor force, Job satisfaction, Wages & salaries, Education, Women, Statistical data, Growth industries

Conflict, Clarity, Tension, and Satisfaction in Chain (347) Store Manager Roles

Role conflict, role clarity, job tension, and job satisfaction are very important dimensions of occupational roles. They have significant implications for the performance of individuals and can also have much impact on the operational effectiveness of organizations. A study was made of 179 retail store managers on these 4 role dimensions. The managers were surveyed via questionnaires. The results of the study suggested that corporate executives would find it worthwhile to consider ways to decrease role conflict, increase role clarity, and decrease job tension. Achieving these 3 objectives would likely help stabilize the fairly high level of job satisfaction found among the managers. Also, many of the managers seemed to believe they were overqualified for their positions. Thus, management should determine whether promotion opportunities are available for these people. Other considerations for management include: 1. determining the adequacy of resources and materials levels supplied to their store managers, 2. improving communications, and 3. instituting a management-by-objectives system. Diagram. Tables. References. —Kelly, J. Patrick; Gable, Myron; and Hise, Richard T.; *Jrnl of Retailing,* Spring 1981, 57(1): pp. 27-42. Avail. ABI 81-22054

> Chain stores, Managers, Roles, Conflict, Job, Tension, Job satisfaction, Studies, Correlation analysis, Organizational behavior

Demographics, Job Satisfaction, and Propensity to (348) Leave of Industrial Salesmen

This study assessed the effects of demographic variables on job satisfaction among salespersons and on salespersons' turnover intentions. Salespersons from a large pharmaceutical firm were surveyed about their satisfaction with their jobs, co-workers, supervisors, pay, promotion and development potential, and customers. Respondents also completed a questionnaire listing age, tenure with the company, income, educational level, and turnover intention. All aspects of job satisfaction were found to be more significant determinants of turnover intention than were demographic characteristics. Turnover intention was negatively related to income, age, and tenure, and positively related to education. Age and tenure were not significant determinants of job satisfaction. However, education had a strong negative association to satisfaction with the job itself and to advancement potential. Income was positively related to all aspects of job satisfaction, except for promotion and development potential. Chart. Tables. References. —

Parasuraman, A. and Futrell, Charles M.; *Jrnl of Business Research,* Mar 1983, 11(1): pp. 33-48. Avail. ABI 83-10715

Personal selling, Salespeople, Employee turnover, Demography, Job satisfaction, Studies

An Empirical Test of Linkages Proposed in the Walker, (349) Churchill, and Ford Model of Sales Force Motivation and Performance

Walker, Churchill, and Ford proposed a model of sales motivation and performance that hypothesized a negative relationship between a salesman's perceived role ambiguity and closeness of supervision, participation in decision-making, selling experience, and both extrinsic and intrinsic job satisfaction. This study extended that research by empirically testing causes and consequences of role ambiguity as influenced by those factors. Data were obtained from 127 questionnaires completed by industrial sales personnel. Responses were examined using a path analysis and revealed a significant negative relationship between participation and closeness of supervision and role ambiguity. The Walker et. al. hypothesis negatively linking experience with role ambiguity was not supported. A positive relationship was found between extrinsic job satisfaction and closeness of supervision, with this factor having only an indirect positive effect on intrinsic rewards. A salesman's intrinsic, but not extrinsic, satisfaction was found to be significantly related to his involvement in decision-making. Tables. Charts. References. Appendix. —Teas, R. Kenneth; *Jrnl of the Academy of Marketing Science,* Winter/Spring 1980, 8(1) ,2: pp. 58-72. Avail. ABI 80-18035

Salespeople, Sales, Job satisfaction, Job attitudes, Roles, Studies, Employee problems, Behavior, Supervision, Personal selling, Performance, Performance evaluation, Motivation, Estimating techniques, Perceptions

Experience Is the Nation's Wealth (350)

Rolls-Royce is being looked upon by other UK manufacturers as taking the lead in setting a new pattern of shop floor relationships. To tap the vast experience and reserve of workers' skills, Quality Control Groups were brought into operation 2 years ago to help in restoring the "old fashioned" spirit of pride. These groups learned the principles of problem analysis using logic and pre-control charts, cause-and-effect diagrams, and capability charts. The groups help to secure everyone's future by both self-improvement and product-improvement and lead to a greater sense of job satisfaction.In bridging the gap between workers and supervision, the company benefits in meeting the product design specification at minimum cost to the company and the customer. The workers' desire to be associated with group application to problem solving has eliminated the myth that the shop floor is not interested in improving efficiency, productivity, and cost. —Rooney, J. P.; *Management Accounting (UK),* Jun 1980, 58(6): pp. 19-20. Avail. ABI 80-13035

Rolls Royce-UK, Quality control, Groups, Job satisfaction, Human relations

Exploring Operator Satisfaction (351)

A survey of word processing (WP) operators was conducted to explore their levels of job satisfaction and to determine the relevance of human factors in

WP systems. Sixty-one WP operators in 22 locations in Dallas and Houston, Texas, took part in the survey. The operators had worked with the system for at least 6 months, and the system had been in operation for at least a year. The operators' levels of job satisfaction were measured by personnel and environmental factors. It was found that turnover was directly related to the level of the operators' job satisfaction, and the average turnover rate in organizations in which the "more-satisfied" operators worked was 26%. Further, there was a strong correlation between the level of operator job satisfaction and their amount of personal contact with system users. The use of slack time was discovered to affect the job satisfaction of those surveyed, with those operators participating in self-improvement activities during slack time reporting higher levels of job satisfaction than those who did not. Interestingly, the operators' yearly salary levels had no impact on job satisfaction. —Mitchell, Robert B.; *Management World,* Apr 1982, 11(4): pp. 12-13. Avail. ABI 82-12133

Word processing, Operators, Job satisfaction, Factors, Surveys

A Facet Structure for Nurses' Evaluations of Ward Design (352)

Although difficult to quantify in service professions, the physical environment of the workplace contributes to worker satisfaction. Several facets of the physical layout of a hospital ward as related to nurses' job satisfaction were introduced as criteria for evaluation of wards. A model was developed and nurses throughout England were given a questionnaire generated from the model. Levels of patient-nurse interaction as well as the object of nurses' interaction and whether the object necessitates direct or indirect patient care were measured. Findings showed that nurses wanted to work in a physical setting that allowed them to care for patients at bedside and allowed them to observe the patients. Since design of a ward can be a job satisfier for nurses, and since nurses want to care for patients, then in the interest of patients' care, nurses should be consulted during the stages in which the ward floor plan is being designed. Diagrams. Tables. References. —Kenny, Cheryl and Canter, David; *Jrnl of Occupational Psychology (UK),* 1981, 54(2): pp. 93-108. Avail. ABI 81-15940

Design, Work environment, Effects, Job satisfaction, Studies, Nurses, Hospitals, Models, Evaluation

Factors Contributing to the Performance and Satisfaction of Branch Managers (353)

A study was undertaken of the factors involved in the performance and satisfaction of branch managers in the financial services industry. The managers used in the study were selected from 2 financial institutions in Arizona. Data were collected by using a questionnaire, and analysis was performed via 2 multiple regression models. The results indicated that satisfaction is significantly related to leadership style, internal locus of control, and mutually accepted and acceptable measures of performance. Performance is related significantly to leadership style, gender, and the financial institution itself. A statistically significant correlation exists between performance and satisfaction, but it is too weak to treat them as being directly related. Strengthening the relationship between the branch manager and the regional manager and having a well-defined performance-based management system contributes to performance and satisfaction. Tables. References. —Euske, Kenneth J.; Jackson, Donald W., Jr.; and Reif, William E.; *Arizona Business,* Feb/Mar 1982, 29(2): pp. 3-7. Avail. ABI 82-10616

Financial services, Branch, Managers, Studies, Job satisfaction, Performance evaluation

The Financial Institution Marketer (354)

Marketing has become an increasingly important function in commercial banks and thrift institutions. However, little has been written about the financial services marketer. A study has been conducted of the job perceptions of the members of the Bank Marketing Association (BMA) and the Savings Institutions Marketing Society of America (SIMSA). Data were gathered by means of a questionnaire. The study indicates that most members considered seeing a particular program through to its successful completion as the most satisfying aspect of the job. On the other hand, the perception of lack of top management support for the marketing function was most often named as the most frustrating aspect of the job. Being in marketing was perceived as helping upward mobility by increasing exposure to other personnel. In the 1980s, the marketing function will be very important. In order to attract qualified people, these individuals must feel they have a future and will be heard. Tables. —Lingren, John H., Jr.; Berry, Leonard L.; and Kehoe, William J.; *Jrnl of Retail Banking,* Sep 1980, 2(3): pp. 39-45. Avail. ABI 80-22489

Financial institutions, Marketing, Bank marketing, Personnel, Surveys, Profiles, Job satisfaction, Career advancement

How Bank Marketers View Their Jobs (355)

Although bank marketing has been a frequent topic, there has been little published research on the bank marketer. In order to answer questions about the satisfactions of the bank marketing job, the frustrations of the job, and marketing in relation to upward mobility within the bank, a study was conducted by means of a questionnaire sent to a random sample of members of the Bank Marketing Association (BMA). It was indicated that satisfactions of the job include: 1. results orientation aspects, 2. involvement with other bank personnel, and 3. creative aspects of the job. Frustration was found to stem from: 1. lack of management support, 2. lack of interdepartmental cooperation, and 3. short deadlines and jumping from project to project. In many banks, upward mobility is hampered if the marketing person has no experience in other bank functions, most notably, commercial lending. In the 1980s it will be important for a bank to have good people in the marketing area. Attracting good people to marketing requires a bank climate in which marketing work does not hinder upward mobility. Charts. —Berry, Leonard L.; Kehoe, William J.; and Lindgren, John H., Jr., *Bankers Magazine,* Nov/Dec 1980, 163(6): pp. 35-40. Avail. ABI 81-01415

Bank marketing, Studies, Job satisfaction, Job attitudes, Mobility, Barriers, Perceptions, Qualifications, Bank management, Implications

Job Satisfaction of Physical Therapists (356)

Studies of hospital and health care employees have shown some correlation between job satisfaction and productivity. To measure job satisfaction among physical therapists, a survey was made of a sample of physical therapists in an eastern US metropolitan area. Data were collected from 225 physical therapists via a revised Porter questionnaire that covered: 1. background and demographic information, 2. job characteristics, and 3. level of job characteristic importance. The survey instrument was based on Maslow's hierarchy of needs. The respondents reported uniformly high satisfaction in their work. Physical therapists tend to be strongly self-motivated and less concerned with job status and the esteem of others. Employee job satisfaction benefits the employer as it results in lowered absenteeism and turnover, which in turn reduce recruitment, selection, placement, and training costs. The findings implied that work that combines significant skill requirements with autonomy, accountability, and reasonable income will likely produce high job satisfaction for those who perform it. Charts. References. —Atwood, Carol Ann and Woolf, Donald Austin; *Health Care Mgmt Review,* Winter 1982, 7(1): pp. 81-86. Avail. ABI 82-06282

Job satisfaction, Therapy, Surveys, Health care industry

The Job Satisfaction of Higher Level Employees in (357) Large Certified Public Accounting Firms

This research examines the differences between audit, tax, and management services (MS) specialists holding positions of Senior or higher and employed by large certified public accounting (CPA) firms. Three dimensions are examined: 1. job satisfaction, 2. personal characteristics, and 3. job features. Using multivariate analysis, no statistically significant differences were found on the 3 dimensions between audit and tax specialists, but differences were found between MS specialists and the audit and tax specialists as a combined group. MS specialists are currently paid more than their contemporaries in audit and tax; therefore, they are more satisfied with their pay, even though their promotional opportunities are more limited than audit and tax specialists. MS specialists scored higher on the personal characteristic dimension, sociability/ascendancy, than did audit or tax specialists. The second part of the study, using personal characteristics and job features as independent variables in multiple regression, was moderately successful in predicting the job satisfaction of audit and tax specialists, but predicting the level of job satisfaction of MS specialists was unsuccessful. Tables. References. —Benke, Ralph L., Jr. and Rhode, John Grant; *Accounting, Organizations & Society (UK),* 1980, 5(2): pp. 187-201. Avail. ABI 80-18621

CPAs, Accounting firms, Job satisfaction, Job attitudes, Management services (DP), Personnel, Characteristics, Statistical analysis, Studies

Job Satisfaction Among a Select Group of Coal Miners (358)

Job satisfaction among a particular group of coal miners was studied. A sample of 132 trainees who were enrolled in a 10-week West Virginia University Mining extension program was chosen. In 1973, the trainees completed an extensive questionnaire dealing with personal characteristics, educational background, job history, and attitudes towards their jobs.The statistical technique used is discriminant analysis, which allows the investigation of the direction and magnitude of influence of independent variables having a hypothesized relationship to job satisfaction. Five variables are concerned with personal background and job history, 6 are concerned with specific dimensions of the job, 11 are concerned with the flow of information and communication, and the final set of 13 are concerned with health and safety attitudes. The information and communication variables were particularly valuable, and concern of the boss and belief that mining has a high degree of telling others what to do were also effective variables. Overall, the discriminant model was very successful, predicting almost 95% of the cases correctly. References. Tables. Appendix −Palomba, Catherine A. and Palomba, Neil A.; *Energy Communications,* 1980, 6(1): pp. 53-71. Avail. ABI 80-15374

Job satisfaction, Coal mining, Employees, Discriminant analysis, Studies, Models, Variables, Statistical analysis, Job attitudes

Job Satisfaction Among Urban Planners: A Discriminant Analysis (359)

Since the planning occupation can be seen as one of extreme importance in terms of directing the future of American cities, serious research focusing upon factors affecting planners' potential societal contribution is warranted. From a cursory review of planning literature, it can be concluded that planners committed to the traditional model of the planning process, one free from the restraints of politics yet founded in community participation and oriented toward plan implementation as proof of societal efficacy, invite frustration. The study population includes planning professionals who work for the city planning departments of Los Angeles, San Francisco, and San Diego. A mail-out questionnaire was used to obtain data, and the data are analyzed through the use of discriminant analysis. Ten variables were found to be important in predicting the willingness of planners to select urban planning as a career choice if they had the chance to choose a career again. These factors ranged from opportunities to use abilities to job security. Of the extrinsic factors, an absence of leadership and associated poor delegation of responsibility proved to be critical factors of satisfaction. Tables. References. −Rea, Louis M.; Clapp, James A.; and Corso, Anthony W.; *Midwest Review of Public Administration,* Mar 1980, 14(1): pp. 15-28. Avail. ABI 80-20905

Job satisfaction, Urban planning, Urban, Planners, Discriminant analysis, Research, Design, Data analysis

Job Satisfaction and the Systems Professional (360)

A systems staff is composed of transient systems personnel that use the system job as a stepping stone to management or other careers, unmotivated personnel, and dedicated-to-professional systems personnel. The dedicated systems personnel represent professionals who want to develop, but do not care for a management position. This special group is important for any organization and for the continuance of the profession.In order to avoid losing these dedicated professionals, organizations must make a special effort to assist them in becoming very good specialists in their area of interests. Once their goal is achieved, they should be promoted to a position of inside consultant rather than given a management position. The professional should be encouraged to interact within his profession and to do his own applied research. If organizations become more knowledgeable about the things that motivate the individual systems person, they will see more dedicated systems professional and fewer transients within their firms. Graph. Charts. References. —Tomeski, Edward Alexander and Sadek, Konrad E.; *Jrnl of Systems Mgmt,* Jun 1980, 31(6): pp. 6-10. Avail. ABI 80-13048

Professional, Systems management, Personnel, Job satisfaction, Career advancement, Promotions (MAN), Career development planning

Leader Behavior in a Police Organization Revisited (361)

An attempt is made to extend prior research on the nature of the police officer's role by assessing the influence of police leader behavior under different conditions of task structure in the context of a panel design. These hypotheses were tested: 1. For the aggregate sample, role clarification behaviors exhibited by leaders will be positively related to job satisfaction of subordinates and to favorability of their attitudes toward the citizenry. 2. When skill variety is perceived to be relatively high, perceived role clarification behaviors will seem causally related to job satisfaction and police attitudes towards citizens. 3. For the aggregate sample, perceived skill variety will be positively related to job satisfaction and to favorability of attitudes toward the citizenry. It is also predicted that job longevity will moderate the relationships between skill variety and police responses. Only limited support is provided for the hypothesis that leader role clarification behaviors may be positively linked with job satisfaction and favorability of attitudes toward citizenry. Moreover, while static correlations of perceived skill variety to job satisfaction were significantly positive for the aggregate sample, neither the path coefficient relating skill variety to job satisfaction nor any of the relationships of skill variety to attitudes toward citizenry were significant. Hypotheses regarding the moderating roles of skill variety and job longevity were unvaryingly disproved. Charts. References. —Brief, Arthur P.; Aldag, Ramon J.; Russell, Craig J.; and Rude, Dale E.; *Human Relations,* Dec 1981, 34(12): pp. 1037-1051. Avail. ABI 82-02781

Police, Officers, Leadership, Roles, Behavior, Perceptions, Skills, Subordinates, Job satisfaction, Attitudes, Citizens, Organization theory, Correlation analysis, Organizational behavior

Looking at the Age of Salespersons (362)

Salespersons were segmented into age groups in order to identify and measure their attitudes and how they perceive their self-development opportunities. The major proposition of the investigation was that attitudes toward self-development potential may be different among age groups. The method used was a Self-Development Opportunity Index, the scores of which were measured on a 5-point Likert-type scale. The youngest salespersons exhibit a high level of enthusiasm for their job situations. The attitudes of the 26-35 age group showed an erratic deviation. These persons are in the phase of life where financial interests are strong and expectations of rewards for performance are high. In the 36-45 age group, personal growth matters are valued above monetary matters. There is a shifting focus from extrinsic to intrinsic rewards. Older salespersons exhibit the lowest level of positive attitudes. Second careers and new directions of career growth may be in order for this group. Employees have changed and there is a challenge to management to deal with these changes. References. —Apostolides, Panos; *Jrnl of the Academy of Marketing Science,* Fall 1980, 8(4): pp. 322-331. Avail. ABI 81-06452

Salespeople, Job attitudes, Job satisfaction, Employee attitude (PER), Age, Groups, Behavior, Studies

Managing the Sales Manager (363)

The sales manager is the critical link between the salesforce and top management; the manager's primary task is to make the salesforce more profitable and productive. A study of 234 sales managers investigated the factors that bring them satisfaction or dissatisfaction. About 67% reported that they are motivated by a challenging job that provides a feeling of achievement or that earns recognition, advancement, or responsibility. A large number of sales managers pointed to growth and success of subordinates as a key factor in their own job satisfaction. The major factor causing dissatisfaction was found to be trouble with the boss in such areas as lack of appreciation and unfair evaluations. Other problem areas cited included unpopular company policies, poor relationships with subordinates, and lack of accomplishment of required goals. To maintain a staff of satisfied sales managers, management must see to it that the factors that cause them to be dissatisfied be minimized as much as possible. Table. —Stilwell, William P.; *Business Marketing,* Dec 1983, 68(12): pp. 37,40-41. Avail. ABI 84-01316

Sales managers, Surveys, Job satisfaction, Job attitudes, Salespeople

The Measurement of Shop-Floor Job Satisfaction: The (364)
Convergent and Discriminant Validity of the Worker
Opinion Survey

The Worker Opinion Survey (WOS) developed by Cross (1973) to measure shop-floor job satisfaction was examined to determine its validity in relation to the well-established Job Descriptive Index (JDI). Shop-floor workers of a medium-sized urban Australian factory were questioned about their attitudes towards: 1. promotion, 2. pay, 3. work content, 4. co-workers, 5. supervision, and 6. the organization as a whole. The data were converted to the 5 JDI subscales, and a multitrait-multimethod (MTMM) matrix, which relates the correlation coefficients of the various subscales to each other, was computed. Strong support for the WOS's convergent and discriminant validity in relation to the JDI was shown by each of the 4 analysis methods. The WOS has considerable appeal because: 1. it is level-specific to the shop-floor, 2. it contains 6 subscales, 3. each subscale has an equal number of items, and there are an equal number of positive and negative items, 4. the total number of items is relatively small (48), and 5. workers accept the instrument. Tables. References. —Soutar, Geoffrey N. and Weaver, John R.; *Jrnl of Occupational Psychology (UK),* 1982, 55(1): pp. 27-33. Avail. ABI 82-09982

Shop, Job satisfaction, Measurement, Statistical analysis, Studies, Blue collar workers

The Nature and Causes of Self-Esteem, Performance, (365) and Satisfaction in the Sales Force: A Structural Equation Approach

Salesmen experience 3 broad outcomes on the job: 1. self-esteem, 2. performance, and 3. job satisfaction. These job outcomes are hypothesized to be affected by job tension, role ambiguity, and motivation. Data were obtained from a sample of industrial salespeople operating in a market that has little product differentiation, no price competition, and in which products and customers' needs are technical and well defined. Performance was measured as the dollar volume of sales. Self-esteem was measured through 6 Likert items constructed for this particular study, and job satisfaction was measured with an 8-item Likert scale. The Job Related Tension Index and the Work Orientation Index were used to measure job tension and motivation. A structural equation methodology was used that explicitly models errors in equations and errors in variables. Role ambiguity appears to have the greatest adverse effect on self-esteem. Motivation has the strongest effect on job satisfaction. The data do not support the propositions relating job tension to job outcomes. Tables. Figure. Equations. References.
—Bagozzi, Richard P.; *Jrnl of Business (Univ of Chicago)*, Jul 1980, 53(3) (Part 1): pp. 315-331. Avail. ABI 81-06877

Salespeople, Behavior, Performance, Job satisfaction, Motivation, Job, Tension, Roles, Self, Attitudes, Studies

Performance and Satisfaction of Bank Managers (366)

Branch managers are important to the effective operation of a bank because they are frequently accountable for the branch's operating income, meeting targets for commercial loans, consumer loans and deposits, and meeting standards for number of calls, referrals, and bad debts. However, little is known about the elements that are associated with their performance and satisfaction. Thus, a study is made of branch managers and their supervisors and regional managers to determine factors that contribute to the satisfaction and performance of branch managers. Branch managers were selected from 2 publicly held banks in the Southwest; performance data were furnished by regional managers, and the balance of the data were furnished by the branch managers. It is shown that a supervisor's leadership style is an important variable influencing both job satisfaction and performance. To increase job satisfaction, regional managers should try to establish a work situation in which the performance measures used for evaluation are ones which branch managers would prefer to have used for that purpose. Finally, it can not be assumed that satisfaction inevitably leads to high performance, or that high performers are inevitably satisfied with their jobs. Charts. References. —Euske, Kenneth J. and Jackson, Donald W., Jr.; *Jrnl of Bank Research*, Spring 1980, 11(1): pp. 36-42. Avail. ABI 80-09373

Bank management, Managers, Studies, Performance, Job satisfaction, Branch banking, Leadership

Public Administrators: Some Determinants of Job **(367)**
Satisfaction

To determine a generalized view of the status of job satisfaction in public government, a national study was made in 1977. The study's sample was drawn from a random list of members of the American Society for Public Administration. Of 1500 questionnaires mailed, 805 usable responses were received. The Job Descriptive Index was selected to measure job satisfaction in relation to 5 components: 1. promotion, 2. pay, 3. supervision, 4. the work itself, and 5. co-workers.While the findings showed many similarities in job satisfaction and related variables in the private and public sectors, they indicated that interpersonal relations in the public sector could be improved. Female respondents were more unhappy with co-workers than males who were not very happy themselves. As more women enter the higher administrative levels and agencies formerly dominated by men, further tensions are indicated unless an attempt is made to help women see themselves in leadership capacities and to provide a more open and equitable opportunity structure. The study identified potential problem areas for government employees. Factors of job dissatisfaction may be more acute among the general population of public sector employees. Tables. References. —Lynn, Naomi B. and Vaden, Richard E.; *Bureaucrat,* Summer 1979, 8(2): pp. 66-71. Avail. ABI 80-05984

Public administration, Job satisfaction, Surveys, Studies, Government employees, Factors

Resolving Contradictions in Technical Careers or What **(368)**
If I Like Being an Engineer?

Interviews were conducted with technical professionals in 3 high-technology research and development laboratories, all of which were involved in shifting their emphasis from developing optimal products to improving sales. The process of adjusting to these new circumstances created 4 contradictions which interfered with the efficiency of work and career satisfaction. First, a conflict existed between the scientists' autonomy and control. Researchers could choose which problems to work on, but managers determined how those problems were worked on; the reverse should have held sway. A second contradiction came from the impulse to reorganize. In the face of new external constraints, organizations often removed common functions from divisions or project groups and centralized them into new departments, which caused frustration in all the labs studied. The third contradiction involved the fear of stagnating too long in one position and the fear that any change to a new position would create more problems than it would solve. In the last contradiction, it was found that effective work, which requires involvement and low visibility, is a less effective way of being promoted than is being visible to management. Temporary assignments and career rewards are 2 ways to better manage technical professionals. References. —Bailyn, Lotte; *Technology Review,* Nov/Dec 1982, 85(8): pp. 40-47. Avail. ABI 82-29938

Engineers, Technical, Careers, Scientists, Job satisfaction, Career advancement, Job status

Role Clarity and Job Satisfaction in Purchasing (369)

Among all business functions, the purchasing function is probably responsible for the largest segment of the value of products sold by US manufacturing firms. The effectiveness of this function depends on the people who perform and manage it. Research on employee effectiveness indicates that role clarity and job satisfaction are 2 factors that are particularly relevant for effective purchasing. Research was conducted to examine the role clarity and job satisfaction of purchasing professionals. Usable questionnaires were obtained from 267 purchasing professionals from a wide variety of industries. Both role clarity and job satisfaction were measured. The results indicated that while overall role clarity of purchasing employees was fairly high, such employees appeared to have a clearer grasp of self-perceived, informal role specifications than of formally stated policies. The overall job satisfaction of people in the purchasing profession also seemed quite high. Results showed that the number of employees in the purchasing department and the number of product categories bought were associated significantly with overall role clarity. Tables. References. – Parasuraman, A.; *Jrnl of Purchasing & Materials Mgmt,* Fall 1981, 17(3): pp. 2-7. Avail. ABI 82-10137

Purchasing, Job satisfaction, Characteristics, Surveys, Roles, Statistical analysis

Role Conflict, Role Clarity, Job Tension and Job Satisfaction in the Brand Manager Position (370)

Brand managers in consumer product firms often have diverse responsibilities and problems in the areas of authority, information, number of interfaces, lack of job continuity, triviality, lack of assistance, too many products, and conflicting responsibilities to superiors. This study attempted to determine: 1. whether the relationships for role conflict, role clarity, job tension, and job satisfaction hold true for product managers as reported in relevant literature, 2. whether these areas were influenced by demographic or job-related factors, and 3. what suggestions might be made for restructuring the brand manager's role. Data were obtained from questionnaires completed by 198 product managers in which they indicated the extent to which they agreed with statements relevant to the concepts being studied. The results confirmed expected relationships-that role clarity was related to job tension and job satisfaction and that tension was significantly related to job satisfaction. Four independent variables were analyzed: 1. personal factors, 2. organizational concepts, 3. participation in product decisions, and 4. level of contact with others. Only involvement in decisions and level of contact were found to have a significant relationship. Chart. Tables. References. –Kelly, J. Patrick and Hise, Richard T.; *Jrnl of the Academy of Marketing Science,* Winter/Spring 1980, 8(1) ,2: pp. 120-137. Avail. ABI 80-18040

Brands, Managers, Job satisfaction, Motivation, Product, Managers, Roles, Stress, Marketing management, Organizational plans, Responsibilities, Surveys

Role Conflict, Role Ambiguity, and Organizational Climate in a Public Accounting Firm

(371)

Little effort has been made to analyze the relationships between role conflict and ambiguity experienced by members of the public accounting profession, although the profession has been characterized as having the potential for conflict and ambiguity. Drawing on role theory, a model was developed to act as a framework to analyze both the potential consequences, and sources, of role conflict and ambiguity of audit seniors in a large public accounting firm. Job-related tension, job satisfaction, and propensity to leave the organization are 3 potential consequences of role conflict and role ambiguity. Using Pearson product-moment correlations and multiple regression, both role conflict and ambiguity were found to be significantly related to job-related tension, and job satisfaction. Most of the specific variables significantly related to stress arose from the relationship between seniors and their superiors. To help reduce stress, firms should make an effort to reduce violations in chain of command, which result in incompatible orders, or in different expectations from more than one superior. Tables. References. – Senatra, Phillip T.; *Accounting Review,* Oct 1980, 55(4): pp. 594-603. Avail. ABI 80-21638

Roles, Conflict, Auditors, Models, Organizational behavior, CPAs, Studies, Job satisfaction, Employee turnover, Job, Tension, Multiple regression, Accounting firms, Accounting theory

Role Orientations and Job Satisfaction in a Public Bureaucracy

(372)

Increasing levels of job satisfaction is important for public administrators for 2 reasons: 1. Low levels of job satisfaction are linked to negative mental health effects. 2. Some evidence suggests a relationship between satisfaction and productivity. Selected factors related to job satisfaction among State of Georgia Merit System personnel are examined. Data were obtained by a mail questionnaire distributed in 1978 to a random sample of 1,100 State of Georgia Merit System personnel at the 6-00 pay grade and above. Data suggest the plausibility of a 2-tiered approach to the analysis of job satisfaction. The strongest and most direct influences are derived from role orientation measures. To a modest degree, managers can affect job satisfaction in a manner conducive to the psychological health of employees. Tables. References. –DeCotiis, Allen R. and Gryski, Gerard S.; *Southern Review of Public Administration,* Spring 1981, 5(1): pp. 22-33. Avail. ABI 81-21731

Public administration, Job satisfaction, Bureaucrats, Government employees, Public sector, Roles, Statistical analysis

Salesmen and Saleswomen Job Satisfaction

(373)

A study was originated by 2 companies which were interested in discovering the differences in the job related attitudes of their male and female salespeople. Survey data in the form of questionnaires were collected from the sales forces of 2 national pharmaceutical companies. The results showed that saleswomen differed from salesmen in job perception. Women cited lower satisfaction with superiors and fellow salespeople. Female respondents reported receiving less from their work in terms of intrinsic rewards, while experiencing greater role conflict and role ambiguity.Managers can help instill a positive attitude and confidence in women by use of training programs. However, an underlying problem that saleswomen often experience is communication. Informal meetings held to discuss better sales techniques often do not include women, especially women entering the force. Managers must recognize that women experience greater work pressures than men, and they must help remove the barriers of lingering chauvinism. Table. References. —Futrell, Charles M.; *Industrial Marketing Mgmt,* Feb 1980, 9(1): pp. 27-30. Avail. ABI 80-06653

    Salespeople, Men, Women, Job satisfaction, Industrial, Sales, Job attitudes, Studies, Comparative analysis

Salespeople and Their Managers: An Exploratory Study   (374) of Some Similarities and Differences

Very little is known about the behavior and characteristics of salespeople and even less about the persons who manage them. In order to gain insight into this area, the salespeople and sales managers of an industrial salesforce were asked to complete an extensive questionnaire. Additional data were obtained from company accounting records, interviews with executives and personnel close to the selling situation, and participant observation of salespeople and their managers on the job. A total of 135 salespeople and 35 managers were surveyed, with useable responses from 122 salespeople and 33 managers. Sales managers generally expressed higher levels of job satisfaction. This can be attributed to their compensation, both tangible and intangible, being greater than that received by the salesforce. It was also found that internal control affects positively new business generated by sales managers, but not salespeople. Further, sales managers seem to cope better with ambiguity and tension on the job than do salespeople. For salespeople, the greater the task specific self-esteem and the less the felt role ambiguity and job tension, on the one hand, the higher the dollar sales, new business generated, and job satisfaction on the other hand. Tables. Charts. References. —Bagozzi, Richard P.; *Sloan Mgmt Review,* Winter 1980, 21(2): pp. 15-26. Avail. ABI 80-10362

    Salespeople, Sales managers, Job satisfaction, Characteristics, Performance, Studies, Motivation, Internal, Control, Statistical analysis

Salespeople Satisfaction and Performance Feedback   (375)

A study was conducted to examine the impact of supervisory behavior on salesforce job satisfaction. The relationship between sales supervisory behavior and salesforce job satisfaction was explored using a model. Two important dimensions of the model were the degree to which the supervisor initiates structure and provides consideration, and the degree to which the employee participates in decision making and receives feedback about performance. The data used were obtained from surveys of the industrial sales personnel of 3 midwestern corporations. The study found that sales supervision is an important determinant of salesforce job satisfaction. Salespeople were more satisfied with their jobs when they perceived their supervisors to be considerate. Job satisfaction also increased when participation in supervisory decisions resulted in the clarification of performance expectations. Performance feedback was found to be positively related to all the components of job satisfaction. Equations. Tables.

Appendix. References. —Teas, R. Kenneth and Horrell, James F.; *Industrial Marketing Mgmt,* Feb 1981, 10(1): pp. 49-57. Avail. ABI 81-05942

Salespeople, Job satisfaction, Performance, Feedback, Supervision, Models, Regression analysis, Communication

Scientists, Engineers and the Organization of Work (376)

The problems of job dissatisfaction and low productivity appear to arise in scientists and engineers due to a fundamental conflict between professionalism and bureaucracy. Studies indicate both problems could be somewhat alleviated by a sharing of authority between management and the scientists and engineers. Change, however, normally comes from the current holders of power-management-and researchers feel it is unlikely that members of management will voluntarily relinquish their power and status. Unionism has been suggested as a means of dealing with this reluctance, but efforts in this direction have been unsuccessful among scientists and engineers because these people view unionization as a move that lowers their status. The current power balance leaves too little power to the professionals and too much to the managers, but the outlook seems to be one of slow, marginal change. There is a direct economic relevance in proper work organization for scientists and engineers, but human capital literature has ignored its effect on productivity and job satisfaction by assuming that all human capital is utilized to its full potential. Economically, such an erroneous assumption is expensive. References. —Alexander, Kenneth O.; *American Jrnl of Economics & Sociology,* Jan 1981, 40(1): pp. 51-66. Avail. ABI 81-05884

Scientists, Engineers, Power, Work environment, Job satisfaction, Bureaucracy, Unions

Sources of Job Related Ambiguity and Their (377) Consequences upon Salespersons' Job Satisfaction and Performance

An analysis is made of a conceptual model relating 2 individual difference variables-need for clarity and locus of control-and 4 sources of job-related ambiguity to salesperson job performance and job satisfaction. The conceptual model constructed to gauge the impacts of individual differences and job-related ambiguity on job outcomes is presented; and a review of related research is included. Five industrial seller firms were identified through executive interviews, and both managers and salespersons participated in the study questionnaires. Results show that ambiguity involving sales manager and customer expectations relates negatively to performance. Ambiguity involving family expectations relates positively to performance. The explanation for lower levels of satisfaction is given as managerial-expectation ambiguity. Variables of individual differences are found to relate to job outcomes. Diagram. Tables. Graph. Chart. References. —Behrman, Douglas N.; Bigoness, William J.; and Perreault, William D., Jr.; *Management Science,* Nov 1981, 27(11): pp. 1246-1260. Avail. ABI 82-01578

Salespeople, Performance, Job satisfaction, Models, Management science, Regression analysis, Motivation

Spectrum/Harris Poll: The Job   (378)

In a recent survey, IEEE Spectrum teamed with Louis Harris & Associates Inc. to study the job views of electrical engineers (EE). According to the study, the most important factors influencing EEs' job satisfaction involve human relations. The study includes a survey of 4,000 engineers. The response was more than 50%. An overwhelming number of respondents prefer design and development, the 2 principal tasks of most EEs, over management, research, consulting, or teaching. This underlines the importance of creativity in the jobs of EEs. Three factors were cited most often for improving the engineer's productivity: 1. more and better information from managers about decisions that affect engineers, 2. more say in decisions that affect engineers, and 3. a greater chance for recognition and promotion. According to 63% of the respondents, the design of new high-technology products has improved in the last 10 years. Engineers indicated that the number of hours they work today is essentially unchanged from 10 years ago. However, over 60% said that engineers are less loyal to their employers than 10 years ago, and 38% said they are less motivated. Table. Graphs. —Guterl, Fred; *IEEE Spectrum,* Jun 1984, 21(6): pp. 38-43. Avail. ABI 84-22687

Electric, Engineers, Surveys, Job satisfaction, Job attitudes, Management styles

A Test of a Model of Department Store Salespeople's   (379) Job Satisfaction

A study was made of the relationship between the retail salesperson's perceptions of specific job characteristics and job satisfaction. Data were derived from surveys of sales personnel in 5 department stores. Several hypotheses related to job satisfaction were tested by means of multiple regression analysis. The findings indicate the salespersons' perceptions of supervision, organizational communication, and job characteristics may be important determinants of job satisfaction. Retail salespeople seem to experience greater job satisfaction when they perceive that they are closely supervised in terms of high leader consideration and initiation of structure. Thus, if a work climate is characterized by mutual trust, respect, and friendliness, supervisors will likely see a favorable effect on employees' satisfaction with work, supervision, pay, and other job aspects. The enrichment of retail selling jobs may have a significant positive effect on employees' job satisfaction. Tables. References. —Teas, R. Kenneth; *Jrnl of Retailing,* Spring 1981, 57(1): pp. 3-25. Avail. ABI 81-22053

Department stores, Retail stores, Models, Salespeople, Job satisfaction, Perceptions, Supervision, Performance, Feedback, Job attitudes, Leadership, Job, Characteristics, Studies, Regression analysis

Toward Increased Job Satisfaction of Practicing CPAs   (380)

Job satisfaction is crucial in reversing the high turnover rates that are so costly to CPA firms. A survey was taken of 296 CPA practitioners from firms throughout the US, asking respondents to gauge their job satisfaction. Satisfaction levels were analyzed on the basis of sex, position within the firm, specialty, office size, and educational level. The survey found males were generally more satisfied in their jobs than females. Salary was a point of contention with female practitioners. It showed as employees advanced, they tended to become more satisfied, and that while partners may be satisfied, senior and junior staff and managers generally were not. Specialty did not correlate to job satisfaction as strongly as did firm position and sex. Practitioners in offices employing staffs of 50-200 were more satisfied than those from firms with staffs of fewer than 50 or more than 200. Practitioners with master's degrees were less satisfied than those with bachelor's degrees. Tables. —Albrecht, W. Steve; Brown, Scott W.; and Field, David R.; *Jrnl of Accountancy,* Aug 1981, 152(2): pp. 61-66. Avail. ABI 81-21947

CPAs, Accountants, Job satisfaction, Evaluation, Studies, Surveys

Up-Front with Retail Clerks-Morale Is High   (381)

A nationwide Drug Topics survey revealed that drugstore retail clerks are happy to be part of the drugstore business. In a poll of more than 200 chain and independent retail clerks, it was found that the typical retail clerk is female, under 30, working an average of 39 hours per week, and earning an average salary of $3.79 per hour. The average clerk has been on the job for almost 8 years.The clerks indicated that they preferred working in a drugstore rather than any other type of retail setting. However, a comparison of chain store clerks and independent store clerks revealed that chain store clerks were less satisfied, earn less, and are less involved with the more preferred functions of drugstore clerking. While a recent annual meeting of the National Association of Chain Drug Stores emphasized the "traditional neighborhood drugstore concept", the survey indicated that such an effort should start with the retail clerks. Tables. —Anonymous; *Drug Topics,* Jun 13, 1980, 124(12): pp. 33-37,45. Avail. Drug 80-13011

Pharmacies, Clerical personnel, Surveys, Statistical data, Job satisfaction

5

Waste in the Workforce

MANAGING STRESS, BURNOUT, ALIENATION

Accounting for Performance: Stressful-but Satisfying   (382)

Two major areas of behavior affected by the accountant's role as evaluator are his job satisfaction and role stress. Job satisfaction is defined as a pleasurable or positive emotional state resulting from the appraisal of one's job or job experience, while role stress is job-induced tension resulting from the necessity of facing either incompatible performance expectations or unclear job expectations. This study involved a sample of 3,600 managerial accountants who were employed in manufacturing companies throughout the US. Results validated the hypothesis that role stress is negatively related to job satisfaction. Also, the accountant's involvement in the control/performance measurement process correlates positively with all dimensions of job satisfaction. Tables. References. —Sapp, Richard W. and Seiler, Robert E.; *Management Accounting*, Aug 1980, 62(2): pp. 29-35. Avail. ABI 80-16129

Management, Accounting, Stress, Accountants, Job satisfaction, Roles, Correlations, Statistical analysis, Studies, Surveys

Alcohol and Drugs: Poor Remedies for Stress   (383)

Employees who rely on drugs and alcohol are frequently victims of stress. The stressful personality is overly achievement oriented, aggressive, competitive, and ambitious. The work environment itself may produce stress. One way is through organizational frustration, which produces acts of direct aggression and nonaggressive responses such as compensation, conversion, fantasy, projection, or repression. Job stress may also produce stress, either through job ambiguity or job conflict. Stress may also be produced by underutilization, work overload, resource inadequacy, insecurity, and nonparticipation. Many employees turn to alcohol to unwind. Industry is not usually concerned until the heavy drinker becomes a problem drinker-someone whose work is adversely affected by the drinking. Even the alcoholic is frequently able to remain on the job for some time after he or she has already begun to cause severe damage in terms of work-time lost and higher accident rates. An alcohol treatment program is important, preferably accompanied by a clear company policy. To some extent, the signs of drug abuse are similar to those of alcohol abuse. As with alcohol, the focus should be on understanding, confidentiality, and treatment, rather than on termination of the abusing employee. It is more cost-effective to deal with stress in the work environment and to attempt treatment of its damaging effects. —Milbourn, Gene, Jr.; *Supervisory Mgmt,* Mar 1981, 26(3): pp. 35-42. Avail. ABI 81-07047

Employee problems, Alcoholism, Drug abuse, Programs, Job, Stress, Work environment, Behavior

All Work and No Play (384)

The truly effective, successful salesperson is not the one who constantly works at a hectic pace. By not taking formally scheduled play periods, the natural instinct to break the tensions of the day will be suppressed and will come out in unproductive behavior. To prescribe the right amount of play, begin by reading such stress signs as expressions of anger, tightened muscles, and increasing indulgence in nervous habits. Take time to trace where, when, and with whom these signs occur and the thoughts pertaining to them. It would not be uncommon to discover 2 or 3 high stress periods during the workweek or workmonth cycle. These high stress periods are the time best suited to be either followed or preceded by play periods. However, some forms of play are stress producing rather than relaxing. The form of play recommended by most consultants involves outgoing self-expression, such as writing or painting. —Aiello, Ralph; *American Salesman,* Sep 1983, 28(9): pp. 34-36. Avail. ABI 83-31087

Salespeople, Stress, Recreation, Leisure time, Employee problems

Alleviating Worker Stress (385)

Employee behavior at quitting time often reveals the general emotional atmosphere of an office. A certain amount of job stress, inevitable in today's high-pressure world, can be traced to: 1. anxiety regarding one's personal life, 2. the future of the company, or 3. potential cutbacks in production, salary, or jobs. Company growth may lead to an increased workload, a rapid influx of additional personnel, overtime, and lowered service standards. Managers can protect employees from the physical and psychological problems associated with job stress by following certain guidelines. These include: 1. Try to be sensitive to the signs and symptoms of stress. 2. Avoid consistent lack of communication with subordinates. 3. Provide straightforward, accurate updates to clear up misinformation. 4. Tell employees about any corporate changes that will affect them. 5. Do not demean or embarrass workers. 6. Make an effort to acknowledge a job well done. 7. Encourage a sense of teamwork. 8. Avoid being distant and unapproachable. 9. Let workers know that they are trusted. 10. Inform workers of the latest department codes and standards. 11. Help subordinates develop their career goals and objectives. —Miles, Mary; *Computer Decisions,* May 1984, 16(6): pp. 252-256. Avail. ABI 84-20792

Employee problems, Stress, Management, Effectiveness, Guidelines

Are You a Potential Burnout?   (386)

Workers with high expectations and a sense of purpose are most likely to experience burnout. These people set unrealistic goals for themselves and eventually find themselves overloaded. People in the "helping professions" (medicine, religion, law enforcement, education, and social work, among others) are the prime candidates for burnout. Quick solutions are not the answer. Solutions that can help a burnout victim regain control are: 1. setting goals for one's life, 2. examining one's self-defeating attitudes, 3. leaving a job or relationship that is causing burnout, 4. reducing concern that one cannot get out of the situation, 5. spending time with one's family, 6. finding people to talk to, 7. cultivating outside interests, 8. being good to oneself, 9. learning to say "no", 10. becoming more tolerant of others rights, 11. not feeling sorry for oneself, 12. simplifying one's life, 13. keeping strictly to a five-day, 40-hour week, 14. reminding oneself "I don't have to be perfect", 15. taking courses that will help, and 16. reading in the areas of meditation, nutrition, and relaxation. Charts. —Helliwell, Tanis; *Training & Development Jrnl,* Oct 1981, 35(10): pp. 24-29. Avail. ABI 81-24053

Stress, Occupations, Personality, Lifestyles

Are You "Humoring" Your Employees?   (387)

Humor can be an effective tool in dealing with job-related stress. Given the fact that we usually laugh at someone else's expense, it follows that humor has its roots in aggression, and aggression does permeate the workplace. The many uses of humor can be seen in the workplace, i.e., attracting attention, making a point, relieving tension, etc. A good manager must understand humor and its uses in the workplace and be able to use this knowledge effectively. A manager without a sense of humor is at a distinct disadvantage because such individuals are filled with inhibition and cannot easily show emotions. Laughter can take away stress, and productivity will increase in the absence of stress. It is essential that the manager be able to laugh at himself if the situation warrants. For businessmen who are in the public eye, humor can serve to make audiences more receptive and more entertained. —Sleeter, Michael; *Management World,* May 1981, 10(5): pp. 25-27. Avail. ABI 81-13381

Humor, Effectiveness, Stress, Management

Assessing the Substained Effects of a Stress   (388)
Management Intervention on Anxiety and Locus of
Control

The degree to which locus of control and anxiety level (both state and trait) can be modified by a stress management intervention is investigated, and the extent to which these effects are sustained in a later real-life stressful event is assessed. The extent to which the type A/B characteristic mediates response to treatment is also investigated. The results provide further support for the efficacy of short-term, cognitive-behavior intervention programs for anxiety reduction. The sustaining effects of such interventions during real-life stressful events is also demonstrated. It appears that some of the pessimism frequently directed at the long-term effects of behaviorally oriented interventions may be unwarranted. However, the experimental treatment failed to promote significant increases in internality. Also, although it may be contended that type As should benefit more than type Bs from such programs, no significant differences exist between the reductions achieved by type As and type Bs. Tables. Graph. References. —Rose, Robin L. and Veiga, John F.; *Academy of Mgmt Jrnl,* Mar 1984, 27(1): pp. 190-198. Avail. ABI 84-11390

Stress, Employee problems, Anxieties, Organizational behavior, Studies, Statistical analysis

Auditor Stress and Time Budgets (389)

Studies indicate that accountants are in a profession with extremely high stress levels. Four recent studies examine the impact of time-budget pressures on the stress level of public accountants, with results indicating that the impacts of time-budget pressures can be: 1. misreported chargeable time by auditors, 2. employee turnover, and 3. the likelihood of an early sign-off on some step of the program. Results of a recent questionnaire indicate that time-budget pressures are perceived as being heavier at the senior level than by those at other levels. The responses measure the beliefs concerning the optimal degree of budget goal difficulty across levels, with most respondents believing that the goals can be attained with reasonable effort. Behavior responses to overly tight budgets across levels indicate harder work would be given to meet the schedule. Other means of meeting the required schedule would be to ask for more time, to underreport chargeable time, and to shift the time actually worked to other categories. An implication of budget pressures is that most managers and partners do not feel that time-budget pressures are a problem, while the seniors and staff are reporting relatively high levels of dysfunctional stress. Tables. References. —Kelley, Tim and Seiler, Robert E.; *CPA Jrnl,* Dec 1982, 52(12): pp. 24-34. Avail. ABI 83-02946

Auditors, Stress, Behavior, Time, Budgets, Studies, Public accountants

Back from Burnout - Tools for Recovery for Credit Personnel (390)

Job burnout is a difficult problem to solve, requiring recognition by the individual that he/she is burned out and determination to make the changes required to remedy the situation. According to Morton Ziven of Temple University, the job and all elements surrounding it are the root cause of burnout. Early treatment should involve reestablishing the individual's sense of self through such actions as making a career change, if indicated, or learning to function within the limits of the present job. The individual seeking to recover from burnout must assess where he/she is personally and professionally and make changes one step at a time. Credit managers affected by burnout might try changing the way they approach old, familiar tasks, such as how they arrive at the credit-granting decision. Trying some new analysis techniques may serve to remove the tedium and burnout from the task. Individuals must realize that they are not powerless to change the situation, and they would be well-advised to spend more time with people they admire as mentors or role models to pattern their lifestyles after such role models. Management support and understanding of the employee suffering from burnout will aid the recovery process. —Poe, Susannah Grimm and Scherr, Frederick C.; *Credit & Financial Mgmt,* Jun 1982, 84(6): pp. 26-30. Avail. ABI 82-15666

Employee problems, Stress, Credit management

Bankers and Occupational Stress (391)

A national survey conducted by Robert L. Kahn, University of Michigan Institute for Social Research, revealed the following: 1. 35% of all employees surveyed complained about job ambiguity, 2. 48% experienced conflicts in job expectations from supervisors, and 3. 45% were unable to fulfill heavy daily work loads. Customer reaction to changes in bank policy has created a stressful climate for bankers, who must cope with irate customers. Many job-related stresses involve confrontation with customers or arguments with other employees. Overstress normally occurs when work pressures, combined with outside conflicts, are more than the individual can handle. Health-care professionals have found that the stressfulness of our industrial environment contributes to cancer, heart disease, stroke, and other serious disorders. Emotional manifestations of stress range from vague discontent accompanied by fatigue and depression to mental illness. Poor job performance can be linked to high stress levels among workers. Methods for coping with stress vary. However, in the work environment, compromise, open lines of communication, delegation of responsibilities, withdrawal to sort issues out, and not expecting more than is humanly feasible are effective instruments toward diminishing pressure. If pressures become too difficult to cope with, professionals trained to work with physical and/or emotional disorders should be called upon. –Ashley, Janelle C.; *Bankers Magazine,* Sep/Oct 1981, 164(5): pp. 68-72. Avail. ABI 81-27076

Banks, Occupational, Stress, Management, Employee problems

Bankers Under Stress (392)

Stress is a nonspecific physiological response to any demand made on it. Things which cause stress (stressors) can be either positive or negative. A research team from the Illinois Institute of Technology conducted a study, involving 117 National Association of Bank Women (NABW) members, to determine the kinds of levels of work tension bank women experience, their methods of coping with stress, and the relationship between work tension and physical and psychological health. The factors that stimulate stress in their order of importance are: 1. work overload, 2. organizational climate, 3. decision making and information processing, 4. supervision, and 5. promotion. The principal factors of coping are: 1. cognitive coping, 2. give up, 3. information seeking, 4. withdraw from situation and seek help, 5. emotional ventilation, 6. cognitive distortion, 7. goal substitution, and 8. active confrontation. The study results show a high level of alienation from work reported by a majority of the NABW members. Banks should seriously consider the social, physical, ecological, and interpersonal circumstances of their employees, because these individuals hold the keys to success for such financial institutions. Tables. –Hartigan, Kevin J.; Alpert, Barry; Gots, Lynne S.; Ellis, Michael V.; and Bassi, Robert A.; *NABW Jrnl (National Assn of Bank Women),* Mar/Apr 1982, 58(3): pp. 4-10. Avail. ABI 82-27121

Women, Bank management, Managers, Stress, Organizational behavior, Banks, Work environment

A Basis for Stress Management (393)

Participants in stress management courses for Canadian public service managers receive training in the holistic management of stress. Course participants receive a computerized health assessment on body fat, serum lipids, blood pressure, pulmonary function, muscular endurance, and cardiorespiratory fitness. Data on over 300 managers revealed that many managers were physically unfit and had a lifestyle that did not prepare them to manage stress successfully. The first step in stress management is identifying the sources of stress which are incompatible with health and productivity. Increasing resistance to stress through an emphasis on health, fitness, and a balanced lifestyle must follow. Sources of stress which cannot be eliminated or that are unavoidable must be coped with through relaxation, assertiveness training, or professional assistance. Charts. References. –Jette, Maurice; *Optimum (Canada),* 1982, 13(1): pp. 35-46. Avail. ABI 82-22121

> Government employees, Canada, Stress, Management, Programs, Employee problems, Physical fitness, Managers, Case studies

Before You Reach Your Breaking Point (394)

Stress is a growing problem for data processing managers faced with long hours, tight deadlines, and impossible user demands. The ability to handle stress varies with different individuals. The need to have control over one's own fate and one's self-image influence reactions to stress. Stressful situations include: 1. a gap between responsibilities and authority to carry them out, 2. unclear job descriptions, 3. ambiguity of how superiors regard one's performance, 4. uncertainty about future job prospects, and 5. personal and work-related transitions. A technician who has been promoted to manager may be prone to stress problems. Good, basic management practices can keep stress to a minimum. Methods to treat stress include biofeedback, transcendental meditation, hypnosis, Samadhi tank treatments, and assertiveness training. Managers must deal with the shock of change to others as well as to themselves. Because changes on the job are stressful, there is a need for good orientation, training, and group support. To cope with political pressures, a manager might occasionally go back to comfortable, familiar routines. Because stagnation in a job is also stressful, people must be given room to grow. –Lasden, Martin; *Computer Decisions,* Feb 1982, 14(2): pp. 84-98. Avail. ABI 82-18061

> Data processing, Managers, Stress, Tension, Health

Between Service and Servility: Role Conflict in (395) Subordinate Service Roles

Organizational role stress has been studied in recent theoretical and research literature in Organizational/Industrial Psychology and Organizational Sociology fields. Job-related stress can possibly interfere with the physical and psychological functioning of the individual, and lead to undesirable organizational consequences. There is belief that the level of conflict in subordinate service roles (SSRs) is even higher than the level of conflict in organizational leadership roles. These reasons are related to the 4 characteristics of SSRs: 1. relatively high boundary relevance, 2. high degree of exposure to role senders outside the organization, 3. lower status relative to role senders outside the organization, and 4. low status relative to role senders inside the organization. There are several typical person-role conflicts in SSRs: 1. inequality dilemmas, 2. feeling vs. behavior, and 3. conflict over territory. Intersender conflicts include: 1. organization vs. client, and 2. interclient conflicts. People in SSRs may avoid contact, withdraw psychologically, overact, or resort to automatic behavior to deal with conflicts. References. –Shamir, Boas; *Human Relations,* Oct 1980, 33(10): pp. 741-756. Avail. ABI 80-22357

Subordinates, Service, Roles, Conflict, Stress, Behavior, Human relations

Beware Understress: Opportunity + Danger = Benign (396) Crisis

When combined, the Chinese symbols for danger and opportunity mean crisis. Crisis is, in turn, often called stress. Stress actually helps an individual to function, and it is understress that must be guarded against. Understress denotes a work underload that does not challenge the individual's potential nearly enough. People suffering from understress are characterized by such factors as feeling low or flat at work, being dissatisfied with jobs for no apparent reason, and finding that their minds wander during meetings. The individual needs manageable stress to get work done and make life meaningful. Managers expect stress and can take it since they have learned to manage it, but of course, there is a limit to the stress with which they can successfully deal. Successful salespeople and air traffic controllers are among those who perform best under stress. It is necessary to understand stress, manage it, and use it constructively and creatively, without allowing harmful side effects to occur. Winners accept the challenge and risk of stress, while also-rans just run away from it and its challenges. –Stern, Frances Meritt; *Marketing Times,* Jan/Feb 1983, 30(1): pp. 26-28. Avail. ABI 83-07221

Stress, Tension, Salespeople

Beyond Freud: Widening Choices in Executive Mental (397) Health

There are a number of schools of therapeutic thought for solving problems such as depression, anxiety, hysteria, and phobias. Some of these include: 1. Psychoanalysis, which is expensive, can last for years, and involves the patient talking about dreams, fantasies, and early memories to get at the root of the problem. 2. Behavior therapy, lasting a few months, with a wide range of costs, involves efforts to change some bad habit. 3. Group therapies, lasting from a few months to a few years, rely on interrelating with others, and may be either traditional or avant garde. 4. Biological therapies are generally used in conjunction with other therapy. Before a person chooses a psycho-therapeutic cure, it is wise for him/her to get a complete physical check-up, for assurance that the problem is not medically-based. For instance, depression can have biological roots. Drug therapy can be indicated in some chemical imbalances. It is believed that stress can change people's body chemistry. Even if the depression is real, caused by some event in real life, it may respond to drugs. —Anonymous; *Business Week,* Sep 28, 1981, (2707) (Industrial Edition): pp. 128-132. Avail. ABI 81-22594

Executives, Mental health, Stress, Therapy

Brain Processing-Leadership Stress or Success (398)

Stress among administrators and executives appears to be at an all time high. Leadership positions have become more stressful as evidenced by increasing physiological and emotional problems. One theory suggests that stress is the result of a person working in a career position that does not fit his/her needs, abilities, styles, etc. Brain processing may be added to this theory. Each person has 2 separate and unique brains which are each capable of high order thinking and problem solving and vary in functional areas. A right brain (R/B) person whose dominant brain is on the right side will view a problem differently than a left brain (L/B) person. The dominant brain does the initial processing of incoming stimuli. The point in regard to stress is to help leaders understand their brain processing modes, the reasons behind thinking and operation patterns, and how to integrate both hemispheres so that their tolerance is wide and accepting. Conflict between left and right (logical and creative) brains must be resolved. References. —Piatt, James G.; *Manage,* Jul 1980, 32(3): pp. 10-13. Avail. ABI 80-17340

Leadership, Stress, Information processing

Burn Out-Business's Most Costly Expense (399)

Burn out is an affliction which strikes people in self-imposed, high-intensity situations. Once burned out executives were seen as being simply overworked; however, simplistic explanations are no longer accepted. Burn out, in fact, appears to be a necessary transition time for some employees. What occurs in a normal and healthy grief reaction is that the life forces are diverted from the normal range of problem-solving and life-sustaining functions, and during this period, the person is developing a new life support system. Further, mid-career is often the classical time in life when people start to deal with some of the unrealistic expectations that they and others may have placed on their lifestyle.Personnel managers can perform an important role in the burn out situation. Management needs to create a climate of working conditions which raises the level of self-worth and morale. There is also a need to get the employee to deal with himself in the employment situations by such techniques as talking about issues bothering him, learning to be reflective, and not accepting his condition. The result may be an employee who is comfortable with himself and his business, and the company may not lose a highly-skilled and loyal employee. —Nelson, John G.; *Personnel Administrator,* Aug 1980, 25(8): pp. 81-87. Avail. ABI 80-16041

Employee problems, Career advancement, Personnel management, Employee morale, Job attitudes, Employee attitude (PER)

Burnout (400)

Periods of crisis occurring in an executive's career are sometimes defined in terms of burnout. It is possible to view executive burnout as a positive experience if it is properly understood and respected. The first step to resolution of burnout is proper diagnosis. There are 3 views of executive burnout: 1. symptomatic view, 2. management view, and 3. dynamic view. The symptomatic view, which is the most common, focuses on the physical and emotional reactions an executive exhibits but does not address the root causes. The management view is limited in that only workplace-related problems are addressed. The management approach uses a formal structure consisting of: 1. identification, 2. documentation, 3. confrontation, and 4. follow-up. The multi-disciplinary, comprehensive approach of the dynamic view addresses all facets of the executive's problem, including personal problems, by using an outside, confidential counsellor. Too often, executives are reluctant to admit to feeling burned out because of corporate attitudes that work against any type of positive resolution. –Meyer, John H.; *Executive (Canada)*, Jul 1982, 24(7): pp. 26-30. Avail. ABI 82-20440

Stress, Employee problems, Cases

BURNOUT! (401)

Ottis Stull, top manager of a $2.4 million electrical contracting business, found that he had burned himself out at age 35. He became exhausted, frustrated, and could not relax. Most victims of burnout have worked too hard, too long, and have tried to bear excessive stress without respite. Dr. Edward Stambaugh, a clinical psychologist, helped to resolve Stull's burnout by approaching it in a businesslike manner. With Stambaugh's aid, Stull identified his problem, determined his goals, and developed specific methods for achieving his objectives. Among Stull's objectives were: 1. recognizing tension and learning to relax, 2. improving his self-image, and 3. spending more time with his family. Stull now limits himself to an 8-5 workday, and takes a few minutes to relax whenever possible. He spends time with his family and enjoys his days off. He can avoid a recurrence of burnout by not taking his work too seriously. –Sammons, Donna L.; *Inc.*, Dec 1980, 2(12): pp. 56-58,60,62. Avail. ABI 80-23678

Stress, Tension, Work environment, Profiles, Workloads

Burnout (402)

Burnout is a disease of disappointment and disillusionment. Its most susceptible victims are those who do not get what they want at work and those who do, but who often discover their rewards are not what they expected. The physical symptoms are: chronic fatigue, low energy, headaches, muscle tension, susceptibility to sickness, and frequent bouts with flue or virus. Psychological symptoms can include depression, and feelings of hopelessness, helplessness, and entrapment. One definition of the syndrome is the excessive striving to reach an unrealistic expectation that is imposed by the values of society or oneself. Burnout victims usually have unrealistic expectations. One expert relates it to the threshold for stress one has. Most people probably experience burnout at some time in their careers. The process can be long term. The bureaucracy of a company can contribute to the problem, but burnout can also be the problem of the individual. A firm can strive to limit stress in the workplace, recognize individual accomplishments, and provide a positive workforce in order to reduce the effects of burnout. —Wakin, Edward; *Today's Office,* Apr 1983, 17(11): pp. 40-45. Avail. ABI 83-20622

Burnout, Employee problems, Executives, Stress

Burnout: A Real Threat to Human Resources Managers (403)

Burnout is an extreme condition; it is the end product of a process that, with such problems as stress and depression, forms a continuum. Distinguishing characteristics of the burnout candidate are: 1. They have job-related stresses. 2. They tend to be idealists and self-motivating achievers. 3. They tend to seek unattainable goals. The human resources manager can prevent stress by: 1. promoting stress management through relaxation, exercise, attitude and awareness, and diet; 2. altering working conditions, and 3. exercising a sense of humor. Human resource managers must set realistic goals as a basic support for preventing burnout. If burnout is reached, the rebuilding process will take time and patience and will involve an attitudinal change that can be difficult to attain. Table. Chart. References. —Niehouse, Oliver L.; *Personnel,* Sep/Oct 1981, 58(5): pp. 25-32. Avail. ABI 81-25044

Human resources, Managers, Stress, Factors

Burnout: Summary and Future Research (404)

Research literature on burnout is reviewed. Burnout is defined as a response to stress which results in emotional or physical exhaustion, lowered productivity, and depersonalization. Most research on burnout has been descriptive. Few statistical analyses have been performed for individual and organizational variables. Future research is required to answer major questions about the causes and prevention of burnout. A model is presented for 4 stages of burnout: 1. the potential for burnout in a given situation, 2. the perceived stress of individuals in the situation, 3. the response to stress, and 4. the effects of burnout. Other research factors and variables which need to be considered include: 1. valid measurements for burnout, 2. methodology, 3. norms to define level and intensity of burnout, 4. gains associated with burnout, 5. social and psychological impact of burnout, 6. individual predispositions to burnout, and 7. types of burnout. Charts. References. —Perlman, Baron and Hartman, E. Alan; *Human Relations,* Apr 1982, 35(4): pp. 283-305. Avail. ABI 82-14065

Defined, Stress, Research, Literature, Models, Studies

Burnout: Victims and Avoidances (405)

Employees in data processing get fed up with their jobs primarily when they become locked into a routine. The routine may involve maintaining the same system for a number of years because nobody else knows the system and the budget does not contemplate redeveloping it. Or the routine may be that of training users or implementing software, with each training session or implementation being a carbon copy of many others that were done before. Such routines in data processing, and the instances of employee burnout that develop from them, are more common in the larger, more sophisticated and specialized installations. The best way to prevent burnout is for programming managers to schedule their work on the premise that they will have a programmer or analyst for three or four years, after which time that person must move on. It must be recognized that keeping people interested in their jobs requires flexibility and the opportunity to meet new challenges. —Cherlin, Merrill; *Datamation,* Jul 1981, 27(7): pp. 92-99. Avail. ABI 81-17946

Data processing, Employee attitude (PER), Job attitudes, Employee turnover, Programmers, Job satisfaction

Can Companies Kill? Is the Corporation Responsible for   (406) Employee Mental Health?

Recent court cases have raised the question of whether an employer can, by its own action or inaction, kill with stress. The issue revolves around the extent to which a company can be held responsible, beyond the provisions of workers' compensation laws, for psychiatric injury to employees. Workers' compensation laws provide financial coverage for employees disabled by industrial accidents without having to bring the employer to court. The law aids the worker and protects the employer from damage suits for larger amounts. In the last 20 years, 15 states have changed their worker compensation laws to allow payments in job-related cases of anxiety, depression, and other mental disorders severe enough to be disabling. One viewpoint takes the position that preexisting emotional conditions and personality and family factors all influence an employee's mental health. Despite this view, many companies now offer their employees stress-reduction programs or psychological counseling either in-house or outside. Perhaps companies should consider offering their employees job security and emotional security, within reason. —Rice, Berkeley; *Personnel Administrator,* Dec 1981, 26(12): pp. 54-59. Avail. ABI 82-00442

Employers, Liability, Employee, Mental health, Working conditions, Stress, Mental illness, Psychological, Workers compensation, State laws, Litigation

Career Burnout   (407)

Job burnout is caused by a variety of factors ranging from the "me generation" emphasis on getting more out of a job than just a pay check to the pressures resulting from changing technology and a volatile economy. For blacks, add the pressures of coping with unfamiliar corporate environments and job-related racial bias. Corporations are realizing that the burnout syndrome is forcing as much as 10% of all managers and executives to quit. Experts say that burnout is a withdrawal caused by stress. Several symptoms of burnout include incapacitating anxiety, loss of confidence, inability to make decisions, resentment, irritability, and fatigue. The classic response is to quit or get fired. The black person in a white organization has the additional stress of institutionalized racism. One method of handling the stress is to plan more carefully and to direct career goals more cautiously. Another is to create support networks with coworkers, friends, and family. It is necessary to distinguish between racially inspired or other types of limitations in different stress situations. —Norman, Beverly; *Black Enterprise,* Jul 1981, 11(12): pp. 45-48. Avail. ABI 81-14821

Stress, Blacks, Managers

Career Success and Personal Failure: Alienation in   (408)
Professionals and Managers

It has long been assumed in US society that professional and managerial careers are desirable because individuals in these positions are more satisfied in both the job and the nonjob aspects of their lives. Among the reasons suggested for this high degree of satisfaction are that professionals and managers have greater societal prestige, an increased range and challenge of job activities, and more autonomy in meeting the demands of their positions. However, today these assumptions are being questioned. Alienation, an emotional attitude considered to be conceptually and empirically distinct from job dissatisfaction, must be considered. Expectancy disconfirmation, contradictory role demands, sense of external control, loss of affiliative satisfactions, and developmental life changes are proposed as significant factors in the personal and social alienation among professionals and managers. Of the factors examined, the loss of affiliative satisfactions was consistently the most significant. Chart. Tables. References. –Korman, Abraham K.; Wittig-Berman, Ursula; and Lang, Dorothy; *Academy of Mgmt Jrnl,* Jun 1981, 24(2): pp. 342-360. Avail. ABI 81-14525

Professional, Managers, Social, Alienation, Job satisfaction, Organizational behavior, Conflicts, Emotions, Studies, Statistical analysis

Caution for Communicators: Take Stress in Moderation   (409)

The organizational communicator is often faced with the occupational hazard of job stress. Stress can have negative consequences, but when it occurs in moderation, the individual can benefit since stress energizes and motivates the individual to greater productivity. The goal of the communicator should be to develop constructive methods for identifying and coping with stress. The first step is to recognize stress when it is occurring. Major stress factors are role ambiguity, conflict, and overload, but anxiety and frustration can also contribute. Some guidelines designed to reduce the adverse effects of stress include: 1. keeping a job diary to identify stress patterns, 2. using exercise and music to reduce a stressful atmosphere, 3. taking breaks during the working day, 4. talking out a problem with a friend, 5. expressing anger through such harmless means as jogging or punching a bag, 6. avoiding the mistake of procrastinating on an important project, and 7. having the good sense to get professional counseling when stress problems become too great. Graph. –Huber, Vandra L.; *Jrnl of Organizational Communication,* 1980, 10(1): pp. 20-23. Avail. ABI 81-02922

Job, Stress, Public relations, Personnel, Roles, Conflict, Factors, Reduction, Guidelines

Control Stressful Situations Before They Control You   (410)

Lifestyle changes, such as foregoing social activities for career-oriented priorities, are needed to meet exceptionally high self-set standards for achieving success. If the change is major, there may be a question of the validity of the goals. Stress may result. The reaction to stress depends on many factors, such as the cause for the need to achieve. Positive stress usually results from factors such as personal growth and willingness to take a risk. Indicators of harmful stress include: 1. irritation over minor incidents, 2. trouble sleeping, 3. loss of sense of humor, and 4. excessive worrying.Before trying to deal with the stressors, it is useful to identify what activities occurred during "negative hours" to change to a positive profile. It is necessary to determine goals before a positive profile can be developed. Ways to handle stress include: 1. physical activity, 2. talking the problem over with a trusted person, 3. avoiding self-medication, 4. balancing work and recreation, and 5. getting enough rest and sleep. —McCullough, Rose V.; *Rough Notes,* Aug 1980, 123(8): pp. 52-56. Avail. ABI 80-16375

Stress, Management, Health care, Goal setting

Controlling Burnout: A Leadership Guide for Managers   (411)

Burnout is an increasingly occurring, destructive condition whose related problems cost US businesses billions yearly in lost production. The symptoms of stress and burnout are comparable, but people who suffer stress will not necessarily suffer burnout. Burnout candidates predominantly experience job-related stress. They tend to be idealistic and/or self-motivating achievers seeking unattainable goals. There are no consistent characteristics for leadership because the details of each situation and the people involved are different. Leadership must be a continuous, flexible process. When it is not, an unnecessarily stressful situation is created. In addition to choosing an appropriate style of leadership, a manager can use leadership to control or minimize burnout in several ways: 1. maintaining realistic goals, 2. removing job ambiguities, 3. introducing major changes gradually, 4. altering working conditions that are physically and mentally stressful, 5. knowing the signs of burnout, and 6. initiating and promoting a stress management program where needed. Chart. Graph. —Niehouse, Oliver I.; *Business Horizons,* Jul/Aug 1984, 27(4): pp. 80-85. Avail. ABI 84-26621

Burnout, Stress, Employee problems, Leadership, Human relations

Coping with Entrepreneurial Stress   (412)

Although entrepreneurs express a high degree of satisfaction from owning their own businesses, many also pay a high price: their health. A survey of 450 entrepreneurs showed that the 2 most positive aspects of business ownership were the income and the psychic rewards of control and achievement. The interviews also revealed 4 causes of stress: 1. loneliness - no one in whom to confide, 2. immersion in the business, which deprives them of outside activities, 3. people problems, particularly frustrations and disappointment in relationships with partners and subordinates, and 4. the need to achieve, which can drive entrepreneurs relentlessly. In order for entrepreneurs to combat such stress, they must first be aware of its existence and its potential for destructiveness. They must then clarify the causes of stress, and in addition to the proven stress-reduction techniques, they must use networking, take frequent vacations and breaks, communicate with subordinates, and seek satisfaction outside the company. Charts. References. Boyd, David P. and Gumpert, David E.; *Harvard Business Review,* Mar/Apr 1983, 61(2): pp. 44-64. Avail. ABI 83-08663

Entrepreneurs, Small business, Stress, Studies, Job satisfaction, Personal income, Psychic income, Advantages, Problems

Coping with Job-Related Stress   (413)

A certain amount of tension spurs productivity and creativity, but problems arise when tensions persist on a high level or when a body reacting to a stress cannot let down after the crisis. Thresholds for tension vary, and each individual has an optimum tension level. A variety of symptoms accompany tension. One serious consequence is chronic fatigue. Excessive tension is caused by many different things, including work addiction. Job-related tensions can sometimes be eased by listing and organizing things which need to be done. Tension can also be caused by conditions outside of the job situation, and these can spill over into the job. Those who suffer from tension tend to eat on the run, have few extra-curricular interests, average 6 or fewer hours of sleep per night, smoke, drink, and use sedatives or tranquilizers. Ways to combat tensions include: 1. reducing overtime, 2. making sure you are in the right line of work, 3. changing physical positions often while working, and 4. making time for recreation. —Raudsepp, Eugene; *Supervision,* Mar 1981, 43(3): pp. 10-14. Avail. ABI 81-07130

Job, Stress, Tension, Employee problems, Guidelines

Coping with Managerial Stress   (414)

Stress is generally thought of as being harmful to performance and, therefore, must be eradicated. However, stress is frequently accompanied by, and indeed may be a necessary part of, the process of change and growth. Without stress, perhaps nothing would be achieved. But a world of difference exists between healthy occupational stress and harmful distress. In order to determine whether the manager's experience with different stress influences will be positive or negative, it is worthwhile to examine 5 aspects of the manager's experience: 1. direction of influence, 2. predictability, 3. acceptance by significant others, 4. success of work efforts, and 5. perceived agreement among significant others. Further, 5 different patterns of problem-solving can be considered, which have been adopted by managers in coping with differences in expectations, pressures and needs from their reference groups: 1. compartmentalized loyalty, 2. dominant loyalty, 3. rejection of all references, 4. striking a balance, and 5. seeking alternatives. —Pendleton, Barbara; *Management World,* Jan 1981, 10(1): pp. 25-27. Avail. ABI 81-04597

Managers, Stress, Multiple, Loyalty, Problems, Strategy

Coping with Personal Problems at Work   (415)

Given that, at any one time, 20% of a company's workforce faces some personal problem and some 8% face a major problem, it is surprising how little effort companies are making to help. In 1981, Control Data Ltd. set up a program called Employee Advisory Resource (EAR) to improve the quality of life for all employees and their families by providing greater support. While many managers favor the program, others fear that employees will use it to bypass them or to reverse management decisions. The guiding principles of the program are: 1. independence, 2. confidentiality, 3. availability, 4. wide scope, and 5. voluntary and free. The program works by providing one or more of 3 basic services: information, counseling, and referral. While the qualitative benefits of the program are difficult to measure, it is estimated that the company's US program saves at least $10 million annually in lower turnover, absenteeism, and medical costs. There are plans to expand EAR in the future. References. —Hall, John and Fletcher, Ben; *Personnel Mgmt (UK),* Feb 1984, 16(2): pp. 30-33. Avail. ABI 84-07239

Employee problems, Stress, Employee counseling, Assistance, Employee benefits, Control Data-Minneapolis, Case studies

Coping with Stress in a Time of Transition   (416)

Technology is causing changes in the way Americans work. While improving productivity, the changes are also producing stress among workers, which contributes to a variety of physical and mental illnesses. Indirectly, stress costs industry an estimated $75 billion to $100 billion annually, due to: 1. absenteeism, 2. medical costs, and 3. diminished productivity. Job-related stress can be caused by: 1. lack of control over job performance, 2. boredom, 3. supervisor and coworker relationships, 4. exclusion from decision making, 5. over- or under-utilization of abilities, and 6. role ambiguity. Stress studies conducted by the National Institute for Occupational Safety & Health showed clerical and blue-collar workers to be more susceptible to stress than executives. Many companies have reacted to worker stress by providing stress-reduction programs or counseling and these techniques have been successful for both office and industrial workers. Chart. —Palisano, Peg; *Occupational Hazards,* Oct 1983, 45(10): pp. 88-92. Avail. ABI 83-31746

Job, Stress, Health hazards, Studies, Poultry, Inspectors, Postal service, Workers, Office automation, Problems, VDTs, Programs, Manycompanies

Cost Effective Stress Management Training   (417)

Many firms are recognizing the benefits, such as increased productivity, of teaching their employees to manage stress. A good program will usually combine educational material on the nature of stress, its health implications, and methods of coping with stress in the work environment with instruction in techniques for deep relaxation. By alternating exercises with lectures and small group sharing it is possible to handle groups of 25-30 persons with no loss of skill development. Self-analysis exercises are provided as homework along with a stress management plan which includes a scheme for continuing these efforts into the future. For long-range success it is important that the participants be motivated to continue using the techniques.There are several relaxation techniques which work. Ranked in order of their teachability in the classroom, development of skills in a short time, long-term productivity, and likelihood of continued utilization, these techniques are: 1. self-hypnosis, 2. progressive relaxation, 3. transcendental meditation, 4. biofeedback, 5. yoga/zen, and 6. physical exercise. Reference. —Shea, Gordon F.; *Training & Development Jrnl,* Jul 1980, 34(7): pp. 25-33. Avail. ABI 80-14253

Stress, Management, Training, Productivity, Meditation, Cost, Effectiveness, Tension

A Costly Employee Benefit 'Myth'   (418)

Stress in the workplace has often been thought to be a result of working conditions, but this is a myth. The idea that employees should be compensated for disability as a result of this mythical influence is ridiculous. The stress myth takes away the prerogative to control the way we deal with life and enslaves us to the uncertainties with which the world confronts us. There are 2 misunderstandings on which this myth is based: 1. the definition of stress, and 2. the ability of the human being to deal emotionally with the events of life. Stress is often believed to be caused by situations, but it is really a series of specific biological reactions which occur in the human body to help prepare it to deal physically with some real or perceived assault on its stability. Many workers' compensation claims for injuries are purported to result from work-related stress. The validity of these claims relies on the assumption that the work environment is responsible for the occurrence of stress in the on-the-job lives of the employees. This stress myth must be overcome because it is the biggest single promoter of stress. —Ecker, Richard E.; *National Underwriter (Life/Health)*, May 7, 1983, 87(19): pp. 17,28-29. Avail. ABI 83-15265

Stress, Employee problems, Workers compensation, Heart diseases, Occupational, Injuries

A Counseling Approach to Employee Burnout   (419)

Organizational changes can effectively treat some employee burnout, but the counseling approach, which firms often ignore, is more effective with employees who do not experience the organizational changes, or with those whose serious state of burnout calls for further treatment. Burnout affects work-related behavior and may also carry over to an employee's personal life. The employer must recognize the symptoms of burnout and be aware that certain personality types are more susceptible. Career Enhancement Therapy (CET) helps workers design new coping strategies through: 1. evaluating and understanding the causes of burnout, 2. determining necessary changes, 3. developing sensitivity to symptoms to help cope with future episodes, and 4. developing communications skills to discuss feelings with others. CET is most effective when offered to groups of 12-15 employees. CET is not a replacement for psychotherapy, but it is one step an organization may take to remedy the problem of burnout. While the individual is chiefly responsible for recognizing and dealing with burnout, the organization can employ strategies to reduce burnout and help treat the problem where it exists. References. —Glicken, Morley D.; *Personnel Jrnl,* Mar 1983, 62(3): pp. 222-228. Avail. ABI 83-09439

Burnout, Stages, Predictions, Employee counseling, Therapy, Programs, Employee problems

Critical Job Events, Acute Stress, and Strain: A   (420)
Multiple Interrupted Time Series

A study was made of the acute stress of critical job events (CJEs) to determine psychological and physiological effects on individuals. A CJE occurs when a time-bounded peak performance job demand is made. The study sample comprised 39 first-year nursing students. An interrupted time series with multiple replications was used to measure job stress during 2 applications of CJE-anticipation and 3 low-stress occasions. The 5 measurements showed a consistent pattern of notable changes in anxiety, systolic blood pressure, and pulse rate. Qualitative overload and serum uric acid changed significantly 3 out of 4 times. Except for cholesterol, the other variables (quantitative overload, ambiguity, depression, psychosomatic complaints, and self-esteem) also showed changes during stress producing anticipation of events. Stress anticipation and its consequences occurred during an interval, rather than at one time. Although the study showed CJEs to produce the same strains as chronic stress, future research is needed to determine if CJE-derived stress affects individuals differently than chronic stress or organization-change events. Tables. References. –Eden, Dov; *Organizational Behavior & Human Performance,* Dec 1982, 30(3): pp. 312-329. Avail. ABI 83-01878

Critical, Job, Stress, Anticipation, Studies, Anxieties, Hospitals, Nurses

Cumulative Trauma and Stress at Work (421)

Work stress represents a serious cost for industry both in human and financial terms. This is being experienced most seriously in the US, and particularly California, due to the workers' compensation laws regarding cumulative trauma. Cumulative trauma is a type of workers' compensation claim in which an employee contends that a major illness or disability is the cumulative result of minor job stresses and strains stretching back over a period of years. The courts and appeal boards are accepting many of these claims. California allows a very liberal interpretation of stress-induced illness, and 20% of the workers' compensation claims that will be paid in 1977 in California are expected to be cumulative trauma types. The precedent was set in 1960, in the Carter versus General Motors case where the Michigan Supreme Court sustained a compensation award to James Carter, a machine operator, for an emotional breakdown resulting from job pressure. These cases provide a new urgency to the development of methods of accounting for human resources. Table. Bibliography. –Cooper, Cary L.; *Accounting, Organizations & Society (UK),* 1980, 5(3): pp. 357-359. Avail. ABI 80-22705

Cumulative, Stress, Work environment, Workers compensation, Insurance claims, Litigation, California, Michigan, Court decisions

Dealing with Employee Stress (422)

The stress episode model has been developed to help managers reduce the human and economic cost of worker stress. The model depicts factors involved in stress and the responses to stress. The first factor in the model is the objective situation or the environmental stimuli facing the worker. The second is anxiety or the tendency to respond to threatening situations with increased arousal. Anxiety determines how the worker perceives the objective situation. This picture is the subjective situation which, if threatening, triggers arousal, psychological adjustment, or behavioral responses. The worker responds to stress by altering his perception of the situation through defenses or by altering the objective situation (coping). Intervention strategies for managers involve managers becoming more sensitive to situations and taking action to help reduce stress or to increase the worker's capacity to cope with it. They can manipulate the task, the social environment, or the individual's behavior. Intervention can mix and match situations with employees for the good of the individual and the organization. Diagrams. References. –Behling, Orlando and Holcombe, F. Douglas; *MSU Business Topics,* Spring 1981, 29(2): pp. 53-61. Avail. ABI 81-13043

Personnel management, Managers, Employee, Stress, Behavior, Models, Anxieties, Psychological, Adjustments, Intervention, Strategy, Behavior modification

Dealing with Information Overload (423)

The human mind is capable of processing only a limited quantity of information. When a person is subjected to too high a communication input load, efficiency declines. If overload conditions persist, people may make more errors, become forgetful or absent-minded, and become less tolerant of frustration. The stress may even cause personality changes and health deterioration resulting in job-burnout. Environmental stimuli can be eliminated by installing room dividers and sound-absorbing materials to reduce noise, and by rearranging furniture so that desks face away from main traffic areas. Memory aids such as lists and calendars free the mind for the task at hand. Schedule the activities so that tasks can be done one at a time and in the most efficient manner. Delegate tasks in a responsible manner. Organize communications by their importance by delegating message screening to a secretary. Eliminate redundancy in meetings by using a time limit. These are among the ways information-overload stress can be reduced.
—Rader, Martha H.; *Personnel Jrnl,* May 1981, 60(5): pp. 373-375. Avail. ABI 81-11523

Stress, Management, Time management, Information

Decision Making by Socialist Managers in Complex (424) Organizations

An analysis was made of the decision making process by managers in Poland. The model used in the analysis is based on a continuum which defines decision making techniques, emotional states, and levels of activity as the decision process becomes more difficult. The analysis was based on questionnaires and interviews with 165 managers.The results of the study showed that when difficulties continue to which previous efforts have been ineffective, most managers reassess the situation in order to eliminate difficulties by new means (87.6%). Some 30.6% use force and categorical demands, 27% try previous methods again, 20% develop an idea for solving difficulties, and 11.8% compromise the situation. A point is generally reached where the manager addresses a problem not with the goal of accomplishing the task but to defend his interests. Response to the means by which these managers retain emotional balance show that 86.5% used overcompensation at any cost, 56% suppressed their anxieties about situations, and 63.5% were not able to forget their problems away from the job. Charts. Table. References. —Kiezun, Witold; *International Studies of Mgmt & Organization,* Winter 1979/ 1980, 9(4): pp. 63-77. Avail. Sharpe 80-03924

Decision making, Socialism, Managers, Behavior, Planned economy, Case studies, Research, Stress, Problems

Definition and Conceptualization of Stress in (425) Organizations

Stress in organizations is becoming an increasingly important phenomenon in both academic research and organizational practices. Although stress is often associated with several vital individual physiological, psychological, and behavioral symptoms, little is known about it.A definition and conceptualization of stress in organizations is offered to facilitate a greater understanding of the phenomenon. This definition attempts to reflect consideration of the existing multiple uses, paradigms, and research results of stress both inside and outside organizations. The major elements of the stress definition are: uncertainty, opportunity, constraint, and demand. It appears that the intensity of a stress condition is determined by the value of the outcome and the uncertainty attached to the resolution of the stress condition. It is possible for individual strategies to be developed to reduce stress and the symptoms associated with it. Table. Figures. References. – Schuler, Randall S.; *Organizational Behavior & Human Performance,* Apr 1980, 25(2): pp. 184-215. Avail. ABI 80-09152

Stress, Tension, Organizational, Health, Conditions, Studies, Research

Designing an Effective Stress-Management Training Program/Are You Ready for a Stress Management Program? (426)

The conversion of stress from a liability into an asset is a challenging task for trainers. The trainer should make goals of the stress management program as realistic as possible, solicit the support of upper management, and focus on specific attitudinal changes. Steps in the actual program itself include: 1. Assess and measure the stress level of each employee. 2. Assess adaptive and nonadaptive coping strategies. 3. Determine primary stressors in the workplace. 4. Explain clearly what stress is. 5. Explain the health implications of positive and negative stress. 6. Identify the symptoms of each employee that result from excessive stress. 7. Identify their causes, and describe stress management strategies. 8. Develop a personalized stress management program. While all organizations are subject to on-the-job stress, not all organizations need to take active steps to remedy the situation. Using a survey will help gauge the firm's readiness to take action. The survey assesses such questions as: 1. whether the firm's medical department has tabulated data that indicate a need, 2. whether the stress reduction course has been reviewed as to just what it is to accomplish, and 3. whether upper management has mandated that a program be undertaken. Chart. –Griffin, Darrell R.; Everly, George; Fuhrmann, Calvin; and Bright, Deborah K.; *Training,* Sep 1982, 19(9): pp. 20-34. Avail. ABI 82-23958

Stress, Management, Training, Strategy, Goals, Goal setting, Surveys, Guidelines

Determinants of Leader-Subordinate Exchange Relationships (427)

The attempt to produce a tractable, empirically supported model consistently predicting leader effectiveness has been frustrating for leadership theorists and researchers. One empirical generalization stands out from descriptive-focused research conducted in the last 10 years: leaders react differently to different subordinates. A conceptual dimension is offered for ordering the differences in behavior shown to different subordinates. This dimension is treated as a variable to be accounted for, and the effect on it of certain antecedent variables is examined. The value of the concept "noncontractual social exchange" (NSE) as a dimension describing leader behavior is assessed. The results of an experiment employing an in-basket memo device demonstrated that subordinate competence best predicted the intentions of NSE by a sample of working adults. Subjects were more likely to initiate

NSE with highly competent subordinates. When the situation contained stress in the form of pressure for effective task outcomes, this discrimination was more pronounced. Results also showed that low-"least preferred co-worker" (LPC), or task-oriented leaders showed greater variation in NSE as a function of subordinate competence and task stress, as well as a generally lower level of NSE, than high-LPC, or relationship-oriented leaders. Implications for selecting, training, and organizational support of leaders are discussed. Charts. References. –Kim, Ken I. and Organ, Dennis W.; *Group & Organization Studies,* Mar 1982, 7(1): pp. 77-89. Avail. ABI 82-11283

Organizational behavior, Leadership, Social, Exchange, Theory, Studies, Task, Stress, Variance analysis

Developing a Corporate Policy for Managing Stress (428)

Research has suggested that job-related stress may cause poor productivity, low morale, and a wide range of other dysfunctional organizational outcomes. In an attempt to reduce this problem, a process has been designed to establish a workable and meaningful corporate policy on stress. The process begins with detecting problem areas. This is the monitoring stage. At this step, it is necessary to distinguish between stress and undesirable stress outcomes. During the next step, or the analysis stage, the nature and scope of the problems must be understood. An in-depth examination of identified problem areas is necessary to pinpoint the roots and extent of the trouble. The last stage involves formulating corrective policy. The corrective policy may be "individual-oriented" or "organization-oriented," depending upon where the undesirable stress outcomes are located. Some of the common sources and suggested causes of organizational stress are discussed, as well as corrective policies. Charts. –Stoner, Charles R. and Fry, Fred L.; *Personnel,* May/Jun 1983, 60(3): pp. 66-76. Avail. ABI 83-17243

Employee problems, Organizational, Stress, Programs, Corporate, Policy making, Organizational behavior

Diagnosing and Treating Managerial Malaise (429)

Increasingly, human resources (HR) professionals are facing a problem that is often difficult to identify and even harder to treat: the problem of previously productive managers who start to plateau or burn out. A self-reporting inventory is presented to help HR professionals identify those who are prone to or have "managerial malaise." Managerial malaise is the feeling of not being as productive as possible, or of not being challenged enough by current projects or excited by the prospect of future ones. Causes of managerial malaise include: 1. a "mid-life crisis," 2. economic recession, and 3. decreased or eliminated compensation increases. The remedy for managerial malaise depends on the individual. Both the organization and the manager must understand the seriousness of the problem and become involved in careful planning and action to alleviate the symptoms and underlying causes of the malaise. Specific actions and preventive measures are discussed. –Ginsburg, Sigmund G.; *Personnel,* Jul/Aug 1984, 61(4): pp. 34-41. Avail. ABI 84-25982

Employee morale, Job satisfaction, Managers, Employee problems, Rehabilitation, Effectiveness, Goal setting

The Effects of Emotional Support on Perceived Job   (430)
Stress and Strain

A national sample of 553 social workers - mental health professionals - is used to examine the relationship between work stress and strain and emotional support. The central issue dealt with is the ability of emotional support to buffer or moderate the impact of work stress. The data indicate that emotional support is negatively associated with perceived stress and strain, a finding which supports all of the previous research on this issue. In contrast, no evidence is found that buffering effects occur with either work-related strain or health-related strain; this contradicts the findings reported by LaRocco, House, and French (1980) and Pinneau (1976). According to the present data, if emotional support can reduce stress and thereby the strain one feels, then it has not demonstrated its potential. A simple explanation may exist in the differences in populations and measures employed in the various studies. Chart. Tables. References. —Jayaratne, Srinika and Chess, Wayne A.; *Jrnl of Applied Behavioral Science,* May 1984, 20(2): pp. 141-153. Avail. JAI 84-23334

Stress, Emotions, Burnout, Job satisfaction, Behavioral sciences, Social services, Correlation analysis, Employee problems

Effects of Life and Job Stress on Information Search   (431)
Behaviors of Organizational Members

Persons employed in a wide variety of organizations completed questionnaires designed to measure both life-related and work-related stress. The questionnaires also produced information on subsequent role-related information search in on the job and off-the-job settings. It is suggested that stressful events provoke a person to question the appropriateness of typical modes of role enactment. Results of the study showed that stressful events do in fact provoke such questions and, as a result, predict role-relevant information search activities. Moreover, the study revealed that work-related stressful events predict information search conducted on the job. On the other hand, life stress situations predict information searches off-the-job. It is suggested that stressful events can serve a positive function, whether work-related or life-related, because they can produce a significant reevaluation of habitual role enactment, and can occasion subsequent adaptation to a changing environment. References. —Weiss, Howard M.; Ilgen, Daniel R.; and Sharbaugh, Michael E.; *Jrnl of Applied Psychology,* Feb 1982, 67(1): pp. 60-66. Avail. ABI 82-07416

Personal, Job, Stress, Effects, Behavior, Job hunting, Organizational behavior, Feedback, Continuing education, Studies

Effects of Stressful Life Events on Individual   (432)
Performance Effectiveness and Work Adjustment
Processes Within Organizational Settings: A Research
Model

In administrative and organizational sciences, the effect of stress on valued work outcomes has generally been conceptualized in terms of work. A selective overview of some of the significant findings of life stress research is presented, and a conceptual model for examining the effects of stressful life events on employee job involvement, performance effectiveness, and other related work adjustment processes is proposed. The etiological significance of stressful life events in one's personal life is integrated with stresses originating from one's organizational life. Intervention strategies and techniques for improving work life should consider the development of research-based personal and organizational mechanisms for the "stressed" employee to cope with stressful life events. Other implications for future research are noted. Table. References. –Bhagat, Rabi S.; *Academy of Mgmt Review,* Oct 1983, 8(4): pp. 660-671. Avail. ABI 83-29189

Stress, Effects, Performance, Social psychology, Organizational behavior, Studies, Models, Personality, Organization theory, Employee problems

Emotional Exhaustion in a High Stress Organization (433)

Stress has become a key concept in studies of employee health and welfare. Emotional exhaustion is an extremely affective and chronic type of work-related strain. Sources of emotional exhaustion are investigated via interviews and questionnaires completed by 169 police officers in a police force struggling with the impact of major changes. Findings suggest that emotional exhaustion is the result of interaction among personal characteristics of the individual employee, of the interpersonal milieu, and of the type of work. However, emotional exhaustion is profoundly affected by departmental context, administrative policy and practices, and the conflicting mandates of police in society. All stress in police work is not created by the work itself; some is the result of organizational processes. Little can be done to remedy many of these process-related stresses, such as hours of monotony interspersed with periods of frantic activity. Chart. Tables. References. –Gaines, Jeannie and Jermier, John M.; *Academy of Mgmt Jrnl,* Dec 1983, 26(4): pp. 567-586. Avail. ABI 84-01702

Stress, Burnout, Studies, Law enforcement, Police, Emotions, Employee problems, Statistical analysis, Organizational behavior

An Empirical Investigation of Job Stress, Social (434) Support, Service Length, and Job Strain

Stress can be defined in terms of a relationship between a person (P) and the environment (E). To further explore the problem of stress, the hypothesized relationship between job stress and 2 job strains-job dissatisfaction and ineffective job performance-were examined. A sample of 166 bus operators across 4 bus stations within a midwestern transit authority was employed. A pretested questionnaire was administered which included job stress, social support, and job satisfaction measures. The French job-stress model was used. Results furnished only limited support for the French model, and length of service was discovered to be an important variable to consider. Although very little relationship was discovered between job stress elements and ineffective job performance, stronger support was found in the job-stress-job dissatisfaction relationship. A P-E fit approach to job stress was found to be methodologically defensible. Chart. Tables. Appendix. References. –Blau, Gary; *Organizational Behavior & Human Performance,* Apr 1981, 27(2): pp. 279-302. Avail. ABI 81-26135

Job, Stress, Models, Organizational behavior, Social, Support, Job satisfaction, Studies

An Examination of the Organizational Antecedents of Stressors at Work   (435)

Seven sources of stress in the work environment and their relationship to contextual, task, and role-related variables were examined. The stressors included: inter-unit conflict, technical problems, efficiency problems, role frustration, staff shortages, short lead times, and too many meetings. Subsystem and work shift were the contextual variables, and job level or hierarchical position were the role-related characteristics. Five task dimensions were utilized. Data were obtained from a medium-sized food processing firm which had 5 subsystems and 3 job levels. Multivariate analysis of covariance was performed. Contextual and role-related variables of subsystem and job level were found to be significantly and independently related to the reported magnitude of 5 stressors; the pattern of stressors across job levels differed systematically. Task dimensions of complexity, routinization, interdependence, and closeness of supervision demonstrated weak to moderate relationships with several stressors. Chart. Tables. References. —Parasuraman, Saroj and Alutto, Joseph A.; *Academy of Mgmt Jrnl,* Mar 1981, 24(1): pp. 48-67. Avail. ABI 81-06617

Organizational, Stress, Organizational behavior, Variance analysis, Roles, Conflicts, Studies

The Experience of Tedium in Life and Work   (436)

Tedium, which is the experience of physical, emotional, and mental exhaustion, is assumed to arise from chronic daily pressures. It was predicted that tedium was related to: 1. internal features which include pressures inherent in the individual's roles and imposed on the cognitive capacity and the need for meaningfulness and achievement, and 2. external features which include the pressures imposed on the individual by physical, organizational, and social environment. A trilogy of studies was conducted to develop a tedium measure, to test its reliability and validity, and to examine its relationships to internal and external life and work features. A total of 1187 subjects were involved in the 3 studies. The results indicate that tedium is a highly relevant psychological construct. It was found that tedium was a significant correlate of both internal and external life and work features. The results suggest a need to develop a more rigorous causal model of tedium. Tables. References. —Kafry, Ditsa and Pines, Ayala; *Human Relations,* Jul 1980, 33(7): pp. 477-503. Avail. ABI 80-15399

Stress, Tension, Human relations, Social services, Programs, Employees, Statistical analysis, Studies

Experiencing Uncertainty: Organisational Lessons from the Clinic   (437)

Several ambiguous aspects of the work setting may contribute to the development of work stress. The uncertainty of the economic situation affects all workers, whether or not they fear for their own positions. It is the threat and build-up to redundancy, rather than the actual unemployment, that creates the more pronounced psychological and physical symptoms of stress. Another potentially stressful area involves lack of clarity about the work objectives associated with a particular job. This role ambiguity has been related to: 1. lowered self-esteem, 2. life and job dissatisfaction, and 3. a decreased motivation to work. Inadequate feedback can also produce a great deal of stress. Management must recognize that uncertainty is handled differently by each worker and must strive to give the support and encouragement necessary to make uncertainty tolerable. The effects of uncertainty are examined in a case study in which stress was reduced, once the employee was able to look objectively at the work situation. References. —Firth, Jenny; *Personnel Review (UK)*, 1983, 12(2): pp. 11-15. Avail. ABI 83-28577

Organizational behavior, Employment security, Roles, Psychological, Problems, Stress, Employee problems

Goal Specificity and Difficulty and Leader Initiating   (438)
Structure as Strategies for Managing Role Stress

There is a growing concern with stress in the work environment resulting from physical and sociopsychological conditions. Role stress, which is becoming more common and destructive for individuals and companies, occurs when the individual is uncertain of his or her role in an organization of how and where to perform given tasks. It is suggested that role conflict is related to leader-initiating structure and goal-setting. A study suggests strategies for managing role stress based on these two factors. Strategies are presented in the framework of a role perception model permitting examination of several components related to role stress conditions. The object of the study was to determine: 1. the relationship of leader-initiating structure and goal-setting to employee satisfaction, 2. their relationship to role conflict and ambiguity, and 3. the interrelationship among goals and structure, satisfaction, and conflict and ambiguity. Results provided strong support for the model implemented and suggest good cause for goal specificity and leader-initiating structure in reducing role stress. Because this study was cross-sectional, the causal relationships among the variables in the role perception model cannot be specified. The role perception model should also incorporate the role of the organizational structure and the nature of the employee's task, so as to offer alternatives for clarifying employees' expectations. Charts. References. —Lee, Cynthia and Schuler, Randall S.; *Jrnl of Mgmt,* Fall 1980, 6(2): pp. 177-187. Avail. ABI 81-26081

Roles, Conflict, Stress, Management, Goal setting, Employee attitude (PER), Supervision, Organizational behavior, Studies

Hassles, Helplessness and Hurriedness: Three Critical   (439)
Stressors in a Manager's Life

The stress factors of hassles, helplessness, and hurriedness have increased significantly over the past few years. Such daily annoyances as traffic jams, rising prices, or putting on weight may be small, but the cumulative effect can be greater than a major traumatic event. Helplessness is a sense of impotence to influence important factors of life. It is responsibility with no authority or control. Hurriedness, a constant sense of urgency in all aspects of life, is typical of individuals with intense drive and competitiveness. Hassles can be avoided by foresight and planning. Participation and initiative will help relieve helplessness. Hurriedness is best controlled by effective time management. Social support is the crucial buffer between stress and illness. Specific steps to follow in managing stress include: 1. consciously assessing your present pace of life, 2. leaving job tensions at the office, 3. developing alternative methods for coping with stress, and 4. maintaining conscious control of your life. Chart. References. —Howard, John H.; *Business Qtrly (Canada),* Spring 1983, 48(1): pp. 22-27. Avail. ABI 83-13612

Employee problems, Stress, Tension, Time management, Personality

Health, Stress, and the Manager's Life Style   (440)

Of the risk factors associated with 10 leading causes of death, stress is undoubtedly a factor in both the environmental and life-style areas. While tolerance for stress differs with the individual, excessive stress increases the likelihood of ill health, low productivity, and low morale. Those who feel they are in control of their work environment, who are challenged by their work, and who are committed to its importance withstand stress better than others. Individual stress-management techniques must focus on 3 levels of response: 1. removing or avoiding unnecessary stressors, 2. coping effectively with necessary stressors, and 3. building health to buffer the long-term impact of stress. A "Health, Stress and Your Life Style" program has shown positive effects. Implications for human-resource-development professionals include the need to: 1. create educational training events in this area for people at all levels of the organization, 2. work toward building control, challenge, and commitment into every job, 3. help remove unnecessary stressors, 4. support individuals' attempts to take care of themselves, and 5. support and stimulate a more healthful management paradigm. References. Tables. —Adams, John D.; *Group & Organization Studies,* Sep 1981, 6(3): pp. 291-301. Avail. ABI 81-22640

Health, Stress, Lifestyles, Managers, Human resources, Development, Organizational, Behavior, Prevention

Hidden Menace in Pits   (441)

The stresses of the trading business fall into many categories. The most obvious is the stress of actually trading which involves being on the exchange floor daily. In addition to long hours, working conditions at the exchanges are sometimes less than ideal as the pits are often overcrowded, and the noise level is intense. Stress can occur from the reality of outtrades, trades that do not match up the day after they occur. The world places stress on traders or brokers by expecting them to act in a certain way. And there is the stress of needing to make money to pay bills. Carolyn Schuham, a psychotherapist specializing in stress management, says that people in the commodities industry worry too much and have a tendency to catastrophize. She notes that stress is physical - blood pressure, heart rate, breathing, flow of blood to the muscles, and the metabolism of the body. Stress management involves nutrition, fitness, relaxation, and the psychological implications of stress. Schuham suggests establishing peer support groups. Knowing how to best prepare for stress and cope with it when it occurs can give traders and brokers an edge. —Bard, Susan; *Commodities: The Magazine of Futures Trading,* Aug 1982, 11(8): pp. 92-96. Avail. ABI 82-21873

Commodity markets, Trading, Commodity futures, Stress, Tension

Hostility in the Workplace   (442)

Hostility is the child of inferiority and of fear, and no department can function well when hostility is present. As a hostility chain reaction multiplies, motivation, creativity, and productivity can be impaired on every level of a company. If a person senses a feeling of hostility, he should always stop and try to reason why. The real source of anger can be confused when guilt is the offender. Suppressed hostility is the major cause of pilfering, sabotage, and backbiting of one's boss. Check your feelings before starting each day, leaving family problems at home. Show employees that you respect their work, and give them credit for every job well done. The next time a bad incident on the job happens, write it down. Record what happened, what events led up to the incident, were there any clues, and how could it have been prevented. Saving such records for comparison will provide a pattern of one's supervising skills and interpersonal relationships.
—Turecamo, Dorrine Anderson; *Supervision,* Feb 1981, 43(2): pp. 9-11. Avail. ABI 81-05068

Employees, Employee attitude (PER), Behavior, Stress

How Pharmacists Cope with Stress   (443)

Pharmacists are in a segment of the helping professions that is more prone to stress and burnout than the general public, due to the heavy demands placed upon it. Research has shown pharmacists are a high-risk group for suicides, drug/alcohol dependence, and other problems. Stress is induced when pharmacists believe they are: 1. unappreciated and/or unsupported by employees or those receiving services, 2. overtrained and underutilized, and 3. isolated as a group, from their directorship. Younger pharmacists tend to feel the stress of professional/business aspects more than older pharmacists. Work overloads with tight deadlines also create stress in pharmacists, as does: 1. increased competition, 2. paperwork, 3. government regulations, and 4. need for security. Pharmacists can learn to handle stress, beginning with the taking of a stress inventory. As stressful situations are recognized, they may be avoided or handled in a non-stress producing way. Stress can be reduced in non-work hours. While the method of attacking stress may vary, pharmacists are considered to have a stronger sense of wellness than other health professionals. —Chi, Judy; *Drug Topics,* Mar 1, 1982, 126(5): pp. 26-28,32-33. Avail. Drug 82-07680

Stress, Employee problems, Pharmacies

How to Experience the Joy of Burnout   (444)

The post-World War II baby boom has created the increasing incidence of job stress and burnout. Middle management is glutted with the baby boom generation. As a result, new graduates cannot advance. The pressure to produce and the growing fear of making mistakes have also contributed to job burnout. A facetious method is suggested for dealing with today's high pressure environment - enjoy burnout. There are 6 ways to enjoy job burnout and avoid working: 1. Be negative to avoid progress. 2. Collect irrelevant data to delay decision making. 3. Never write down anything that might be useful. 4. Pile up the distractions. 5. Follow the rules. 6. Quit. Another way to enjoy job burnout is to try to make burnout the latest organizational fad.

Time management is one way to get out of the workstream, and if someone notices the practitioner's lack of work, massive denial is a useful technique. —Davis, Robert H.; *Communication World,* Jan 1984, 1(3): pp. 18-20. Avail. ABI 84-05373

Burnout, Organizational behavior, Employee problems, Guidelines

How to Manage Managerial Stress (445)

There are many external and internal contacts that place demands on the skills and abilities of the manager, which leads to stress. Managers are also taxed by a set of self-imposed expectations. Furthermore, the demands that a manager faces are often in conflict with one another. The high volume of work and the disjointed work load make the manager's job stressful in psychological and physical ways. Role conflict and role ambiguity are 2 basic causes of managerial stress. Role conflict is found in several forms: 1. generated by a single sender, 2. generated by 2 or more senders, 3. person-role conflict, 4. inter-role conflict, and 5. role overload. There are 3 managerial practices that can be used in managing stress: 1. goal-setting program, 2. performance appraisal system, and 3. formalized reward system. These systems can reduce role ambiguity. The role management process must be understood and managed. Chart. —Brief, Arthur P.; *Personnel,* Sep/Oct 1980, 57(5): pp. 25-30. Avail. ABI 80-22410

Managers, Stress, Roles, Conflict, Personnel management, Management

The How, What and Why of Stress Management Training (446)

Stress is a major and growing problem for employees and employers alike. Many companies have instated some type of stress management program to minimize individual and corporate stress-related problems. Such programs can relieve performance problems created by employees who deal with stressful situations. Also, they may contribute to better employee health since there is a relationship between stress and health problems. Effective stress management training programs feature voluntary attendance. While these programs vary widely in form and content, certain general characteristics contribute to their chances of success. Stress management training may be measured in terms of: 1. skills achieved by participants, 2. self-reports of decreased tension and increased effectiveness, 3. observation and performance ratings, and 4. changes in turnover, absenteeism, grievance rates, etc. Charts. References. —Matteson, Michael T. and Ivancevich, John M.; *Personnel Jrnl,* Oct 1982, 61(10): pp. 768-774. Avail. ABI 82-26349

Stress, Management, Training, Personnel management, Costs, Human resources

The Human Problems in Practicing Law (447)

Twenty-five male attorneys were interviewed to gain their insights on the pressures of law practice. Most of the lawyers noted the piles of paperwork and reading they must go through; they regret the years when their children grew up without them, yet they feel the sacrifice was unavoidable. Older lawyers apparently have proportionately greater career satisfaction. Studies have revealed that lawyers are hypertensive, drink and smoke, and have a higher incidence of alcoholism and coronary artery disease than those who are less dedicated to their work and under less stress. The current study revealed that, although some lawyers hire office managers, many assume that role themselves because they are unable to delegate authority. The lawyers attributed much of their stress to assignment to trial and the accompanying scheduling difficulties. Most lawyers said they constantly work to impress on the staff the importance of contacts with clients; some were interested in the idea of sending the staff to seminars on dealing with the public. How the lawyer manages human resources seems to be the key to success. —Shrager, Joan M.; *Legal Economics,* Jan/Feb 1984, 10(1): pp. 20-28. Avail. ABA 84-06241

Attorneys, Stress, Personality, Law firms, Client relationships, Career development planning

An Interactionist Approach to Measuring Anxiety at Work   (448)

A measure of work anxiety is developed that was guided by the interactionist position, i.e., that behavior is determined by situations in interaction with individual responses. Endler's S-R format was adapted for a sample of 220 male managers between ages 30 and 60. The main measure was the Job Reaction Questionnaire (JRQ), in which respondents reported their psychological and emotional reactions on 8 response dimensions to 20 work situations. The situations ranged from answering the telephone to giving a talk in public. To analyze the JRQ responses, a procedure was used that combines clustering procedures based on an analysis of variance model with a canonical decomposition of each 2-way table associated with a first-order interaction term. The results generally supported 3 hypotheses: 1. that the proportions of variance accounted for by main effects and interactions are determined by the variation designed into the measure itself and by variations with the subject sample, 2. that the existence of statistical interactions that account for sizable variance does not demonstrate that behavior is a function of interaction in any general sense, and 3. that those who had not experienced a situation tended to rate it as more stressful. Tables. Charts. References. Appendix. —Payne, Roy L.; Fineman, Stephen; and Jackson, Paul R.; *Jrnl of Occupational Psychology (UK),* 1982, 55(1): pp. 13-25. Avail. ABI 82-09981

Anxieties, Work environment, Measurement, Hypotheses, Variance analysis, Stress, Studies

Job Stress and Job Performance Controversy: An Empirical Assessment   (449)

An examination of the relationship between job stress and employees' performance and withdrawal behavior was conducted. The subjects were 440 nurses in 2 hospitals in a metropolitan Canadian city on the east coast. Assessment was made of job stressors, including role ambiguity, role overload, role conflict, and resource inadequacy. Employees' performance was operationalized in regard to job performance, motivation, and patient care skill. Absenteeism, tardiness, and anticipated turnover were the withdrawal behaviors assessed. Multiple regressions, curvilinear correlation coefficients, and canonical correlations were figured to test the nature of the relationship between stressors and the criterion variables of the study. Results were more supportive of the negative linear relationship between stress and performance than for positive linear or curvilinear relationship.

The stressor role ambiguity showed a monotonic nonlinear relationship with a number of criterion variables. Chart. Tables. References. —Jamal, Muhammad; *Organizational Behavior & Human Performance,* Feb 1984, 33(1): pp. 1-21. Avail. ABI 84-05763

Stress, Effects, Performance, Studies, Statistical analysis, Effectiveness, Absenteeism, Employee turnover, Employee problems

Job Stress in Small Business Organizations: Causes,   (450) Measurement, Reduction

Some personality factors are linked with stress, but some characteristics of organizations and jobs are as much to blame or more so. To many people, work overload and work underload are sources of endless frustration, and not feeling secure can also cause stress. In small companies, poor utilization of good principles of management is often a serious contributor of high stress levels. Job stress usually appears in the form of job ambiguity or job conflict. Job ambiguity indicates the lack of clarity surrounding a person's job authority, responsibility, task demands, and work methods. Job conflict is the degree of incompatibility of expectations felt by a person on the job. There are several organizational principles to follow which can alleviate sources of job stress. Other techniques to relieve stress range from bio-feedback to simple relaxation exercises aimed at relieving fatigue and helping one to cope with anxieties that can lead to high blood pressure, hardening of the arteries, stroke, and heart attacks. Chart. References. —Milbourn, Gene, Jr.; *American Jrnl of Small Business,* Summer 1980, 5(1): pp. 37-46. Avail. ABI 81-00805

Small business, Job, Stress, Factors, Measurement, Reduction, Personality, Characteristics, Organizational, Principles

Job-Related Stress in Public Accounting   (451)

Accounting has traditionally been a high-stress profession. To be able to control stress to the degree practical, a firm must have an idea of the sources of job-related stress experienced by its staff. It must identify specific employee groups that are experiencing job-related stress. In a study of 7 accounting firms, the problem of job-related stress among accounting practitioners was investigated. Respondents from the large offices of national firms reported highest travel requirements, role conflict, and underuse. Members from small offices reported significantly less role ambiguity, underuse, and travel requirements. The audit group reported greater travel requirements and work load dissatisfaction, but the lowest feeling of autonomy. Managers felt significantly greater stress from role conflict and unwanted overtime than all other levels. Seniors seemed particularly concerned about job future ambiguity, unwanted overtime, inequity of pay, boredom, and work load dissatisfaction; while juniors reported the most stress resulting from feelings of being underused in an environment filled with ambiguity or uncertainty. Table. References. —Gaertner, James F. and Ruhe, John A.; *Jrnl of Accountancy,* Jun 1981, 151(6): pp. 68-74. Avail. ABI 81-15020

CPAs, Public accountants, Stress, Studies, Causes, Accountants

Ma Bell and the Hardy Boys (452)

The breakup of the Bell System last year allowed 2 psychologists, Suzanne C. Ouellette Kobasa and Salvatore R. Maddi, to test their hypothesis that certain personality traits combine to produce "hardiness." The hardiness characteristic enables people to withstand severe pressure without becoming ill. Kobasa and Maddi have concluded that "hardy" people: 1. are open to change and welcome it as a challenge, 2. get deeply involved in whatever they are doing, 3. find their work interesting and important, and 4. have a sense of control over events. The members of a sample of 259 male executives at Illinois Bell who rated high in psychological hardiness seemed to take the breakup in stride. Some were even exhilarated by the changes. These hardy individuals reported far fewer physical or mental difficulties in the wake of divestiture. The researchers have developed a model that explains how psychological hardiness works to preserve health. They believe hardiness is learned in early childhood, but it can be taught by one's environment later in life. Graphs. —Pines, Maya; *Across the Board,* Jul/Aug 1984, 21(7) /8: pp. 37-42. Avail. ABI 84-25081

Stress, Personality, Studies, Telephone companies, Executives, Psychological aspects, Employee problems, Divestiture, ATT

Managerial Burnout: Causes and Cures (453)

Job burnout is characterized by mental and physical exhaustion and feelings of disgust, dread, or boredom toward the job. Burnout engenders a kind of helplessness. However, burnout can be rectified if recognized while one still possesses a good standing with the employer, a high energy level, and a good self-image. Factors contributing to manager burnout are: 1. the belief that the freedom to take on professional risks and challenges is vanishing, 2. unionization, 3. governmental regulation, 4. the pressures of consumerism, 5. worker groups that lack a sense of occupational mobility, and 6. "crazymakers," those "double-bind, mixed-message" situations. Further, new managers and administrators sometimes see themselves as "change agents" sent to "deliver" the organization from the "ruin" caused by the regular hands. Administrators who exhibit a high degree of openness - delegating, assigning, explaining, and sharing duties and responsibilities - are less susceptible to burnout than others. References. —Sloan, R. B., Jr.; *Management Qtrly,* Fall 1982, 23(3): pp. 12-18. Avail. ABI 82-29332

Managers, Stress, Causes, Prevention

Managerial/Organizational Stress: Identification of (454)
Factors and Symptoms

To manage stress, managers must understand its dynamics and effects. Stress is an internal reaction to an environmental event and may eventually lead to a breakdown of the system if the short-term body reactions exist for prolonged time periods. Organizations tend to foster stress through their competitiveness. As they become more upwardly mobile, managers suffer stress from their success. Suppressed conflicts within subordinates and managers or between them may lead to frustration and anxiety. Rivalry over promotions and underutilization of managers may also create stress.Thirty job-related and 25 individual factors, such as work overload, ambiguous roles, financial problems, and a low self-esteem have been identified as major causes of stress. The severity of stress increases with the importance of the motives being blocked, the duration of the situation, the adjustments required, etc. Symptoms of stress include irritability, high blood pressure, fatigue, inability to concentrate, etc. Task-oriented reactions to stress occurring in an organization evolve around attack, withdrawal, or compromise. Tables. Chart. References. –Appelbaum, Steven H.; *Health Care Mgmt Review*, Winter 1980, 5(1): pp. 7-16. Avail. ABI 80-04717

Managers, Stress, Organizational, Factors, Identification, Changes, Promotions (MAN), Mobility

Managing Organization Caused Stress: The Challenge (455) for Employers and Employees

Many people work in organizations whose environments are not conducive to productivity and personal health. They suffer from stress which is directly related to their work settings. Stress is the body's reaction to both negative and positive demands made on it. The symptoms of workplace stress include increased absenteeism and accidents. Factors which contribute to a stress buildup include the lack of a support network in the individual's work and personal life. The physical setting of the workplace can also cause stress. Stress must be managed effectively, and for such management to be fruitful, it must be a joint responsibility of employers and employees. Both must develop an awareness of the symptoms of stress at work. Workers must bring to management's attention stressful circumstances in their work settings, and management must listen with the goal of improving the quality of work life. References. –Lynn, George and Lynn, Joanne Barrie; *Manage*, May 1983, 35(2): pp. 20-23. Avail. ABI 83-18043

Stress, Employee problems, Tension, Attitudes, Work environment, Health, Problems, Alcoholism, Absenteeism

Managing Stress for Increased Productivity (456)

There is an inverted-U curve depicting the relationship of stress and productivity. Productivity is low both when stress is too low and the individual's natural energizers are not charged and when stress is too high or prolonged due to a loss of vitality. It is necessary for managers to develop useful and constructive methods for identifying and managing stress, since it is an inevitable and inherent part of the manager's job. For managers, the sources of job stress include: 1. role overload resulting from expectations which are too high, 2. role ambiguity concerning job responsibilities, and 3. role conflict imposed by the various groups with which the manager works. Managers also face stress caused by life events and by their own personality types. There are a number of ways to reduce or alleviate sources of job stress which also help to clarify job responsibilities, including: 1. regular and frequent meetings with supervisors, 2. job descriptions, and 3. management by objectives statements. Other ways to reduce stress include: 1. talking it out, 2. leaving the situation for a short time, 3. taking some kind of action, and

4. obtaining professional counseling. Diagram. Table. —Huber, Vandra L.; *Supervisory Mgmt,* Dec 1981, 26(12): pp. 2-12. Avail. ABI 82-02220

Supervisors, Job, Stress, Management, Performance, Roles, Conflict

Managing Stress: A Model for the Human Resource Staff   (457)

Stress can rob organizations of potential daily success by sapping the emotional energy of their employees. Handling stress is a long-term goal-a process necessitating patience, practice, and commitment to changing behavior. A model that is useful in approaching stress management includes: 1. identifying sources of stress, 2. choosing a target, 3. looking for barriers-planning to succeed, 4. developing a stress management plan, and 5. evaluating the plan. To identify sources of stress, a checklist can be used by the trainer. Another effective way to do this is through group sharing. After identifying sources of stress on the job, employees can decide on a target problem with the goal of managing that problem. For about a week, they should record what happens when the problem occurs. In the planning stage, trainers can use cognitive restructuring. Thus, a stress-management plan is actually a problem-solving effort, with long-range goals being established and accomplished through a series of steps that usually last one or 2 weeks. Charts. References. —Weigel, Randy and Pinsky, Sheldon; *Personnel Administrator,* Feb 1982, 27(2): pp. 56-60. Avail. ABI 82-05540

Stress, Management, Programs, Training, Planning, Guidelines

Marriage: DP Style   (458)

The job-related demands in the data processing field have contributed to a very high divorce rate among data processing personnel. Excessive stress, long hours, and midnight trouble calls create an environment many marriages cannot tolerate. John Van Zwieten, a stress management consultant, says the high divorce rate in data processing is a natural result of the high degree of stress it generates. To combat this stress, people need to be aware of the fact that they have control over stress. Each area of stress must be addressed. Finally, an action plan must be developed to change behavioural patterns to eliminate the stress. New software development techniques may eliminate some job stress by making projects more manageable and less likely to fall behind schedule. Predictable software systems will allow better scheduling. As software development progresses from an art to a science, many of the classical job stresses will be eliminated. —Cherlin, Merrill; *Datamation,* Sep 1980, 26(9): pp. 184-188. Avail. ABI 80-18827

Marriage, Divorce, Data processing, Problems, Stress, Work hours

Meditation at the Telphone Company   (459)

The New York Telephone (NYT) company has instituted an unusual program that is aimed at helping its employees use meditation-relaxation to overcome stress and its physical effects. The program is largely based on Clinically Standardized Meditation (CSM) and is open to all employees. NYT participants report that the CSM program has helped them become more calm and more positive about themselves. Participants in the CSM pilot project were recruited through company circulars featuring a self-scoring quiz, aimed at measuring an individual's "scream index" by rating 10 possible symptoms of stress. The program itself featured 3 methods of achieving relaxation: 1. progressive muscle relaxation, 2. respiratory one method, and 3. CSM. Evaluation of the pilot program showed that CSM offered the most benefits, but failed to predict what kind of person would be best suited for a particular method. As the CSM program and evaluations continue, indications are that meditating can be helpful in reducing symptoms of stress and improving people's efficiency. References. – McGeveran, William A., Jr.; *Wharton Magazine,* Fall 1981, 6(1): pp. 28-32. Avail. ABI 81-25375

Telephone companies, Stress, Reduction, Meditation, Programs, Case studies

Mental Distress: Possible Implications for the Future   (460)

In recent years, organizations have become more concerned with the emotional well-being of their workers. Programs for job enrichment and improving the quality of work life are an indication of a growing awareness that the organization's productivity and long-term prosperity depend heavily on employee dedication and commitment. Another trend is the extent to which employees, aided by both statutes and the common law, are trying to hold their employers legally liable for psychological and mental distress said to be job and work related. Not only is this an area of potential financial burden, but the problems in measuring, assessing, and controlling something as intangible as emotional distress make its management particularly challenging. There are 3 major areas of the law where this development is taking place: 1. mental injury resulting from work stresses and related factors for which the employer is liable under programs of workers' compensation, 2. compensation beyond "make-whole" remedies for mental anguish resulting from the employer's violation of certain anti-discrimination statutes, and 3. emotional distress from intentional acts by the employer designed to humiliate and degrade. References. –Novit, Mitchell S.; *Personnel Administrator,* Aug 1982, 27(8): pp. 47-53. Avail. ABI 82-21250

Stress, Emotions, Mental health, Damages, Discrimination, Effects, Work environment, Workers compensation, Litigation, Court decisions

Mid-Career Crisis - Is It a Myth?   (461)

Little empirical data has been provided to document the existence or the extent of the mid-life crisis and its symptoms. John Hunt of the London Business School interviewed a cross-section of 574 male managers in Australia to determine the extent of the problem and whether it was "created" by behavioral scientists. Three problems were approached: 1. if the crisis exists, 2. if it is restricted to a certain age, and 3. if people in certain organizations are more susceptible. Hunt found that in age groups under 50 years, 20%-27% of managers had been or were depressed. Most depression occurs in the late 30s and early 40s, but age alone does not define the problem. The major cause of the crisis is the locked-in effect where progression from middle management to the superstar level is blocked. The greatest incidence of mid-career crisis was found in industries with highly structured hierarchical organizations. Two major groups were found to exhibit mid-life crisis - the loners and the solid middle managers. Hunt suggests some areas in which companies can act: 1. counselling, 2. stress-reduction programs, 3. life/career planning, 4. sabbatical leave, and 5. greater opportunity for career change. Tables. —Anonymous; *Work & People (Australia),* 1981, 7(3): pp. 36-38. Avail. ABI 82-23103

Australia, Mid career, Crisis, Depression, Behavior, Stress, Health, Employee problems

Mid-Career Crisis and the Organization   (462)

"Mid-career crisis" is characterized by certain growing dissatisfaction with one's job and one's self-perception. The most severe crises often occur at the height of a person's career, despite previously outstanding work records. The causes are many and complex. A mid-career crisis will have consequences for both the individual and the organization; either party can react to the crisis either negatively or positively. Negative reactions from both worker and employer may ultimately result in termination. Positive employer reaction and negative worker reaction will result in a "marginal" employee whose feelings of incompetence eventually result in the organization moving the employee to a less demanding job or encouraging early retirement. Positive worker reaction and negative employer reaction will produce a worker who becomes satisfied with putting forth only limited effort to be productive. Positive reactions from both worker and employer will result in a well-adjusted worker who can be a valuable organizational asset. Organizations can help employees adjust to mid-life crises in a variety of mutually beneficial ways. Chart. References. —Thomas, Joe; *Business Horizons,* Nov/Dec 1982, 25(6): pp. 73-78. Avail. ABI 83-01334

Mid career, Crisis, Employee problems, Stress

Middle Management Stress: Recognizing and Treating   (463)
Burnout Victims

Burnout, which is a term used to describe a person's physical and mental deterioration, has a number of signs or symptoms, including: 1. lack of energy, 2. denial of stress, 3. lack of creativity, and 4. tight muscles. According to Randy Kunkle, director of a consulting firm in Colorado Springs, Colorado, there are 5 stages in the burnout process: 1. chronic but minor physical ailments, 2. overindulgence in eating, drinking, or sleeping, 3. intellectual boredom and a shortened attention span, 4. greater emotional involvement such as alienation from colleagues, and 5. a loss of skills and strengths to the point of being unable to make decisions. The middle manager often has duties assigned but is not able to share the decision-making role with the top manager. Because of this situation, the middle manager can begin to feel trapped and unproductive. Effective handling of burnout requires changing the internal and external factors which caused the burnout. It is also important for middle managers to receive feedback from their colleagues and superiors. Table. Graph. References. —Tanner, L. Art; *Healthcare Financial Mgmt,* Jan 1983, 37(1): pp. 12-22. Avail. ABI 83-04119

Middle management, Burnout, Stages, Stress, Managers, Probability

Models to Combat Stress   (464)

Job burnout is an emotional condition created by chronic and excessive on-the-job stress. Job burnout reduces an employee's job performance and negatively affects his personal life. Credit management is a particularly stressful occupation, and credit executives and credit analysts face more possibility of burnout. One stress-producing area is the making of credit decisions and explaining the decision procedure. In this area, credit-granting decision models can be helpful. As they can be "put down on paper," their use and decisions can be easily explained to the sales and other departments. These models are usually one of 3 types: 1. Judgmental Scoring Models, 2. Judgmental-Statistical Hybrids, and 3. Fully Statistical-Analytical Models. Another stress area in credit is the interpersonal dealings between credit personnel and customers. Other sources of stress on credit executives and analysts are common to manager-subordinate situations. Burnout can be avoided or reduced by: 1. holding informative employee meetings, 2. group problem solving, 3. employee-defined training, and 4. open communications. Recognizing stress as it affects employees is a key to heading off burnout. —Poe, Susannah Grimm and Scherr, Frederick C.; *Credit & Financial Mgmt,* Oct 1981, 83(9): pp. 35-37,46. Avail. ABI 81-23445

Stress, Credit management, Decision making models, Credit manager

Monitoring Psychological Stress Means Preventive Management (465)

A stress overload can be detrimental to both organizations and individuals. Organizations should act to create a supportive health culture which promotes preventive stress management. Stress can take a physiological, psychological, or behavioral form. Psychological symptoms are usually developed first, which means its monitoring is probably of the most benefit to an organization. A validated psychological stress audit has been developed to test psychological stress reactions by 5 constructs - anxiety, fatigue, depression, dissatisfaction, and low self-esteem. The benefits of this approach are that it is: 1. empirically verified and more reliable, 2. short and easy to fill out, and 3. general and can be used in many specific types of work environments. The audit can identify organizational trouble spots and individuals who need counseling. Chart. Table. References. —Hsu, Mu-Lan; *Industrial Mgmt,* Jul/Aug 1982, 24(4): pp. 7-11. Avail. ABI 82-24443

Stress, Audits, Prevention, Management

A Multi-Dimensional Model for Assessing Factors Associated with Burnout in Human Service Organizations (466)

Although burnout in human service organizations has been discussed widely, little direction has been offered to organizations on how to prevent or alleviate the factors that cause burnout and the symptoms associated with it. After a comprehensive research project at a child-care organization, a process and model were developed for evaluating individual, group, and organizational dynamics that seem to be associated with burnout. The researchers' perspective was based on a model of person-peer organization (PPO) interactions. Questionnaires were developed, and returned by 236 agency staffers. Problem areas in the agency, such as organizational communications patterns, especially between administrators and direct staff, were identified from the questionnaire. References. —Eldridge, William; Blostein, Stanley; and Richardson, Virginia; *Public Personnel Mgmt,* Fall 1983, 12(3): pp. 314-321. Avail. ABI 83-31772

Burnout, Personnel policies, Social services, Agencies, Organizational behavior, Studies, Employee problems, Personnel management

Nervous Strain, Anxiety and Symptoms Amongst 32-   (467) Year-Old Men at Work in Britain

Employees reporting they are under nervous strain at work tend also to complain about problems with their health. However, problems have arisen in interpreting many studies that link health symptoms with stressful features of a job. A study is described wherein a longitudinal group of 1,052 men was followed from birth in 1946. Periodic contacts were made with the men. The study confirmed that reports of nervous strain at work related to features of the job. Those in highly demanding jobs reported more strain, earlier indications of prior susceptibility to anxiety, and more frequent sleep problems, headaches, and stomach pains. The report of these symptoms, however, related to the indicators of susceptibility to anxiety rather than to the apparently stressful features of their jobs. Exposure to job demands per se apparently did not affect the frequency of symptom reporting. Tables. References. —Cherry, Nicola; *Jrnl of Occupational Psychology (UK),* Jun 1984, 57(2): pp. 95-105. Avail. ABI 84-22769

Stress, Anxieties, Employee problems, UK, Studies, Statistical analysis

NIOSH Puts Job Stress Under the Microscope/Coping   (468) with Stress

The National Institute of Occupational Safety & Health (NIOSH) has studied stress and found that both jobs that are too complex and those that are too simple can cause stress. Stress producers were pinpointed to include low utilization of abilities, lack of participation in decision making, and role ambiguity. Workers in highly stressful jobs suffer more illnesses, have higher absentee rates, and seem more vulnerable to accidents than those in jobs with less stress. Jobs in which stress turned out to be higher than anticipated include general and construction laborers, secretaries, office managers, and foremen. NIOSH is presently engaged in additional studies to review stress/ strain effects and to obtain a clearer picture of health problems related to machine-paced work. A list of guidelines designed to reduce worker stress, gathered by Occupational Hazards, includes: 1. match the job requirements to the individual's capabilities, 2. set up machine-paced jobs so the operator does not become a complete captive of the machine, 3. avoid rotating shifts which tend to increase stress, and 4. provide workers with clear-cut responsibilities. Workers' compensation savings constitute an incentive for employers to seek means of reducing stress. —Sheridan, Peter J.; *Occupational Hazards,* Apr 1981, 43(4): pp. 70-73,75-76. Avail. ABI 81-10163

NIOSH, Studies, Stress, Occupations, Rotating, Shifts, Operators, Blue collar workers, White collar workers, Occupational safety

Occupational Health in Organizations: Strategies for (469) Personnel Effectiveness

Occupational health addresses the physiological/physical and psychological conditions of an organization's workforce, and many personnel functions and activities are devoted to it. Altering it for the better can improve overall organizational effectiveness, given the fact that accidents and sickness cost US companies a large sum yearly. Organizations also suffer significant costs due to stress and lack of a suitable quality of work life. The firm that improves occupational health among its workers will realize many benefits, including money saved, absenteeism reduced, and productivity improved. Many steps can be taken to improve occupational health: 1. Diseases can be reduced by measuring chemicals in the workplace and setting objectives for the removal and treatment of chemical-related disease. 2. The sociopsychological work environment can be improved by such steps as job redesign, participation, stress management, and improved communications. 3. Time management can be taught to employees as a means of reducing stress. Charts. References. –Schuler, Randall S.; *Personnel Administrator*, Jan 1982, 27(1): pp. 47-55. Avail. ABI 82-01870

Occupational, Health, Improvements, Work environment, Quality of work, Life, Prevention, Accidents, Occupational diseases, Job, Design, Stress, Reduction, Strategy

Occupational Stress in Female Managers: A (470) Comparative Study

Male and female managers working in a wide cross section of UK industries were surveyed about their occupational stressors and stress outcomes. In general, female managers experienced higher levels of stress than did male managers, with junior and middle-level female managers having the highest stress levels and male senior managers having the lowest. The primary workplace stressors for female managers were associated with sexual discrimination and occupancy in traditionally male positions, with respondents reporting stress due to feelings that they: 1. were "tokens" in their positions, 2. had to work harder than their male counterparts, and 3. had poorer career development opportunities. Female managers also experienced higher levels of stress than male managers due to work/home conflicts. Stress outcomes for female managers included nervousness, tiredness, less flexible management style, and poor health. These results suggest the need for management training and stress reduction programs for women, as well as corporate policy changes directed to their career development needs. Charts. References. –Davidson, M. J. and Cooper, C. L.; *Jrnl of Mgmt Studies (UK)*, Apr 1984, 21(2): pp. 185-205. Avail. ABI 84-22427

Stress, Women, Managers, UK, Studies, Employee problems, Management styles

Occupational Stress in Female Managers - A Review of (471) the Literature/Counterpoint/Rejoinder/Counterpoint

A multifaceted approach to occupational stress affecting women managers is presented in the form of a literature review and model depicting the sources of occupational stress and subsequent stress outcomes. The literature stresses the combined influence of organizational and extra-organizational stressors, i.e., the home/work interface, as being particularly pertinent to women managers. This male-dominated home/work interface constitutes a set of stressors unique to women and not dependent on women's ability to cope with stress. Clearly, organizational policymakers should recognize this unique stress in women managers and adopt more positive action to alleviate some of these pressures. McKenna and Ellis argue that the approach used here concentrates on life hazards rather than work stress, and that the "positivist assertions" of Davidson and Cooper do not form a well-grounded analysis. This charge is flatly denied in the Davidson-Cooper rejoinder. Reynolds points out the difficulty in finding all the literature described by Davidson and Cooper. She suggests that their out-of-context extracts may be subject to different interpretations. Charts. Graph. References. –Davidson, Marilyn J.; Cooper, Cary L.; McKenna, Eugene; Ellis, Tony; and Reynolds, Mary; *Jrnl of Enterprise Mgmt,* 1981, 3(2): pp. 115-147. Avail. ABI 83-07875

Managers, Women, Occupational, Stress, Models, UK, Trends, Surveys, Work environment, Executives, Sources, Skills, Organizational, Structure, Roles, Sex discrimination, Research

Occupational Stress Management: A Review and Appraisal   (472)

Thirteen published and unpublished studies evaluating the merits of occupational stress management are reviewed. These studies vary considerably in terms of: 1. work groups involved, 2. program orientation and format, 3. stress management techniques, 4. nonspecific effects, and 5. presence and type of follow-up. The studies used such stress management methods as biofeedback, muscle relaxation, and cognitive restructuring. Future studies are needed to cover such topics as: 1. nonspecific factors, 2. proportion of successful and unsuccessful participants, 3. maintenance of benefits, and 4. cost-benefit determinations. Although too few studies have been conducted to state unequivocally general conclusions, worksite stress management programs appear to offer promise for improving worker well-being and partially offsetting the costs of job stress. Table. References. – Murphy, Lawrence R.; *Jrnl of Occupational Psychology (UK),* Mar 1984, 57(1): pp. 1-15. Avail. ABI 84-13602

Stress, Studies, Employee, Health, Programs

Occupational Stress Among Purchasing Managers   (473)

Job stress in purchasing can undermine effective cooperation with vendors and hinder the establishment of material specifications. A study was undertaken to examine sources of stress among purchasing managers. Some stress results from conflict with user departments and suppliers and from goal complexity. Environmental sources of stress include technological advances, product innovations, economic conditions, and government regulation. The final source of stress is inherent in the individual. Characteristics which help to mitigate stress are: 1. the ability to effectively handle interpersonal relationships, 2. identifying closely with one's organization, and 3. flexibility. The organization should increase self-awareness among its managers as to how stress can be reduced. Managers can reduce stress through: 1. role clarification, and 2. supportive leadership in the work environment, which includes a pleasant interpersonal work climate, performance feedback, and job autonomy. References. —Trinkaus, Robert J. and Vredenburgh, Donald J.; *Jrnl of Purchasing & Materials Mgmt,* Winter 1982, 18(4): pp. 2-7. Avail. ABI 83-09344

Purchasing, Managers, Stress, Sources, Conflict, Roles, Functions, Studies, Materials management

On Top of the Job   (474)

Stress-related disabilities are costing Canadian businesses $13 billion a year according to the Canadian Institute of Stress. These losses come in the form of lower productivity, lost working days, medical payments, and worker replacement costs. According to the Clarke Institute of Psychiatry, 4 factors make some jobs more stressful than others: 1. lack of control over flow of work or management decisions, 2. job/home interaction, 3. interaction with the public, and 4. role underload or overload when too few or too many demands are made of the employee. A study conducted by the Clarke Institute uncovered 5 extremely stressful occupation groups: 1. stock exchange floor traders, 2. long-distance traveling salespeople, 3. psychiatrists, 4. pool typists, and 5. farmers. Methods for coping with stress in these occupations are discussed in profiles of members of each group. — MacBeth, Mike; *Canadian Business (Canada),* Dec 1982, 55(12): pp. 69-76. Avail. ABI 83-01379

Stress, Employee problems, Manypeople, Occupations

Optimizing Human Resources: A Case for Preventive   (475)
Health and Stress Management

Organizations have a particularly acute interest in the advancement of employee health, for humanitarian as well as business reasons. Stress can have an adverse effect on employee productivity and creativity. Ideally, stress should be approached from a perspective of prevention. However, elimination of all stress would not only be impractical but possibly counterproductive, since creative work is spurred by some levels of stress. Some executives have not yet recognized that preventive health management is just as important as preventive equipment maintenance. Steps an organization can take to improve employee health and reduce stress include: 1. Get top management involved. 2. Encourage workers to talk about job stress, etc. 3. Place emphasis on self-awareness. Other steps include: 1. charting stressors, 2. health profiling, 3. providing stress inoculation training, 4. role clarification, 5. altering organizational climate, and 6. providing employee exercise facilities. Many responsibilities with which a manager already deals can be effectively redefined as preventive health and stress management concerns. Charts. References. —Ivancevich, John M. and Matteson, Michael T.; *Organizational Dynamics,* Autumn 1980, 9(2): pp. 4-25. Avail. ABI 81-02245

Human resources, Stress, Management, Preventive medicine, Quality of work, Tension, Guidelines, Management by objectives

Organizational Determinants of Job Stress   (476)

Job stress is a particular individual's awareness of personal dysfunction as a result of perceived conditions or happenings in the work setting. A model of job stress that focuses on organizational and job-related stress is presented. An organizational model of job stress is created which lists 6 categories of stressors: 1. characteristics and conditions of the job itself, 2. conditions associated with the organization's structure, climate, and information flow, 3. role-related factors, 4. relationships at work, 5. perceived career development, and 6. external commitments and responsibilities. Participants in the study were 367 managers employed by a major restaurant chain. The results indicate that emphasis on achievement, fairness, decision making and feedback - variables that were expected to be related to stress - were not related to stress. Chart. Tables. References. – Parker, Donald F. and DeCotiis, Thomas A.; *Organizational Behavior & Human Performance,* Oct 1983, 32(2): pp. 160-177. Avail. ABI 83-29213

Stress, Studies, Research, Problems, Psychological aspects, Anxieties, Statistical analysis, Employee development (PER), Employee problems

Overdue for a Vacation (477)

An increasing number of professionals are forfeiting their annual vacation, causing concern among physicians who fear that this may negatively affect health and productivity. Although month-long vacations are standard in many European countries, a 1980 Department of Labor survey reports that the average US vacation lasts 10 days. Many professionals merely extend weekends as vacations; however, such vacations are too busy and too short to give professionals time to unwind. Stress management consultant Stephen Shapiro believes that lack of vacation time can result in job burnout, and that professionals must get away from work to rejuvenate themselves and to stimulate creativity. Shapiro blames the compulsive work habits of executives for the scant vacation time taken, and management for doing little to encourage employees to take vacations. The current trend toward in-house health programs reflects many corporations' realization of the importance of vacation time. –Lau, Barbara; *Management Qtrly,* Fall 1983, 24(3): pp. 29-32. Avail. ABI 83-31063

Employee benefits, Vacations, Employee problems, Job, Burnout, Stress

The Personnel Profession Looks at Stress and Burnout (478)

The results of a study of stress and burnout, as it affects people who are involved in personnel work, are reported. In addition, this analysis explores the intensity of the problem, the personnel professionals it affects, the type of organizations in which they work, and the probable reasons for stress and burnout in the personnel field. Questionnaires were sent to randomly selected persons whose names were drawn from the membership list of 4 personnel organizations in the Los Angeles County (California) geographical area. Replies were received from 103 individuals. The conclusions include the following: 1. Burnout is a major problem, with 41% of respondents stating that they were experiencing burnout. 2. The sources of stress are found in the job, as well as outside of the job. 3. Relationships with upper management show up repeatedly as a major source of stress. Tables. References. –Glogow, Eli; *Review of Public Personnel Administration,* Spring 1984, 4(2): pp. 68-78. Avail. ABI 84-17746

Stress, Burnout, Surveys, Employee problems

Person/Role Conflict: Holland's Model Extended to Role-Stress Research, Stress Management, and Career Development (479)

One type of role stress, role conflict, occurs when incongruous expectations are associated with a role, and role ambiguity is the extent to which information is lacking on expectations, methods, and consequences of role performance. The different kinds of role conflict have been conceptually distinguished, but the conceptualization of person/role conflict seems to be ambiguous. An extension of Holland's person/environment congruence model to research on person/role conflict can assist in clarifying this construct. Three types of research to develop better understanding of this kind of employee stress are: 1. development of a scale to measure perceptions of person/role conflict separately from other kinds of role conflict, 2. application of the Holland model as a conceptual foundation as well as an objective measure of one aspect of person/role conflict-person/role incongruence, and 3. empirical tests of the propositions suggested by the Holland model. Holland suggests individuals seek environments that are compatible with their personality orientations. Career choice represents an attempt to express one's personality orientation. Figure. Tables. References.
—Latack, Janina C.; *Academy of Mgmt Review,* Jan 1981, 6(1): pp. 89-103. Avail. ABI 81-03787

Research, Job, Stress, Roles, Conflicts, Personality, Orientations, Careers, Choices, Models, Behavior

Perspectives on a Fast-Paced Public Project: Personal Reactions of MARTA Executives (480)

The current nature of society and its institutions requires that public administrators deal with projects and events that proceed at an ever-increasing pace. Enhanced productivity will be the result of anticipating and moderating the effects of this accelerated pace on people in organizations. A study was done to examine the impacts of fast-paced projects on those people involved with them. Focus was placed on personal health, individual learning and coping, and effects on organization dynamics and processes. A separate, prescriptive analysis emphasized policies, procedures, and practices. Information was obtained from interviews with 8 executives involved in the development of the Metropolitan Atlanta Rapid Transit Authority (MARTA). Executives learned from and dealt with their experiences in ways that reflect significant similarities and differences. References. —Golembiewski, Robert T. and Kiepper, Alan; *Public Administration Review,* May/Jun 1983, 43(3): pp. 246-254. Avail. ASPA 83-18107

Public, Projects, Case studies, Rapid transit, Mass transit, Stress, Employee problems, Organizational behavior

Phases of Progressive Burnout and Their Work Site Covariants: Critical Issues in OD Research and Praxis (481)

Studies of worker burnout have generally been descriptive, providing no basis for comparative analysis of burnout across organizations. The present study attempts to provide a basis for comparative burnout analysis by: 1. evaluating the applicability of a burnout survey designed for persons involved in people-intensive work to those working in commercial enterprises, 2. analyzing the progressive phases of burnout, and 3. relating burnout phases to work site characteristics. Maslach's Burnout Inventory (1981) was administered to workers in a multidivisional firm and was found to measure burnout reliably in the commercial setting. A series of burnout phases was identified, progressing from an initial depersonalization of work relationships, to a reduction in personal accomplishments, and finally, to emotional exhaustion. It was found that the burnout phases could be successfully related to 22 work site characteristics related to degree of supervisory support, compensation satisfaction, work attractiveness, job meaningfulness, and activity level. Tables. References. —Golembiewski, Robert T.; Munzenrider, Robert; and Carter, Diane; *Jrnl of Applied Behavioral Science,* Nov 1983, 19(4): pp. 461-481. Avail. JAI 84-07321

Burnout, Organization development, Studies, Statistical analysis, Organizational behavior, Job satisfaction

Predicting Job Stress Using Data from the Position Analysis Questionnaire   (482)

Complaints by striking air traffic controllers in 1981 affirmed the common belief that some jobs are more stressful than others. A study was done to investigate whether any consistent relationship exists between the behavioral characteristics of different jobs and the levels of various stresses undergone by groups of people working in those jobs. Using data from the Position Analysis Questionnaire (PAQ) database, behavioral characteristics of 92 jobs were assessed. Correlational and regression analyses were conducted to determine the relationship between job dimension scores derived from the PAQ and 18 indices of job stress obtained from 3 archival sources. PAQ and stress data were matched through job titles and codes obtained from the Dictionary of Occupational Titles. The analysis revealed a strong relationship between PAQ scores and stress data. Tables. References. —Shaw, James B. and Riskind, John H.; *Jrnl of Applied Psychology,* May 1983, 68(2): pp. 253-261. Avail. ABI 83-14632

Stress, Occupational, Differences, Characteristics, Studies, Correlation analysis, Mental health

Pressure-Prone Information Managers Can Avoid Stress   (483)

Stress results in a loss of control and can often lead to cardiovascular disease, particularly when managers are physically inactive. Stress causes organizations an estimated $17 billion to $25 billion per year in lost performance, absenteeism, and health benefit payments. Stress can be combatted through employee fitness and recreational opportunities. For example, Texas Instruments (Dallas, Texas) has a program called Positive Approach to Total Health (P.A.T.H.). The program involves the development of personal health profiles, cardiovascular/flexibility/body fat testing, exercise prescriptions, regular monitoring, consultation, and ongoing education programs. Xerox Corp. (Rochester, New York) also offers its employees a variety of recreational and physical pursuits. In addition, some companies offer nonphysical activities in the form of company picnics,

Christmas parties, and cultural opportunities. Charts. —Anonymous; *Data Mgmt,* Sep 1983, 21(9): pp. 24-27. Avail. ABI 83-25741

Stress, Information processing, Managers, Prevention, Recreation programs (PER), Leisure time, Physical fitness, Employee counseling, Employee problems

Preventing Employee Burnout (484)

Burnout is a feeling of emotional exhaustion in one's work. Personal characteristics, such as idealistic expectations and goals, and certain organizational conditions can contribute to employee burnout. Burnout results in: 1. withdrawal behaviors, 2. interpersonal friction, 3. a decline in job performance and health, and 4. family problems. Organizations can help prevent burnout several ways: 1. developing anticipatory socialization programs, which give new employees a realistic picture of their jobs, 2. increasing employees' participation in decision making, and 3. increasing feedback about job performance. Chart. —Jackson, Susan E. and Schuler, Randall S.; *Personnel,* Mar/Apr 1983, 60(2): pp. 58-68. Avail. ABI 83-14787

Employee problems, Job satisfaction, Organizational behavior, Employee, Participation, Performance, Feedback

Preventing Environmental Stress in the Open Office (485)

An increasing number of companies are converting offices to an open landscape plan, replacing floor-to-ceiling walls with partitioned work areas separated by freestanding partitions and movable screens. Employees and managers alike have voiced reservations about the change to open offices due to environmental stress problems such as increased noise, lack of privacy, and overcrowding. A number of steps can be taken to prevent most of the problems encountered with open offices: 1. Provide adequate space in which the worker can do the job, taking into account the degree of concentration required for the task. 4. Reduce noise by such means as acoustical padding under typewriters and heavy carpeting and drapes. 3. Minimize distractions by such means as facing desks away from aisles, locating departments with the most traffic nearest the office entrance, and separating workstations with solid acoustical panels. 4. Provide comfortable temperature and adequate lighting, and isolate offensive odors from such sources as chemicals. In all cases, human basic needs must take precedence over aesthetic and space considerations if the open office is to work for the people who use it. —Rader, Martha and Gilsdorf, Jeanette; *Jrnl of Systems Mgmt,* Dec 1981, 32(12): pp. 25-27. Avail. ABI 82-01706

Open, Offices, Work environment, Stress, Working conditions, Office layout, Planning

Relieving Sales Stress (486)

Prospecting and sales stress are forces self-inflicted on the insurance agent. One of the most damaging aspects of stress is overreaction to the act of prospecting. A person's body reacts to a rejection in much the same way that it reacts to the anxiety created by a life threatening situation. When stress gets out of hand, a person becomes aware of the importance of controlling it. If stress control is overlooked, the physical and emotional costs can be overwhelming. In controlling stress, the first step is to recognize stress indicators, which include memory lapses, procrastination, excessive family conflicts, and recurring headaches. The next step is to associate those indicators with what is happening at the moment. When the source of the problem is identified, it is possible to solve it. Stress can be controlled by learning how to relax. There are methods for learning how to relax the mind. Planned physical exercise can also help eliminate stress. —Hemsley, Aaron; *Life Association News,* May 1983, 78(5): pp. 63-68. Avail. ABI 83-16394

Life insurance, Insurance agents & brokers, Physical, Psychological, Stress, Exercise

Remedies for Depression and Burnout (487)

Many people in the US workforce suffer from psychological depression and productivity burnout caused by the increasing abstraction of work and work relationships. Managing these afflictions is the responsibility of the leader-managers in organizations, not the psychiatrists. Several ways that managers can improve or alleviate the problems of insecurity, depression, and productivity burnout are: 1. Improve management's understanding of the main products and services which the organization provides. 2. Give people responsibility for serving a client, train them in all areas of the job, and hold them accountable for doing it. 3. Make the job a sensory growth experience by imparting a thorough knowledge of the products. 4. Separate the rewards system from that for supporting the content of what people do to get a quality job done. 5. Replace human-relations training with education in the humanities. For supply-side economics to be successful, a feeling for products and people must be redeveloped. —Herzberg, Frederick; *Industry Week,* Feb 7, 1983, 216(3): pp. 38-39. Avail. ABI 83-06508

Corporate management, Burnout, Working conditions, Employee attitude (PER), Employee morale, Personnel management

The Road to Burnout in the Public Sector (488)

The intensity of the interpersonal relationship that evolves between helping professionals in the public sector and the individuals they are attempting to help, involving such professions as police and social workers, is the cause of burnout in these professions. There are usually 3 stressors in public sector positions: 1. role ambiguity, 2. the power-powerlessness paradox, and 3. politics. The increased complexity of government at federal, state, and local levels is the case of role ambiguity. Overlapping in function and responsibility occurs often and creates bureaucratic nightmares. Not only is responsibility ill-defined but often accountability as well, with some public employees having several bosses. In many public sector positions, power and powerlessness co-exist as a result of the power which some outside agencies have over the position. It is possible for burnout to result from the frustrations caused by this paradox. Although a political environment exists in the private sector, the public sector works in an extremely political environment. Political pressures often lead to unrealistic goals, which are a major factor in burnout. Recent federal government attempts at reducing the size of government have increased both stress and the chance of burnout. —Niehouse, Oliver L.; *Supervisory Mgmt,* Mar 1983, 28(3): pp. 22-28. Avail. ABI 83-08334

Occupational, Stress, Burnout, Government employees, Roles

Role Conflict and Role Ambiguity: Integration of the (489)
Literature and Directions for Future Research

While extensive research has been done on role conflict and ambiguity, there has resulted only moderate consistency in the focus and findings of the research. Several areas of role conflict and ambiguity are still relatively unexamined. A framework is proposed for organizing recent research which may assist in consolidating the field and providing an understanding of the condition of present research, what remains to be done, and directions for future research in role conflict and ambiguity. Three approaches are recommended for future research efforts: 1. use of longitudinal and experimental multivariate designs with the incorporation of additional theoretical perspectives, 2. investigation of methods for coping with role stress, and 3. assessment of links among role conflict, role ambiguity, and organizational information processing. Current study designs fail to allow for the specification of causal relationships. Diagram. References. —Van Sell, Mary; Brief, Arthur P.; and Schuler, Randall S.; *Human Relations,* Jan 1981, 34(1): pp. 43-71. Avail. ABI 81-09597

Roles, Conflict, Expectations, Stress, Job satisfaction, Personal, Interpersonal, Organizational, Factors, Organizational behavior, Research, Studies

Rx for Stress: One Hospital's Approach (490)

"Burnout" is a psychological state in which a person feels alienated and isolated, is physically and emotionally exhausted, and often feels victimized by the organizational system. Burnout is progressive in nature and results from chronically high levels of stress. It is a contributing factor in high rates of absenteeism, frequent complaints of illness, cynicism, lowered work performance, low morale, and turnover. Burnout frequently is found in acute-care hospitals - especially with nurses. Stanford University Hospital has implemented a program to combat burnout. After conducting a stress audit of 129 intensive-care-unit (ICU) nurses through a free-response questionnaire to determine the nature of their stress, a stress management program was implemented based on an analysis of the audit. The program for ICU nurses included the development of 15 training modules, a number of workshops for dealing with specific stressors, and the hiring of a nurse consultant and a counselor to help the nurses cope with their stress. Charts. —Bailey, June T. and Walker, Duane D.; *Supervisory Mgmt,* Aug 1982, 27(8): pp. 32-37. Avail. ABI 82-20220

Stress, Factors, Health care industry, Hospitals, Nurses, Case studies

The Science of Stress (491)

Stress can be of two major types: 1. psychological stress, which includes emotional, behavioral, mental and social stress responses, and 2. physiological stress, which can be chemical/neurological in origin, or from some other bodily system response. Stress is really a process that involves both the stimulus and the response. The physiological manifestation of stress may have the greatest impact in the form of physical disorders. To understand the effects of stress, one must be able to identify it by looking at the obvious and subtle stress signals and signs. There may be behavioral signs, somatic indicators, or internal physiological system responses that are less visible. There are both effective and ineffective ways of coping with stress. A number of mini-strategies can be effective in dealing with "everyday" stress. These include mini-relaxation exercises, internal cue words, calming through self-hypnosis, and meditation techniques. To deal with stress, a person might make such changes in lifestyle as: 1. planning idle time into the daily schedule, 2. exercise, 3. developing greater awareness for greater enjoyment of life, 4. avoiding irritating events and people, and 5. planning leisurely, non-structured vacations. —Fuller, George D. and Peters, John T.; *Credit & Financial Mgmt,* Feb 1982, 84(2): pp. 20-23,26. Avail. ABI 82-04958

Physical, Psychological, Stress, Effects, Behavior, Management, Techniques, Guidelines, Lifestyles, Attitudes, Changes

Scientific Evaluation of Rest Allowances (492)

Menneer, Minter, and Williamson developed a simplified calculation of rest allowance (RA) as figured by recovery from physical work. The calculation accounts for the worker's skill level, weight of the load, and how posture affects recovery time. Experimental observations were divided into 2 sets of measurement: 1. energy involvement related to work done, and 2. heart rate and oxygen values during recovery. The ill-motivated or non-qualified worker needs more recovery time than the qualified worker as the day progresses, and even qualified workers will do inferior work if they do not have enough RA. The minimum requirement of RA is 10% taken within 90 minute periods. To determine physical fatigue, allow 1% of RA per kilogram multiplied by an appropriate posture factor on a time-weighted basis. References. —Hamley, E. J. and Menneer, R. R.; *Management Services (UK),* Sep 1983, 27(9): pp. 12-14. Avail. ABI 83-29450

Work environment, Working conditions, Physical, Stress, Recovery, Time, Ergonomics

Social Stressors on the Job: Recommendations for a (493) Broadened Perspective

Recent job-stress research indicating the effect of psychosocial stressors on employees is reviewed. Four suggestions are presented to broaden the job-stress research while keeping the psychosocial emphasis: 1. Search for additional psychosocial stressors. 2. Expand the kinds of social support investigated as moderating variables. 3. Research outcomes of job stress other than employee strains. 4. Consider the use of theories other than role theory in developing research hypotheses. It also is recommended that research be integrated with stress management programs, and particular research designs are suggested for the evaluation of such programs. It is recommended that job-stress researchers increase their investigations both within the context of psychosocial variables and theories related to the work situation and between psychosocial job concepts and other, usually more application-oriented, topics. In this manner, job-stress researchers can avoid the error of researching and treating only a small part of a very complex phenomenon. Chart. References. —Love, Kevin G. and Beehr, Terry A.; *Group & Organization Studies,* Jun 1981, 6(2): pp. 190-200. Avail. ABI 81-16785

Job, Occupational, Stress, Research, Behavioral sciences, Social psychology

The Sources and Consequences of Stress in a Public (494) Accounting Firm

The potential effects of stress, as perceived by audit seniors in a Big Eight public accounting firm, have been examined. The effects of stress can be costly to the individual, in terms of emotional consequences, and to the organization, in terms of lower quality of performance and turnover. The study examines potential consequences of stress experienced by audit seniors and attempts to identify conditions which have the potential to contribute to stressful situations in certified public accountant (CPA) firms of all sizes. There are 3 potential consequences of role conflict and ambiguity: 1. increased job-related tension, 2. decreased job satisfaction, and 3. increased propensity to leave the firm. The study data provides support to the contention that the difficulties people have with their organizational roles increase as conflict and ambiguity increase. However, the propensity to leave the firm is not significantly related to the measures of stress. Some suggestions for the reduction of stress are: 1. provision for adequate opportunities for formal and informal training, 2. prompt response by superiors to a senior's problems and recommendations, and 3. firm communications should be accurate, timely, complete, and flow both up and down. Tables. References. —Senatra, Phillip T.; *Woman CPA*, Apr 1982, 44(2): pp. 16-20. Avail. ABI 82-13303

Public accountants, Accounting firms, Stress, Roles, Conflict, Studies, Regression analysis, Senior, Auditors

Sources and Outcomes of Stress in Organizational (495) Settings: Toward the Development of a Structural Model

An integrated structural model of the sources and outcomes of job stress is presented. According to the model, job stress is a function of: 1. the organizational subsystem in which the individual works, 2. the individual's job level, 3. the individual's sensitivity to stress, and 4. the situational factors that may produce stress reactions, i.e., job stressors. Job stressors include: 1. inter-unit conflict, 2. technical and efficiency problems, 3. role frustrations, 4. staff shortages, 5. short lead times, and 6. too many meetings. The consequences of stress include low organizational commitment, poor performance, and turnover. A test of the model based on path analysis of data gathered from employees of a food processing company provided qualified support for the causal assumptions. The individual's location within the organization and stress sensitivity were especially strong predictors of felt stress, as were role frustration and short lead times. Tables. Charts. References. —Parasuraman, Saroj and Alutto, Joseph A.; *Academy of Mgmt Jrnl*, Jun 1984, 27(2): pp. 330-350. Avail. ABI 84-22058

Stress, Employee problems, Correlation analysis, Organizational behavior, Job satisfaction

Sources of Stress and Type A Behaviour in a Public (496) Service Management Population

While a certain degree of stress is beneficial to productivity, a high degree of stress which is not properly managed can produce debilitating physical and emotional effects on job performance. Canadian public service managers were surveyed about sources of job stress. The most commonly cited sources of stress involved: 1. the constant deadlines associated with work overload, 2. interpersonal relationships with supervisors, subordinates, and peers, 3. personal limitations, 4. occupational situations, and 5. poor organizational management. A majority of the managers were found to be Type A personalities - those overly involved in work, very ambitious, insecure, and prone to tachycardiac and vasomoter reactions to stress. Public service seems to be promoting and reinforcing this type of behavior which leads to reduced productivity, job dissatisfaction, and disease. Public service organizations must take responsibility for eliminating sources of employee stress and provide rehabilitative assistance for those suffering from excess stress. Charts. References. —Jette, Maurice; *Optimum (Canada)*, 1982, 13(1): pp. 22-34. Avail. ABI 82-22120

Canada, Studies, Government employees, Stress, Employee problems, Managers, Public administration

Stress - Not a Management Monopoly (497)

Work-related stress is a problem at the shop or office floor as well as at the management level. An important contributing factor to stress is job content. Work underload, as well as overload, can lead to stress. This is common for the person who feels ill-equipped for the job. This also is found in jobs that are repetitive in nature. Certain factors can be designed into a job to lessen the degree of stress. One factor allows employees to make decisions and exercise some control over their own immediate work situations. The regulation of pressures by employees will lead to reduced levels of stress. Social support and control over future prospects also are stress-reducing factors. Companies are helping employees cope with stress through physical fitness, relaxation, and meditation programs. A job design that allows for human contribution and self-determination will reduce the level of stress. Table. Figures. References. —Tacy, Lynne; *Work & People (Australia)*, 1982, 8(2): pp. 17-21. Avail. ABI 83-08900

Stress, Tension, Heart diseases, Technological change, Job attitudes, Design

Stress and Performance: Effects of Subjective Work (498) Load and Time Urgency

The traditional view of the effects of stress on work performance is that low levels of stress help performance at first, but once optimum performance is reached, increases in stress negatively affect performance. A study was conducted in which objective work load was constant, but subjective work load differences could exist. The study involved 39 management personnel engaged in a 2-week management training course in which they were given test problems requiring steps of logical inference and/or numerical calculations. Subjective work load, time urgency, and involvement were measured using a self-report questionnaire at the end of the course. Results indicated that high levels of subjective work load and time urgency are associated with substantially lower performance, instead of the expected higher performance due to increased motivation; involvement did not relate negatively to performance. These results suggest that eliminating a high sense of work load and great time urgency in management jobs could be potentially beneficial, and that involvement can encourage high motivation without the detrimental effects of these other 2 variables. Tables. References. —Friend, Kenneth E.; *Personnel Psychology,* Autumn 1982, 35(3): pp. 623-633. Avail. ABI 82-27138

Stress, Performance evaluation, Performance appraisal, Management development, Studies, Psychological aspects

Stress and Work: A Review and Theoretical Framework, I (499)

A critical review of the extensive literature on stress and work examines the identification, causation, and measurement of stressors and strains in work situations in order that management can cope intelligently with the problem. Although 8-10% of the working population are under sufficient strain to cause concern, few guidelines can be established from the literature due to lack of adequate measurement techniques and lack of consideration of non-work factors in past research. In order to integrate and assess all the data, better definitions of the important concepts are needed as well as a model which delineates the relationships between the concepts. Some of the most common stressors identified are: 1. role overload, 2. role underload, 3. job pressure, and 4. role conflict. Some of the primary supports/constraints are: 1. role clarity, 2. quality of equipment, 3. financial resources, and 4. participation in decisions. Tables. References. —Fletcher, Ben (C.) and Payne, Roy L.; *Personnel Review (UK),* Winter 1980, 9(1): pp. 19-29. Avail. ABI 81-02561

Stress, Research, Reviews, Literature, Occupations, Measurement

Stress at Work: A Review and Theoretical Framework, II (500)

At any time, about 8% of the workforce experience strain or distress, with more strain appearing in the lower social classes and with repetitive work tasks. With physiological strain, the body is attempting to return to its normal homeostatic state. With psychological strain, a person is experiencing cognitive or emotional discomfort, which can include boredom from under-stimulation. Stressors, the strain-producing factors, can tip the ideal balanced state in either direction. Strain may be either acute or chronic, and treatment will need to differ. Reactions to stressors can include: 1. changing the stressors, 2. denying the effects, and 3. riding it out. The individual under strain may also habituate himself to the level of strain so that it is no longer stressful. However, the psychological and physiological thresholds permanently shift, so reactions to all stressors will change. An assembly line worker may habituate so that there is no boredom strain, but may not be able to raise his threshold for dealing with complex situations. Treatment must identify whether the present problem is actually a secondary stressor or is, in fact, the primary stressor. Chart. References. —Fletcher, Ben C. and Payne, Roy L.; *Personnel Review (UK),* Spring 1980, 9(2): pp. 5-8. Avail. ABI 81-01040

Job, Stress, Models, Studies

Stress: Causes, Consequences, and Coping Strategies   (501)

Organizations are becoming more sensitive to the impact of stress on employee health and productivity. The size of the problem may be illustrated by a recent survey in which 80% of the respondent job holders indicated that they wanted information on stress management. Sources of stress are: 1. family, 2. individual, 3. social and environmental, and 4. organizational. Types of reactions to stress are subjective, behavioral, cognitive, physiological, and organizational. Employees and organizations deal with stress by various strategies that include: 1. physical maintenance, 2. internal assistance, such as meditation and relaxation, 3. personal organization, 4. outside assistance, such as psychoanalysis and behavior-change techniques, 5. stress-directed, such as dynamic psychotherapy, 6. situational and support group, and 7. negative, such as avoiding substance abuse. Tables. —Sailer, Heather R.; Schlacter, John; and Edwards, Mark R.; *Personnel,* Jul/Aug 1982, 59(4): pp. 35-48. Avail. ABI 82-22279

Stress, Causes, Management, Strategy, Reduction, Models

Stress in Accounting Systems   (502)

Stress is an important accompaniment to accounting practices. Auditors are being urged to study the attitudes of management toward its own internal controls and be cautious when a client consistently chooses the least conservative approach. This study suggests that normal pressures intensify when accounting is done in hard economic times. Accounting requires the constant critical study of data and its source, but many accountants cannot stop being critical when they go home to their families. The inability to accept human beings as imperfect usually leads to severe interpersonal problems and stress. Stress can originate in actual or perceived conditions. It is affected by the kinds of adjustment an individual is able to make, and is partially shown by a nonspecific response. To help lower the stress factors people should be given controllable features of a situation as much as possible. If a person has to be given uncontrollable variables, at least try to unconfound controllability and predictability. The most effective accounting systems may be those that impose control on people but also allow them to predict when the potentially aversive events will occur. References. —Weick, Karl E.; *Accounting Review,* Apr 1983, 58(2): pp. 350-369. Avail. ABI 83-17653

Organizational, Stress, Accounting procedures, Organizational behavior, Accountants

Stress Management Training in the Banking Profession   (503)

Stress exists when the demands of a situation outweigh the available resources, thereby requiring adaptation or readjustment. A seminar was conducted to provide stress management training to a group of banking professionals in a medium-sized, midwestern bank. The premise was to identify the primary sources of stress within the profession and to develop a set of strategies designed to deal with each stressor identified. A pre-session questionnaire asked respondents to list what they felt to be the primary obstacles to successful job performance. The stressors listed were placed in 4 groups depending upon their frequency. The most frequent stressor was customer demands/contact. The 2nd phase of the seminar involved addressing specific stressors by suggesting possible methods for effectively managing that stressor. Relaxation techniques were presented to participants to supplement the verbal content of the stress management concept. Some of the suggested strategies for handling customer demands/contact included job rotation, assertiveness, and improved exercise/diet. Charts. References. —Mirabile, Richard J.; *Training & Development Jrnl,* Aug 1983, 37(8): pp. 40-43. Avail. ABI 83-22824

Stress, Management, Banking industry, Surveys, Employee problems, Training

Stress Management: Separating Myth from Reality   (504)

Management has an educated self-interest in maintaining a healthy, stimulated, and productive workforce, and among the primary means of achieving such a workforce is the reduction of stress and its damaging effects in the workplace. Stress casualties can be reduced through recognition of signs of overload. A number of myths exist today about stress. These myths include: 1. All stress is harmful. 2. Little can be done to help the individual who is naturally stress-prone. The medical community estimates that half to 3/4 of routine medical practice is concerned with people whose complaints are directly related to the stress response, and due to escalating health care costs, businesses in the future will have to pay increased attention to behavioral medicine that reduces stress. There are 3 parts to the manager's role in handling employee stress: 1. being aware of employee stress, 2. referring affected workers to programs that can help, and 3. following up on the success of the assistance. Charts. —Pesci, Michael; *Personnel Administrator,* Jan 1982, 27(1): pp. 57-67. Avail. ABI 82-01871

Stress, Effects, Management, Behavior, Medicine, Managers, Roles

The Stress of Productivity   (505)

Stress can be divided into 2 forms-physiological and psychological. In industry, psychological stress is the more serious problem. If the individual cannot adapt to stress, "distress" occurs and can result in ill health and premature death. If there is a successful adaptation, a condition called "eustress" occurs; this allows employees to express their talents and energies and can result in increased productivity. Managers must realize that people are assets and that, in most cases, because of poor management techniques, employees do not utilize more than 30% of their potential. Since the organizational potential is dependent upon the employee, the organizational climate created by management will determine the success of the entity. By stimulating positive work activity involving the entire human organism, a condition of eustress will be created. This increases productivity by decreasing absenteeism, hostility, illness, and workers' compensation claims. Diagram. References. —Zausmer, Fred and Farris, Roy; *Mid-South Business Jrnl,* Jan 1982, 2(1): pp. 15-19. Avail. ABI 82-07687

Stress, Human resources, Psychological aspects, Organizational behavior, Productivity

Stress: Organizational Consequences and Occupational   (506)
Differences

There are many different definitions of stress. Some regard it as a nonspecific response to demands made on the body, while others say it involves an interaction with the environment. The interactional definition which considers individual differences is the best. Stress effects fall into 3 groups, beginning with: 1. physical and mental health and illness, such as heart disease, ulcers, and neuroticism, 2. behavioral/cognitive responses such as nervous symptoms, fatigue, and withdrawal, and 3. organizational consequences, such as high absenteeism, turnover, and job dissatisfaction. The results of studies on stress and its relationship to various occupations tend to be flawed because they ignore individual differences. These differences may moderate the stress/stressor relationship, or stressors may produce different stress levels in different people at different times. The lack of a widely accepted concept of what stress is has hurt the studies on occupational stress. The definition of stress that is used can greatly influence the results obtained. References. —Kolvereid, Lars; *International Studies of Mgmt & Organization,* Fall 1982, 12(3): pp. 14-32. Avail. Sharpe 83-06123

Stress, Effects, Mental health, Illnesses, Organizational behavior, Employee problems

Teaching Stress Management: Meeting Individual and Organizational Needs (507)

Organizations pay a high economic penalty for the poor stress management practices of their employees, but some companies are introducing programs to alleviate the stress coping problem. Mead Corporation's Packaging Division, for example, has found a solution with a program for hourly and salaried employees that teaches the 3Rs of stress management: recreation, relaxation, and reorientation of negative or unproductive attitudes. Companies that are considering the implementation of similar stress-management programs would do well to observe several important principles: 1. Program objectives should reflect reasonable expectations. 2. Those entrusted with the program should have a solid working knowledge of the interactive nature of stress. 3. Whenever possible, it is best to link classroom efforts with continuing counseling services. Mead's program of stress management is still in its infancy, but the early results are encouraging. Using a systematic, internally integrated approach has shown that stress and good health are not mutually exclusive. Charts. —Pelligrino, John F.; *Advanced Mgmt Jrnl,* Spring 1981, 46(2): pp. 27-30,35-39. Avail. ABI 81-12941

Stress, Management, Training, Employee problems, Employee counseling, Programs, Case studies

Testing for Demographic Covariants of Psychological Burn-Out: Three Sources of Data Rejecting Robust and Regular Associations (508)

The relationship between burnout and numerous demographic variables is examined. The little literature available concerning burnout and demographics, which emphasizes people-helping professions and settings, is critically examined. Original research is conducted analyzing the demographics of burnout in a commercial organization. No robust association of demographic variables with psychological burnout is found. The available literature provides no evidence of significant and sizable covariation of burnout and demographic variables. This finding is confirmed by the unsuccessful test for such relationships which employed 3 Maslach

Burnout Inventory sub-scale scores, a total score, and progressive burnout phases. It is concluded that simple demographics do not identify high-probability targets or indicate the usefulness of "class-action" designs for coping with burnout and its effects. Tables. References. —Golembiewski, Robert T. and Sccichitano, Michael; *International Jrnl of Public Administration,* 1983, 5(4): pp. 435-447. Avail. ABI 84-00292

Burnout, Demography, Variables, Studies, Personality, Statistical analysis, Employee problems

Time Out for Stress Management Training   (509)

Employers benefit from effective stress management through reduced absenteeism, lower health care costs, fewer accidents, and improved job performance. Employees benefit by reduced risk of serious illness, better interpersonal relationships, and more energy. Effective implementation of a stress management program depends upon 3 elements: 1. Get employees involved. 2. Encourage experimentation and reinforce changed behavior. 3. Provide organizational support from the top down. Among the first enrollees in a stress management program should be upper-level management. This will make attendance from all other levels "safe." A good sign of organizational support is changing the work environment to provide better facilities for employees. This will show that a stress management program has top-level support and is worthy of employee involvement. Chart. References. —Kindler, Herbert S.; *Training & Development Jrnl,* Jun 1984, 38(6): pp. 64-66. Avail. ABI 84-20816

Stress, Management, Training

Toward a Theory of Burnout   (510)

The job burnout phenomenon has been widely acknowledged as an important issue. However, the study of burnout has lacked substantial empirical foundation. A new model of burnout is presented; it is based largely on the work of Bandura (1977). In this model, burnout is defined as the state in which individuals expect little reward and considerable punishment from work because of a lack of value reinforcement, control of outcomes, or personal competence. The burnout model predicts that reinforcement expectations, outcome expectations, and efficacy expectations directly influence the subjective experience of burnout. Such experiences are thought to result from repeated learning experience on the job. An examination of the elements involved indicates that individuals may differ in how they cope with the processes leading to burnout. References. —Meier, Scott T.; *Human Relations,* Oct 1983, 36(10): pp. 899-910. Avail. ABI 83-31510

Burnout, Expectancy theories (PER), Studies, Organizational behavior, Stress, Employee problems, Employee attitude (PER)

Understanding and Managing Stress in the Workplace: (511)
An Overview

Most models of stress in the workplace, including the Person-Environment Fit model (French, 1974) conclude that stress results from a poor fit between worker and job environment. The job environment comprises the physical, social, and organizational settings within which a job is done. A more appropriate 2-way supply-and-demand model would consider that stress results when the job environment does not have supplies to meet the motives and needs of workers. To improve stress management and mental health in the workplace, managers must acknowledge that responsibility for effective stress management rests with the worker and the organization jointly. Both should take steps to reduce or eliminate unnecessary sources of stress and improve strategies for dealing with unavoidable sources of stress. Organizational approaches to stress management include involving workers in policy decisions and building social support structures. Individual approaches to stress management include developing outside hobbies and interests and improving support networks. Chart. Graph. References. – MacBride, Arlene; *MTM Jrnl of Methods-Time Measurement,* 1983, 10(2): pp. 15-19. Avail. ABI 83-24787

Stress, Work environment, Models, Organizational behavior, Employee problems

Viewpoint Before Impairment: Physician Stress and the   (512) Organization's Responsibility

Stress management by professional providers of health care has not been a topic of significant concern in the health care delivery area. It is often thought that after surviving medical school, the new physician faces less stress, but it is suggested that physicians' stress may actually increase when they are faced with several psychological and environmental pressures. Such pressures include: 1. expansion of their medical knowledge base, 2. awareness of legal liability, 3. challenges to professional dominance, and 4. the image of physicians. The results of physician stress are high suicide and divorce rates, alcoholism, and drug addiction. The health care system has contributed to stress suffered by physicians by establishing conditions that perpetrate and foster it. Little allowance is made for limitations on a person's stress-handling capabilities during training to be a physician. It is often assumed that a person who cannot deal with the stress is unsuited to be a physician. The health care system should develop support mechanisms to deal with stress; the first step should involve recognition of the problem. References. –Numerof, Rita E. and Abrams, Michael N.; *Health Care Mgmt Review,* Fall 1981, 6(4): pp. 77-82. Avail. ABI 81-27796

Physicians, Stress, Effects, Behavior, Hospitals, Roles

The Wages of Overwork - Burnout   (513)

Burnout occurs when a person is overworked and gradually wears down his or her reserves, resulting in mental, physical, and emotional exhaustion. The prime candidate for burnout is a person with high expectations who tries very hard to be perfect. Overachieving accountants are typically burnout victims and often do not realize that there is a problem until burnout becomes serious. The shortage of chartered accountants has aggravated the situation, as have alienation, a sense of powerlessness, and organizational changes brought on by computers and microprocessors. Some organizational solutions to burnout which are being tried include: 1. a 4-day workweek, 2. job sharing, and 3. encouraging socializing. Among the individual solutions are: 1. spending time alone to set life goals, 2. being good to oneself, 3. developing a support system of people to whom one can talk freely, 4.

simplifying one's life, and 5. recognizing that it is not necessary to be perfect. Questionnaires. —Helliwell, Tanis; *CA Magazine (Canada),* Aug 1982, 115(8): pp. 83-87. Avail. ABI 82-22865

Stress, Employee problems, Accountants, Guidelines, Mental health

What Causes Stress for Management Accountants? (514)

A survey of 138 management accountants revealed that, of 15 personal and job-related variables, the factors most related to high job stress were age and higher-level positions. The mean average of stress fell between 3 and 4 on a scale of 5, which is generally considered above a comfortable level for professionals. Job stress factors were separated into: 1. role conflict, 2. role clarity, and 3. job satisfaction. Many of the variables relating to stress can be controlled. Programs should be initiated to alleviate stress. For example, before promoting to a higher level position, the candidate's ability to handle stress should be considered. Tables. References. —Strawser, Robert H.; Kelly, J. Patrick; and Hise, Richard T.; *Management Accounting,* Mar 1982, 63(9): pp. 32-35. Avail. ABI 82-08861

Management accounting, Management, Accountants, Job, Stress, Factors

When People Are Pushed Too Far (515)

Too much stress on the job can lead to physical, emotional, and family problems. The causes of the stress syndrome include performing repetitive and monotonous tasks, and exposure at the workplace to excessive heat, cold, vibrations, or toxic fumes. People are often pushed too far, even though there are warning signals. Experiments have shown that the highest level of stress is present not among top executives, but on the shop floor among foremen, supervisors, assemblers, and relief workers. In order to relieve stress, workers must receive more "satisfiers" - wages, job security, prestige and status, opportunity for advancement, creativeness, sympathetic supervision, friendly atmosphere, and competent management. Employees who are satisfied and motivated can maintain a high level of performance despite work pressures. —Anonymous; *Worklife (Canada),* 1983, 3(2): pp. 5-6. Avail. ABI 83-16823

Working conditions, Effects, Stress, Employee problems, Job satisfaction

Work and Nonwork Influences on Health: A Research (516) Agenda Using Inability to Leave as a Critical Variable

A basic path analytic model of stressor-health relationships is constructed from a multidisciplinary literature base. Nonwork factors are introduced along with work and individual difference factors as exogenous stressors in a path analytic model of stress-health relationships in an attempt to approach stress research from a multidisciplinary perspective. In integrating the organizational withdrawal literature, expanded conceptualizations of stress by McGrath (1976) and Schuler (1980) are utilized. Inability to leave is identified as a research variable that emerges from both perspectives as a variable of potentially significant stressor-health consequences. Through the causal process model, empirical investigations of how and where inability to leave interrelates with multiple and varied stressors to produce direct and indirect effects on one's health are conducted. Chart. References. —Martin,

Thomas N. and Schermerhorn, John R., Jr.; *Academy of Mgmt Review,* Oct 1983, 8(4): pp. 650-659. Avail. ABI 83-29188

Stress, Effects, Mental health, Physical, Health, Studies, Work environment, Job satisfaction, Models, Organization theory, Employee problems

Work Overload (517)

The consequences of role overload-inadequate time or resources to complete all jobs-are detrimental to both the employee and the organization. Overload is often created by the manager or organization in an effort to increase motivation. The adverse effects of overload for employees are: 1. lower performance ratings, 2. increased work avoidance, 3. job dissatisfaction, and 4. association with the Type A behavior pattern-a personality pattern which has been causally related to coronary heart disease and which appears to be conceptually independent of other important coronary risk factors, such as cigarette smoking and high blood pressure. It is important for employees and management to avoid long-term overload. The best method of achieving this is effective planning and time utilization. References. —Bateman, Thomas S.; *Business Horizons,* Sep/Oct 1981, 24(5): pp. 23-27. Avail. ABI 81-21343

Workloads, Stress, Impacts, Motivation, Employee problems

Work Role Transitions and Stress in Managers: (518) Illustrations from the Clinic

Work-role transitions such as promotions sometimes lead to stress. The study of case histories can often be useful in identifying circumstances which can result in stress. There are 4 components of the occupational role: 1. job requirements, 2. job expectations of employees, 3. job experience of the employees, and 4. job performance. There can be 2 problems for employees: 1. occupational role integration, when the employee perceives no discrepancies, and 2. differentiation, when the employee sees discrepancies in the aspects of the occupational role. The case studies identified work transition which was accompanied by ambiguity in the new job requirements. Each manager in the case studies had no clear standard of job performance. Each manager had high personal standards which, coupled with a lack of specific job requirements, created anxiety. Solutions include: 1. training courses, and 2. close supervision during the transition, emphasizing realistic goals. References. —Brewin, Chris; *Personnel Review (UK),* Summer 1980, 9(3): pp. 27-30. Avail. ABI 81-06323

Managers, Executives, Stress, Work, Job, Roles, Transitions, Promotions (MAN)

Workaholism: Fears a Job Can't Solve (519)

Many psychologists find that the compulsive personality of the workaholic is self-defeating, although a few analysts congratulate the workaholic as the backbone of America. The workaholic is generally an individual who suppresses pent-up anger or fear of failure by grasping on to work for emotional fulfillment. He may temporarily gain successes, but by overtaxing his physical and mental resources, the stage is set for an eventual collapse. Perhaps worst of all, the workaholic is virtually destined to fail.Pushing and pulling by bosses, resentment of threatened colleagues, and frustration at slow mobility make the corporate setting potentially unbearable for the workaholic. The workaholic's best recourse might be in starting his own business. However, the danger of overwork and deteriorated health exists even in self-employment. Besides health problems, the workaholic also faces the casualty of marital and family problems. A number of highly creative, but workaholic, artists have produced rewarding but short, furious, and agonizing lives. In essence, the workaholic races against time, and time becomes the controlling factor. —Price, Margaret; *Industry Week,* Mar 3, 1980, 204(5): pp. 56-63. Avail. ABI 80-05653

Work, Workloads, Performance appraisal, Stress, Tension, Studies, Productivity, Health

Work-Role Stress and Attitudes Toward Co-Workers   (520)

Role theory has been employed to conceptualize the findings regarding job stress, suggesting that the source of job stress is one's co-workers. Role stress is any aspect of a role that is associated with role strain. If co-workers are the source of stress, individuals in stressful jobs are likely to be particularly dissatisfied with their co-workers. In interviews with 651 employees of 5 Midwestern work organizations, it was illustrated that 3 role stresses (role ambiguity, role overload, and underutilization of skills) were associated with 5 employee outcomes: overall job dissatisfaction, life dissatisfaction, low self-esteem, depressed mood, and fatigue. As hypothesized, each stress was most strongly correlated with dissatisfaction with the stress itself, second most strongly correlated with dissatisfaction with co-workers, and least strongly correlated with dissatisfaction with the nonsocial aspects of the work role. It was concluded that people who experience job stress blame the social system in the organization, resulting in their dissatisfaction with co-workers, who are parts of that system. Tables. References. —Beehr, Terry A.; *Group & Organization Studies,* Jun 1981, 6(2): pp. 201-210. Avail. ABI 81-16786

Job, Occupational, Stress, Roles, Organizational behavior, Job satisfaction, Studies, Attitudes, Workers

DEALING WITH EXECUTIVE STRESS

Coming to Grips with Executive Burnout   (521)

As executive burn-out takes a heavy toll on employee productivity, companies should be alert to its symptoms, causes, and remedies. The most common symptoms are: 1. fatigue, 2. tendencies to blame others for work-related problems, 3. complaints about job aspects that were not previous areas of concern, 4. tardiness and leaving work early, 5. quarrels with co-workers, 6. day-dreaming or sleeping on the job, and 7. frequent illnesses. The causes of burn-out are complex, but some broad categories include: 1. over-stimulation at work, as in an unstable environment without clear objectives; 2. under-stimulation at work, as where job duties become routine and predictable; 3. mis-matching of individual and job or organization, as where one or the other is too free-wheeling or too structured; 4. low organizational productivity, as where declining production appears beyond control; or 5. problems outside work. Prevention strategies include: 1. matching characteristics of the individual, the job, and the organizational structure; 2. developing company programs to treat stress; and 3. teaching and encouraging self-diagnosis and the adoption of individual strategies for dealing with burn-out, which may include group or individual counseling. – Glicken, Morley D. and Janka, Katherine; *International Mgmt (UK)*, Oct 1981, 36(10): pp. 27-30. Avail. ABI 81-25485

Executives, Stress, Health care, Employee problems

The Current Status of Executive Health Programs   (522)

The principal asset at most organizations is the calibre and efficiency of their executive decision-makers. For that reason, executive health is being recognized as a major concern. While the thrust of most medical activity is toward avoidance and treatment of disease, executive health programs are beginning to emphasize healthy lifestyles and quality of life. It is now being argued that well over half of all medical disorders are stress-related. Bringing about changes in the health status of individuals involves 2 stages: 1. assessment and diagnosis, and 2. treatment and intervention. Assessment and diagnosis can be done by self appraisal or by a professional medical and psychological examination. An ideal treatment and intervention stage involves simultaneous improvements in 4 areas: 1. exercise, 2. diet, 3. psychological, and 4. medical. For an executive health program to become cost effective, it must manifest realistic objectives, comprehensive assessment, and individually prescribed multi-disciplinary interventions. Table. References. –Kretsch, Andrey and Boyce, Roger; *Work & People (Australia)*, 1981, 7(2): pp. 20-24. Avail. ABI 82-07659

Executives, Health, Rankings, Lifestyles, Factors, Stress, Health hazards, Prevention

Executive Health: Ways to Keep Fit   (523)

In a recent interview, Dr. Ronald E. Costin, medical director for eastern operations of the Life Extension Institute in New York City, stated that stress-related illnesses such as hypertension and heart disease are increasing among executives but that some stress-related illnesses such as peptic ulcer disease are decreasing. Evidence shows that the health problems of male and female executives are more alike than in the past. There is no evidence of a direct link between excessive tension and drinking, and there is less use of drugs than in the general population. Depression which may stem in part from boredom with the job is increasing, but it is treatable although difficult to identify. A regular routine exercise program is beneficial, although it need not be rigorous to be effective. Today, examinations try to spot potential risk factors and prevent development of diseases. Preventive medicine has reduced or nearly eliminated many infectious diseases and now can do much the same for chronic diseases such as cardiovascular disease. –Anonymous; *Association Mgmt*, Jan 1981, 33(1): pp. 58-61,63. Avail. ABI 81-03260

Executives, Tension, Stress, Health, Health care, Depression, Alcohol, Exercise, Physical fitness

Executive Stress Goes Global   (524)

Stress has long been considered strictly a phenomenon of the affluent, industrialized Western world. Now, a survey of 10 countries affirms that executive stress is a global phenomenon. Overall, executives in Brazil, Nigeria, Egypt, Singapore, and Japan have a higher incidence of stress symptoms and a greater tendency toward mental instability than do their counterparts in such Western nations as the US, UK, and Germany. A sampling of survey findings includes: 1. US respondents appear to have gained the upper hand on stress, with very low mental health problems and the lowest percentage of executives at risk of instability. 2. Swedish executives reflect stability, with just 6% taking sleeping pills and only 4% using tranquilizers. 3. Executives in Japan, Brazil, and Singapore report the highest rates of job dissatisfaction. 4. Nigerian executives show signs of stress resulting from having to perform in a growing economy with insufficient infrastructure; they have the 2nd-highest rate of "pill-popping." Graphs. – Cooper, Cary and Arbose, Jules; *International Mgmt (UK),* May 1984, 39(5) (European Edition): pp. 42-48. Avail. ABI 84-17813

Stress, Executives, Manycountries, Surveys

Executive Stress: Pressure in a Grey Flannel Suit   (525)

Chronic stress in business executives is usually found more in middle management than in top management. It is characterized by a continuous sense of time urgency and an incessant need to accomplish too much. Such changes in work pattern as concentrating on only the important items, taking frequent "day dreaming" breaks, and staying an extra half hour to avoid rush hour traffic can help relieve stress. Transcendental Meditation, biofeedback, encounter groups, and yoga are also useful in understanding and relieving tensions and stress. However, more important than any artificial technique is an individual's self-realization that he is exhibiting outward symptoms of stress and inner tension and that he must personally take action to reduce this pressure-building situation. The current emphasis on stress-relieving techniques helps make the public aware of the dangers of stress. –Lourie, Roger H.; *Direct Marketing,* Dec 1981, 44(8): pp. 46-49. Avail. ABI 82-01738

Executives, Stress, TM, Transactional analysis, Management, Techniques

The Executive Under Stress: A Profile   (526)

A profile of the executive who is both physically and emotionally at risk from stress includes the following characteristics: 1. He is age 35-45. 2. He is ambitious and dedicated. 3. He is in a highly competitive job atmosphere. 4. He is under pressure to meet the demands of superiors, co-workers, or customers. 5. He feels that the demands of his job conflict with those of his personal life. This profile is the result of a longitudinal study of stress on 500 senior executives in the UK. Subjects completed questionnaires and had physical exams at specific points during the study. The preliminary results show that the executives, on the whole, are not smokers, but a rather high percentage do drink. Most participants indicated that their job was the main source of stress in their lives, and a significant number said that family problems were a close second. Job insecurity appears to be a prime factor in the mental health of the executives. The stress that these executives experience can lead to physical and mental illness. –Zippo, Mary; *Personnel,* Sep/ Oct 1980, 57(5): pp. 41-43. Avail. ABI 80-22412

Executives, Stress, Profiles, Surveys, UK

Executives Under Fire: The Burnout Syndrome (527)

Burnout is a type of existential crisis in which work is no longer a meaningful function. Burned-out workers see work as tedious, redundant, and insignificant. Burned-out executives may have a tendency to blame others for their burnout, to complain bitterly about aspects of their work, to miss work, to daydream or sleep on the job, to be the last to come to work and the first to leave, or to become increasingly isolated from others. Executive burnout can stem from work overstimulation, work understimulation, personal problems, job mismatch, or low organizational productivity. Treatment and prevention are possible within the organizational framework. Without an effort to remedy burnout, organizations stand to lose top level resources. Three elements crucial to prevention are: 1. recognition of early warning signals, 2. diagnosis of causes, and 3. development of prevention. Prevention strategies include: 1. seeking a fit between the worker's characteristics, the complexity of the job, and the type of organization, 2. developing a program to help individuals cope with stress, and 3. teaching self-diagnosis. Techniques used to combat burnout include sanctioned timeouts. The Career Enhancement Therapy Approach is suggested for counselors. Reference. – Glicken, Morley D. and Janka, Katherine; *California Mgmt Review,* Spring 1982, 24(3): pp. 67-72. Avail. ABI 82-18573

Employee problems, Executives, Stress, Behavior, Prevention, Methods, Therapy

The Extra Pressures on Women Executives (528)

Research in the UK and the US shows few women with high status positions. A survey of managers listed in the Women's Who's Who showed that these women had an average age of 40, were well educated, and received a salary well above the mean for British working women. Less than half the respondents were married, but most married women had children. Women who rejected marriage were found to experience more stress. Women managers experience unique stresses and often encounter male-dominated policy-making.Respondents felt that stress was related to the job and the amount of control over the situation. Women appear to suffer additional stress factors and higher levels of work-related stress which contribute to: 1. deterring women from seeking or staying in management positions, 2. deterring women from seeking promotions, 3. more "Type A" behavior, and 4. detrimental effects on physical and mental well-being. Tables. References. –Davidson, Marilyn and Cooper, Cary; *Personnel Mgmt (UK),* Jun 1980, 12(6): pp. 48-51. Avail. ABI 80-14160

Women, Executives, UK, Surveys, Stress, Qualifications, Tension, Managers

Facing Up to Executive Anger (529)

Organizations are more concerned than ever before with the degree of self-control possessed by executives, and table-pounding is no longer acceptable. The professional manager is expected to conduct himself in a professional manner. There is a current lull in executive displays of anger, and there are several explanations for this executive calm. Psychologist Harry Levin has provided an explanation of executive calm in the assumption that today's managers use angry energy against themselves. The greater the separation between the executive's ideal and image, the fiercer the individual's attack on himself. US executives will have to find ways of expressing anger, and it seems in order that the solution should be a new civility that accommodates the expression of angry emotions. The currently popular assertiveness training legitimizes the expression of angry feelings within an organization. Also, some organizations offer courses in handling anger. –Kiechel, Walter, III; *Fortune,* Nov 16, 1981, 104(10): pp. 205,208,210. Avail. ABI 81-25698

Executives, Emotions, Control, Communication, Stress

The High Cost of Stress on Women Managers (530)

An investigation of 135 top female executives in the UK demonstrated the existence of greater stress on women managers than on men. Professional women tend to have higher self-esteem and better mental health than homemakers, but they lack relaxation time. This inability to relax may result in depression, anxiety, high blood pressure and headaches. In turn, this can lead to poorer work performance, changed sleeping habits, alcohol, drug, and tobacco abuse, and poor interpersonal relationships with colleagues. Society appears to demand that women managers successfully handle both career and home responsibilities. With the proportion of women in the workforce increasing, society must try to understand the unique pressures that bear on them. Tables. References. –Cooper, Cary L. and Davidson, Marilyn J.; *Organizational Dynamics,* Spring 1982, 10(4): pp. 44-53. Avail. ABI 82-15836

Men, Women, Managers, Stress, Executives, Health, Heart diseases, Mental health, Studies, UK, Smoking, Alcoholism, Drug abuse

Suicide: An Executive Suite Hazard? (531)

Every year, some executives take their own lives, and the reasons for their actions are not clear. It is undeniable that stress is a primary contributing factor since the executive is a human being affected by the same tensions and motivations as everyone else. Guilt is involved with most executive suicides, either guilt for doing the wrong thing or guilt for feeling that one is not doing enough. Companies are reluctant to discuss suicides at all, and no reliable statistics exist to indicate just how many executive suicides actually take place. The US rate is about average, with Denmark being the leader and Greece having the lowest suicide rate. Clues almost always exist as to a suicidal tendency in an individual, a verbal allusion to despair being the most common. An executive suicide seldom is the result of a single crisis, and depression is typically present. Job loss and poor corporate promotion policies are significant causes of despair/suicide, and problems in family life can exert a significant influence on the suicide danger. –Horovitz, Bruce; *Industry Week,* Mar 9, 1981, 208(5): pp. 40-43,45. Avail. ABI 81-07249

Executives, Mental health, Mental illness, Causes, Stress

What Puts Stress on Executives (532)

Organizational complexity increases stress in managers. Factors that influence executive health were identified by a large-scale longitudinal study of 523 male and female managers attending management courses at Henley Management College and working at 2 nearby firms. Besides interviews and follow-up questionnaires, the 10-year study includes current and follow-up medical examinations. The major health differences between male and female managers that emerged were that male managers tended to be less physically fit and females less healthy mentally. The follow-up examinations reveal that female managers are becoming "male" in their attitudes to challenge and work, as well as in the diseases they suffer. Responses to annual questionnaires indicate that stress is alleviated by: 1. regular exercise, 2. relaxation, and 3. a supportive home life. The most effective coping skill was the ability to leave work behind when the manager goes home. —Cooper, Cary L. and Melhuish, Andrew; *Management Today (UK),* Sep 1983, pp. 41-46. Avail. ABI 83-32555

   Executives, Stress, Factors, Health, Studies, UK

When Executives Burn Out   (533)

Burn-out, like generalized stress, cuts across executive and managerial levels. Managing people, the most difficult administrative task, has a built-in frustration which can cause burn-out, if carried to extremes. Contributing to the situation are increasing time pressures, the complexity of modern organizations, increasing numbers of people to be dealt with, changing organizational values, and employee demands. Some steps to mitigate the occurrence of burn-out include: 1. recognition and acknowledgement of the problem, and periodic rotation of duties and changes of pace, 2. placement of time constraints on the job and planned recreation, 3. discovery of a systematic way of letting people know that they are important, 4. establishment of management teams to generate mutual support, 5. provision of avenues through which people can express all their emotions, 6. public defense against outside attacks on the organization, 7. provisions to retrain and upgrade managers as technology changes, 8. maintenance of personal interaction with subordinates in times of unmitigated strain. References. —Levinson, Harry; *Harvard Business Review,* May/Jun 1981, 59(3): pp. 72-81. Avail. ABI 81-11686

   Executives, Job, Stress, Characteristics, Prevention, Managers, Psychological, Behavior, Organizational behavior

When Executives Burn Out   (534)

Burnout cuts across executive and managerial levels. Those suffering burnout have identifiable characteristics: 1. chronic fatigue, 2. anger at those making demands, 3. self-criticism for putting up with the demands, 4. cynicism, 5. a sense of being besieged, and 6. hair-trigger displays of emotion. Frequently, other types of destructive behavior accompany these feelings. Most people probably experience a near burnout at some time in their careers. This exhaustion has been observed among many kinds of professionals. Many contemporary managerial situations provide the perfect breeding ground for burnout. Prevention is the best cure. Steps which can be taken include: 1. Recognize that burnout does happen. 2. Time constraints on a job are crucial. 3. Make sure there is a systematic way of letting people know their contributions are important. 4. Send groups of people from one task to another. 5. Provide avenues for the expression of anger and disappointment. 6. Defend publicly against outside attacks. 7. Retrain and upgrade your managers as technology changes. 8. Provide support for managers who are burning out. Loss of a leader should not be allowed to cripple an organization. References. —Levinson, Harry; *Canadian Banker & ICB Review (Canada),* Dec 1981, 88(6): pp. 52-58. Avail. ABI 82-02599

Executives, Stress, Factors, Prevention, Guidelines

Author Index

Author Index

Subject Index

Absenteeism 43, 82, 86, 87, 88, 92, 94, 101, 113, 142, 154, 224, 225, 236, 248, 274, 275, 449, 455
Accidents 49, 469
Accountants 380, 382, 451, 502, 513, 514
Accounting firms 357, 371, 494
Accounting procedures 502
Accounting theory 371
Accounts payable 296
Advertising 344
Aetna Life & Casualty-Hartford 46
Affirmative action 6, 128, 162, 323
Age 270, 295, 299, 362
Alcohol 523
Alcoholism 383, 455, 530
Alienation 342, 408
Anxieties 138, 388, 420, 422, 448, 467, 476
Arizona 119
Assembly lines 18
Associations 163, 272
ATT 452
Attitude surveys 119, 239, 294
Attorneys 447
Auditing procedures 174
Auditors 371, 389, 494
Audits 465
Australia 62, 114, 118, 333, 461
Automation 51

Bank management 355, 366, 392
Bank marketing 354, 355
Banking 230, 278
Banking industry 503
Banks 391, 392
Behavior modification 32, 422

Behavioral sciences 430, 493
Belgium 25
Benefit cost analysis 62
Blacks 325, 407
Blue collar workers 148, 161, 364, 468
Branch banking 366
Budgets 389
Bureaucracy 376
Bureaucrats 372
Burnout 48, 272, 402, 411, 419, 430, 433, 444, 463, 466, 477, 478, 481, 487, 488, 508, 510
Business ownership 225

California 421
Canada 222, 321, 393, 496
Career advancement 6, 126, 127, 128, 134, 136, 137, 138, 139, 147, 150, 168, 178, 182, 214, 216, 221, 327, 354, 360, 368, 399
Case studies 5, 20, 24, 27, 46, 49, 61, 68, 71, 74, 79, 86, 100, 111, 131, 135, 142, 296, 298, 306, 338, 393, 415, 424, 459, 480, 490, 507
Causality 315, 336
Chain stores 347
Chief executive officer 157, 276, 303
Child care 154, 159, 170
Children 162
Civil service 293
Classification 243
Clerical personnel 43, 52, 93, 381
Client relationships 447
Coal industry 346
Coal mining 346, 358